GMAT National Test Dates

Test Dates	Registration Deadlines	
	Regular	Late
October 22, 1983	September 19, 1983	September 26, 1983
January 28, 1984	December 26, 1983	January 3, 1984
March 17, 1984	February 13, 1984	February 21, 1984
June 16, 1984	May 14, 1984	May 21, 1984

FEES: Registration (U.S.) $30.00
           Registration (outside U.S.) $36.00
           Late registration (U.S. only) $10.00

D0609979

Test-Taker's Checklist for the GMAT

BASIC STRATEGIES

1. *Be Prepared.* Make sure you bring several sharpened number two pencils, a good eraser, and a watch (the test center may not have a visible clock).

2. *Budget Your Time.* Calculate the time you may spend on each question. Don't linger on questions you can't answer.

3. *Read questions carefully.* Make sure you answer the questions that are asked. Consider *all* choices. Remember you must pick the *best* choice, not just a good choice.

4. *Mark answers carefully.* Use your pencil and blacken your answer choices completely. Be sure erasures are done cleanly.

5. *When to Guess.* There is a penalty for wrong answers. Guess only if you can eliminate at least one wrong answer.

6. *Get plenty of rest before the exam.* The GMAT exam takes over four hours, with only one fifteen-minute break. Try to get as much rest as possible before the exam.

THE FINER POINTS

Reading Comprehension Questions test your ability to understand *main points* and *significant details* contained in material you have read, and your ability to draw inferences from this material. Tactics to use:

1. Identify the central theme of the passage.

2. Organize mentally how the passage is put together and determine how each part is related to the whole.

3. Determine the opinion or viewpoint that the writer wants the reader to follow or assume.

Analysis of Situations Questions test your ability to understand a business problem requiring decision making by one or more of the characters. You are required to classify each question according to its importance in the decision to be made. Tactics to use:

1. Before reading the passage, read the questions pertaining to it.

2. Use only information mentioned in the passage.

3. Learn by heart the five classifications used in the questions.

Writing Ability Questions test your understanding of the basic rules of English grammar and usage. Tactics to use:

1. Read the sentence carefully, paying more attention to the *underlined* part.

2. Assume any part of the sentence that is *not* underlined is correct.

3. Verb and pronoun errors are the most common examples—check for these first.

4. Other common errors include mis-use of adjectives and adverbs.

Problem Solving Questions test your ability to work with numbers and require a basic knowledge of arithmetic, algebra and geometry. Tactics to use:

1. Don't waste time on questions you can't figure out in two or three minutes.

2. Budget your time so that you will have a chance to try each question.

3. Try to answer questions by *estimating* or doing a rough calculation.

4. Make sure your answer is in the units asked for.

5. Remember that it is worthwhile to guess if you eliminate any answers.

Data Sufficiency Questions test your reasoning ability. Like the Problem Solving questions, they require a basic knowledge of arithmetic, algebra, and geometry. Each Data Sufficiency question consists of a mathematical problem and two statements containing information relating to it. You must decide whether the problem can be solved by using information from: (A) the first statement alone, but not the second statement alone; (B) the second statement alone, but not the first statement alone; (C) both statements together, but neither alone; or (D) either of the statements alone. Choose (E) if the problem cannot be solved, even by using both statements together. Tactics to use:

1. Don't waste time figuring out the exact answer.

2. Use the strategies in Chapter 5 to make intelligent guesses, if you can't answer the questions.

BARRON'S

BASIC TIPS
on the Graduate Management Admission Test
GMAT

By

Eugene D. Jaffe, M.B.A., Ph.D.
Associate Professor and
Director of the Management Training Center,
Bar-Ilan University, Israel
Formerly Professor of Marketing,
Graduate School of Business, St. John's University

and

Stephen Hilbert, Ph.D.
Associate Professor of Mathematics
Ithaca College

BARRON'S EDUCATIONAL SERIES, INC.
Woodbury, New York • London • Toronto • Sydney

© Copyright 1983 by Barron's Educational Series, Inc.

All rights reserved.
No part of this book may be reproduced
in any form, by photostat, microfilm, xerography,
or any other means, or incorporated into any
information retrieval system, electronic or
mechanical, without the written permission
of the copyright owner.

All inquiries should be addressed to:
Barron's Educational Series, Inc.
113 Crossways Park Drive
Woodbury, New York 11797

Library of Congress Catalog No. 83-18767
International Standard Book No. 0-8120-2733-7

Library of Congress Cataloging in Publication Data
Jaffe, Eugene D.
  Basic tips on the graduate management admission test,
GMAT.

  1. Management—Examinations, questions, etc.
2. Business—Examinations, questions, etc. I. Hilbert,
Stephen. II. Title.
HD30.413.J34   1983   650'.076   83-18767
ISBN 0-8120-2733-7

PRINTED IN THE UNITED STATES OF AMERICA
345   550   987654321

CONTENTS

Preface

How ready are you for the Graduate Management Admission Test (GMAT)? How familiar are you with the sorts of questions the exam contains? Do you know what level of mathematical and grammatical ability is necessary to get a high score on the GMAT? This book will provide you with strategies, review, and practice for taking the actual test. Since the results of the GMAT are used by many graduate schools of business as a means for measuring the qualifications of their applicants, it is important that you do as well as you can on this exam. Your admission to business school may well depend on it.

This book described in detail the question types found on the GMAT exam. It offers you invaluable advice on how to prepare for the exam, including a step-by-step program designed to help you discover and correct weak points.

If you have scored well on the sample tests in this book, you may take the actual exam with confidence. If this book has shown that you need further practice, then you may wish to begin working with *Barron's How to Prepare for the Graduate Management Admission Test*. The most complete GMAT study guide available, it covers all areas on the test with explanations and numerous practice exercises. The book also features a diagnostic test and five additional full-length model exams with answer analyses and self-scoring charts.

Acknowledgments

The authors gratefully acknowledge the kindness of all organizations concerned with granting us permission to reprint passages, charts, and graphs. The copyright holders and publishers of quoted passages are listed on this and the following pages.

Page 112, Passage 2: From *Our Dynamic World: A Survey in Modern Geography* by A. Joseph Wraight. © 1966 by the author. Reproduced by permission of the publisher Chilton Book Company, Radnor, Pennsylvania.

Page 127, Passage 2: Reprinted with permission from Boyd, Clewett, and Westfall, *Cases in Marketing Strategy* (Homewood, Ill.: Richard D. Irwin, Inc., 1957), pp. 55–58, © 1957.

Pages 137–142, Section V, 25 Questions (with Explained Answers): Samuel C. Brownstein and Mitchel Weiner, *Barron's How to Prepare for College Entrance Examinations (SAT)*, © 1982 Barron's Educational Series, Inc., Woodbury, N.Y.

Page 146, Passage 2: Reprinted with permission from Boyd, Clewett, and Westfall, *Cases in Marketing Strategy* (Homewood, Ill.: Richard D. Irwin, Inc., 1957), pp. 124–128, © 1957.

Pages 152–158, Section VII, 5 Questions (with Explained Answers): Murray Rockowitz et al., *Barron's How to Prepare for the New High School Equivalency Examination (GED)*, © 1979 Barron's Educational Series, Inc., Woodbury, N.Y.

Page 191, Passage 1: *Improving Executive Development in the Federal Government*, copyright 1964 by the Committee for Economic Development.

Page 194, Passage 2: from *Legal Aspects of Marketing* by Marshall C. Howard. Copyright 1964 by McGraw-Hill Book Company. Used with permission of McGraw-Hill Book Company.

Page 216, Passage 2: Reprinted with permission from Cateora and Hess, *International Marketing*, Third Edition (Homewood, Ill.: Richard D. Irwin, Inc., 1975), pp. 721–727, © 1975.

Page 236, Passage 1: Reprinted with permission from Cruickshank and Davis, *Cases in Management* (Homewood, Ill.: Richard D. Irwin, Inc., 1954), © 1954.

Page 239, Passage 2: Reprinted with permission from Cateora and Hess, *International Marketing*, Third Edition (Homewood, Ill.: Richard D. Irwin, Inc., 1975), pp. 727–732, © 1975.

Pages 246–252, Section VIII, 21 Questions (with Explained Answers): Samuel C. Brownstein and Mitchel Weiner, *Barron's How to Prepare for College Entrance Examinations (SAT)*, © 1982 Barron's Educational Series, Inc., Woodbury, N.Y.

Pages 246–252, Section VIII, 3 Questions (with Explained Answers): Murray Rockowitz et al., *Barron's How to Prepare for the New High School Equivalency Examination (GED)*, © 1979 Barron's Educational Series, Inc., Woodbury, N.Y.

Page 283, Passage 1: Petra Karin Kelly, "Cancer A European Conquest?" *European Community*, April–May, 1976, pp. 23–24.

Page 285, Passage 2: Walter Sturdivant, "Loch Ness Monster," *European Community*, April–May, 1976, pp. 36–37.

Page 290, Passage 4: Reprinted from *The Bible on Broadway* by Arthur T. Buch. © Arthur T. Buch 1968, Hamden, CT., Archon Books, with the permission of The Shoe String Press, Inc.

Page 297, Passage 1: Reprinted by special permission from the July 1977 issue of *International Management*. Copyright © 1977 McGraw-Hill International Publications Company Limited. All rights reserved.

Page 317, Passage 1: Reprinted by special permission from the May 1978 issue of *International Management*. Copyright © 1978 McGraw-Hill International Publications Company Limited. All rights reserved.

Page 325, Passage 2: From *The Social Bond*, by Robert A. Nisbet. Copyright © 1970 by Alfred A. Knopf, Inc. Reprinted by permission of the publisher.

1
An Introduction to the GMAT

The most productive approach to undertaking the actual study and review necessary for any examination is first to determine the answers to some basic questions: What? Where? When? and How? In this case, what is the purpose of the Graduate Management Admission Test (GMAT)? What does it measure? Where and when is the exam given? And most important, how can you prepare to demonstrate aptitude and ability to study business at the graduate level?

The following discussion centers on the purpose behind the Graduate Management Admission Test and presents a study program to follow in preparing for this exam, including a special section to acquaint you with the general format and procedure used on the GMAT.

THE PURPOSE OF THE GMAT

The purpose of the GMAT is to measure your ability to think systematically and to employ the reading and analytical skills that you have acquired throughout your years of schooling. The types of questions that are used to test these abilities are discussed in the next chapter. It should be noted that the test does not aim to measure your knowledge of specific business or academic subjects. No specific business experience is necessary, nor will any specific academic subject area be covered. You are assumed to have knowledge of basic algebra, geometry, and arithmetic.

In effect, the GMAT provides business school admission officers with an objective measure of academic abilities to supplement subjective criteria used in the selection process, such as interviews, grades, and references. Suppose you are an average student in a college with high grading standards. Your overall grade average may be lower than that of a student from a college with lower grading standards. The GMAT allows you and the other student to be tested under similar conditions using the same grading standard. In this way, a more accurate picture of your all-around ability can be established.

WHERE TO APPLY

Information about the exact dates of the exam, fees, testing locations, and a test registration form can be found in the "GMAT Bulletin of Information" for candidates published by ETS. You can obtain a copy by writing:

Graduate Management Admission Test
Educational Testing Service
Box 966-R
Princeton, New Jersey 08541

The GMAT is generally given in October, January, March, and June. Since the majority of business schools send out their acceptances in the spring, it is wise to take the exam as early as possible to ensure that the schools you are applying to receive your scores in time.

THE TEST FORMAT

In recent years, the GMAT has contained questions of the following types: Reading Comprehension, Problem Solving, Analysis of Situations, Data Sufficiency, Writing Ability (2 types: Usage and Sentence Correction), Verbal Ability, and Reading Recall. The most recent tests, however, have contained the following types: Reading Comprehension, Problem Solving, Analysis of Situations, Data Sufficiency, and Writing Ability (only Sentence Correction).

Recent GMAT examinations have contained eight sections, with each section allotted thirty minutes. Some possible test formats are:

FORM A

SECTION	TYPE OF QUESTION	NUMBER OF QUESTIONS	TIME (MIN.)
I	Reading Comprehension	20–25	30
II	Reading Comprehension	20–25	30
III	Problem Solving	20	30
IV	Analysis of Situations	35	30
V	Data Sufficiency	25	30
VI	Analysis of Situations	35	30
VII	Writing Ability	25	30
VIII	Problem Solving	20	30
Total		200–210	240

FORM B

SECTION	TYPE OF QUESTION	NUMBER OF QUESTIONS	TIME (MIN.)
I	Reading Comprehension	20–25	30
II	Analysis of Situations	35	30
III	Problem Solving	20	30
IV	Analysis of Situations	35	30
V	Data Sufficiency	25	30
VI	Writing Ability	25	30
VII	Writing Ability	25	30
VIII	Problem Solving	20	30
Total		205–210	240

Additional forms are possible wherein sections may be repeated—e.g., Problem Solving or Analysis of Situations may appear three times in one test. However, the content of question types has not changed. Usually only six of the eight sections are counted in your score. The other two sections either contain experimental questions or are used to calibrate different versions of the GMAT. However, you will not know which sections are going to count, so you must do your best on every section.

Each section of the GMAT must be completed within the specified time limit. If you finish the section before the allotted time has elapsed, you must spend the remaining time working on that section *only*. You may *not* work on other sections of the test at all.

Specific directions telling you exactly how to answer the questions appear at the beginning of each section of the exam. Keep in mind that although the directions for answering the sample questions in this guide are designed to simulate as closely as possible those on the actual test, the format of the test you take may vary: Therefore, it is important that you read the directions on the actual test very carefully before attempting to answer the questions. You also should be certain of the exact time limit you are allowed.

YOUR SCORES AND WHAT THEY MEAN

You will receive three scores on the GMAT exam: a total score, a verbal score, and a quantitative score. The total score ranges from 200 to 800; the verbal and quantitative scores range from 0 to 60. You will also be given a percentile ranking for each of the three scores. The percentile ranking gives you the percentage of the test scores in the last three years lower than yours. Thus, a percentile ranking of 75 would mean that 75% of the test scores in the last three years were below your score.

All of the scores you receive are *scaled scores.* Since there are many different versions of the exam, the use of scaled scores allows test results based on different versions of the exam to be compared. The same *raw score* (total number of correct answers minus one fourth of the number of wrong answers) will be converted into a higher scaled score if you took a more difficult version of the exam. If you take several versions of the exam, your scaled scores should cluster about your "true" scaled score. Thus, your scaled score in some sense represents a range of possibilities. A score of 510 means that your "true" score is probably between 480 and 540.

In general, no particular score can be called good or bad, and no passing or failing grade has been established. Scores above 700 or below 300 are unusual. In recent years, about two thirds of all scores have fallen between 350 and 570, with the average between 460 and 470. In the verbal and quantitative scores, grades above 46 or below 10 are unusual. About two thirds of these scores fall between 22 and 38, with the average about 30.

Your score on the GMAT is only one of several factors examined by admissions officers. Your undergraduate record, for example, is at least as important as your GMAT score. Thus, a low score does not mean that no school will accept you, nor does a high GMAT score guarantee acceptance at the school of your choice. However, since your score is one important factor, you should try to do as well as you can on the exam. Using this book should help you to maximize your score.

HOW TO PREPARE FOR THE GMAT

You should now be aware of the purpose of the GMAT and have a general idea of the format of the test. With this basic information, you are in a position to begin your study and review. The rest of this guide represents a study plan which will enable you to prepare for the GMAT. If used properly, it will help you diagnose your weak areas and take steps to remedy them.

Begin your preparation by becoming as familiar as possible with the various types of questions that appear on the exam. Chapters 2–5 are designed for this purpose. When you feel you understand this material completely, take the sample tests and evaluate your results on the self-scoring tables provided at the end of each test. (An explanation of how to use these tables appears below.) A low score in any area indicates that you should spend more time reviewing that particular material. For best results, try to simulate exam conditions as closely as possible when taking sample tests: no unscheduled breaks or interruptions, strict adherence to time limits, and no use of outside aids.

The Self-scoring Tables

The self-scoring tables for each sample test in this guide can be used as a means of evaluating your weaknesses in particular subject areas and should help you plan your study program most effectively.

After completing a sample test, first determine the number of *correct* answers you had for each section. Next, subtract *one-fourth* the number of *wrong* answers for each part from the number of correct answers. This is done to eliminate the benefits of wild guessing. Do *not* subtract for any answers left blank. For example, suppose that in Section I you answered 15 out of 25 questions correctly, with 6 incorrect responses and 4 blanks. Subtract ¼ of 6 (1½) from 15 to obtain a final score of 13½. Record this score in the appropriate score box in the Self-scoring Table as shown below.

SELF-SCORING TABLE

SECTION	SCORE	RATING
1	13½	FAIR
2		
3		
4		
5		
6		
7		
8		

Then compare this score with those contained in the Self-scoring Scale. Insert your rating, either POOR, FAIR, GOOD, or EXCELLENT, in the appropriate box in the Self-scoring Table.

SELF-SCORING SCALE—RATING

SECTION	POOR	FAIR	GOOD	EXCELLENT
1	0–12+	13–17+	18–21+	22–25
2	0–9+	10–13+	14–17+	18–20
3	0–17+	18–24+	25–31+	32–35
4	0–12+	13–17+	18–21+	22–25
5	0–12+	13–17+	18–21+	22–25
6	0–17+	18–24+	25–31+	32–35
7	0–12+	13–17+	18–21+	22–25
8	0–9+	10–13+	14–17+	18–20

In the table, numbers such as 12+ mean numbers larger than 12 but less than 13. For example, if your raw score on Section 6 of the exam was 24½, then this translates to FAIR on the self-scoring table.

A rating of FAIR or POOR in any area indicates that you need to spend more time reviewing that material.

Scaled Scores

The rules below will give you a method for converting your raw score on a practice exam into a scaled score. This is not the same procedure that the GMAT uses, but it should give you some idea of what your scaled score would be on the exam. Note that your raw score on an exam is the number of correct answers minus one fourth of the incorrect answers, with no deduction for answers left blank.

Use the following rule to convert your raw score into a scaled score.

Call N the number of questions in the test. Then the rule is:

> SCALED SCORE = 3.5 × (RAW SCORE) + (800 − 3.45 N)

If the rule gives a scaled score greater than 800, then the scaled score is 800. If the rule gives a scaled score less than 200, then the scaled score is 200.

EXAMPLE: You have a raw score of 142.5 on a test with 200 questions.

(A) Use the rule SCALED SCORE = 3.5 × (RAW SCORE) + (800 − 3.45N).
(B) Since N = 200, (800 − 3.45N) = 800 − 690 = 110.
(C) So the scaled score is 3.5 (142.5) + 110 = 498.75 + 110 = 609.

If your scaled scores are low on the first practice exams you take, don't get discouraged. Your scaled score should improve on the later practice exams after you have used the various reviews to strengthen your weaknesses. The tests were made hard. That way you can discover your weaknesses and try to correct them. Easy practice tests are not good practice for a difficult exam. Remember that, on the GMAT itself, you shouldn't expect to be able to answer every single question. Don't worry about that. To maximize your score, you want to answer as many questions as you can correctly in the given amount of time.

AFTER YOU TAKE THE EXAM

You will usually receive your scores about four weeks after the exam.

You may take the GMAT as many times as you wish. However, if you repeat the test, your scores from that test and the two most recent previous test results will be sent to all institutions you designate as score recipients. Many schools average your scores if you take the test more than once. So unless there is a reason to expect a substantial improvement in your score, it usually is *not* worthwhile to retake the exam.

Currently, you can receive a copy of your answer sheet, a booklet containing all questions that were counted in scoring your exam, an answer key, and the scale used to translate your raw scores into scaled scores. You should obtain this information if you are considering retaking the exam. You can see if there was any particular section which hurt your score and concentrate on those questions as you study.

You can also cancel your scores if you act *before* receiving them. If you wish to cancel your scores, you must indicate this on your answer sheet, notify the supervisor before you leave the test center, or notify ETS by mail within 7 days of the test administration. If you cancel your scores, the fact that you took the test will be reported to all the places you designated as score recipients. Thus, it is generally not advantageous to cancel your scores unless there is reason to believe that you have done substantially worse on the test than you would if you took the test again; for example, if you became ill while taking the exam. Once a score is cancelled from your record it cannot be put back on your record or reported at a later date.

As a general rule, it is better to retake the exam after looking over your previous results (questions, answers, and so on) than it is to cancel your scores. You can do well on the exam without finishing every section of the exam. In addition, each version of the exam contains questions or sections which are experimental and are not counted towards your score, so your score may be better than you expect. Thus, you usually are better off waiting to see your score before deciding whether or not to retake the exam.

2
Reading Comprehension Review

The Reading Comprehension section tests your ability to analyze written information and includes passages from the humanities, the social sciences, and the physical and biological sciences.

The typical Reading Comprehension section consists of three or four passages with a total of 25 questions which must be completed in 30 minutes. You will be allowed to turn back to the passages when answering the questions. However, many of the questions may be based on what is *implied* in the passages, rather than on what is explicitly stated. Your ability to draw inferences from the material is critical to successfully completing this section. You are to select the best answer from five alternatives. For example:

According to the passage, the main reason for Napoleon's withdrawal from Russia was the

    (A) disloyalty of the French troops
    (B) Russian winter
    (C) burned buildings
    (D) planned revolts in other countries
    (E) Russian army

TIPS TO HELP YOU COPE

1. Read the passage, underlining important points, names, and so on.
2. Determine the central thought. Is there a topic sentence that expresses the main idea succinctly? What title would you give the passage?

3. Notice the specific details or statements that the writer gives to support the main idea.

4. Note the special techniques used by the author. These may include reasoning from experimental data (inductive method) or from principles accepted in advance (deductive method) and the use of examples, anecdotes, analogies, and comparisons.

5. Determine the author's purpose. Is he or she seeking to inform, to persuade, to satirize, to evoke pity, to amuse, to arouse to action?

6. Look at the questions, noting the type of information called for.

7. Pay attention to the wording of each question. A question that begins "The main idea of the passage is . . ." calls for a different kind of reasoning from a question that begins "Which of the following is mentioned . . . ?" Watch out for questions which specify "All of the following EXCEPT" or "Which of the following is NOT . . ." since these phrases mean you should look for the *false* or *inapplicable* answer rather than the *true* one.

8. All reading comprehension questions on the GMAT can be answered on the basis of information provided in the passage. Therefore, don't bring in your own prior knowledge or your personal opinions when answering the questions; they may be inapplicable, inaccurate, or misleading.

9. Read all five answer choices carefully before selecting an answer. Sometimes two or more choices will have elements of truth; however, only one answer will be the best. Don't overlook the best answer by hastily choosing the first choice that seems reasonable.

The following discussion is designed to help you formulate an approach to reading passages that will enable you to better understand the material you will be asked to read on the GMAT. The practice exercise at the end of this review will give you an opportunity to try out this approach.

BASIC READING SKILLS

A primary skill necessary for good reading comprehension is the understanding of the meanings of individual words. Knowledge of a wide and diversified vocabulary enables you to detect subtle differences in sentence meaning that may hold the key to the meaning of an entire paragraph or passage. For this reason, it is important that you familiarize yourself with as many words as possible.

A second reading skill to be developed is the ability to discover the central theme of a passage. By making yourself aware of what the entire passage is about, you are in a position to relate what you read to this central theme, logically picking out the main points and significant details as you go along. Although the manner in which the central theme is stated may vary from passage to passage, it can usually be found in the title (if one is presented), in the "topic sentence" of a paragraph in shorter passages, or, in longer passages, by reading several paragraphs.

A third essential skill is the capacity to organize mentally how the passage is put together and determine how each part is related to the whole. This is the skill you will have to use to the greatest degree on the GMAT, where you must pick out significant and insignificant factors, remember main details, and relate information you have read to the central theme.

In general, a mastery of these three basic skills will provide you with a solid basis for better reading comprehension wherein you will be able to read carefully to draw a conclusion from the material, decide the meanings of words and ideas presented and how they in turn affect the meaning of the passage, and recognize opinions and views that are expressed.

APPLYING BASIC READING SKILLS

The only way to become adept at the three basic reading skills outlined above is to practice using the techniques involved as much as possible. Studying the meanings of new words you encounter in all your reading material, will soon help you establish a working knowledge of many words. In the same manner, making an effort to locate topic sentences, general themes, and specific details in material you read will enable you to improve your skills in these areas. The following drills will help. After you have read through them and answered the questions satisfactorily, you can try the longer practice exercise at the end.

FINDING THE TOPIC SENTENCE

The term "topic sentence" is used to describe the sentence that gives the key to an entire paragraph. Usually the topic sentence is found in the beginning of a paragraph. However, there is no absolute rule. A writer may build his paragraph to a conclusion, putting the key sentence at the end. Here is an example in which the topic sentence is located at the beginning:

EXAMPLE 1:
The world faces a serious problem of overpopulation. Right now many people starve from lack of adequate food. Efforts are being made to increase the rate of food production, but the number of people to be fed increases at a faster rate.

The idea is stated directly in the opening sentence. You know that the passage will be about "a serious problem of overpopulation." Like a heading or caption, the topic sentence sets the stage or gets your mind ready for what follows in that paragraph.

Before you try to locate the topic sentence in a paragraph you must remember that this technique depends upon reading and judgment. Read the whole passage first. Then try to decide which sentence comes closest to expressing the main point of the paragraph. Do not worry about the position of the topic sentence in the paragraph; look for the most important statement. Find the idea to which all the other sentences relate.

Try to identify the topic sentence in this passage:

EXAMPLE 2:
During the later years of the American Revolution, the Articles of Confederation government was formed. This government suffered severely from a lack of power. Each state distrusted the others and gave little authority to the central or federal government. The Articles of Confederation produced a government which could not raise money from taxes, prevent Indian raids, or force the British out of the United States.

What is the topic sentence? Certainly the paragraph is about the Articles of Confederation. However, is the key idea in the first sentence or in the second sentence? In this instance, the *second* sentence does a better job of giving you the key to this paragraph—the lack of centralized power that characterized the Articles of Confederation. The sentences that complete the paragraph relate more to the idea of "lack of power" than to the time when the government was formed. Don't assume that the topic sentence is always the first sentence of a paragraph. Try this:

EXAMPLE 3:
There is a strong relation between limited education and low income. Statistics show that unemployment rates are highest among those adults who attended school the fewest years. Most jobs in a modern industrial society require technical or advanced training. The best pay goes with jobs that demand thinking and decisions based on knowledge. A few people manage to overcome their limited education by personality or a "lucky break." However, studies of lifetime earnings show that the average high school graduate earns more than the average high school dropout, who in turn earns more than the average adult who has not finished eighth grade.

Here, the first sentence contains the main idea of the whole paragraph. One more example should be helpful:

EXAMPLE 4:
They had fewer men available as soldiers. Less than one third of the railroads and only a small proportion of the nation's industrial production was theirs. For most of the war their coastline was blockaded by Northern ships. It is a tribute to Southern leadership and the courage of the people that they were not defeated for four years.

In this case you will note that the passage builds up to its main point. The topic sentence is the last one. Practice picking out the topic sentences in other material you read until it becomes an easy task.

FINDING THE GENERAL THEME

A more advanced skill is the ability to read several paragraphs and relate them to one general theme or main idea. The procedure involves careful reading of the entire passage and deciding which idea is the central or main one. You can tell you have the right idea when it is most frequent or most important, or when every sentence relates to it. As you read the next passage, note the *underlined* parts.

EXAMPLE:

True democaracy means direct rule by the people. A good example can be found in a modern town meeting in many small New England towns. All citizens aged twenty-one or over may vote. They not only vote for officials, but they also get together to vote on local laws (or ordinances). The small size of the town and the limited number of voters make this possible.

In the cities, voters cast ballots for officials who get together to make the laws. Because the voters do not make the laws directly, this system is called indirect democracy or representative government. There is no problem of distance to travel, but it is difficult to run a meeting with hundreds of thousands of citizens.

Representation of voters and a direct voice in making laws are more of a problem in state or national governments. The numbers of citizens and the distances to travel make representative government the most practical way to make laws.

Think about the passage in general and the underlined parts in particular. Several examples discuss voting for officials and making laws. In the first paragraph both of these are done by the voters. The second paragraph describes representative government in which voters elect officials who make laws. The last paragraph emphasizes the problem of size and numbers and says that representative government is more practical. In the following question, put all these ideas together.

The main theme of this passage is that
  (A) the United States is not democratic
  (B) citizens cannot vote for lawmakers
  (C) representative government does not make laws
  (D) every citizen makes laws directly
  (E) increasing populations lead to less direct democracy

The answer is choice (E). Choices (B), (C), and (D) can be eliminated because they are not true of the passage. Choice (A) may have made you hesitate a little. The passage makes comments about *less direct* democracy, but it never says that representative government is *not democratic*.

In summary, in order to find the general theme:
  1. Read at your normal speed.
  2. Locate the topic sentence in each paragraph.

3. Note ideas that are frequent or emphasized.
4. Find the idea to which most of the passage is related.

FINDING LOGICAL RELATIONSHIPS

In order to fully understand the meaning of a passage, you must first look for the general theme and then relate the ideas and opinions found in the passage to this general theme. In this way, you can determine not only what is important but also how the ideas interrelate to form the whole. From this understanding, you will be better able to answer questions that refer to the passage.

As you read the following passages, look for general theme and supporting facts, words or phrases that signal emphasis or shift in thought, and the relation of one idea to another.

EXAMPLE:

The candidate who wants to be elected pays close attention to statements and actions that will make the voters see him favorably. In ancient Rome candidates wore pure white togas (the Latin word *candidatus* means "clothed in white") to indicate that they were pure, clean, and above any "dirty work." However, it is interesting to note that such a toga was not worn after election.

In more modern history, candidates have allied themselves with political parties. Once a voter knows and favors the views of a certain political party, he may vote for anyone with that party's label. Nevertheless, divisions of opinion develop, so that today there is a wide range of candidate views in any major party.

The best conclusion to be drawn from the first paragraph   Ⓐ Ⓑ Ⓒ Ⓓ Ⓔ
is that after an election
(A) all candidates are dishonest
(B) candidates are less concerned with symbols of integrity
(C) candidates do not change their ideas
(D) officials are always honest
(E) policies always change

You noted the ideas about a candidate in Rome. You saw the word "however" signal a shift in ideas or thinking. Now the third step rests with your judgment. You cannot jump to a conclusion; you must see which conclusion is reasonable or fair. Choices (A), (D), and (E) should make you wary. They say "all" or "always" which means without exception. The last sentence is not that strong or positive. Choices (B) and (C) must be considered. There is nothing in the paragraph that supports the fact that candidates do not change their ideas. This forces you into choice (B) as the only statement logically related to what the paragraph said.

MAKING INFERENCES

An inference is not stated. It is assumed by the reader from something said by the writer. An inference is the likely or probable conclusion rather than the direct, logical one. It usually involves an opinion or viewpoint that the writer wants the reader to follow or assume. In another kind of inference, the reader figures out the author's opinion even though it is not stated. The clues are generally found in the manner in which facts are presented and in the choice of words and phrases. Opinion is revealed by the one-sided nature of a passage in which no opposing facts are given. It is shown further by "loaded" words that reveal the author's feelings.

It is well worth noting that opinionated writing is often more interesting than straight factual accounts. Some writers are very colorful, forceful, or amusing in presenting their views. You should understand that there is nothing wrong with reading opinion. You should read varied opinions, but know that they are opinions. Then make up your own mind.

Not every writer will insert his opinion obviously. However, you can get clues from how often the same idea is said (frequency), whether arguments are balanced on both sides (fairness), and the choice of wording (emotional or loaded words). Look for the clues in this next passage.

EXAMPLE:
Slowly but surely the great passenger trains of the United States have been fading from the rails. Short-run commuter trains still rattle in and out of the cities. Between major cities you can still find a train, but the schedules are becoming less frequent. The Twentieth Century Limited, The Broadway Limited, and other luxury trains that sang along the rails at 60 to 80 miles an hour are no longer running. Passengers on other long runs complain of poor service, old equipment, and costs in time and money. The long distance traveller today accepts the noise of jets, the congestion at airports, and the traffic between airport and city. A more elegant and graceful way is becoming only a memory.

1. With respect to the reduction of long-run passenger   1. Ⓐ Ⓑ Ⓒ Ⓓ Ⓔ
   trains, this writer expresses
   - (A) regret
   - (B) pleasure
   - (C) grief
   - (D) elation
   - (E) anger

Before you choose the answer, you must deduce what the writer's feeling is. He does not actually state his feeling, but clues are available so that you may infer what it is. Choices (B) and (D) are impossible, because he gives no word that shows he is pleased by the change. Choice (C) is too strong, as is choice (E). Choice (A) is the most reasonable inference to make. He is sorry to see the change. He is expressing regret.

2. The author seems to feel that air travel is   2. Ⓐ Ⓑ Ⓒ Ⓓ Ⓔ
   - (A) costly
   - (B) slow
   - (C) streamlined
   - (D) elegant
   - (E) uncomfortable

Here we must be careful because he says very little about air travel. However, his one sentence about it presents three negative or annoying points. The choice now becomes fairly clear. Answer (E) is correct.

PRACTICE EXERCISE   Time: 9 minutes

Directions: This part contains a reading passage. You are to read it carefully. When answering the questions, you *will* be able to refer to the passages. The questions are based on what is *stated* or *implied* in the passage. You have nine minutes to complete this part.

Above all, colonialism was hated for its explicit assumption that the civilizations of colonized peoples were inferior. Using slogans like *The White Man's Burden* and *La Mission Civilicatrice*, Europeans asserted their moral obligation to impose their way of life on those endowed with
(5) inferior cultures. This orientation was particularly blatant among the French. In the colonies, business was conducted in French. Schools used that language and employed curricula designed for children in France. One scholar suggests that Muslim children probably learned no more about the Maghreb than they did about Australia. In the Metropole, in-
(10) tellectuals discoursed on the weakness of Arabo-Islamic culture. A noted historian accused Islam of being hostile to science. An academician wrote

that Arabic—the holy language of religion, art and the Muslim sciences—
is "more of an encumbrance than an aid to the mind. It is absolutely
devoid of precision." There was of course an element of truth in the
(15) criticisms. After all, Arab reformists had been engaging in self-criticism
for decades. Also, at least some Frenchmen honestly believed they were
helping the colonized. A Resident General in Tunisia, for example, told
an assemblage of Muslims with sincerity, "We shall distribute to you all
that we have of learning; we shall make you a party to everything that
(20) makes for the strength of our intelligence." But none of this could change
or justify the cultural racism in colonial ideologies. To the French, North
Africans were only partly civilized and could be saved only by becoming
Frenchmen. The reaction of the colonized was of course to defend his
identity and to label colonial policy, in the words of Algerian writer Malek
(25) Hadad, "cultural asphyxia." Throughout North Africa, nationalists made
the defense of Arabo-Islamic civilization a major objective, a value in
whose name they demanded independence. Yet the crisis of identity,
provoked by colonial experiences, has not been readily assured and lin-
gers into the post-colonial period. A French scholar describes the dev-
(30) astating impact of colonialism by likening it to "the role played for us (in
Europe) by the doctrine of original sin." Frantz Fanon, especially in his
Studies in a Dying Colonialism, well expresses the North African per-
spective.

Factors producing militant and romantic cultural nationalism are an-
(35) chored in time. Memories of colonialism are already beginning to fade
and, when the Maghreb has had a few decades in which to grow, dis-
locations associated with social change can also be expected to be fewer.
Whether this means that the cultural nationalism characteristic of the
Maghreb today will disappear in the future cannot be known. But a preoc-
(40) cupation with identity and culture and an affirmation of Arabism and Islam
have characterized the Maghreb since independence and these still remain today important elements in North African life.

A second great preoccupation in independent North Africa is the pro-
motion of a modernist social revolution. The countries of the Maghreb
(45) do not pursue development in the same way and there have been variations in policies within each country. But all three spend heavily on
development. In Tunisia, for example, the government devotes 20–25%
of its annual budget to education, and literacy has climbed from 15% in
1956 to about 50% today. A problem, however, is that such advances are
(50) not always compatible with objectives flowing from North African na-

tionalism. In Morocco, for instance, when the government decided to give children an "Arab" education, it was forced to limit enrollments because, among other things, most Moroccans had been educated in French and the country consequently had few teachers qualified to teach in Arabic.

(55) Two years later, with literacy rates declining, this part of the Arabization program was postponed. The director of Arabization declared, "We are not fanatics; we want to enter the modern world."

1. Which of the following titles best describes the content of the passage? 1. Ⓐ Ⓑ Ⓒ Ⓓ Ⓔ
   (A) *Education in the Levant*
   (B) *Nationalism in North Africa*
   (C) *Civilization in the Middle East*
   (D) *Muslim Science*
   (E) *Culture and Language*

2. Which of the following is *not* used by the author in the presentation of his arguments? 2. Ⓐ Ⓑ Ⓒ Ⓓ Ⓔ
   (A) Colonialism demoralized the local inhabitants.
   (B) Colonialism produced an identity crisis.
   (C) Cultural nationalism will soon disappear.
   (D) Decolonization does not always run smoothly.
   (E) Colonialists assumed that local cultures were inferior.

3. The author's attitude toward colonialism is best described as one of 3. Ⓐ Ⓑ Ⓒ Ⓓ Ⓔ
   (A) sympathy
   (B) bewilderment
   (C) support
   (D) hostility
   (E) ambivalence

4. Which of the following does the author mention as evidence of cultural colonialism? 4. Ⓐ Ⓑ Ⓒ Ⓓ Ⓔ
   (A) Native children in North Africa learned little about local culture.
   (B) Science was not taught in the Arabic language.
   (C) Colonial policy was determined in France.
   (D) Colonialists spent little on development.
   (E) Native teachers were not employed in public schools.

5. The author provides information that would answer   5. Ⓐ Ⓑ Ⓒ Ⓓ Ⓔ
   which of the following questions?
   (A) What was the difference between French and Ger-
       man attitudes toward their colonies?
   (B) Why did Europeans impose their way of life on
       their colonies?
   (C) Why was colonialism bad?
   (D) Why was colonialism disliked?
   (E) When did colonialism end in North Africa?

Answers and Analysis

1. **(B)** Clearly, the main subject of the passage is nationalism. This is given in
   the statement on line 1, "Above all, colonialism was hated . . ." and in lines
   25ff. and 34ff.

2. **(C)** Choice (E) is given in lines 1–2, (D) in lines 49–51, (B) in lines 27–29,
   and (A) is implied throughout; while the opposite of (C) is found in lines 38–
   41.

3. **(D)** See, for instance, the reference to "cultural racism" in lines 20–21, as
   well as the general tone of paragraph 1.

4. **(A)** This is mentioned in lines 6–9. The fact that children were taught very
   little about their own culture and history was due to cultural colonialism.

5. **(D)** This theme begins on line 1 and continues throughout much of the
   passage.

3
Analysis of Situations Review

The Analysis of Situations section of the GMAT is usually comprised of *Data Evaluation* questions. A second set of questions, *Data Application*, has not appeared on recent tests. For both question types, you are asked to read a passage (the most recent test contained two passages) that presents some business problem requiring decision making by one or more of the characters. After you complete the passage, you are given questions to answer.

TIPS TO HELP YOU COPE

1. *Before reading the passage, read the questions pertaining to it.* By reading the questions first, *carefully*, you familiarize yourself with the type of problem being presented and the factors you will have to take into consideration in choosing your answers.

2. *Use only information mentioned in the passage.* Even if the subject of a passage is one about which you have personal knowledge, use only information specifically mentioned in the passage. Inferences and assumptions should be based on the perceptions of the characters in the passage.

3. *Learn by heart the five classifications used in Data Evaluation questions.* Once you have decided that a certain item is a Major or Minor Factor, you should not have to waste time leafing back and forth to find out if you want to mark (B) or (C) on your answer sheet.

DATA EVALUATION QUESTIONS

In the Data Evaluation questions, you will be asked to evaluate each item given and classify it as either

    (A) A MAJOR OBJECTIVE in making the decision: one of the goals sought by the decision maker

    (B) A MAJOR FACTOR in making the decision: an aspect of the problem, specifically mentioned in the passage, that fundamentally affects and/or determines the decision

    (C) A MINOR FACTOR in making the decision: a less important element bearing on or affecting a Major Factor, rather than a Major Objective directly

    (D) A MAJOR ASSUMPTION in making the decision: a projection or supposition arrived at by the decision maker before considering the factors and alternatives

    (E) AN UNIMPORTANT ISSUE in making the decision: an item lacking significant impact on, or relationship to, the decision

The Classifications

(A) Major Objective

A situation or condition resulting from the decision to be made will be a Major Objective. A Major Objective will often be introduced by expressions of desire: "He wants . . . ," "He would like . . . ," "It is important to him. . . ." The desired result may be one of business condition or of happiness or prestige for a firm or individual.

  To illustrate a Major Objective, read the following passage:

> Dave Robinson wants to replace his company's present cement mixer with a new model. Dave has been chief building engineer for five years. Dave's calculations show that the newer model can save the company up to $10,000 in operating costs. He is considering ordering one of three models. The three models are all immediately available but vary in cost.

  In Analysis of Situations cases, a major decision considered is almost invariably a Major Objective. In the passage quoted, the major decision is whether to buy a new cement mixer. Another clue to locating the Major Objective is the expression of desire: "Dave Robinson *wants* to replace his company's present cement mixer with a new model."

(B) Major Factor

In the decision-making process, the strengths and weaknesses of various alternatives must be weighed and considered. As a result of these considerations the decision maker will choose one alternative over another. The points used to contrast and compare one alternative to another are Major Factors. The final decision will be based on the results of these considerations.

Let us continue with the passage.

Dave is considering three models: A two-ton fully automatic mixer, a two-ton semi-automatic mixer, and a one-ton fully automatic mixer. Dave's decision will depend on some calculations he has made. He will consider total costs, including the purchase price, amortization, and operating costs of each mixer. Dave will compare these costs with the contribution the mixers can make to company earnings. Dave knows the importance of his decision; a wrong choice can result in an operating loss for his company.

In addition to the cost side, Dave considers the quality of the mixers. After examining the technical literature supplied by the mixer manufacturer and talking with users of the equipment, Dave cataloged each mixer's operating characteristics. In particular, he needs a mixer which will have the least maintenance problems, including downtime. Dave is confident that he will be able to reach a correct decision based on his calculations.

Major factors include the key elements that impinge on the decision to be made. Once alternative choices of action have been identified, the pros and cons, or strengths and weaknesses, of each alternative will be weighed.

To reiterate what we explained above, the Major Objective is to acquire a new mixer. The alternative courses of action are (in addition to a "No go" decision—after all, Dave may decide not to buy any of the proposed models) the choice of one of three different models. The Major Factors, therefore, are the strengths and weaknesses of each model as considered by Dave. Specifically, they are *total costs* and the *quality* of the mixers. Both are criteria by which the pros and cons of each mixer can be assessed.

(C) Minor Factor

Minor factors play a less direct part in the decision-making process. They are usually related to or are part of the considerations comprising Major Factors. A Minor Factor may also pertain to only one or some of the alternatives. A Major Factor will involve consideration of all the elements of an alternative course of action.

Referring to our definition of Minor Factors, we can see that a number of secondary factors or items are related to each Major Factor. For example, we are told that the *total cost* of the mixers is comprised of the *purchase price*, *amortization*, and *operating costs*. A question mentioning one of the parts of the total cost—say, purchase price—should be labeled a Minor Factor. The price of the mixers is only a sub-element of a Major Factor, total cost. Dave Robinson would not consider only the purchase price of the mixers—or any of the other elements of total cost alone—in making his decision. Moreover, we read in the passage that total cost is but one of two major considerations in the decision process. The other is *quality*. Quality is defined as the operating characteristics of the mixers. Operating characteristics consist of the incidence of maintenance problems. A question mentioning the consideration of downtime would be a Minor Factor.

To sum up, Minor Factors are subsets of Major Factors. Minor Factors represent facts that are considered for less than all alternative courses of action or are partial facts considered for less than all alternative courses of action.

(D) Major Assumption

Major Assumptions are feelings, beliefs, or opinions accepted by the decision maker without supporting information. They will mirror expectations of future events and the personal feelings and opinions of the decision maker.

Considering our passage again, note that a Major Assumption is expressed as Dave Robinson's belief or opinion "that he will be able to reach a correct decision based on his calculations." Here, the key word is "confident," which designates an assumption on the part of the decision maker. Dave is assuming that he will be able to choose an alternative course of action based on his calculations. Note that no information is given in the passage about the accuracy of these calculations. Apart from the statement (in paragraph 1) that the newer model can save up to $10,000 in operating costs, nothing more is said about the calculations.

In many cases, Major Assumptions may be based on implications made by the decision maker. Major Assumptions may be identified by such key words as "probability," "likelihood," "estimate," "reliability," and "availability."

(E) Unimportant Issue

Unimportant Issues are those items not significantly influencing the choice of an alternative. Or, by elimination, if an item is not a Major Objective, a Major or Minor Factor, or a Major Assumption, it is an Unimportant Issue.

An example of an Unimportant Issue is that Dave has been chief building engineer for five years. His occupation and length of seniority have no importance in the selection of an alternative course of action and are not Major Objectives, Major or Minor Factors, nor Major Assumptions.

STRATEGY FOR DATA EVALUATION QUESTIONS

The following decision tree will help you visualize the relationships between the question classifications. To use the tree simply start at the top and by answering YES or NO move downwards until you arrive at the correct choice. The first YES is the correct answer.

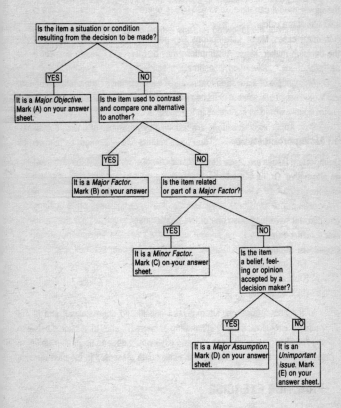

DATA APPLICATION QUESTIONS

A second set of questions, Data Application, which has not appeared on recent tests, contains general questions each requiring selection of the answer that comes closest to describing an objective or objectives in the passage. You may also have to draw inferences or make simple calculations based on data contained in the passage. More often than not, a typical Data Application question will require recall of factors in the passage. Typical questions take such forms as

"Which of the following reasons is (are) given for Dave's decision to sell his business?" or "Dave was opposed to increasing advertising expenditures because of . . ."

An example of a question that requires a calculation or interpretation of data would be: "Total sales in units had increased by _____ percent." Sales figures of course would be contained in the passage.

Data Application questions are followed by a number of possible answers. For example, the question "Total sales in units had . . ." might be followed by these answers:[7]

I. increased every year
II. increased in real terms
III. decreased in 1981

You will have to choose one of five possibilities:

(A) I only
(B) III only
(C) I and II only
(D) II and III only
(E) I, II, and III

In the above question, alternatives I and III and alternatives II and III are mutually exclusive, thereby eliminating answers (D) and (E). A choice between the remaining answers—(A), (B), and (C)—would depend upon your ability to interpret or calculate (if needed) the sales data presented in the passage.

PRACTICE EXERCISE

This part is designed to give you some practice reading and answering an Analysis of Situations test. On the actual test you will have 30 minutes to read two passages and answer thirty-five questions. Because the passage that follows is a shortened version of an actual test, spend no more than 5 minutes reading the passage and answering the questions.

Ed Freed was considering opening a tennis club. Ed was thirty-five years old and had played amateur tennis for over twenty years; the idea of a tennis club would satisfy a long-held dream of making a business out of a favorite pastime. Ed was a traveling salesman for an exporting firm. Because he did not want to give up his present job, he wanted his wife to manage the club. He believed he could convince her to do so because of the extra annual income the club would provide. If his wife would not agree, Ed planned to hire a business manager. Ed spent his spare time looking for a suitable site for the club. He found a piece of real estate on the outskirts of town which was easily accessible by car. The property was large enough to build a club having four indoor courts, showers, restrooms, and a snack bar. There was room for a 30-car outdoor parking lot. Ed had calculated that he needed to operate three courts at a rate of at least 60 percent capacity to break even. The property was particularly attractive because the fourth court would make the operation profitable. Ed estimated that it would take six months to make the club operational. The time necessary to build the club was crucial because Ed could only obtain bank financing for part of the project. Ed had to provide the balance from his savings. If the club was not completed on time, Ed would not be able to repay the bank finance charges. After considering all the facts, Ed decided to make his bid for the property only one day before his option expired.

Data Evaluation Questions

Directions: The questions that follow relate to the preceding passage. Evaluate, in terms of the passage, each of the items given. Then select your answer from one of the following classifications, and indicate your choice in the space provided.

   (A) A MAJOR OBJECTIVE in making the decision: one of the goals sought by the decision maker
   (B) A MAJOR FACTOR in making the decision: an aspect of the problem, specifically mentioned in the passage, that fundamentally affects and/or determines the decision
   (C) A MINOR FACTOR in making the decision: a less important element bearing on or affecting a Major Factor, rather than a Major Objective directly
   (D) A MAJOR ASSUMPTION in making the decision: a projection or supposition arrived at by the decision maker before considering the factors and alternatives
   (E) AN UNIMPORTANT ISSUE in making the decision: an item lacking significant impact on, or relationship to, the decision

1. Location of the property
1. Ⓐ Ⓑ Ⓒ Ⓓ Ⓔ

2. Increasing annual income
2. Ⓐ Ⓑ Ⓒ Ⓓ Ⓔ

3. Likelihood of operating the club within six months
3. Ⓐ Ⓑ Ⓒ Ⓓ Ⓔ

4. Ed's age (thirty-five)
4. Ⓐ Ⓑ Ⓒ Ⓓ Ⓔ

5. Size of the property
5. Ⓐ Ⓑ Ⓒ Ⓓ Ⓔ

6. Likelihood of Ed's wife's managing the club
6. Ⓐ Ⓑ Ⓒ Ⓓ Ⓔ

7. Room for a snack bar
7. Ⓐ Ⓑ Ⓒ Ⓓ Ⓔ

8. Time necessary to build the club
8. Ⓐ Ⓑ Ⓒ Ⓓ Ⓔ

9. Option for purchasing the property
9. Ⓐ Ⓑ Ⓒ Ⓓ Ⓔ

10. Ed's experience as a tennis player
10. Ⓐ Ⓑ Ⓒ Ⓓ Ⓔ

Data Application Questions

Directions: Answer each of the following questions using information contained in the passage.

11. Opening a tennis club appealed to Ed because it would
11. Ⓐ Ⓑ Ⓒ Ⓓ Ⓔ
    I. provide business experience for his wife
    II. allow him to quit his present job
    III. actualize an old dream of Ed's
    (A) I only
    (B) III only
    (C) I and II only
    (D) II and III only
    (E) I, II, and III

12. According to the passage, Ed wanted his wife to manage the club because
12. Ⓐ Ⓑ Ⓒ Ⓓ Ⓔ
    I. his wife had managerial experience
    II. he would not have to pay her a salary
    III. he did not want to leave his present job
    (A) I only
    (B) III only
    (C) I and II only
    (D) II and III only
    (E) I, II, and III

Answers and Analysis

Data Evaluation Questions

1. **(B)** Major Factor. *Note the first word, "location."* The location of the property is important because it is linked to the potential profitability of the club. Location is not a Major Objective; it is not a goal desired by the decision maker. The goal is the establishment of a tennis club. However, location is one of the Major Factors considered by Ed in his decision to build a club.

2. **(A)** Major Objective. A major goal of Ed was to convert his pastime to an income-producing business. Moreover, he wanted his wife to manage the club because he did not plan to leave his present employment as a traveling salesman. Ed's desire to have his wife manage the club is another major goal.

3. **(D)** Major Assumption. *Note the key word in the question, "likelihood."* The key word in the *passage* is "estimated." "Estimated" mirrors a belief on Ed's part that the club could be opened within six months.

4. **(E)** Unimportant Issue. Ed's age has no bearing on a desired goal, nor is it a factor in the consideration of an alternative course of action.

5. **(B)** Major Factor. Like location, size of the property is a major consideration in the selection of a particular site for the club. Size is linked to profitability. The property had to be large enough to accommodate at least three tennis courts.

6. **(D)** Major Assumption. *Note the key word, "likelihood."* Although employing Ed's wife as club manager is a major goal sought, it is stated in the passage that Ed "believed he could convince her" to take the job. There is no information given to support Ed's belief that his wife will accept the position. Therefore, whether she will accept remains an assumption.

7. **(C)** Minor Factor. Room for a snack bar is secondary to the Major Factor of size.

8. **(B)** Major Factor. *Note the first word, "time."* Time is a major consideration in the decision process. It is stated in the passage that if the club is not completed on time, Ed would not be able to repay his bank loan.

9. **(E)** Unimportant Issue. There is nothing in the passage to suggest that the existence of an option deadline played an important role in the decision process. No relationship was shown between the option and the decision to bid for the property.

10. **(E)** Unimportant Issue. There is no explicit link between Ed's *experience* as a tennis player and the business venture. A better link is his *desire* (goal) to combine a pastime with a business.

Data Application Questions

11. **(B)** Alternatives I and II can be quickly eliminated. While there is little doubt that Ed's wife would gain business experience managing the club, it was not mentioned in the passage. Alternative II is incorrect, because the passage states that Ed did not want to give up his present job as a traveling salesman.

12. **(B)** No information is contained in the passage to allow the reader to infer alternatives I and II. Alternative III is given at the very beginning of the passage.

4

Writing Ability Review

In spite of its name, the Writing Ability part of the exam tests not writing ability but rather your understanding of the basic rules of English grammar and usage. To succeed in this section, you need a command of sentence structure including tense and mood, subject and verb agreement, proper case, parallel structure, and other basics. No attempt is made to test for punctuation, spelling, or capitalization.

The Writing Ability section is comprised of *Sentence Correction* questions. You will be given a sentence in which all or part of the sentence is underlined. You will then be asked to choose the best phrasing of the underlined part from five alternatives. (A) will always be the original phrasing.

EXAMPLE:

Not having heard clearly, <u>the speaker was asked to repeat his statement.</u>

  (A) the speaker was asked to repeat his statement
  (B) she asked the speaker to repeat again his statement
  (C) the speaker was asked to repeat his statement again
  (D) she asked the speaker to repeat his statement
  (E) she then asked the speaker again to repeat his statement

ANSWER:

  (D) is the best choice.

TIPS TO HELP YOU COPE

1. Read the sentence concentrating on the underlined part.
2. Check for pronoun errors. (Look for errors in words like *he, him, her, we, us, them, who, whom, whoever, whomever, you, it, which,* or *that.*)

---

3. If there are no pronoun errors, check the verbs.
4. If you find no errors in either verbs or pronouns, look at adjectives and adverbs.
5. Other possible errors include the use of incorrect idioms and faulty parallelism.
6. If the sentence is correct, select (A) as your answer.

REVIEW OF ERRORS COMMONLY FOUND IN THE WRITING ABILITY SECTION

Since you need only *recognize* errors in grammar and usage for this part of the exam, this section of the book will review those errors most commonly presented in the GMAT and teach you *what to look for*. We will not review the *basic* rules of grammar, such as the formation and use of the different tenses and the passive voice, the subjective and objective cases of pronouns, the position of adjectives and adverbs, and the like. We assume that a candidate for the GMAT is familiar with basic grammar, and we will concentrate on error recognition based on that knowledge.

VERB ERRORS

1. Errors in Verb Tense

Check if the correct verb *tense* has been used in the sentence.

INCORRECT: When I came home, the children still didn't finish dinner.
CORRECT: When I came home, the children still <u>hadn't finished</u> dinner.

In REPORTED SPEECH, check that the rule of *sequence of tenses* has been observed.

INCORRECT: She promised she will come.
CORRECT: She promised she <u>would</u> come.

2. Errors in Tense Formation

Check if the tense has been formed correctly. *Know* the past participle of irregular verbs!

INCORRECT: He throwed it out the window.
CORRECT: He threw it out the window.

3. Errors in Subject-Verb Agreement

Check if the subject of the verb is singular or plural. Does the verb agree in number?

Multiple subjects will be connected by the word AND:

Ted, John, and I are going.

If a singular subject is separated by a comma from an accompanying phrase, *it remains singular.*

The bride, together with the groom and her parents, is receiving at the door.

INCORRECT: There is many reasons why I can't help you.
CORRECT: There are many reasons why I can't help you.

4. Errors in Conditional Sentences

In conditional sentences, the word *if* will NEVER be followed by the words *will* or *would*.

Here are the correct conditional forms:

FUTURE: If I have time, I will do it tomorrow.
PRESENT: If I had time, I would do it now.
PAST: If I had had time, I would have done it yesterday.

Sentences using the words *when, as soon as, the moment,* etc., are formed like future conditionals:

I will tell him if I see him.
I will tell him when I see him.

The verb *to be* will ALWAYS appear as *were* in the present conditional:

If I were you, I wouldn't do that.
She wouldn't say so if she weren't sure.

NOTE: Not all sentences containing *if* are conditionals. When *if* appears in the meaning of *whether*, it may take the future:

> I don't know if he will be there. (I don't know whether he will be there.)

INCORRECT: If I would have known, I wouldn't have gone.
CORRECT: If I had known, I wouldn't have gone.

5. Errors in Expressions of Desire

Unfulfilled desires are expressed by the form "_____ had hoped that _____ would (or *could*, or *might*) do _____."

> I had hoped that I would pass the exam.

Expressions with *wish* are formed as follows:

PRESENT: I wish I knew him.
FUTURE: I wish you could (would) come.
PAST: I wish he had come. (or could have come, would have come, might have come)

NOTE: As in conditionals, the verb *to be* will ALWAYS appear as *were* in the present: I wish she were here.

INCORRECT: I wish I heard that story about him before I met him.
CORRECT: I wish I had heard (or could have heard or would have heard) that story about him before I met him.

6. Errors in Verbs Followed by VERB WORDS

The following list consists of words and expressions that are followed by a VERB WORD (the infinitive without the *to*):

ask	prefer	requirement
demand	recommend	suggest
desire	recommendation	suggestion
insist	require	urge

It is essential/imperative/important/necessary that . . .

INCORRECT: She ignored the doctor's recommendation that she stops smoking.
CORRECT: She ignored the doctor's recommendation that she stop smoking.

7. Errors in Negative Imperatives

Note the two forms for negative imperatives:

a. Please <u>don't</u> do that.
b. Would you please <u>not</u> do that.

INCORRECT: Would you please don't smoke here.
CORRECT: Please <u>don't</u> smoke here.

OR

Would you please <u>not</u> smoke here.

8. Errors in Affirmative and Negative Agreement of Verbs

Note the two correct forms for *affirmative* agreement:

a. <u>I am</u> an American and <u>so is she</u>.
b. <u>I am</u> an American and <u>she is too</u>.

a. <u>Mary likes</u> Bach and <u>so does John</u>.
b. <u>Mary likes</u> Bach and <u>John does too</u>.

a. <u>My father will be</u> there and <u>so will my mother</u>.
b. <u>My father will be</u> there and <u>my mother will too</u>.

INCORRECT: I have seen the film and she also has.
CORRECT: <u>I have seen</u> the film and <u>so has she</u>.

OR

<u>I have seen</u> the film and <u>she has too</u>.

Note the two correct forms for *negative* agreement:

a. <u>I'm not</u> American and <u>he isn't either</u>.
b. <u>I'm not</u> American and <u>neither is he</u>.

a. <u>Mary doesn't like</u> Bach and <u>John doesn't either</u>.
b. <u>Mary doesn't like</u> Bach and <u>neither does John</u>.

a. <u>My father won't be</u> there and <u>my mother won't either</u>.
b. <u>My father won't be</u> there and <u>neither will my mother</u>.

INCORRECT: I haven't seen the film and she hasn't neither.
CORRECT: I haven't seen the film and <u>she hasn't either</u>.

OR

I haven't seen the film and <u>neither has she</u>.

9. Errors of Infinitives or Gerunds in the Complement of Verbs

Some verbs may be followed by either an infinitive or a gerund:

I love <u>swimming</u> at night.
I love <u>to swim</u> at night.

Other verbs, however, may require either one *or* the other for idiomatic reasons. Following is a list of the more commonly used verbs in this category:

Verbs requiring an INFINITIVE:

agree	fail	intend	promise
decide	hope	learn	refuse
expect	want	plan	

Verbs requiring a GERUND:

admit	deny	quit
appreciate	enjoy	regret
avoid	finish	risk
consider	practice	stop

Phrases requiring a GERUND.

approve of	do not mind	keep on
be better off	forget about	look forward to
can't help	insist on	think about
count on	get through	think of

INCORRECT: I intend learning French next semester.
CORRECT: I intend <u>to learn</u> French next semester.

10. Errors in Verbs Requiring HOW in the Complement

The verbs KNOW, TEACH, LEARN, and SHOW require the word *HOW* before an infinitive in the complement.

INCORRECT: She knows to drive.
CORRECT: She knows <u>how</u> to drive.

11. Errors in Tag Endings

Check for *three* things in tag endings:
   a. Does the ending use the *same person* as the sentence verb?
   b. Does the ending use the *same tense* as the sentence verb?

c. If the sentence verb is positive, is the ending negative; if the sentence verb is negative, is the ending positive?

It's nice here, isn't it?
It isn't nice here, is it?

She speaks French, doesn't she?
She doesn't speak French, does she?

They'll be here tomorrow, won't they?
They won't be here tomorrow, will they?

EXCEPTIONS:

I'm right, aren't I?
We ought to go, shouldn't we?
Let's see, shall we?

NOTE: If there is a contraction in the sentence verb, make sure you know what the contraction stands for:

INCORRECT: She's been there before, isn't she?
CORRECT: She's been there before, hasn't she?

12. Errors in Idiomatic Verb Expressions

Following are a few commonly used idiomatic verb expressions. Notice whether they are followed by a verb word, a participle, an infinitive, or a gerund. Memorize a sample of each to check yourself when choosing an answer:

a. *must have (done)*—meaning "it is a logical conclusion"

They're late. They must have missed the bus.
There's no answer. They must have gone out.

b. *had better (do)*—meaning "it is advisable"

It's getting cold. You had better take your coat.
He still has fever. He had better not go out yet.

c. *used to (do)*—meaning "was in the habit of doing in the past"

I used to smoke a pack of cigarettes a day, but I stopped.
When I worked on a farm, I used to get up at 4:30 in the morning.

d. *to be used to*—meaning "to be accustomed to"

to get used to
to become used to } —meaning "to become accustomed to"

The noise doesn't bother me; I'm used to studying with the radio on.
In America you'll get used to hearing only English all day long.

e. *make* someone *do*—meaning "force someone to do"
   have someone *do*—meaning "cause someone to do"
   let someone *do*—meaning "allow someone to do"

My mother made me take my little sister with me to the movies.
The teacher had us write an essay instead of taking an exam.
The usher didn't let us come in until the intermission.

f. *would rather*—meaning "would prefer"

I would rather speak to her myself.
I would rather not speak to her myself.

But if the preference is for someone *other than the subject* to do the action, use the PAST:

I would rather you spoke to her.
I would rather you didn't speak to her.

PRONOUN ERRORS

1. Errors in Pronoun Subject-Object

Check if a pronoun is the SUBJECT or the OBJECT of a verb or preposition.

INCORRECT: All of us—Fred, Jane, Alice, and me—were late.
CORRECT: All of us—Fred, Jane, Alice, and I—were late.

2. Errors with WHO and WHOM

When in doubt about the correctness of WHO/WHOM, try substituting the subject/object of a simpler pronoun to clarify the meaning:

I don't know who/whom Sarah meant.

Try substituting *he/him*; then rearrange the clause in its proper order:

he/him Sarah meant / Sarah meant him

Now it is clear that the pronoun is the *object* of the verb *meant*, so *whom* is called for.

CORRECT: I don't know whom Sarah meant.

ANOTHER EXAMPLE:

There was a discussion as to who/whom was better suited.

> Try substituting *she/her*:

>> she was better suited / her was better suited

> Here the pronoun is the *subject* of the verb *suited*:

CORRECT: There was a discussion as to who was better suited.

3. Errors of Pronoun Subject-Verb Agreement

Check if the pronoun and its verb agree in number. Remember that the following are *singular*:

anyone	either	neither	what
anything	everyone	no one	whatever
each	everything	nothing	whoever

These are *plural*:

both	many	several	others
few			

INCORRECT: John is absent, but a few of the class is here.
CORRECT: John is absent, but a few of the class are here.

INCORRECT: Everyone on the project have to come to the meeting.
CORRECT: Everyone on the project has to come to the meeting.

NOTE: In the forms *either. . . or* and *neither. . . nor*, the word directly preceding the verb will determine whether the verb should be singular or plural:

> Either his parent or he is bringing it.
> Either he or his parents are bringing it.

> Neither his parents nor he was there.
> Neither he nor his parents were there.

4. Errors of Possessive Pronoun Agreement

Check if possessive pronouns agree in *person* and *number*.

INCORRECT: If anyone calls, take their name.
CORRECT: If anyone calls, take his name.

5. Errors in Pronouns after the Verb TO BE

TO BE is an intransitive verb and will always be followed by a subject pronoun.

INCORRECT: It must have been her at the door.
CORRECT: It must have been she at the door.

6. Errors in Position of Relative Pronouns

A relative pronoun refers to the word preceding it. If the meaning is unclear, the pronoun is in the wrong position.

INCORRECT: He could park right in front of the door, which was very convenient.

Since it was not the door which was convenient, the "which" is illogical in this position. In order to correct the sentence, it is necessary to rewrite it completely:

CORRECT: His being allowed to park right in front of the door was very convenient.

7. Errors in Parallelism of Impersonal Pronouns

In forms using impersonal pronouns, use *either* "one . . . one's/his or her" *or* "you . . . your."

INCORRECT: One should take your duties seriously.
CORRECT: One should take one's/his or her duties seriously.

OR

You should take your duties seriously.

ADJECTIVE AND ADVERB ERRORS

1. Errors in the Use of Adjectives and Adverbs

Check if a word modifier is an ADJECTIVE or an ADVERB. Make sure the correct form has been used.

An ADJECTIVE describes a noun and answers the question, *What kind?*

She is a good cook. (What kind of cook?)

An ADVERB describes either a verb or an adjective and answers the question, *How?*

She cooks <u>well</u>. (She cooks how?)

This exercise is <u>relatively easy</u>. (How easy?)

Most adverbs are formed by adding *-ly* to the adjective.

EXCEPTIONS:

Adjective	Adverb
early	early
fast	fast
good	well
hard	hard (*hardly* means *almost not*)
late	late (*lately* means *recently*)

INCORRECT: I sure wish I were rich!

CORRECT: I <u>surely</u> wish I were rich!

2. Errors of Adjectives with Verbs of Sense

The following verbs of sense are intransitive and are described by ADJECTIVES:

be	look	smell	taste
feel	seem	sound	

INCORRECT: She looked very well.

CORRECT: She looked very <u>good</u>.

NOTE: "He is well" is also correct in the meaning of "He is healthy" or in describing a person's well-being.

INCORRECT: The food tastes deliciously.

CORRECT: The food tastes <u>delicious</u>.

NOTE: When the above verbs are used as transitive verbs, modify with an adverb, as usual: She tasted the soup <u>quickly</u>.

3. Errors in Comparatives

a. Similar comparison

ADJECTIVE: She is <u>as pretty as</u> her sister.

ADVERB: He works <u>as hard as</u> his father.

b. Comparative (of two things)

ADJECTIVE: She is prettier than her sister.
              She is more beautiful than her sister.
              She is less successful than her sister.

ADVERB: He works harder than his father.
              He reads more quickly than I.
              He drives less carelessly than he used to.

NOTE 1: A pronoun following *than* in a comparison will be the *subject pronoun*:

You are prettier than she (is).
You drive better than he (does).

NOTE 2: In using comparisons, adjectives of one syllable, or of two syllables ending in *-y*, add *-er*: smart, smarter; pretty, prettier. Other words of more than one syllable use *more*: interesting, more interesting. Adverbs of one syllable add *-er*; longer adverbs use *more*: fast, faster; quickly, more quickly.

NOTE 3: The word *different* is followed by *from*:

You are different from me.

c. Superlative (comparison of more than two things)

ADJECTIVE: She is the prettiest girl in her class.
              He is the most successful of his brothers.
              This one is the least interesting of the three.

ADVERB: He plays the best of all.
              He speaks the most interestingly.
              He spoke to them the least patronizingly.

EXCEPTIONAL FORMS:

good	better	best
bad	worse	worst
much/many	more	most
little	less	least

INCORRECT: This exercise is harder then the last one.
CORRECT: This exercise is harder than the last one.

4. Errors in Parallel Comparisons

In parallel comparisons, check if the correct form has been used.

INCORRECT: The more you practice, you will get better.
CORRECT: The more you practice, the better you will get.

5. Errors of Illogical Comparatives

Check comparisons to make sure they *make sense*.

INCORRECT: Texas is bigger than any state in the United States.
CORRECT: Texas is bigger than any other state in the United States. (If Texas were bigger than *any state*, it would be bigger than itself!)

6. Errors of Identical Comparisons

Something can be *the same as* OR *like* something else. Do not mix up the two forms.

INCORRECT: Your dress is the same like mine.
CORRECT: Your dress is like mine.

OR

Your dress is the same as mine.

7. Errors in Idioms Using Comparative Structures

Some idiomatic terms are formed like comparatives, although they are not true comparisons:

as high as   as much as   as few as
as little as   as many as

INCORRECT: You may have to spend so much as two hours waiting.
CORRECT: You may have to spend as much as two hours waiting.

8. Errors in Noun-Adjectives

When a NOUN is used as an ADJECTIVE, treat it as an adjective. Do not pluralize or add *'s*.

INCORRECT: You're talking like a two-years-old child!
CORRECT: You're talking like a two-year-old child!

9. Errors in Ordinal and Cardinal Numbers

Ordinal numbers (first, second, third, etc.) are preceded by *the*. Cardinal numbers (one, two, three, etc.) are not.

> We missed the first act.
> We missed Act One.

NOTE: Ordinarily, either form is correct. There are two exceptions:

a. In *dates* use only *ordinal* numbers:

> May first (*not* May one)
> the first of May

b. In terms dealing with *travel*, use only *cardinal* numbers, as "Gate Three" may not actually be the third gate. It is Gate Number Three.

INCORRECT: We leave from the second pier.
CORRECT: We leave from Pier Two.

10. Errors in Modifying Countable and Noncountable Nouns

If a noun can be preceded by a number, it is a countable noun and will be modified by these words:

a few	many, more	some
few, fewer	number of	

If it cannot be preceded by a number, it is noncountable and will be modified by these words:

amount of	little, less	some
a little	much, more	

INCORRECT: I was surprised by the large amount of people who came.
CORRECT: I was surprised by the large number of people who came.

ERRORS IN USAGE

1. Errors in Connectors

There are several ways of connecting ideas. Do not mix the different forms:

and	also	not only . . . but also
too	as well as	both . . . and

INCORRECT: She speaks not only Spanish but French as well.
CORRECT: She speaks Spanish and French.

She speaks Spanish. She also speaks French.

She speaks Spanish and French too.

She speaks not only Spanish but also French.

She speaks both Spanish and French.

She speaks Spanish as well as French.

2. Errors in Question Word Connectors

When a question word such as *when* or *what* is used as a connector, the clause that follows is *not* a question. Do not use the interrogative form.

INCORRECT: Do you know when does the movie start?
CORRECT: Do you know when the movie starts?

3. Errors in Purpose Connectors

The word *so* by itself means *therefore*.

It was too hot to study, so we went to the beach.

So that means *in order to* or *in order that*.

INCORRECT: We took a cab so we would be on time.
CORRECT: We took a cab so that we would be on time.

4. Errors with BECAUSE

It is incorrect to say: *The reason is because* . . . Use: *The reason is that* . . .

INCORRECT: The reason he was rejected was because he was too young.
CORRECT: The reason he was rejected was that he was too young.

OR

He was rejected because of his young age.

OR

He was rejected because he was too young.

5. Errors of Dangling Modifiers

An introductory verbal modifier should be directly followed by the noun or pronoun which it modifies. Such a modifier will start with a gerund or participial phrase and be followed by a comma. Look for the modified noun or pronoun *immediately* after the comma.

INCORRECT: Seeing that the hour was late, it was decided to postpone the committee vote.

CORRECT: <u>Seeing</u> that the hour was late, <u>the committee</u> decided to postpone the vote.

6. Errors in Parallel Construction

In sentences containing a series of two or more items, check if the same form has been used for all the items in the series. Do *not* mix infinitives with gerunds, adjectives with participial phrases, or verbs with nouns.

INCORRECT: The film was interesting, exciting, and it was made well.

CORRECT: The film was <u>interesting</u>, <u>exciting</u>, and <u>well made</u>.

7. Errors of Unnecessary Modifiers

In general, the more simply an idea is stated, the better it is. An adverb or adjective can often eliminate extraneous words.

INCORRECT: He drove in a careful way.

CORRECT: He drove carefully.

Beware of words with the same meaning in the same sentence.

INCORRECT: The new innovations were startling.

CORRECT: The innovations were startling.

Beware of general wordiness.

INCORRECT: That depends on the state of the general condition of the situation.

CORRECT: That depends on the situation.

8. Errors of Commonly Confused Words

Following are some of the more commonly misused words in English:

a. **to lie**	lied	lied	lying	to tell an untruth
to lie	lay	lain	lying	to recline
to lay	laid	laid	laying	to put down (*Idiomatic* usage: LAY THE TABLE, put dishes, etc., on the table; CHICKENS LAY EGGS; LAY A BET, make a bet)

b. **to rise**	rose	risen	rising	to go up; to get up
to arise	arose	arisen	arising	to wake up; to get up (*Idiomatic* usage: A PROBLEM HAS ARISEN, a problem has come up)
to raise	raised	raised	raising	to lift; bring up (*Idiomatic* usage: TO RAISE CHILDREN, to bring up children; TO RAISE VEGETABLES, to grow vegetables; TO RAISE MONEY, to collect funds for a cause)
c. **to set**	set	set	setting	to put down (*Idiomatic* usage: SET A DATE, arrange a date; SET THE TABLE, put dishes, etc., on the table; THE SUN SET, the sun went down for the night; TO SET THE CLOCK, to adjust the timing mechanism of a clock)
to sit	sat	sat	sitting	to be in or get into a sitting position
d. **to let**	let	let	letting	to allow; to rent
to leave	left	left	leaving	to go away

e. **formerly**—previously
   formally—in a formal way

f. **to affect**—to influence (verb)
   effect—result (noun)

INCORRECT: He was laying in bed all day yesterday.
CORRECT: He was <u>lying</u> in bed all day yesterday.

INCORRECT: The price of gas has raised three times last year.
CORRECT: The price of gas <u>rose</u> three times last year.

OR

The price of gas <u>was raised</u> three times last year.

INCORRECT: He raised slowly from his chair.
CORRECT: He <u>arose</u> slowly from his chair.

9. Errors of Misused Words and Prepositional Idioms

a. in spite of; despite

The two expressions are synonymous; use *either* one *or* the other.

INCORRECT: They came despite of the rain.
CORRECT: They came in spite of the rain.

OR

They came despite the rain.

b. scarcely; barely; hardly

All three words mean *almost not at all*; do NOT use a negative with them.

INCORRECT: I hardly never see him.
CORRECT: I hardly ever see him.

INCORRECT: He has scarcely no money.
CORRECT: He has scarcely any money.

c. Note and memorize the prepositions in these common idioms:

approve/disapprove of	agree/disagree with
be ashamed of	compare with (point out
capable/incapable of	similarities between things of a
be conscious of	different order)
be afraid of	compare to (point out differences
independent of	between things of the same
in the habit of	order)
be interested in	be equal to
except for	next to
dependent on	related to
be bored with	similar to

STRATEGY FOR SENTENCE CORRECTION QUESTIONS

The first step in the Sentence Correction part of the exam is to read the sentence carefully in order to spot an error of grammar or usage. Once you have found an error, eliminate choice (A) and ALL OTHER ALTERNATIVES CONTAINING THAT ERROR. Concentrate on the remaining alternatives to choose your answer. Do not select an alternative that has changed the *meaning* of the original sentence.

EXAMPLE 1:

If I knew him better, <u>I would have insisted that he change</u> the hour of the lecture.

    (A) I would have insisted that he change

    (B) I would have insisted that he changed

    (C) I would insist that he change

    (D) I would insist for him to change

    (E) I would have insisted him to change

Since we must assume the unmarked part of the sentence to be correct, this is a PRESENT CONDITIONAL sentence; therefore, the second verb in the sentence should read *I would insist*. Glancing through the alternatives, you can eliminate (A), (B), and (E). You are left with (C) and (D). Remember that the word *insist* takes a *verb word* after it. (C) is the only correct answer.

If you do not find any grammatical error in the underlined part, read the alternatives to see if one of them does not use a clearer or more concise style to express the same thing. Do not choose an alternative that changes the meaning of the original sentence.

EXAMPLE 2:

<u>The couple, who had been married recently, booked their honeymoon passage through an agent who lived near them.</u>

    (A) The couple, who had been married recently, booked their honeymoon passage through an agent who lived near them.

    (B) The couple, who had been recently married, booked their honeymoon passage through an agent who lived not far from them.

    (C) The newlyweds booked their honeymoon passage through a local agent.

    (D) The newlyweds booked their passage through an agent that lived not far from them.

    (E) The couple lived not far from the agent who through him they booked their passage.

Although (A), the original, has no real errors, (C) expresses the same thing more concisely, without distorting the original meaning of the sentence.

Remember: If you find no errors, and if you find that none of the alternatives improve the original, choose (A).

PRACTICE EXERCISE

Directions: This exercise consists of a number of sentences, in each of which some part or the whole is underlined. Each sentence is followed by five alternative versions of the underlined portion. Select the alternative you consider both most correct and most effective according to the requirements of standard written English. Answer (A) is the same as the original version; if you think the original version is best, select answer (A).

In considering the answer choices, be attentive to matters of grammar, diction, and syntax, as well as clarity, precision, and fluency. Do not select an answer which alters the meaning of the original sentence.

1. A good doctor inquires not only about his patients'   1. Ⓐ Ⓑ Ⓒ Ⓓ Ⓔ
   physical health, but about their mental health too.
   (A) but about their mental health too
   (B) but their mental health also
   (C) but also he inquires about their mental health
   (D) but also about their mental health
   (E) but too about their mental health

2. Knowing that the area was prone to earthquakes, all   2. Ⓐ Ⓑ Ⓒ Ⓓ Ⓔ
   the buildings were reinforced with additional steel and
   concrete.
   (A) Knowing that the area was prone to earthquakes,
   (B) Having known that the area was prone to earth-
       quakes,
   (C) Since the area was known to be prone to earth-
       quakes,
   (D) Since they knew that the area was prone to earth-
       quakes,
   (E) Being prone to earthquakes,

3. John would never have taken the job if he had known   3. Ⓐ Ⓑ Ⓒ Ⓓ Ⓔ
   what great demands it would make on his time.
   (A) if he had known
   (B) if he knew
   (C) if he had been knowing
   (D) if he knows
   (E) if he was knowing

4. Anyone wishing to enroll in the program should send   4. Ⓐ Ⓑ Ⓒ Ⓓ Ⓔ
   in their applications before the fifteenth of the month.
   (A) send in their applications
   (B) send their applications in
   (C) send in their application
   (D) send their application in
   (E) send in his application

5. Start the actual writing only after having thoroughly   5. Ⓐ Ⓑ Ⓒ Ⓓ Ⓔ
   researched your subject, organized your notes, and
   you have planned an outline.
   (A) you have planned an outline
   (B) planned an outline
   (C) you having planned an outline
   (D) an outline has been planned
   (E) an outline was planned

Answers and Analysis

1. **(D)** The connective *not only* MUST be accompanied by *but also*. Eliminate
   (A), (B), and (E). (C) repeats *he inquires* unnecessarily. (D) is correct.

2. **(C)** *All the buildings* couldn't have known that the area was prone to earthquakes. Since the unmarked part of the sentence must be assumed to be
   correct, eliminate all alternatives beginning with a dangling modifier: (A),
   (B), and (E). In (D) the word *they* is unclear. Where there is no definite subject,
   the passive is preferable. (C) is correct.

3. **(A)** This is a past conditional sentence. (A) is correct.

4. **(E)** *Anyone* is singular. At one glance eliminate every choice but (E).

5. **(B)** Here is a series of three verbs: having *researched, organized,* and
   planned. (B) is correct.

5

Problem Solving and Data Sufficiency Review

This chapter contains explanations, examples and strategies for the Problem Solving and Data Sufficiency sections on the GMAT. In addition, it contains a brief mathematics review.

PROBLEM SOLVING

The Problem Solving section of the GMAT is designed to test your ability to work with numbers. There are a variety of questions in this section dealing with the basic principles of arithmetic, algebra, and geometry. These questions may take the form of word problems or require straight calculation. In addition, questions involving the interpretation of tables and graphs may be included.

The typical Problem Solving section that has appeared on recent tests consists of 20 questions that must be answered within a time limit of 30 minutes. These questions range from very easy to quite challenging and are not always arranged in order of difficulty. Make sure you budget your time so that you can try each question.

TIPS TO HELP YOU COPE

1. If a problem involves geometry, and a diagram is not provided, draw a picture.
2. Before you start to work a problem, check the answers to see how accurate the answer must be. For example, if all the answers are given in tenths,

don't use five decimal places in your computations.

3. Don't waste time on unnecessary calculations. If you can answer the question by estimating or doing a rough calculation, the time you save can be used to work on other questions. Keep this in mind especially when doing problems that involve tables or graphs.

4. Make sure your answer is in the units asked for. Change all measurements to the same units before you do any calculations.

5. Reread the question to make sure you answered the question that was asked as opposed to the question you THOUGHT would be asked.

6. If possible check your answer. For example, if you solve an equation, check that the number you obtained actually solves the equation. Always ask yourself if an answer makes sense.

7. You will not be allowed to use a calculator on the exam. Practice doing arithmetic without a calculator for a week or two before the test.

8. Don't waste time working on a problem you can't solve in two or three minutes. Be sure to budget your time so that you can try each question. After you have tried each question, then work on questions that you might solve in more than three minutes.

9. Remember that it is worthwhile to guess if you can eliminate any answers.

10. Use the test booklet for scrap work.

Solve the sample questions below, allowing yourself 12 minutes to complete all of them. As you work, try to make use of the above strategy. Any figure that

appears with a problem is drawn as accurately as possible to provide information that may help in answering the question. All numbers used are real
numbers.

SAMPLE PROBLEM SOLVING QUESTIONS

Time: 12 minutes

1. A train travels from Albany to Syracuse, a distance of 120 miles, at the average rate of 50 miles per hour. The train then travels back to Albany from Syracuse. The total traveling time of the train is 5 hours and 24 minutes. What was the average rate of speed of the train on the return trip to Albany?

1. Ⓐ Ⓑ Ⓒ Ⓓ Ⓔ

(A) 60 mph   (D) 50 mph
(B) 48 mph   (E) 35 mph
(C) 40 mph

2. A parking lot charges a flat rate of X dollars for any amount of time up to two hours, and $\frac{1}{6}X$ for each hour or fraction of an hour after the first two hours. How much does it cost to park for 5 hours and 15 minutes?

2. Ⓐ Ⓑ Ⓒ Ⓓ Ⓔ

(A) $3X$ (D) $1\frac{1}{2}X$
(B) $2X$ (E) $1\frac{1}{6}X$
(C) $1\frac{2}{3}X$

Use the following table for questions 3–5.

Number of Students by major in State University		
	1950	1970
Division of Business	990	2,504
Division of Sciences	350	790
Division of Humanities	1,210	4,056
Division of Engineering	820	1,600
Division of Agriculture	630	1,050
TOTAL	4,000	10,000

3. From 1950 to 1970, the change in the percentage of   3. Ⓐ Ⓑ Ⓒ Ⓓ Ⓔ
university students enrolled in Engineering was
(A) roughly no change
(B) an increase of more than 4%
(C) an increase of more than 1% but less than 4%
(D) a decrease of more than 4%
(E) a decrease of more than 1% but less than 4%

4. The number of students enrolled in Business in 1970   4. Ⓐ Ⓑ Ⓒ Ⓓ Ⓔ
divided by the number of Business students in 1950 is
(A) almost 3
(B) about 2.5
(C) roughly 2
(D) about 1
(E) about 40%

5. By 1970 how many of the divisions had an enrollment   5. Ⓐ Ⓑ Ⓒ Ⓓ Ⓔ
greater than 200% of the enrollment of that division in
1950?
(A) 0   (D) 3
(B) 1   (E) 4
(C) 2

6. Which of the following sets of values for w, x, y, and   6. Ⓐ Ⓑ Ⓒ Ⓓ Ⓔ
z respectively are possible if ABCD is a parallelogram?

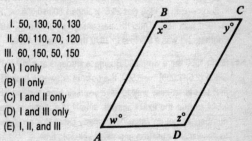

      I. 50, 130, 50, 130
     II. 60, 110, 70, 120
    III. 60, 150, 50, 150
(A) I only
(B) II only
(C) I and II only
(D) I and III only
(E) I, II, and III

7. John weighs twice as much as Marcia. Marcia's weight   7. Ⓐ Ⓑ Ⓒ Ⓓ Ⓔ
is 60% of Bob's weight. Dave weighs 50% of Lee's
weight. Lee weighs 190% of John's weight. Which of
these 5 persons weighs the least?
(A) Bob   (D) Lee
(B) Dave   (E) Marcia
(C) John

Answers and Analysis

Answers:

1. **(C)**	4. **(B)**	7. **(E)**
2. **(C)**	5. **(D)**	
3. **(D)**	6. **(A)**	

Analysis:

1. **(C)** The train took $120/50 = 2\frac{2}{5}$ hours to travel from Albany to Syracuse. Since the total traveling time of the train was $5\frac{2}{5}$ hours, it must have taken the train 3 hours for the trip from Syracuse to Albany. Since the distance traveled is 120 miles, the average rate of speed on the return trip to Albany was $(\frac{1}{3})(120)$ mph $= 40$ mph.

2. **(C)** It costs X for the first 2 hours. If you park 5 hours and 15 minutes there are 3 hours and 15 minutes left after the first 2 hours. Since this time is charged at the rate of $X/6$ for each hour or fraction thereof, it costs $4(X/6)$ for the last 3 hours and 15 minutes. Thus the total $X + \frac{4}{6}X = 1\frac{2}{3}X$.

3. **(D)** Since $820/4,000 = .205$, the percentage of university students enrolled in Engineering in 1950 was 20.5%; since $1,600/10,000 = .16$, the percentage in 1970 was 16%. Thus the percentage of university students enrolled in Engineering was 4.5% less in 1970 than it was in 1950.

4. **(B)** In 1950 there were 990 Business students and in 1970 there were 2,504. Since $(2.5)(1,000) = 2,500$, the correct answer is thus (B), about 2.5. Note that this is an easy way to save yourself time. Instead of dividing 990 into 2,504 to find the exact answer, simply use numbers close to the original numbers to get an estimate. In many cases this gives enough information to answer the question and saves valuable time.

5. **(D)** If a division in 1970 has more than 200% of the number of students it had in 1950 that means that the number of students more than doubled between 1950 and 1970. Therefore simply double each entry in the 1950 column and if this is less than the corresponding entry in the 1970 column, that division has more than 200% of the number of students it had in 1950. Since $(2)(990) = 1980$, which is less than 2,504, the number of Business

students more than doubled. Since $(2)(1,210) = 2,420$, which is less than 4,056, Humanities more than doubled, and because $(2)(350) = 700$, which is less than 790, Sciences more than doubled. Engineering did not double in size because $(2)(820) = 1640$, which is larger than 1,600. Also since $(2)(630) = 1,260$, which is larger than 1,050, the number of Agricultural students in 1970 was less than 200% of the number of Agricultural students in 1950. Therefore three of the divisions (Business, Humanities, and Sciences) more than doubled between 1950 and 1970.

6. **(A)** The sum of the angles of a parallelogram (which is 4-sided) must be $(4 - 2) 180° = 360°$. Since the sum of the values in III is 410, III cannot be correct. The sum of the numbers in II is 360, but in a parallelogram opposite angles must be equal so x must equal z and y must equal w. Since 60 is unequal to 70, II cannot be correct. The sum of the values in I is 360 and opposite angles will be equal, so I is correct.

7. **(E)** John weighs twice as much as Marcia, so John cannot weigh the least. Marcia's weight is less than Bob's weight, so Bob's weight is not the least. Dave's weight is ½ of Lee's weight, so Lee can't weigh the least. The only possible answers are Marcia or Dave. Let $J, M, B, D,$ and L stand for the weights of John, Marcia, Bob, Dave, and Lee respectively. Then $D = .5L = .5(1.9)J$. So $D = .95J$. Since $J = 2M$, we know $M = .5J$. Therefore Marcia weighs the least.

DATA SUFFICIENCY

This section of the GMAT is designed to test your reasoning ability. Like the Problem Solving section, it requires a basic knowledge of the principles of arithmetic, algebra, and geometry. Each Data Sufficiency question consists of a mathematical problem and two statements containing information relating to it. You must decide whether the problem can be solved by using information from: (A) the first statement alone, but not the second statement alone; (B) the second statement alone, but not the first statement alone; (C) both statements together, but neither alone; or (D) either of the statements alone. Choose (E) if the problem cannot be solved, even by using both statements together. A typical section will consist of 25 questions to be worked in 30 minutes. As in the Problem Solving section, time is of the utmost importance. Approaching Data Sufficiency problems properly will help you use this time wisely.

TIPS TO HELP YOU COPE

1. *Don't waste time figuring out the exact answer.* Always keep in mind that you are never asked to supply an answer for the problem; you need only determine if there is sufficient data available to find the answer. Once you know whether or not it is possible to find the answer with the given information, you are through. If you spend too much time doing unnecessary work on one question, you may not be able to finish the entire section.

2. *Don't make extra assumptions.* In particular, don't make inferences based on the diagram supplied with some problems. You can't really tell if an angle is 90 degrees or 89 degrees by looking at a picture.

3. *Use the strategies described below to improve your score on these sections.*

STRATEGY FOR DATA SUFFICIENCY QUESTIONS

A systematic analysis can improve your score on Data Sufficiency sections. By answering three questions, you will always arrive at the correct choice. In addition, if you can answer any one of the three questions, you can eliminate at least one of the possible choices so that you can make an intelligent guess.

The three questions are:

    I Is the first statement alone sufficient to solve the problem?

    II Is the second statement alone sufficient to solve the problem?

    III Are both statements together sufficient to solve the problem?

As a general rule try to answer the questions in the order I, II, III, since in many cases you will not have to answer all three to get the correct choice.

Here is how to use the three questions:

If the answer to I is YES, then the only possible choices are (A) or (D). Now, if the answer to II is YES, the choice must be (D), and if the answer to II is NO, the choice must be (A).

If the answer to I is NO then the only possible choices are (B), (C), or (E). Now, if the answer to II is YES, then the choice must be (B), and if the answer to II is NO, the only possible choices are (C) or (E).

So, finally, if the answer to III is YES, the choice is (C), and if the answer to III is NO, the choice is (E).

A good way to see this is to use a decision tree.

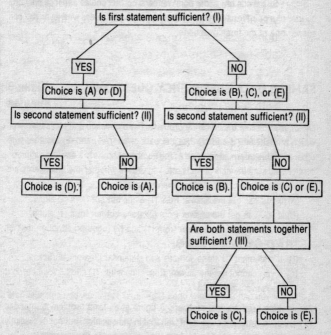

To use the tree simply start at the top and by answering YES or NO move down the tree until you arrive at the correct choice. For example, if the answer to I is YES and the answer to II is NO, then the correct choice is (A). (Notice that in this case you don't need to answer III to find the correct choice.)

The decision tree can also help you make intelligent guesses. If you can only answer one of the three questions, then you can eliminate the choices that follow from the wrong answer to the question.

Example 1. You know the **answer to I is** YES. You can eliminate choices (B), (C), and (E).

Example 2. You know the **answer to II is** NO. You can eliminate choices (D) and (B) since they follow from YES for II.

Example 3. You know the answer to III is YES. You can eliminate choice (E) since it follows from NO for III.

Example 4. You know the answer to I is NO and the answer to III is YES. You can eliminate (E) since it follows from NO to III. You also can eliminate (A) and (D) since they follow from YES to I.

Since you get one raw score point for each correct choice and lose only one quarter of a point for an incorrect choice, you should guess whenever you can answer one of the three questions.

SAMPLE DATA SUFFICIENCY QUESTIONS   Time: 8 minutes

Directions: Each of the following problems has a question and two statements which are labeled (1) and (2). Use the data given in (1) and (2) together with other available information (such as the number of hours in a day, the definition of *clockwise*, mathematical facts, etc.) to decide whether the statements are *sufficient* to answer the question. Then choose

   (A) if you can get the answer from (1) alone but not from (2) alone;
   (B) if you can get the answer from (2) alone but not from (1) alone;
   (C) if you can get the answer from (1) and (2) together, although neither statement by itself suffices;
   (D) if statement (1) alone suffices *and* statement (2) alone suffices;
   (E) if you cannot get the answer from statements (1) and (2) together, but need even more data.

All numbers used are real numbers. A figure given for a problem is intended to provide information consistent with that in the question, but not necessarily consistent with the additional information contained in the statements.

1. A rectangular field is 40 yards long. Find the area of   1. Ⓐ Ⓑ Ⓒ Ⓓ Ⓔ
   the field.
   (1) A fence around the entire boundary of the field is
       140 yards long.
   (2) The field is more than 20 yards wide.

2. Is X a number greater than zero?

    (1) $X^2 - 1 = 0$

    (2) $X^3 + 1 = 0$

2. Ⓐ Ⓑ Ⓒ Ⓓ Ⓔ

3. An industrial plant produces bottles. In 1961 the number of bottles produced by the plant was twice the number produced in 1960. How many bottles were produced altogether in the years 1960, 1961, and 1962?

    (1) In 1962 the number of bottles produced was 3 times the number produced in 1960.

    (2) In 1963 the number of bottles produced was one half the total produced in the years 1960, 1961, and 1962.

3. Ⓐ Ⓑ Ⓒ Ⓓ Ⓔ

4. A man 6 feet tall is standing near a light on the top of a pole. What is the length of the shadow cast by the man?

    (1) The pole is 18 feet high.

    (2) The man is 12 feet from the pole.

4. Ⓐ Ⓑ Ⓒ Ⓓ Ⓔ

5. Find the length of RS if z is 90° and $PS = 6$.

    (1) $PR = 6$

    (2) $x = 45°$

5. Ⓐ Ⓑ Ⓒ Ⓓ Ⓔ

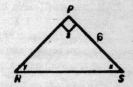

6. Working at a constant rate and by himself, it takes worker U 3 hours to fill up a ditch with sand. How long would it take for worker V to fill up the same ditch working by himself?

    (1) Working together but at the same time U and V can fill in the ditch in 1 hour 52½ minutes.

    (2) In any length of time worker V fills in only 60% as much as worker U does in the same time.

6. Ⓐ Ⓑ Ⓒ Ⓓ Ⓔ

7. Did John go to the beach yesterday?

    (1) If John goes to the beach, he will be sunburned the next day.

    (2) John is sunburned today.

7. Ⓐ Ⓑ Ⓒ Ⓓ Ⓔ

Answers and Analysis

Answers:

1. **(A)**	4. **(C)**	7. **(E)**
2. **(B)**	5. **(D)**	
3. **(E)**	6. **(D)**	

Analysis:

1. **(A)** The area of a rectangle is the length multiplied by the width. Since you know the length is 40 yards, you must find out the width in order to solve the problem. Since statement (2) simply says the width is greater than 20 yards you cannot find out the exact width using (2). So (2) alone is not sufficient. Statement (1) says the length of a fence around the entire boundary of the field is 140 yards. The length of this fence is the perimeter of the rectangle, the sum of twice the length and twice the width. If we replace the length by 40 in $P = 2L + 2W$ we have $140 = 2(40) + 2W$ and solving for W yields $2W = 60$, or $W = 30$ yards. Hence the area is $(40)(30) = 1200$ square yards. Thus (1) alone is sufficient but (2) alone is not.

2. **(B)** Statement (1) means $X^2 = 1$, but there are two possible solutions to this equation, $X = 1$, $X = -1$. Thus using (1) alone you can not deduce whether X is positive or negative. Statement (2) means $X^3 = -1$ but there is only one possible (real) solution to this, $X = -1$. Thus X is not greater than zero which answers the question. And (2) alone is sufficient.

3. **(E)** T, the total produced in the three years, is the sum of $P_0 + P_1 + P_2$, where P_0 is the number produced in 1960, P_1 the number produced in 1961, and P_2 the number produced in 1962. You are given that $P_1 = 2P_0$. Thus $T = P_0 + P_1 + P_2 = P_0 + 2P_0 + P_2 = 3P_0 + P_2$. So we must find out P_0 and P_2 to answer the question. Statement (1) says $P_2 = 3P_0$; thus by using (1) if we can find the value of P_0 we can find T. But (1) gives us no further information about P_0. Statement (2) says T equals the number produced in 1963, but it does not say what this number is. Since there are no relations given between production in 1963 and production in the individual years 1960, 1961, or 1962 you cannot use (2) to find out what P_0 is. Thus (1) and (2) together are not sufficient.

4. **(C)** Sometimes it may help to draw a picture. By proportions or by similar triangles the height of the pole, h, is to 6 feet as the length of shadow, s, + the distance to the pole, x, is to s. So $h/6 = (s + x)/s$. Thus $hs = 6s$

+ 6x by cross-multiplication. Solving for s gives $hs - 6s = 6x$, or $s(h - 6) = 6x$, or, finally we have $s = 6x/(h - 6)$. Statement (1) says $h = 18$; thus $s = 6x/12 = x/2$, but using (1) alone we cannot deduce the value x. Thus (1) alone is not sufficient. Statement (2) says x equals 12; thus, using (1) and (2) together we deduce $s = 6$, but using (2) alone all we can deduce is that $s = 72/(h - 6)$, which cannot be solved for s unless we know h. Thus using (1) and (2) together we can deduce the answer but (1) alone is not sufficient nor is (2) alone.

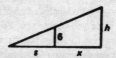

5. **(D)** Since z is a right angle, $(RS)^2 = (PS)^2 + (PR)^2$, so $(RS)^2 = (6)^2 + (PR)^2$, and RS will be the positive square root of $36 + (PR)^2$. Thus if you can find the length of PR the problem is solved. Statement (1) says $PR = 6$, thus $(RS)^2 = 36 + 36$, so $RS = 6\sqrt{2}$. Thus (1) alone is sufficient. Statement (2) says $x = 45°$ but since the sum of the angles in a triangle is 180° and z is 90° then $y = 45°$. So x and y are equal angles and that means the sides opposite x and opposite y must be equal or $PS = PR$. Thus $PR = 6$ and $RS = 6\sqrt{2}$ so (2) alone is also sufficient.

6. **(D)** (1) says U and V together can fill in the ditch in 1⅞ hours. Since U can fill in the ditch in 3 hours, in 1 hour he can fill in one-third of the ditch. Hence, in 1⅞ hours U would fill in $(⅓)(15/8) = 5/8$ of the ditch. So V fills in ⅜ of the ditch in 1⅞ hours. Thus V would take $(8/3)(15/8) = 5$ hours to fill in the ditch working by himself. Therefore statement (1) alone is sufficient. According to statement (2) since U fills the ditch in 3 hours, V will fill ⅗ of the ditch in 3 hours. Thus V will take 5 hours to fill in the ditch working by himself.

7. **(E)** Obviously, neither statement alone is sufficient. John *could* have gotten sunburned at the beach, but he might have gotten sunburned somewhere else. Therefore (1) and (2) together are not sufficient. This problem tests your grasp of an elementary rule of logic rather than your mathematical knowledge.

QUICK MATHEMATICS REVIEW

The Problem Solving and Data Sufficiency areas of the GMAT require a working knowledge of mathematical principles. The following is a brief review of topics that many people need to brush up on. If you want a more comprehensive review of mathematics, we recommend the review that appears in *Barron's How to Prepare for the GMAT*.

ARITHMETIC

Fractions

A *fraction* is a number which represents a ratio or division of two whole numbers (integers). A fraction is written in the form $\frac{a}{b}$. The number on the top, a, is called the numerator; the number on the bottom, b, is called the denominator. The denominator tells how many equal parts there are (for example, parts of a pie); the numerator tells how many of these equal parts are taken. For example, $\frac{5}{8}$ is a fraction whose numerator is 5 and whose denominator is 8; it represents taking 5 of 8 equal parts, or dividing 8 into 5.

> A fraction cannot have 0 as a denominator since division by 0 is not defined.

A fraction with 1 as the denominator is the same as the whole number which is its numerator. For example, $\frac{12}{1}$ is 12, $\frac{0}{1}$ is 0.

If the numerator and denominator of a fraction are identical, the fraction represents 1. For example, $\frac{3}{3} = \frac{9}{9} = \frac{13}{13} = 1$. Any whole number, k, is represented by a fraction with a numerator equal to k times the denominator. For example, $\frac{18}{6} = 3$, and $\frac{30}{5} = 6$.

Mixed Numbers

A *mixed number* consists of a whole number and a fraction. For example, $7\frac{1}{4}$

is a mixed number; it means $7 + \frac{1}{4}$ and $\frac{1}{4}$ is called the fractional part of the

mixed number $7\frac{1}{4}$. Any mixed number can be changed into a fraction:

(A) Multiply the whole number by the denominator of the fractional part.
(B) Add the numerator of the fraction to the result of step A.
(C) Use the result of step B as the numerator and use the denominator of the fractional part of the mixed number as the denominator. This fraction is equal to the mixed number.

EXAMPLE:

Write $7\frac{1}{4}$ as a fraction.

(A) $4 \cdot 7 = 28$ (B) $28 + 1 = 29$ (C)   so $7\frac{1}{4} = \frac{29}{4}$.

In calculations with mixed numbers, change the mixed numbers into fractions.

Multiplying Fractions

To multiply two fractions, multiply their numerators and divide this result by the product of their denominators.

In word problems, *of* usually indicates multiplication.

EXAMPLE:

John saves $\frac{1}{3}$ of $240. How much does he save?

$\frac{1}{3} \cdot \frac{240}{1} = \frac{240}{3} = \$80$, the amount John saves.

Dividing Fractions

One fraction is a *reciprocal* of another if their product is 1. So $\frac{1}{2}$ and 2 are

reciprocals. To find the reciprocal of a fraction, simply interchange the numerator and denominator (turn the fraction upside down). This is called *inverting* the fraction. So when you invert $\frac{15}{17}$ you get $\frac{17}{15}$. When a fraction is inverted the inverted fraction and the original fraction are reciprocals. Thus $\frac{15}{17} \cdot \frac{17}{15} = \frac{255}{255} = \frac{1}{1} = 1$.

To divide one fraction (the dividend) by another fraction (the divisor), invert the divisor and multiply.

EXAMPLE:
$$\frac{5}{6} \div \frac{3}{4} = \frac{5}{6} \cdot \frac{4}{3} = \frac{20}{18}$$

Dividing and Multiplying by the Same Number

Since multiplication or division by 1 does not change the value of a number, you can multiply or divide any fraction by 1 and the fraction will remain the same. Remember that $\frac{a}{a} = 1$ for any nonzero number a. Therefore, if you multiply or divide any fraction by $\frac{a}{a}$, the result is the same as if you multiplied the numerator and denominator by a or divided the numerator and denominator by a.

If you multiply the numerator and denominator of a fraction by the same nonzero number the fraction remains the same.

If you divide the numerator and denominator of any fraction by the same nonzero number, the fraction remains the same.

Consider the fraction $\frac{3}{4}$. If we multiply 3 by 10 and 4 by 10, then $\frac{30}{40}$ must equal $\frac{3}{4}$.

Equivalent Fractions

Two fractions are equivalent or equal if they represent the same ratio or number. In the last section, you saw that if you multiply or divide the numerator and denominator of a fraction by the same nonzero number the result is equivalent to the original fraction. For example, $\frac{7}{8} = \frac{70}{80}$ since $70 = 10 \times 7$ and $80 = 10 \times 8$.

> *In the test there will only be five choices, so your answer to a problem may not be the same as any of the given choices. You may have to express a fraction as an equivalent fraction.*

To find a fraction with a known denominator equal to a given fraction:

(A) divide the denominator of the given fraction into the known denominator;

(B) multiply the result of (A) by the numerator of the given fraction; this is the numerator of the required equivalent fraction.

EXAMPLE:

Find a fraction with a denominator of 30 which is equal to $\frac{2}{5}$:

(A) 5 into 30 is 6;

(B) $6 \cdot 2 = 12$ so $\frac{12}{30} = \frac{2}{5}$.

Reducing a Fraction to Lowest Terms

A fraction has been reduced to lowest terms when the numerator and denominator have no common factors. For example, $\frac{3}{4}$ is reduced to lowest terms, but $\frac{3}{6}$ is not because 3 is a common factor of 3 and 6.

> To reduce a fraction to lowest terms, cancel all the common factors of the numerator and denominator. (Cancelling common factors will not change the value of the fraction.)

For example, $\frac{100}{150} = \frac{10 \cdot 10}{10 \cdot 15} = \frac{10 \cdot}{15} = \frac{5 \cdot 2}{5 \cdot 3} = \frac{2}{3}$. Since 2 and 3 have no common factors, $\frac{2}{3}$ is $\frac{100}{150}$ reduced to lowest terms. A fraction is equivalent to the fraction reduced to lowest terms.

Adding Fractions

If the fractions have the same denominator, then the denominator is called a *common denominator.* Add the numerators, and use this sum as the new numerator with the common denominator as the denominator of the sum.

If the fractions don't have the same denominator, you must first find a common denominator. Multiply all the denominators together; the result is a common denominator.

EXAMPLE:

To add $\frac{1}{2} + \frac{2}{3} + \frac{7}{4}$, $2 \cdot 3 \cdot 4 = 24$ is a common denominator.

There are many common denominators; the smallest one is called the *least common denominator.* For the previous example, 12 is the least common denominator.

Once you have found a common denominator, express each fraction as an equivalent fraction with the common denominator, and add as you did for the case when the fractions had the same denominator.

EXAMPLE:

$\frac{1}{2} + \frac{2}{3} + \frac{7}{4} = ?$

(A) 24 is a common denominator.

(B) $\frac{1}{2} = \frac{12}{24}, \frac{2}{3} = \frac{16}{24}, \frac{7}{4} = \frac{42}{24}.$

(C) $\frac{1}{2} + \frac{2}{3} + \frac{7}{4} = \frac{12}{24} + \frac{16}{24} + \frac{42}{24} = \frac{12 + 16 + 42}{24} = \frac{70}{24} = \frac{35}{12}.$

Subtracting Fractions

When the fractions have the same denominator, subtract the numerators and place the result over the denominator.

When the fractions have different denominators:

(A) Find a common denominator.

(B) Express the fractions as equivalent fractions with the same denominator.

(C) Subtract.

Complex Fractions

A fraction whose numerator and denominator are themselves fractions is called a *complex fraction*. For example $\dfrac{2/3}{4/5}$ is a complex fraction. A complex fraction can always be simplified by dividing the fraction.

EXAMPLE:

$$\frac{2}{3} \div \frac{4}{5} = \frac{\overset{1}{2}}{3} \cdot \frac{5}{\underset{2}{4}} = \frac{1}{3} \cdot \frac{5}{2} = \frac{5}{6}$$

Converting a Fraction into a Decimal

To convert a fraction into a decimal, divide the denominator into the numerator. For example, $\dfrac{3}{4} = \dfrac{3.00}{4} = .75$. Some fractions give an infinite decimal when you divide the denominator into the numerator, for example, $\dfrac{1}{3} = .333\ldots$ where the three dots mean you keep on getting 3 with each step of division. $.333\ldots$ is an *infinite decimal*.

If a fraction has an infinite decimal, use the fraction in any computation.

EXAMPLE:

What is $\dfrac{2}{9}$ of \$3,690.90?

Since the decimal for $\dfrac{2}{9}$ is $.2222\ldots$ use the fraction $\dfrac{2}{9}. \dfrac{2}{9} \times \$3,690.90 = 2 \times \$410.10 = \$820.20$.

Percentage

Percentage is another method of expressing fractions or parts of an object. Percentages are expressed in terms of hundredths, so 100% means 100 hundredths or 1, and 50% would be 50 hundredths or ½.

A decimal is converted to a percentage by multiplying the decimal by 100. Since multiplying a decimal by 100 is accomplished by moving the decimal point two places to the right, *you convert a decimal into a percentage by moving the decimal point two places to the right*. For example, .134 = 13.4%.

If you wish to convert a percentage into a decimal, you divide the percentage by 100. There is a shortcut for this also. To divide by 100 you move the decimal point two places to the left.

Therefore, *to convert a percentage into a decimal, move the decimal point two places to the left*. For example, 24% = .24.

A fraction is converted into a percentage by changing the fraction to a decimal and then changing the decimal to a percentage. A percentage is changed into a fraction by first converting the percentage into a decimal and then changing the decimal to a fraction.

> *When you compute with percentages, it is usually easier to change the percentages to decimals or fractions.*

EXAMPLE 1:

A company has 6,435 bars of soap. If the company sells 20% of its bars of soap, how many bars of soap did it sell?

Change 20% into .2. Thus, the company sold (.2)(6,435) = 1287.0 = 1,287 bars of soap. An alternative method would be to convert 20% to $\frac{1}{5}$. Then, $\frac{1}{5} \times 6,435$ = 1,287.

EXAMPLE 2:

If the population of Dryden was 10,000 in 1960 and the population of Dryden increased by 15% between 1960 and 1970, what was the population of Dryden in 1970?

The population increased by 15% between 1960 and 1970, so the increase was (.15)(10,000) which is 1,500. The population in 1970 was 10,000 + 1,500 = 11,500.

A quicker method: The population increased 15%, so the population in 1970 is 115% of the population in 1960. Therefore, the population in 1970 is 115% of 10,000 which is (1.15)(10,000) = 11,500.

Interest and Discount

Two of the most common uses of percentages are in interest and discount problems.

The rate of interest is usually given as a percentage. The basic formula for interest problems is:

$$\text{INTEREST} = \text{AMOUNT} \times \text{TIME} \times \text{RATE}$$

You can assume the rate of interest is the annual rate of interest unless the problem states otherwise; so you should express the time in years.

EXAMPLE 1:

What annual rate of interest was paid if $5,000 earned $300 in interest in 2 years?

Since the interest was earned in 2 years, $150 is the interest earned in one year. $\dfrac{150}{5,000} = .03 = 3\%$, so the annual rate of interest was 3%.

This type of interest is called *simple interest*.

There is another method of computing interest called *compound interest*. In computing compound interest, the interest is periodically added to the amount (or principal) which is earning interest.

EXAMPLE 2:

What will $1,000 be worth after three years if it earns interest at the rate of 5% compounded annually?

Compounded annually means that the interest earned during one year is added to the amount (or principal) at the end of each year. The interest on $1,000 at 5% for one year is $(1,000)(.05) = $50. So you must compute the interest on $1,050 (not $1,000) for the second year. The interest is $(1,050)(.05) = $52.50. Therefore, during the third year interest will be computed for $1,102.50. During the third year the interest is $(1,102.50)(.05) = $55.125 = $55.13. Therefore, after 3 years the original $1,000 will be worth $1,157.63.

If you calculated simple interest on $1,000 at 5% for three years, the answer would be $(1,000)(.05)(3) = $150. Therefore, using simple interest, $1,000 is worth $1,150 after 3 years. Notice that this is not the same as the money was worth using compound interest.

You can assume that interest means simple interest unless a problem states otherwise.

The basic formula for discount problems is:

$$\text{DISCOUNT} = \text{COST} \times \text{RATE OF DISCOUNT}$$

EXAMPLE 1:
What is the discount if a car which cost $3,000 is discounted 7%?

The discount is $3,000 × .07 = $210 since 7% = .07.

If we know the cost of an item and its discounted price, we can find the rate of discount by using the formula

$$\text{rate of discount} = \frac{\text{cost} - \text{price}}{\text{cost}}.$$

After an item has been discounted once, it may be discounted again. This procedure is called *successive* discounting.

EXAMPLE 2:
A bicycle originally cost $100 and was discounted 10%. After three months it was sold after being discounted 15%. How much was the bicycle sold for?

After the 10% discount the bicycle was selling for $100(.90) = $90. An item which costs $90 and is discounted 15% will sell for $90(.85) = $76.50, so the bicycle was sold for $76.50.

Notice that if you added the two discounts of 10% and 15% and treated the successive discounts as a single discount of 25%, your answer would be that the bicycle sold for $75, which is incorrect. Successive discounts are *not* identical to a single discount of the sum of the discounts. The previous example shows that successive discounts of 10% and 15% are not identical to a single discount of 25%.

Signed Numbers

A number preceded by either a plus or a minus sign is called a *signed number*. For example, $+5$, -6, -4.2, and $+\frac{3}{4}$ are all signed numbers. If no sign is given with a number, a plus sign is assumed; thus, 5 is interpreted as $+5$.

Signed numbers can often be used to distinguish different concepts. For example, a profit of $10 can be denoted by $+\$10$ and a loss of $10 by $-\$10$. A temperature of 20 degrees below zero can be denoted $-20°$.

Absolute Value

The absolute value of a signed number is the distance of the number from 0. The absolute value of any nonzero number is *positive*. For example, the absolute value of 2 is 2; the absolute value of -2 is 2. The absolute value of a number a is denoted by $|a|$, so $|-2| = 2$. The absolute value of any number can be found by dropping its sign, $|-12| = 12$, $|4| = 4$. *Thus $|-a| = |a|$ for any number a.* The only number whose absolute value is zero is zero.

Adding Signed Numbers

Case I. Adding numbers with the *same sign:*
    (A) The sign of the sum is the same as the sign of the numbers being added.
    (B) Add the absolute values.
    (C) Put the sign from step (A) in front of the number you obtained in step (B).

EXAMPLE 1:
What is $-2 + (-3.1) + (-.02)$?

    (A) The sign of the sum will be $-$.
    (B) $|-2| = 2$, $|-3.1| = 3.1$, $|-.02| = .02$, and $2 + 3.1 + .02 = 5.12$.
    (C) The answer is -5.12.

Case II. Adding *two* numbers with *different signs:*
    (A) The sign of the sum is the sign of the number which is largest in absolute value.
    (B) Subtract the absolute value of the number with the smaller absolute value from the absolute value of the number with the larger absolute value.
    (C) The answer is the number you obtained in step (B) preceded by the sign from part (A).

EXAMPLE 2:
How much is $-5.1 + 3$?

    (A) The absolute value of -5.1 is 5.1 and the absolute value of 3 is 3, so the sign of the sum will be $-$.

(B) 5.1 is larger than 3, and $5.1 - 3 = 2.1$.

(C) The sum is -2.1.

Case III. Adding *more than two* numbers with *different signs:*

(A) Add all the positive numbers; the result is positive (this is Case I).

(B) Add all the negative numbers; the result is negative (this is Case I).

(C) Add the result of step (A) to the result of step (B), by using Case II.

EXAMPLE 3:

Find the value of $5 + 52 + (-3) + 7 + (-5.1)$.

(A) $5 + 52 + 7 = 64$.

(B) $-3 + (-5.1) = -8.1$.

(C) $64 + (-8.1) = 55.9$, so the answer is 55.9.

Subtracting Signed Numbers

When subtracting signed numbers:

(A) Change the sign of the number you are subtracting (the subtrahend).

(B) <u>Add</u> the result of step (A) to the number being subtracted from (the minuend) using the rules of the preceding section.

EXAMPLE 1:

Subtract 4.1 from 6.5.

(A) 4.1 becomes -4.1.

(B) $6.5 + (-4.1) = 2.4$.

EXAMPLE 2:

What is $7.8 - (-10.1)$?

(A) -10.1 becomes 10.1.

(B) $7.8 + 10.1 = 17.9$.

So we subtract a negative number by adding a positive number with the same absolute value, and we subtract a positive number by adding a negative number of the same absolute value.

Multiplying Signed Numbers

Case I. Multiplying two numbers:

(A) Multiply the absolute values of the numbers.

(B) If both numbers have the same sign, the result of step (A) is the answer—i.e. the product is positive. If the numbers have different signs, then the answer is the result of step (A) with a minus sign.

EXAMPLE 1:

$(4)(-3) = ?$

(A) $4 \times 3 = 12$

(B) The signs are different, so the answer is -12. You can remember the sign of the product in the following way:

$$(-)(-) = +$$
$$(+)(+) = +$$
$$(-)(+) = -$$
$$(+)(-) = -$$

Case II. Multiplying more than two numbers:

(A) Multiply the first two factors using Case I.

(B) Multiply the result of (A) by the third factor.

(C) Multiply the result of (B) by the fourth factor.

(D) Continue until you have used each factor.

EXAMPLE 2:

$(-5)(4)(2)(-\frac{1}{2})(\frac{3}{4}) = ?$

(A) $(-5)(4) = -20$

(B) $(-20)(2) = -40$

(C) $(-40)(-\frac{1}{2}) = 20$

(D) $(20)(\frac{3}{4}) = 15$, so the answer is 15.

The sign of the product is $+$ *if there are no negative factors or an even number of negative factors. The sign of the product is* $-$ *if there are an odd number of negative factors.*

Dividing Signed Numbers

Divide the absolute values of the numbers; the sign of the quotient is determined by the same rules as you used to determine the sign of a product. Thus,

$$+ \div + = +$$
$$- \div - = +$$
$$+ \div - = -$$
$$- \div + = -$$

EXAMPLE:
Divide 53.2 by -4.

53.2 divided by 4 is 13.3. Since one of the numbers is positive and the other negative, the answer is -13.3.

Averages and Medians

Mean

The *average* or *arithmetic mean* of a collection of N numbers is the result of dividing the sum of all the numbers in the collection by N.

EXAMPLE:
The scores of 9 students on a test were 72, 78, 81, 64, 85, 92, 95, 60, and 55. What was the average score of the students?

Since there are 9 students, the average is the total of all the scores divided by 9.

So the average is $\frac{1}{9}$ of $(72 + 78 + 81 + 64 + 85 + 92 + 95 + 60 + 55)$,

which is $\frac{1}{9}$ of 682 or $75\frac{7}{9}$.

Median

The number which is in the middle if the numbers in a collection of numbers are arranged in order is called the *median*. In the example above, the median score was 78. Notice that the median was different from the average.

> In general, the median and the average of a collection of numbers are different.

If the number of objects in the collection is even, the median is the average of the two numbers in the middle of the array. For example, the median of 64, 66, 72, 75, 76, and 77 is the average of 72 and 75, which is 73.5.

Powers, Exponents, and Roots

If b is any number and n is a whole number greater than 0, b^n means the product of n factors each of which is equal to b. Thus,

$$b^n = b \times b \times b \times \cdots \times b \text{ where there are } n \text{ copies of } b.$$

If $n = 1$, there is only one copy of b so $b^1 = b$. Here are some examples: $2^5 = 2 \times 2 \times 2 \times 2 \times 2 = 32$, $(-4)^3 = (-4) \times (-4) \times (-4) = -64$, $\dfrac{3^2}{4} = \dfrac{3 \times 3}{4} = \dfrac{9}{4}$,

$$1^n = 1 \text{ for any } n, \ 0^n = 0 \text{ for any } n.$$

b^n is read as "b raised to the nth power." b^2 is read "b squared." b^2 is always greater than 0 (positive) if b is not zero, since the product of two negative numbers is positive. b^3 is read "b cubed." b^3 can be negative or positive.

If you raise a fraction, $\dfrac{p}{q}$, to a power, then $\left(\dfrac{p}{q}\right)^n = \dfrac{p^n}{q^n}$. For example,

$$\left(\frac{5}{4}\right)^3 = \frac{5^3}{4^3} = \frac{125}{64}.$$

Exponents

In the expression b^n, b is called the base and n is called the *exponent*. In the expression 2^5, 2 is the base and 5 is the exponent. The exponent tells how many factors there are.

The *two basic formulas for problems involving exponents* are:
   (A) $b^n \times b^m = b^{n+m}$
   (B) $a^n \times b^n = (a \cdot b)^n$
(A) and (B) are called *laws of exponents*.

EXAMPLE:
What is 6^3?

Since $6 = 3 \times 2$, $6^3 = 3^3 \times 2^3 = 27 \times 8 = 216$.
                    or
$$6^3 = 6 \times 6 \times 6 = 216.$$

Roots

If you raise a number d to the nth power and the result is b, then d is called the nth root of b, which is usually written $\sqrt[n]{b} = d$. Since $2^5 = 32$, then $\sqrt[5]{32} = 2$. The second root is called the square root and is written $\sqrt{}$; the third root is called the cube root. For example, $\sqrt{225} = 15$; $\sqrt{81} = 9$; $\sqrt[3]{64} = 4$.

There are two possibilities for the square root of a positive number; the positive one is called the square root. Thus we say $\sqrt{9} = 3$ although $(-3) \times (-3) = 9$.

Since the square of any nonzero number is positive, *the square root of a negative number is not defined as a real number.* Thus $\sqrt{-2}$ is not a real number. There are cube roots of negative numbers. $\sqrt[3]{-8} = -2$, because $(-2) \times (-2) \times (-2) = -8$.

You can also write roots as exponents; for example,

$$\sqrt[n]{b} = b^{1/n}; \text{ so } \sqrt{b} = b^{1/2}, \sqrt[3]{b} = b^{1/3}.$$

Since you can write roots as exponents, formula (B) above is especially useful.

$a^{1/n} \times b^{1/n} = (a \cdot b)^{1/n}$ or $\sqrt[n]{a \times b} = \sqrt[n]{a} \times \sqrt[n]{b}$. This formula is the basic formula for simplifying square roots, cube roots and so on. *On the test you must state your answer in a form that matches one of the choices given.*

EXAMPLE:
$\sqrt{54} = ?$

Since $54 = 9 \times 6$, $\sqrt{54} = \sqrt{9 \times 6} = \sqrt{9} \times \sqrt{6}$. Since $\sqrt{9} = 3$, $\sqrt{54} = 3\sqrt{6}$.

You cannot simplify by adding square roots unless you are taking square roots of the same number. For example,

$$\sqrt{3} + 2\sqrt{3} - 4\sqrt{3} = -\sqrt{3}, \text{ but } \sqrt{3} + \sqrt{2} \text{ is not equal to } \sqrt{5}.$$

ALGEBRA

Algebraic Expressions

Often it is necessary to deal with quantities which have a numerical value which is unknown. For example, we may know that Tom's salary is twice as much as Joe's salary. If we let the value of Tom's salary be called T and the value of

Joe's salary be J, then T and J are numbers which are unknown. However, we do know that the value of T must be twice the value of J, or $T = 2J$.

T and $2J$ are examples of algebraic expressions. An algebraic expression may involve letters in addition to numbers and symbols; however, *in an algebraic expression a letter always stands for a number*. Therefore, you can multiply, divide, add, subtract and perform other mathematical operations on a letter. Thus, x^2 would mean x times x. Some examples of algebraic expressions are: $2x + y$, $y^3 + 9y$, $z^3 - 5ab$, $c + d + 4$, $5x + 2y(6x - 4y + z)$. When letters or numbers are written together without any sign or symbol between them, multiplication is assumed. Thus $6xy$ means 6 times x times y. $6xy$ is called a *term*; terms are separated by $+$ or $-$ signs. The expression $5z + 2 + 4x^2$ has three terms, $5z$, 2, and $4x^2$. Terms are often called monomials (mono $=$ one). If an expression has more than one term, it is called a *polynomial* (poly $=$ many). The letters in an algebraic expression are called *variables* or *unknowns*. When a variable is multiplied by a number, the number is called the *coefficient* of the variable. So in the expression $5x^2 + 2yz$, the coefficient of x^2 is 5, and the coefficient of yz is 2.

Simplifying Algebraic Expressions

Since there are only five choices of an answer given for the test questions, you must be able to recognize algebraic expressions that are equal. It will also save time when you are working problems if you can change a complicated expression into a simpler one.

Case I. Simplifying expressions that don't contain parentheses:

(A) Perform any multiplications or divisions before performing additions or subtractions. Thus, the expression $6x + y \div x$ means add $6x$ to the quotient of y divided by x. Another way of writing the expression would be $6x + \dfrac{y}{x}$. This is not the same as $\dfrac{6x + y}{x}$.

(B) The order in which you multiply numbers and letters in a term does not matter. So $6xy$ is the same as $6yx$.

(C) The order in which you add terms does not matter; for instance, $6x + 2y - x = 6x - x + 2y$.

(D) If there are roots or powers in any terms, you may be able to simplify the term by using the laws of exponents. For example, $5xy \cdot 3x^2y = 15x^3y^2$.

(E) Combine like terms. *Like terms* (or similar terms) are terms which have exactly the same letters raised to the same powers. So x, $-2x$, $\frac{1}{3}x$

are like terms. For example, $6x - 2x + x + y$ is equal to $5x + y$. In combining like terms, you simply add or subtract the coefficients of the like terms, and the result is the coefficient of that term in the simplified expression. In the example given, the coefficients of x were $+6$, -2, and $+1$; since $6 - 2 + 1 = 5$ the coefficient of x in the simplified expression is 5.

(F) Algebraic expressions which involve divisions or factors can be simplified by using the techniques for handling fractions and the laws of exponents. Remember dividing by b^n is the same as multiplying by b^{-n}.

EXAMPLE 1:

$$3x^2 - 4\sqrt{x} + \sqrt{4x} + xy + 7x^2 = ?$$

(D) $\sqrt{4x} = \sqrt{4}\sqrt{x} = 2\sqrt{x}$.

(E) $3x^2 + 7x^2 = 10x^2$, $-4\sqrt{x} + 2\sqrt{x} = -2\sqrt{x}$.

The original expression equals $3x^2 + 7x^2 - 4\sqrt{x} + 2\sqrt{x} + xy$. Therefore, the simplified expression is $10x^2 - 2\sqrt{x} + xy$.

Case II. Simplifying expressions that have parentheses:

The first rule is to perform the operations inside parentheses first. So $(6x + y) \div x$ means divide the sum of $6x$ and y by x. Notice that $(6x + y) \div x$ is different from $6x + y \div x$.

The main rule for getting rid of parentheses is the distributive law, which is expressed as $a(b + c) = ab + ac$. In other words, if any monomial is followed by an expression contained in parentheses, then *each* term of the expression is multiplied by the monomial. Once we have gotten rid of the parentheses, we proceed as we did in Case 1.

If an expression has more than one set of parentheses, get rid of the *inner parentheses first* and then *work out* through the rest of the parentheses.

EXAMPLE 2:

$$2x - (x + 6(x - 3y) + 4y) = ?$$

To remove the inner parentheses we multiply $6(x - 3y)$ getting $6x - 18y$. Now we have $2x - (x + 6x - 18y + 4y)$ which equals $2x - (7x - 14y)$. Distribute the minus sign (multiply by -1), getting $2x - 7x - (-14y) = -5x + 14y$. Sometimes brackets are used instead of parentheses.

Adding and Subtracting Algebraic Expressions

Since algebraic expressions are numbers, they can be added and subtracted.

> The only algebraic terms which can be combined are like terms.

EXAMPLE:

$(3x + 4y - xy^2) + (3x + 2x(x - y)) = ?$

The expression $= (3x + 4y - xy^2) + (3x + 2x^2 - 2xy)$, removing the inner parentheses;

$= 6x + 4y + 2x^2 - xy^2 - 2xy$, combining like terms.

Multiplying Algebraic Expressions

When you multiply two expressions, you multiply *each term of the first by each term of the second.*

EXAMPLE 1:

$(2h - 4)(h + 2h^2 + h^3) = ?$

$= 2h(h + 2h^2 + h^3) - 4(h + 2h^2 + h^3)$

$= 2h^2 + 4h^3 + 2h^4 - 4h - 8h^2 - 4h^3$

$= -4h - 6h^2 + 2h^4$, which is the product.

If you need to multiply more than two expressions, multiply the first two expressions, then multiply the result by the third expression, and so on until you have used each factor. Since algebraic expressions can be multiplied, they can be squared, cubed, or raised to other powers.

EXAMPLE 2:

$(x - 2y)^3 = (x - 2y)(x - 2y)(x - 2y).$

Since $(x - 2y)(x - 2y) = x^2 - 2yx - 2yx + 4y^2$

$= x^2 - 4xy + 4y^2,$

$(x - 2y)^3 = (x^2 - 4xy + 4y^2)(x - 2y)$

$= x(x^2 - 4xy + 4y^2) - 2y(x^2 - 4xy + 4y^2)$

$= x^3 - 4x^2y + 4xy^2 - 2x^2y + 8xy^2 - 8y^3$

$= x^3 - 6x^2y + 12xy^2 - 8y^3.$

The order in which you multiply algebraic expressions does not matter. Thus $(2a + b)(x^2 + 2x) = (x^2 + 2x)(2a + b).$

Factoring Algebraic Expressions

If an algebraic expression is the product of other algebraic expressions, then the expressions are called factors of the original expression. For instance, we claim that $(2h - 4)$ and $(h + 2h^2 + h^3)$ are factors of $-4h - 6h^2 + 2h^4$. We can always check to see if we have the correct factors by multiplying; so by example 1 above we see that our claim is correct. We need to be able to factor algebraic expressions in order to solve quadratic equations. It also can be helpful in dividing algebraic expressions.

First remove any monomial factor which appears in every term of the expression. Some examples:

$$3x + 3y = 3(x + y): 3 \text{ is a monomial factor.}$$
$$15a^2b + 10ab = 5ab(3a + 2): 5ab \text{ is a monomial factor.}$$
$$\frac{1}{2}hy - 3h^3 + 4hy = h\left(\frac{1}{2}y - 3h^2 + 4y\right),$$
$$= h\left(\frac{9}{2}y - 3h^2\right): h \text{ is a monomial factor.}$$

You may also need to factor expressions which contain squares or higher powers into factors which only contain linear terms. (Linear terms are terms in which variables are raised only to the first power.) The first rule to remember is that since $(a + b)(a - b) = a^2 + ba - ba - b^2 = a^2 - b^2$, the difference of two squares can always be factored.

EXAMPLE 1:

Factor $(9m^2 - 16)$.

$9m^2 = (3m)^2$ and $16 = 4^2$, so the factors are $(3m - 4)(3m + 4)$. Since $(3m - 4)(3m + 4) = 9m^2 - 16$, these factors are correct.

You also may need to factor expressions which contain squared terms and linear terms, such as $x^2 + 4x + 3$. The factors will be of the form $(x + a)$ and $(x + b)$. Since $(x + a)(x + b) = x^2 + (a + b)x + ab$, you must look for a pair of numbers a and b such that $a \cdot b$ is the numerical term in the expression and $a + b$ is the coefficient of the linear term (the term with exponent 1).

EXAMPLE 2:

Factor $y^2 + y - 6$.

Since -6 is negative, the two numbers a and b must be of opposite sign. Possible pairs of factors for -6 are -6 and $+1$, 6 and -1, 3 and -2, and

-3 and 2. Since $-2 + 3 = 1$, the factors are $(y + 3)$ and $(y - 2)$. So $(y + 3)(y - 2) = y^2 + y - 6$.

There are some expressions which cannot be factored, for example, $x^2 + 4x + 6$. In general, if you can't factor something by using the methods given above, don't waste a lot of time on the question. Sometimes you may be able to check the answers given to find out what the correct factors are.

Dividing Algebraic Expressions

The main things to remember in division are:

(1) When you divide a sum, you can get the same result by dividing each term and adding quotients. For example, $\dfrac{9x + 4xy + y^2}{x} = \dfrac{9x}{x} + \dfrac{4xy}{x} + \dfrac{y^2}{x} = 9 + 4y + \dfrac{y^2}{x}$.

(2) You can cancel common factors, so the results on factoring will be helpful. For example, $\dfrac{x^2 - 2x}{x - 2} = \dfrac{x(x - 2)}{x - 2} = x$.

Equations

An *equation* is a statement that says two algebraic expressions are equal. $x + 2 = 3$, $4 + 2 = 6$, $3x^2 + 2x - 6 = 0$, $x^2 + y^2 = z^2$, $\dfrac{y}{x} = 2 + z$, and $A = LW$ are all examples of equations. We will refer to the algebraic expressions on each side of the equals sign as the left side and the right side of the equation. Thus, in the equation $2x + 4 = 6y + x$, $2x + 4$ is the left side and $6y + x$ is the right side.

If we assign specific numbers to each variable or unknown in an algebraic expression, then the algebraic expression will be equal to a number. This is called *evaluating* the expression. For example, if you evaluate $2x + 4y^2 + 3$ for $x = -1$ and $y = 2$, the expression is equal to $2(-1) + 4 \cdot 2^2 + 3 = -2 + 4 \cdot 4 + 3 = 17$.

If we evaluate each side of an equation and the number obtained is the same for each side of the equation, then the specific values assigned to the unknowns are called a *solution of the equation*. Another way of saying this is that the choices for the unknowns satisfy the equation.

EXAMPLE:

Consider the equation $s^2 + y^2 = 5x.$

If $x = 1$ and $y = 2$, then the left side is $1^2 + 2^2$ which equals $1 + 4 = 5$. The right side is $5 \cdot 1 = 5$; since both sides are equal to 5, $x = 1$ and $y = 2$ is a solution.

If $x = 1$ and $y = 1$, then the left side is $1^2 + 1^2 = 2$ and the right side is $5 \cdot 1 = 5$. Therefore, since $2 \neq 5$, $x = 1$ and $y = 1$ is not a solution.

There are some equations that *do not have any solutions that are real numbers*. Since the square of any real number is positive or zero, the equation $x^2 = -4$ does not have any solutions that are real numbers.

Equivalence

One equation is *equivalent* to another equation, if they have exactly the same solutions. The basic idea in solving equations is to transform a given equation into an equivalent equation whose solutions are obvious.

The two main tools for solving equations are:
- (A) If you add or subtract the same algebraic expression to or from *each side* of an equation, the resulting equation is equivalent to the original equation.
- (B) If you multiply or divide both sides of an equation by the same *nonzero* algebraic expression, the resulting equation is equivalent to the original equation.

Solving Linear Equations with One Unknown

The most common type of equation is the linear equation with only one unknown. $6z = 4z - 3, 3 + a = 2a - 4, 3b + 2b = b - 4b$, are all examples of linear equations with only one unknown.

Using (A) and (B), you can solve a linear equation in one unknown in the following way:
- (1) Group all the terms which involve the unknown on one side of the equation and all the terms which are purely numerical on the other side of the equation. This is called *isolating the unknown*.

(2) Combine the terms on each side.

(3) Divide each side by the coefficient of the unknown.

EXAMPLE 1:

Solve $3x + 15 = 3 - 4x$ for x.

(1) Add $4x$ to each side and subtract 15 from each side; $3x + 15 - 15 + 4x = 3 - 15 - 4x + 4x$.

(2) $7x = -12$.

(3) Divide each side by 7, so $x = \dfrac{-12}{7}$ is the solution.

CHECK: $3\left(\dfrac{-12}{7}\right) + 15 = \dfrac{-36}{7} + 15 = \dfrac{69}{7}$ and $3 - 4\left(\dfrac{-12}{7}\right) = 3 + \dfrac{48}{7}$

$= \dfrac{69}{7}$.

If you do the same thing to each side of an equation, the result is still an equation but it may not be equivalent to the original equation. Be especially careful if you square each side of an equation. For example, $x = -4$ is an equation; square both sides and you get $x^2 = 16$ which has both $x = 4$ and $x = -4$ as solutions. *Always check your answer in the original equation.*

If the equation you want to solve involves square roots, get rid of the square roots by squaring each side of the equation. Remember to check your answer since squaring each side does not always give an equivalent equation.

EXAMPLE 2:

Solve $\sqrt{4x + 3} = 5$.

Square both sides: $(\sqrt{4x + 3})^2 = 4x + 3$ and $5^2 = 25$, so the new equation is $4x + 3 = 25$. Subtract 3 from each side to get $4x = 22$ and now divide each side by 4. The solution is $x = \dfrac{22}{4} = 5.5$. Since $4(5.5) + 3 = 25$ and $\sqrt{25} = 5$, $x = 5.5$ is a solution to the equation $\sqrt{4x + 3} = 5$.

If an equation involves fractions, multiply through by a common denominator and then solve. Check your answer to make sure you did not multiply or divide by zero.

Solving Two Equations in Two Unknowns

You may be asked to solve two equations in two unknowns. Use one equation to solve for one unknown in terms of the other; now change the second equation into an equation in only one unknown which can be solved by the methods of the preceding section.

EXAMPLE:

Solve for x and y: $\begin{cases} \dfrac{x}{y} = 3 \\ 2x + 4y = 20. \end{cases}$

The first equation gives $x = 3y$. Using $x = 3y$, the second equation is $2(3y) + 4y = 6y + 4y$ or $10y = 20$, so $y = \dfrac{20}{10} = 2$. Since $x = 3y$, $x = 6$.

CHECK: $\dfrac{6}{2} = 3$, and $2 \cdot 6 + 4 \cdot 2 = 20$, so $x = 6$ and $y = 2$ is a solution.

Solving Quadratic Equations

If the terms of an equation contain squares of the unknown as well as linear terms, the equation is called *quadratic*. Some examples of quadratic equations are $x^2 + 4x = 3$, $2z^2 - 1 = 3z^2 - 2z$, and $a + 6 = a^2 + 6$.

To solve a quadratic equation:

  (A) Group all the terms on one side of the equation so that the other side is *zero*.
  (B) Combine the terms on the nonzero side.
  (C) Factor the expression into linear expressions.
  (D) Set the linear factors equal to zero and solve.

The method depends on the fact that if a product of expressions is zero then at least one of the expressions must be zero.

EXAMPLE:
Solve $x^2 + 4x = -3$.

  (A) $x^2 + 4x + 3 = 0$
  (C) $x^2 + 4x + 3 = (x + 3)(x + 1) = 0$
  (D) So $x + 3 = 0$ or $x + 1 = 0$. Therefore, the solutions are $x = -3$ and $x = -1$.

CHECK: $(-3)^2 + 4(-3) = 9 - 12 = -3$
$(-1)^2 + 4(-1) = 1 - 4 = -3$, so $x = -3$ and $x = -1$ are solutions.

A quadratic equation will usually have 2 different solutions, but it is possible for a quadratic to have only one solution or even no real solution.

Word Problems

The general method for solving word problems is to translate them into algebraic problems. The quantities you are seeking are the unknowns, which are usually represented by letters. The information you are given in the problem is then turned into equations. Words such as "is," "was," "are," and "were" mean equals, and words like "of" and "as much as" mean multiplication.

EXAMPLE 1:

A coat was sold for $75. The coat was sold for 150% of the cost of the coat. How much did the coat cost?

You want to find the cost of the coat. Let C be the cost of the coat. You know that the coat was sold for $75 and that $75 was 150% of the cost. So $75 = 150\%$ of C or $75 = 1.5C$. Solving for C you get $C = \dfrac{75}{1.5} = 50$, so the coat cost $50.

CHECK: $(1.5)\$50 = \$75$.

EXAMPLE 2:

Tom's salary is 125% of Joe's salary; Mary's salary is 80% of Joe's salary. The total of all three salaries is $61,000. What is Mary's salary?

Let M = Mary's salary, J = Joe's salary and T = Tom's salary. The first sentence says $T = 125\%$ of J or $T = \dfrac{5}{4}J$, and $M = 80\%$ of J or $M = \dfrac{4}{5}J$. The second sentence says that $T + M + J = \$61,000$. Using the information from the first sentence, $T + M + J = \dfrac{5}{4}J + \dfrac{4}{5}J + J = \dfrac{25}{20}J + \dfrac{16}{20}J + J = \dfrac{61}{20}J$. So $\dfrac{61}{20}J = 61,000$; solving for J you have $J = \dfrac{20}{61} \times 61,000 = 20,000$. Therefore, $T = \dfrac{5}{4} \times \$20,000 = \$25,000$ and $M = \dfrac{4}{5} \times \$20,000 = \$16,000$.

CHECK: $\$25,000 + \$16,000 + \$20,000 = \$61,000$.
So Mary's salary is $16,000.

EXAMPLE 3:

Steve weighs 25 pounds more than Jim. The combined weight of Jim and Steve is 325 pounds. How much does Jim weigh?

Let S = Steve's weight in pounds and J = Jim's weight in pounds. The first sentence says $S = J + 25$, and the second sentence becomes $S + J = 325$.

Since $S = J + 25$, $S + J = 325$ becomes $(J + 25) + J = 2J + 25 = 325$. So $2J = 300$ and $J = 150$. Therefore, Jim weighs 150 pounds.

CHECK: If Jim weighs 150 pounds, then Steve weighs 175 pounds and $150 + 175 = 325$.

EXAMPLE 4:

A carpenter is designing a closet. The floor will be in the shape of a rectangle whose length is 2 feet more than its width. How long should the closet be if the carpenter wants the area of the floor to be 15 square feet?

The area of a rectangle is length times width, usually written $A = LW$, where A is the area, L is the length, and W is the width. We know $A = 15$ and $L = 2 + W$. Therefore, $LW = (2 + W)W = W^2 + 2W$; this must equal 15. So we need to solve $W^2 + 2W = 15$ or $W^2 + 2W - 15 = 0$. Since $W^2 + 2W - 15$ factors into $(W + 5)(W - 3)$, the only possible solutions are $W = -5$ and $W = 3$. Since W represents a width, -5 cannot be the answer; therefore the width is 3 feet. The length is the width plus two feet, so the length is 5 feet. Since $5 \times 3 = 15$, the answer checks.

Distance Problems

A common type of word problem is a distance or velocity problem. The basic formula is

---

DISTANCE TRAVELED = RATE × TIME

The formula is abbreviated $d = rt$.

EXAMPLE:

A train travels at an average speed of 50 miles per hour for $2\frac{1}{2}$ hours and then travels at a speed of 70 miles per hour for $1\frac{1}{2}$ hours. How far did the train travel in the entire 4 hours?

The train traveled for $2\frac{1}{2}$ hours at an average speed of 50 miles per hour, so it traveled $50 \times \frac{5}{2} = 125$ miles in the first $2\frac{1}{2}$ hours. Traveling at a speed of 70 miles per hour for $1\frac{1}{2}$ hours, the distance traveled will be equal to $r \times t$ where $r = 70$ m.p.h. and $t = 1\frac{1}{2}$, so the distance is $70 \times \frac{3}{2} = 105$ miles. Therefore, the total distance traveled is $125 + 105 = 230$ miles.

Work Problems

In this type of problem you can always assume all workers in the same category work at the same rate. The main idea is: If it takes k workers 1 hour to do a job then *each worker does $\frac{1}{k}$ of the job in an hour* or he works at the rate of $\frac{1}{k}$ of the job per hour. If it takes m workers h hours to finish a job then each worker does $\frac{1}{m}$ of the job in h hours so he does $\frac{1}{h}$ of $\frac{1}{m}$ in an hour. Therefore, each worker *works at the rate of $\frac{1}{mh}$ of the job per hour.*

EXAMPLE:

If 5 men take an hour to dig a ditch, how long should it take 12 men to dig a ditch of the same type?

Since 5 workers took an hour, each worker does $\frac{1}{5}$ of the job in an hour. So 12 workers will work at the rate of $\frac{12}{5}$ of the job per hour. Thus if T is the time it takes for 12 workers to do the job, $\frac{12}{5} \times T = 1$ job and $T = \frac{5}{12} \times 1$, so $T = \frac{5}{12}$ hours or 25 minutes.

Inequalities

A number is positive if it is greater than 0, so 1, $\frac{1}{1000}$, and 53.4 are all positive numbers. Positive numbers are signed numbers whose sign is $+$. If you think of numbers as points on a number line, positive numbers correspond to points to the right of 0.

A number is negative if it is less than 0. $-\frac{4}{5}$, -50, and $-.0001$ are all negative numbers. Negative numbers are signed numbers whose sign is $-$. Negative numbers correspond to points to the left of 0 on a number line.

0 is the only number which is neither positive nor negative.

$a > b$ means the number a is greater than the number b; that is, $a = b + x$ where x is a positive number. If we look at a number line, $a > b$ means a is to the right of b. $a > b$ can also be read as b is less than a, which is also written $b < a$. For example, $-5 > -7.5$ because $-5 = -7.5 + 2.5$ and 2.5 is positive.

The notation $a \leqslant b$ means a is less than or equal to b, or b is greater than or equal to a. For example, $5 \geqslant 4$; also $4 \geqslant 4$. $a \neq b$ means a is not equal to b.

If you need to know whether one fraction is greater than another fraction, put the fractions over a common denominator and compare the numerators.

EXAMPLE:

Which is larger, $\dfrac{13}{16}$ or $\dfrac{31}{40}$?

A common denominator is 80. $\dfrac{13}{16} = \dfrac{65}{80}$, and $\dfrac{31}{40} = \dfrac{62}{80}$; since $65 > 62$, $\dfrac{65}{80} > \dfrac{62}{80}$, so $\dfrac{13}{16} > \dfrac{31}{40}$.

Inequalities have certain properties which are similar to equations. We can talk about the left side and the right side of an inequality, and we can use algebraic expressions for the sides of an inequality. For example, $6x < 5x + 4$. A value for an unknown *satisfies an inequality*, if when you evaluate each side of the inequality the numbers satisfy the inequality. So if $x = 2$, then $6x = 12$ and $5x + 4 = 14$ and since $12 < 14$, $x = 2$ satisfies $6x < 5x + 4$. Two inequalities are equivalent if the same collection of numbers satisfies both inequalities.

The following basic principles are used in work with inequalities:

    (A) Adding the same expression to *each* side of an inequality gives an equivalent inequality (written $a < b \leftrightarrow a + c < b + c$ where $\leftrightarrow$ means equivalent).

(B) Subtracting the same expression from *each* side of an inequality gives an equivalent inequality ($a < b \leftrightarrow a - c < b - c$).

(C) Multiplying or dividing *each* side of an inequality by the same *positive* expression gives an equivalent inequality ($a < b \leftrightarrow ca < cb$ for $c > 0$).

(D) Multiplying or dividing each side of an inequality by the same *negative* expression *reverses* the inequality ($a < b \leftrightarrow ca > cb$ for $c < 0$).

(E) If both sides of an inequality have the same sign, inverting both sides of the inequality *reverses* the inequality.

$$0 < a < b \leftrightarrow 0 < \frac{1}{b} < \frac{1}{a}$$

$$a < b < 0 \leftrightarrow \frac{1}{b} < \frac{1}{a} < 0$$

(F) If two inequalities are of the same type (both greater or both less), adding the respective sides gives the same type of inequality.

$$(a < b \text{ and } c < d, \text{ then } a + c < b + d)$$

Note that the inequalities are *not* equivalent.

(G) If $a < b$ and $b < c$ then $a < c$.

EXAMPLE 1:

Find the values of x for which $5x - 4 < 7x + 2$.

Using principle (B) subtract $5x + 2$ from each side, so $(5x - 4 < 7x + 2) \leftrightarrow -6 < 2x$. Now use principle (C) and divide each side by 2, so $-6 < 2x \leftrightarrow -3 < x$.

So any x greater than -3 satisfies the inequality. It is a good idea to make a spot check. -1 is > -3; let $x = -1$ then $5x - 4 = -9$ and $7x + 2 = -5$. Since $-9 < -5$, the answer is correct for at least the particular value $x = -1$.

EXAMPLE 2:

Find the values of a which satisfy $a^2 + 1 > 2a + 4$.

Subtract $2a$ from each side, so
$(a^2 + 1 > 2a + 4) \leftrightarrow a^2 - 2a + 1 > 4$.
$a^2 - 2a + 1 = (a - 1)^2$ so
$a^2 - 2a + 1 > 4 \leftrightarrow (a - 1)^2 > 2^2$.

We need to be careful when we take the square roots of inequalities. If

$q^2 > 4$ and if $q > 0$, then $q > 2$; **but if $q < 0$, then $q < -2$.** We must look at two cases in example 2. First, **if $(a - 1) \geq 0$** then

$(a - 1)^2 > 2^2 \leftrightarrow a - 1 > 2$ or $a > 3$.

If $(a - 1) < 0$ then $(a - 1)^2 > 2^2 \leftrightarrow a - 1 < -2 \leftrightarrow a < -1$.

So the inequality is satisfied if $a > 3$ or if $a < -1$.

CHECK: $(-2)^2 + 1 = 5 > 2(-2) + 4 = 0$, and $5^2 + 1 = 26 > 14 = 2 \cdot 5 + 4$.

Some inequalities are not satisfied by *any* real number. For example, since $x^2 \geq 0$ for all x, there is no real number x such that $x^2 < -9$.

You may be given an inequality and asked whether other inequalities follow from the original inequality. You should be able to answer such questions by using principles (A) through (G).

If there is any property of inequalities you can't remember, try out some specific numbers. If $x < y$, then what is the relation between $-x$ and $-y$? Since $4 < 5$ but $-5 < -4$, the relation is probably $-x > -y$, which is true by (D).

Probably the most common mistake is forgetting to reverse the inequalities if you multiply or divide by a negative number.

GEOMETRY

Angles

If two straight lines meet at a point they form an *angle*. The point is called the *vertex* of the angle and the lines are called the *sides* or *rays* of the angle. The sign for angle is $\angle$.

If two lines intersect at a point, they form 4 angles. The angles opposite each other are called *vertical* angles. $\angle 1$ and $\angle 3$ are vertical angles. $\angle 2$ and $\angle 4$ are vertical angles.

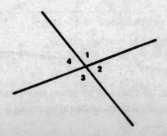

> *Vertical angles are equal.*

A straight angle is an angle whose sides lie on a straight line. *A straight angle equals 180°.*

If the sum of two adjacent angles is a straight angle, then the angles are *supplementary* and each angle is the supplement of the other.

If an angle of $x°$ and an angle of $y°$ are supplements, then $x + y = 180$.

If two supplementary angles are equal, they are both *right angles.* A right angle is half of a straight angle. A right angle $= 90°$.

If the sum of two adjacent angles is a right angle, then the angles are *complementary* and each angle is the complement of the other.

If an angle of $x°$ and an angle of $y°$ are complementary, then $x + y = 90$.

Lines

A line is understood to be a straight line. A line is assumed to extend indefinitely in both directions. *There is one and only one line between two distinct points.*

Parallel Lines

Two lines in the same plane are *parallel* if they do not intersect no matter how far they are extended.

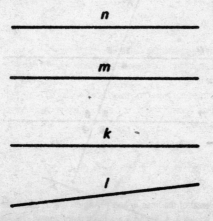

m and n are parallel, but k and l are not parallel since if k and l are extended they will intersect. Parallel lines are denoted by the symbol $\parallel$; so $m \parallel n$ means m is parallel to n.

If two lines are parallel to a third line, then they are parallel to each other.

If a third line intersects two given lines, it is called a *transversal*. A transversal and the two given lines form eight angles. The four inside angles are called *interior* angles. The four outside angles are called *exterior* angles. If two angles are on opposite sides of the transversal they are called *alternate* angles.

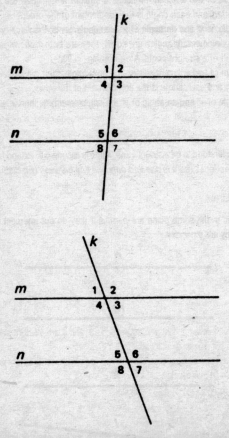

k is a transversal of the lines m and n. Angles 1, 2, 7, and 8 are the exterior angles, and angles 3, 4, 5, and 6 are the interior angles. $\angle 4$ and $\angle 6$ are an example of a pair of alternate angles. $\angle 1$ and $\angle 5$, $\angle 2$ and $\angle 6$, $\angle 3$ and $\angle 7$, and $\angle 4$ and $\angle 8$ are pairs of *corresponding* angles.

If two parallel lines are intersected by a transversal then:
   (1) Alternate interior angles are equal.
   (2) Corresponding angles are equal.
   (3) Interior angles on the same side of the transversal are supplementary.

If we use the fact that vertical angles are equal, we can replace "interior" by "exterior" in (1) and (3).

Perpendicular Lines

When two lines intersect and all four of the angles formed are equal, the lines are said to be *perpendicular*. If two lines are perpendicular, they are the sides of right angles whose vertex is the point of intersection.

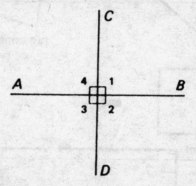

AB is perpendicular to CD, and angles 1, 2, 3, and 4 are all right angles. $\perp$ is the symbol for perpendicular; so $AB \perp CD$.

If *any one* of the angles formed when two lines intersect is a right angle, then the lines are perpendicular.

Polygons

A *polygon* is a closed figure in a plane which is composed of line segments which meet only at their endpoints. The line segments are called *sides* of the polygon, and a point where two sides meet is called a *vertex* (plural *vertices*) of the polygon.

Polygons are classified by the number of angles or sides they have. A polygon with three angles is called a *triangle*; a four-sided polygon is a *quadrilateral*; a polygon with five angles is a *pentagon*; a polygon with six angles is a *hexagon*; an eight-sided polygon is an *octagon*. The number of angles is always equal to the number of sides in a polygon, so a six-sided polygon is a hexagon. The term *n*-gon refers to a polygon with *n* sides.

If the corresponding sides and the corresponding angles of two polygons are equal, the polygons are *congruent*. Congruent polygons have the same size and the same shape

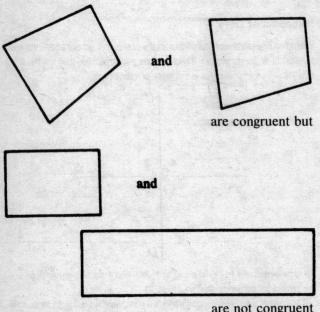

and

are congruent but

and

are not congruent

The sum of all the angles of an *n*-gon is $(n - 2)180°$. So the sum of the angles in a hexagon is $(6 - 2)180° = 720°$.

Triangles

A *triangle* is a 3-sided polygon. If two sides of a triangle are equal, it is called *isosceles*. If all three sides are equal, it is an *equilateral* triangle. The symbol for a triangle is △; so △*ABC* means a triangle whose vertices are *A*, *B*, and *C*.

The sum of the angles in a triangle is 180°.

The sum of the lengths of any two sides of a triangle must be longer than the remaining side.

If two angles in a triangle are equal, then the lengths of the sides opposite the equal angles are equal. If two sides of a triangle are equal, then the angles opposite the two equal sides are equal. In an equilateral triangle all the angles are equal and each angle = 60°. If each of the angles in a triangle is 60°, then the triangle is equilateral.

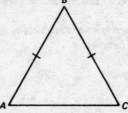

If $AB = BC$, then $\angle BAC = \angle BCA$.

In a right triangle, the side opposite the right angle is called the *hypotenuse*, and the remaining two sides are called *legs*.

The Pythagorean Theorem states that the square of the length of the hypotenuse is equal to the sum of the squares of the lengths of the legs.

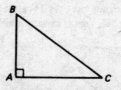

$$(BC)^2 = (AB)^2 + (AC)^2$$

If $AB = 4$ and $AC = 3$ then $(BC)^2 = 4^2 + 3^2 = 25$ so $BC = 5$. If $BC = 13$ and $AC = 5$, then $13^2 = 169 = (AB)^2 + 5^2$. So $(AB)^2 = 169 - 25 = 144$ and $AB = 12$.

If the lengths of the three sides of a triangle are, a, b, and c and $a^2 = b^2 + c^2$, then the triangle is a right triangle where a is the length of the hypotenuse.

Congruence

Two triangles are congruent, if two pairs of corresponding sides and the corresponding *included* angles are equal. This is called *Side-Angle-Side* and is denoted by S.A.S.

Two triangles are congruent if two pairs of corresponding angles and the corresponding *included* sides are equal. This is called *Angle-Side-Angle* or A.S.A.

If all three pairs of corresponding sides of two triangles are equal, then the triangles are congruent. This is called *Side-Side-Side* or S.S.S.

In general, if two corresponding sides of two triangles are equal, we cannot infer that the triangles are congruent.

The symbol ≅ means congruent.

Similarity

Two triangles are similar if all three pairs of corresponding angles are equal. Since the sum of the angles in a triangle is 180°, it follows that if two corresponding angles are equal, the third angles must be equal. The symbol ~ means similar.

Quadrilaterals

A *quadrilateral* is a polygon with four sides. The sum of the angles in a quadrilateral is 360°. If the opposite sides of a quadrilateral are parallel, the figure is a *parallelogram*.

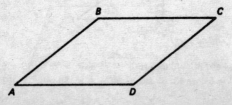

ABCD is a parallelogram.

In a parallelogram:

(1) The opposite sides are equal.

(2) The opposite angles are equal.

(3) Any diagonal divides the parallelogram into two congruent triangles.

(4) The diagonals bisect each other. (A line *bisects* a line segment if it intersects the segment at the midpoint of the segment.)

If *any* of the statements (1), (2), (3) and (4) are true for a quadrilateral, then the quadrilateral is a parallelogram.

If all the angles of a parallelogram are right angles, the figure is a *rectangle*.

ABCD is a rectangle.

Since the sum of the angles in a quadrilateral is 360°, if *all* the angles of a quadrilateral are equal then the figure is a rectangle. The diagonals of a rectangle are equal. The length of a diagonal can be found by using the Pythagorean Theorem.

If all the sides of a rectangle are equal, the figure is a *square*.

A quadrilateral with two parallel sides and two sides that are not parallel is called a *trapezoid*. The parallel sides are called *bases*, and the nonparallel sides are called *legs*.

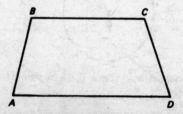

If *BC* ‖ *AD* then *ABCD* is a trapezoid; *BC* and *AD* are the bases.

Circles

A *circle* is a figure in a plane consisting of all the points which are the same distance from a fixed point called the *center* of the circle. A line segment from any point on the circle to the center of the circle is called a *radius* (plural: *radii*) of the circle. All radii of the same circle have the same length.

A line segment whose endpoints are on a circle is called a *chord*. A chord which passes through the center of the circle is a *diameter*. *The length of a diameter is twice the length of a radius.* A diameter divides a circle into two congruent halves which are called *semicircles*.

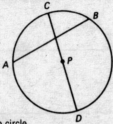

P is the center of the circle.
AB is a chord, *CD* is a diameter, and *PC* and *PD* are radii.

A diameter which is perpendicular to a chord bisects the chord.

If a line intersects a circle at one and only one point, the line is said to be a *tangent* to the circle. The point common to a circle and a tangent to the circle is called the *point of tangency*. The radius from the center to the point of tangency is perpendicular to the tangent.

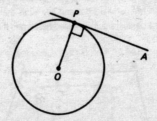

AP is tangent to the circle with center *O*. *P* is the point of tangency and *OP* ⊥ *PA*.

An angle whose vertex is a point on a circle and whose sides are chords of the circle is called an *inscribed angle*. An angle whose vertex is the center of a circle and whose sides are radii of the circle is called a *central angle*.

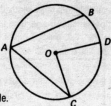

∠*BAC* is an inscribed angle.
∠*DOC* is a central angle.

An *arc* is a part of a circle.

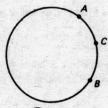

ACB is an arc. Arc *ACB* is written $\overset{\frown}{ACB}$.

An arc can be measured in degrees. The entire circle is 360°; thus an arc of 120° would be ⅓ of a circle.

A central angle is equal in measure to the arc it intercepts.

An inscribed angle is equal in measure to ½ the arc it intercepts.

Area and Perimeter

Area

The *area of a square* equals s^2, where s is the length of a side of the square. Thus, $A = s^2$.

If *AD* = 5 inches, the area of square *ABCD* is 25 square inches.

The *area of a rectangle* equals length times width; if L is the length of one side and W is the length of a perpendicular side, then the area $A = LW$.

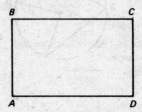

If $AB = 5$ feet and $AD = 8$ feet, then the area of rectangle $ABCD$ is 40 square feet.

The *area of a parallelogram* is base × height; $A = bh$, where b is the length of a side and h is the length of an altitude to the base.

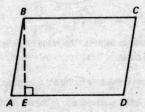

If $AD = 6$ yards and $BE = 4$ yards, then the area of the parallelogram $ABCD$ is 6 · 4 or 24 square yards.

The *area of a trapezoid* is the (average of the bases) × height. $A = [(b_1 + b_2)/2]h$ where b_1 and b_2 are the lengths of the parallel sides and h is the length of an altitude to one of the bases.

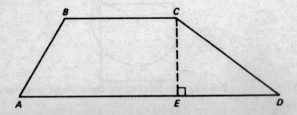

If $BC = 3$ miles, $AD = 7$ miles, and $CE = 2$ miles, then the area of trapezoid $ABCD$ is $[(3 + 7)/2] \cdot 2 = 10$ square miles.

The *area of a triangle* is $\frac{1}{2}$ (base × height); $A = \frac{1}{2}bh$, where b is the length of a side and h is the length of the altitude to that side.

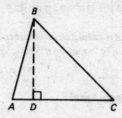

If $AC = 5$ miles and $BD = 4$ miles, then the area of the triangle is $\frac{1}{2} \times 5 \times 4 = 10$ square miles.

If we want to find the *area of a polygon* which is not of a type already mentioned, we break the polygon up into smaller figures such as triangles or rectangles, find the area of each piece, and add these to get the area of the given polygon.

The *area of a circle* is πr^2 where r is the length of a radius. Since $d = 2r$ where d is the length of a diameter, $A = \pi \left(\frac{d}{2}\right)^2 = \pi \frac{d^2}{4}$. π is a number which is approximately $\frac{22}{7}$ or 3.14; however, there is *no fraction which is exactly equal to π*. π is called an *irrational number*.

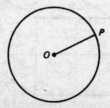

If $OP = 2$ inches, then the area of the circle with center O is $\pi 2^2$ or 4π square inches.

Perimeter

The *perimeter of a polygon* is the sum of the lengths of the sides.

The *perimeter of a rectangle* is $2(L + W)$ where L is the length and W is the width.

The *perimeter of a square is 4s* where s is the length of a side of the square.

The *perimeter of a circle* is called the *circumference* of the circle. The *circumference of a circle is πd or $2\pi r$*, where d is the length of a diameter and r is the length of a radius.

Volume and Surface Area

Volume

The *volume of a rectangular prism or box* is length times width times height.

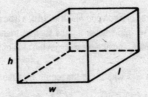

If each of the faces of a rectangular prism is a congruent square, then the solid is a *cube*. the *volume of a cube* is the length of a side (or edge) cubed.

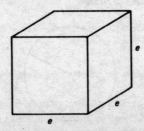

If the side of a cube is 4 feet long, then the volume of the cube is 4^3 or 64 cubic feet.

This solid is a circular cylinder. The top and the bottom are congruent circles. Most tin cans are circular cylinders. The *volume of a circular cylinder* is the product of the area of the circular base and the height.

A *sphere* is the set of points in space equidistant from a fixed point called the center. The length of a segment from any point on the sphere to the center is called the radius of the sphere. *The volume of a sphere of radius r is $\frac{4}{3}\pi r^3$.*

The volume of a sphere with radius 3 feet is $\frac{4}{3}\pi 3^3 = 36\pi$ cubic feet.

Surface Area

The *surface area of a rectangular prism* is $2LW + 2LH + 2WH$ where L is the length, W is the width, and H is the height.

The *surface area of a cube* is $6e^2$ where e is the length of an edge.

The *area of the circular part of a cylinder* is called the lateral area. *The lateral area of a cylinder is $2\pi rh$,* since if we unroll the circular part, we get a rectangle whose dimensions are the circumference of the circle and the height of the cylinder. The total surface area is the lateral surface area plus the areas of the circles on top and bottom, so the total surface area is $2\pi rh + 2\pi r^2$.

Coordinate Geometry

In coordinate geometry, every point in the plane is associated with an ordered pair of numbers called *coordinates*. Two perpendicular lines are drawn; the horizontal line is called the x-axis and the vertical line is called the y-axis. The point where the two axes intersect is called the *origin*. Both of the axes are number lines with the origin corresponding to zero. Positive numbers on the x-axis are to the right of the origin, negative numbers to the left. Positive numbers on the y-axis are above the origin, negative numbers below the origin. The coordinates of a point P are (x,y) if P is located by moving x units along the x-axis from the origin and then moving y units up or down. *The distance along the x-axis is always given first.*

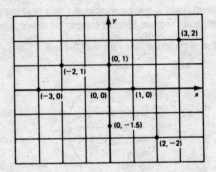

The numbers in parentheses are the coordinates of the point. Thus "P = (3,2)" means that the coordinates of P are (3,2). *The distance between the point with coordinates (x,y) and the point with coordinates (a,b) is $\sqrt{(x-a)^2 + (y-b)^2}$.* You should be able to answer most questions by using the distance formula.

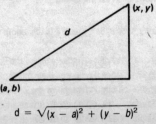

$$d = \sqrt{(x-a)^2 + (y-b)^2}$$

Answer Sheet—Sample Test 1

**Section I
Reading
Comprehension**

1. Ⓐ Ⓑ Ⓒ Ⓓ Ⓔ
2. Ⓐ Ⓑ Ⓒ Ⓓ Ⓔ
3. Ⓐ Ⓑ Ⓒ Ⓓ Ⓔ
4. Ⓐ Ⓑ Ⓒ Ⓓ Ⓔ
5. Ⓐ Ⓑ Ⓒ Ⓓ Ⓔ
6. Ⓐ Ⓑ Ⓒ Ⓓ Ⓔ
7. Ⓐ Ⓑ Ⓒ Ⓓ Ⓔ
8. Ⓐ Ⓑ Ⓒ Ⓓ Ⓔ
9. Ⓐ Ⓑ Ⓒ Ⓓ Ⓔ
10. Ⓐ Ⓑ Ⓒ Ⓓ Ⓔ
11. Ⓐ Ⓑ Ⓒ Ⓓ Ⓔ
12. Ⓐ Ⓑ Ⓒ Ⓓ Ⓔ
13. Ⓐ Ⓑ Ⓒ Ⓓ Ⓔ
14. Ⓐ Ⓑ Ⓒ Ⓓ Ⓔ
15. Ⓐ Ⓑ Ⓒ Ⓓ Ⓔ
16. Ⓐ Ⓑ Ⓒ Ⓓ Ⓔ
17. Ⓐ Ⓑ Ⓒ Ⓓ Ⓔ
18. Ⓐ Ⓑ Ⓒ Ⓓ Ⓔ
19. Ⓐ Ⓑ Ⓒ Ⓓ Ⓔ
20. Ⓐ Ⓑ Ⓒ Ⓓ Ⓔ
21. Ⓐ Ⓑ Ⓒ Ⓓ Ⓔ
22. Ⓐ Ⓑ Ⓒ Ⓓ Ⓔ
23. Ⓐ Ⓑ Ⓒ Ⓓ Ⓔ
24. Ⓐ Ⓑ Ⓒ Ⓓ Ⓔ
25. Ⓐ Ⓑ Ⓒ Ⓓ Ⓔ

**Section II
Problem
Solving**

1. Ⓐ Ⓑ Ⓒ Ⓓ Ⓔ
2. Ⓐ Ⓑ Ⓒ Ⓓ Ⓔ
3. Ⓐ Ⓑ Ⓒ Ⓓ Ⓔ
4. Ⓐ Ⓑ Ⓒ Ⓓ Ⓔ
5. Ⓐ Ⓑ Ⓒ Ⓓ Ⓔ
6. Ⓐ Ⓑ Ⓒ Ⓓ Ⓔ

7. Ⓐ Ⓑ Ⓒ Ⓓ Ⓔ
8. Ⓐ Ⓑ Ⓒ Ⓓ Ⓔ
9. Ⓐ Ⓑ Ⓒ Ⓓ Ⓔ
10. Ⓐ Ⓑ Ⓒ Ⓓ Ⓔ
11. Ⓐ Ⓑ Ⓒ Ⓓ Ⓔ
12. Ⓐ Ⓑ Ⓒ Ⓓ Ⓔ
13. Ⓐ Ⓑ Ⓒ Ⓓ Ⓔ
14. Ⓐ Ⓑ Ⓒ Ⓓ Ⓔ
15. Ⓐ Ⓑ Ⓒ Ⓓ Ⓔ
16. Ⓐ Ⓑ Ⓒ Ⓓ Ⓔ
17. Ⓐ Ⓑ Ⓒ Ⓓ Ⓔ
18. Ⓐ Ⓑ Ⓒ Ⓓ Ⓔ
19. Ⓐ Ⓑ Ⓒ Ⓓ Ⓔ
20. Ⓐ Ⓑ Ⓒ Ⓓ Ⓔ

**Section III
Analysis of
Situations**

1. Ⓐ Ⓑ Ⓒ Ⓓ Ⓔ
2. Ⓐ Ⓑ Ⓒ Ⓓ Ⓔ
3. Ⓐ Ⓑ Ⓒ Ⓓ Ⓔ
4. Ⓐ Ⓑ Ⓒ Ⓓ Ⓔ
5. Ⓐ Ⓑ Ⓒ Ⓓ Ⓔ
6. Ⓐ Ⓑ Ⓒ Ⓓ Ⓔ
7. Ⓐ Ⓑ Ⓒ Ⓓ Ⓔ
8. Ⓐ Ⓑ Ⓒ Ⓓ Ⓔ
9. Ⓐ Ⓑ Ⓒ Ⓓ Ⓔ
10. Ⓐ Ⓑ Ⓒ Ⓓ Ⓔ
11. Ⓐ Ⓑ Ⓒ Ⓓ Ⓔ
12. Ⓐ Ⓑ Ⓒ Ⓓ Ⓔ
13. Ⓐ Ⓑ Ⓒ Ⓓ Ⓔ
14. Ⓐ Ⓑ Ⓒ Ⓓ Ⓔ
15. Ⓐ Ⓑ Ⓒ Ⓓ Ⓔ
16. Ⓐ Ⓑ Ⓒ Ⓓ Ⓔ
17. Ⓐ Ⓑ Ⓒ Ⓓ Ⓔ
18. Ⓐ Ⓑ Ⓒ Ⓓ Ⓔ
19. Ⓐ Ⓑ Ⓒ Ⓓ Ⓔ
20. Ⓐ Ⓑ Ⓒ Ⓓ Ⓔ

21. Ⓐ Ⓑ Ⓒ Ⓓ Ⓔ
22. Ⓐ Ⓑ Ⓒ Ⓓ Ⓔ
23. Ⓐ Ⓑ Ⓒ Ⓓ Ⓔ
24. Ⓐ Ⓑ Ⓒ Ⓓ Ⓔ
25. Ⓐ Ⓑ Ⓒ Ⓓ Ⓔ
26. Ⓐ Ⓑ Ⓒ Ⓓ Ⓔ
27. Ⓐ Ⓑ Ⓒ Ⓓ Ⓔ
28. Ⓐ Ⓑ Ⓒ Ⓓ Ⓔ
29. Ⓐ Ⓑ Ⓒ Ⓓ Ⓔ
30. Ⓐ Ⓑ Ⓒ Ⓓ Ⓔ
31. Ⓐ Ⓑ Ⓒ Ⓓ Ⓔ
32. Ⓐ Ⓑ Ⓒ Ⓓ Ⓔ
33. Ⓐ Ⓑ Ⓒ Ⓓ Ⓔ
34. Ⓐ Ⓑ Ⓒ Ⓓ Ⓔ
35. Ⓐ Ⓑ Ⓒ Ⓓ Ⓔ

**Section IV
Data
Sufficiency**

1. Ⓐ Ⓑ Ⓒ Ⓓ Ⓔ
2. Ⓐ Ⓑ Ⓒ Ⓓ Ⓔ
3. Ⓐ Ⓑ Ⓒ Ⓓ Ⓔ
4. Ⓐ Ⓑ Ⓒ Ⓓ Ⓔ
5. Ⓐ Ⓑ Ⓒ Ⓓ Ⓔ
6. Ⓐ Ⓑ Ⓒ Ⓓ Ⓔ
7. Ⓐ Ⓑ Ⓒ Ⓓ Ⓔ
8. Ⓐ Ⓑ Ⓒ Ⓓ Ⓔ
9. Ⓐ Ⓑ Ⓒ Ⓓ Ⓔ
10. Ⓐ Ⓑ Ⓒ Ⓓ Ⓔ
11. Ⓐ Ⓑ Ⓒ Ⓓ Ⓔ
12. Ⓐ Ⓑ Ⓒ Ⓓ Ⓔ
13. Ⓐ Ⓑ Ⓒ Ⓓ Ⓔ
14. Ⓐ Ⓑ Ⓒ Ⓓ Ⓔ
15. Ⓐ Ⓑ Ⓒ Ⓓ Ⓔ
16. Ⓐ Ⓑ Ⓒ Ⓓ Ⓔ
17. Ⓐ Ⓑ Ⓒ Ⓓ Ⓔ
18. Ⓐ Ⓑ Ⓒ Ⓓ Ⓔ
19. Ⓐ Ⓑ Ⓒ Ⓓ Ⓔ

20. Ⓐ Ⓑ Ⓒ Ⓓ Ⓔ
21. Ⓐ Ⓑ Ⓒ Ⓓ Ⓔ
22. Ⓐ Ⓑ Ⓒ Ⓓ Ⓔ
23. Ⓐ Ⓑ Ⓒ Ⓓ Ⓔ
24. Ⓐ Ⓑ Ⓒ Ⓓ Ⓔ
25. Ⓐ Ⓑ Ⓒ Ⓓ Ⓔ

Section V
Writing
Ability

1. Ⓐ Ⓑ Ⓒ Ⓓ Ⓔ
2. Ⓐ Ⓑ Ⓒ Ⓓ Ⓔ
3. Ⓐ Ⓑ Ⓒ Ⓓ Ⓔ
4. Ⓐ Ⓑ Ⓒ Ⓓ Ⓔ
5. Ⓐ Ⓑ Ⓒ Ⓓ Ⓔ
6. Ⓐ Ⓑ Ⓒ Ⓓ Ⓔ
7. Ⓐ Ⓑ Ⓒ Ⓓ Ⓔ
8. Ⓐ Ⓑ Ⓒ Ⓓ Ⓔ
9. Ⓐ Ⓑ Ⓒ Ⓓ Ⓔ
10. Ⓐ Ⓑ Ⓒ Ⓓ Ⓔ
11. Ⓐ Ⓑ Ⓒ Ⓓ Ⓔ
12. Ⓐ Ⓑ Ⓒ Ⓓ Ⓔ
13. Ⓐ Ⓑ Ⓒ Ⓓ Ⓔ
14. Ⓐ Ⓑ Ⓒ Ⓓ Ⓔ
15. Ⓐ Ⓑ Ⓒ Ⓓ Ⓔ
16. Ⓐ Ⓑ Ⓒ Ⓓ Ⓔ
17. Ⓐ Ⓑ Ⓒ Ⓓ Ⓔ
18. Ⓐ Ⓑ Ⓒ Ⓓ Ⓔ
19. Ⓐ Ⓑ Ⓒ Ⓓ Ⓔ
20. Ⓐ Ⓑ Ⓒ Ⓓ Ⓔ
21. Ⓐ Ⓑ Ⓒ Ⓓ Ⓔ
22. Ⓐ Ⓑ Ⓒ Ⓓ Ⓔ
23. Ⓐ Ⓑ Ⓒ Ⓓ Ⓔ
24. Ⓐ Ⓑ Ⓒ Ⓓ Ⓔ
25. Ⓐ Ⓑ Ⓒ Ⓓ Ⓔ

Section VI
Analysis of
Situations

1. Ⓐ Ⓑ Ⓒ Ⓓ Ⓔ
2. Ⓐ Ⓑ Ⓒ Ⓓ Ⓔ
3. Ⓐ Ⓑ Ⓒ Ⓓ Ⓔ

4. Ⓐ Ⓑ Ⓒ Ⓓ Ⓔ
5. Ⓐ Ⓑ Ⓒ Ⓓ Ⓔ
6. Ⓐ Ⓑ Ⓒ Ⓓ Ⓔ
7. Ⓐ Ⓑ Ⓒ Ⓓ Ⓔ
8. Ⓐ Ⓑ Ⓒ Ⓓ Ⓔ
9. Ⓐ Ⓑ Ⓒ Ⓓ Ⓔ
10. Ⓐ Ⓑ Ⓒ Ⓓ Ⓔ
11. Ⓐ Ⓑ Ⓒ Ⓓ Ⓔ
12. Ⓐ Ⓑ Ⓒ Ⓓ Ⓔ
13. Ⓐ Ⓑ Ⓒ Ⓓ Ⓔ
14. Ⓐ Ⓑ Ⓒ Ⓓ Ⓔ
15. Ⓐ Ⓑ Ⓒ Ⓓ Ⓔ
16. Ⓐ Ⓑ Ⓒ Ⓓ Ⓔ
17. Ⓐ Ⓑ Ⓒ Ⓓ Ⓔ
18. Ⓐ Ⓑ Ⓒ Ⓓ Ⓔ
19. Ⓐ Ⓑ Ⓒ Ⓓ Ⓔ
20. Ⓐ Ⓑ Ⓒ Ⓓ Ⓔ
21. Ⓐ Ⓑ Ⓒ Ⓓ Ⓔ
22. Ⓐ Ⓑ Ⓒ Ⓓ Ⓔ
23. Ⓐ Ⓑ Ⓒ Ⓓ Ⓔ
24. Ⓐ Ⓑ Ⓒ Ⓓ Ⓔ
25. Ⓐ Ⓑ Ⓒ Ⓓ Ⓔ
26. Ⓐ Ⓑ Ⓒ Ⓓ Ⓔ
27. Ⓐ Ⓑ Ⓒ Ⓓ Ⓔ
28. Ⓐ Ⓑ Ⓒ Ⓓ Ⓔ
29. Ⓐ Ⓑ Ⓒ Ⓓ Ⓔ
30. Ⓐ Ⓑ Ⓒ Ⓓ Ⓔ
31. Ⓐ Ⓑ Ⓒ Ⓓ Ⓔ
32. Ⓐ Ⓑ Ⓒ Ⓓ Ⓔ
33. Ⓐ Ⓑ Ⓒ Ⓓ Ⓔ
34. Ⓐ Ⓑ Ⓒ Ⓓ Ⓔ
35. Ⓐ Ⓑ Ⓒ Ⓓ Ⓔ

Section VII
Writing
Ability

1. Ⓐ Ⓑ Ⓒ Ⓓ Ⓔ
2. Ⓐ Ⓑ Ⓒ Ⓓ Ⓔ
3. Ⓐ Ⓑ Ⓒ Ⓓ Ⓔ
4. Ⓐ Ⓑ Ⓒ Ⓓ Ⓔ
5. Ⓐ Ⓑ Ⓒ Ⓓ Ⓔ
6. Ⓐ Ⓑ Ⓒ Ⓓ Ⓔ

7. Ⓐ Ⓑ Ⓒ Ⓓ Ⓔ
8. Ⓐ Ⓑ Ⓒ Ⓓ Ⓔ
9. Ⓐ Ⓑ Ⓒ Ⓓ Ⓔ
10. Ⓐ Ⓑ Ⓒ Ⓓ Ⓔ
11. Ⓐ Ⓑ Ⓒ Ⓓ Ⓔ
12. Ⓐ Ⓑ Ⓒ Ⓓ Ⓔ
13. Ⓐ Ⓑ Ⓒ Ⓓ Ⓔ
14. Ⓐ Ⓑ Ⓒ Ⓓ Ⓔ
15. Ⓐ Ⓑ Ⓒ Ⓓ Ⓔ
16. Ⓐ Ⓑ Ⓒ Ⓓ Ⓔ
17. Ⓐ Ⓑ Ⓒ Ⓓ Ⓔ
18. Ⓐ Ⓑ Ⓒ Ⓓ Ⓔ
19. Ⓐ Ⓑ Ⓒ Ⓓ Ⓔ
20. Ⓐ Ⓑ Ⓒ Ⓓ Ⓔ
21. Ⓐ Ⓑ Ⓒ Ⓓ Ⓔ
22. Ⓐ Ⓑ Ⓒ Ⓓ Ⓔ
23. Ⓐ Ⓑ Ⓒ Ⓓ Ⓔ
24. Ⓐ Ⓑ Ⓒ Ⓓ Ⓔ
25. Ⓐ Ⓑ Ⓒ Ⓓ Ⓔ

Section VIII
Problem
Solving

1. Ⓐ Ⓑ Ⓒ Ⓓ Ⓔ
2. Ⓐ Ⓑ Ⓒ Ⓓ Ⓔ
3. Ⓐ Ⓑ Ⓒ Ⓓ Ⓔ
4. Ⓐ Ⓑ Ⓒ Ⓓ Ⓔ
5. Ⓐ Ⓑ Ⓒ Ⓓ Ⓔ
6. Ⓐ Ⓑ Ⓒ Ⓓ Ⓔ
7. Ⓐ Ⓑ Ⓒ Ⓓ Ⓔ
8. Ⓐ Ⓑ Ⓒ Ⓓ Ⓔ
9. Ⓐ Ⓑ Ⓒ Ⓓ Ⓔ
10. Ⓐ Ⓑ Ⓒ Ⓓ Ⓔ
11. Ⓐ Ⓑ Ⓒ Ⓓ Ⓔ
12. Ⓐ Ⓑ Ⓒ Ⓓ Ⓔ
13. Ⓐ Ⓑ Ⓒ Ⓓ Ⓔ
14. Ⓐ Ⓑ Ⓒ Ⓓ Ⓔ
15. Ⓐ Ⓑ Ⓒ Ⓓ Ⓔ
16. Ⓐ Ⓑ Ⓒ Ⓓ Ⓔ
17. Ⓐ Ⓑ Ⓒ Ⓓ Ⓔ
18. Ⓐ Ⓑ Ⓒ Ⓓ Ⓔ
19. Ⓐ Ⓑ Ⓒ Ⓓ Ⓔ
20. Ⓐ Ⓑ Ⓒ Ⓓ Ⓔ

6
Three Sample GMATs with Answers and Analysis

This chapter contains three full-length GMAT exams. They have the same formats and degrees of difficulty as typical GMAT exams. A detailed analysis of the answers is included after each exam.

SAMPLE TEST 1

Section I   Reading Comprehension   Time: 30 minutes

Directions: This part contains three reading passages. You are to read each one carefully. When answering the questions, you will be allowed to refer back to the passages. The questions are based on what is *stated* or *implied* in each passage.

PASSAGE 1

This passage was written in 1972.

The United States economy made progress in reducing unemployment and moderating inflation. On the international side, this year was much calmer than last. Nevertheless, continuing imbalances in the pattern of world trade contributed to intermittent strains in the foreign exchange markets. These strains intensified to crisis proportions, precipitating a further devaluation of the dollar.

The domestic economy expanded in a remarkably vigorous and steady fashion. After a few lingering doubts about the strength of consumer demand in the opening weeks, the vitality of the expansion never came again into serious question. The resurgence in consumer confidence was reflected in the higher proportion of incomes spent for goods and services and the marked increase in consumer willingness to take on installment debt. A parallel strengthening in business psychology was manifested in a stepped-up rate of plant and equipment spending and a gradual pickup in outlays for inventory. Confidence in the economy was also reflected in the strength of the stock market and in the stability of the bond market, where rates showed little net change over the year as a whole despite the vigorous economic upturn. On several occasions during the year, the financial markets responded to shifting appraisals of the outlook for peace in Vietnam. For the year as a whole, consumer and business sentiment benefited from rising public expectations that a resolution of the conflict was in prospect and that East-West tensions were easing.

The underpinnings of the business expansion were to be found in part in the stimulative monetary and fiscal policies that had been pursued. Moreover, the restoration of sounder liquidity positions and tighter management control of production efficiency had also helped lay the groundwork for a strong expansion. In addition, the economic policy moves made by the President had served to renew optimism on the business outlook while boosting hopes that inflation would be brought under more effective control. Finally, of course, the economy was able to grow as vigorously as it did because sufficient leeway existed in terms of idle men and machines.

The United States balance of payments deficit declined sharply. Nevertheless, by any other test, the deficit remained very large, and there was actually a substantial deterioration in our trade account to a sizable deficit, almost two thirds of which was with Japan. It was to be expected that the immediate effect of devaluation would be a worsening in our trade accounts, with the benefits coming only later. While the overall trade performance proved disappointing, there are still good reasons for expecting the delayed impact of devaluation to produce in time a significant strengthening in our trade picture. Given the size of the Japanese component of our trade deficit, however, the outcome will depend importantly on the extent of the corrective measures undertaken by Japan. Also important will be our own efforts in the United States to fashion internal policies consistent with an improvement in our external balance.

The underlying task of public policy for the year ahead—and indeed for the longer run—remained a familiar one: to strike the right balance between encouraging healthy economic growth and avoiding inflationary pressures. With the economy showing sustained and vigorous growth, and with the currency crisis highlighting the need to improve our competitive posture internationally, the emphasis seemed to be shifting to the problem of inflation. The Phase Three program of wage and price restraint can contribute to dampening inflation. Unless productivity growth is unexpectedly large, however, the expansion of real output must eventually begin to slow down to the economy's larger run growth potential if generalized demand pressures on prices are to be avoided. Indeed, while the unemployment rates of a bit over five percent were still too high, it seems doubtful whether the much lower rates of four percent and below often cited as appropriate definitions of full employment do in fact represent feasible goals for the United States economy—unless there are improvements in the structure of labor and product markets and public policies influencing their operation. There is little doubt that overall unemployment rates can be brought down to four percent or less, for a time at least, by sufficient stimulation of aggregate demand. However, the resultant inflationary pressures have in the past proved exceedingly difficult to contain. After a point, moreover, it is questionable just how much, if any, additional reduction in unemployment can be permanently "bought" by accepting a stepped-up rate of inflation.

1. The passage was most likely published in a

   (A) popular magazine   (D) financial journal
   (B) general newspaper   (E) textbook
   (C) science journal

2. Confidence in the economy was expressed by all of the following except

   (A) a strong stock market
   (B) a stable bond market
   (C) increased installment debt
   (D) increased plant and equipment expenditures
   (E) rising interest rates

3. During the year in question, public confidence in the economy resulted in part from which of the following occurrences?

   I. Possible peace in Vietnam
   II. Reduction in East-West tensions
   III. An entente with China

   (A) I only
   (B) III only
   (C) I and II only
   (D) II and III only
   (E) I, II, and III

4. According to the author, business expansion for the period under review was caused largely by

   (A) stimulative monetary and fiscal policies
   (B) rising interest rates
   (C) increased foreign trade
   (D) price and wage controls
   (E) implementation of the Phase Three program

5. Most of the trade deficit in the balance of payments was attributed to trade with which country?

   (A) United Kingdom   (D) France
   (B) Japan   (E) Saudi Arabia
   (C) Germany

6. Part of the public policy task, as outlined in the passage, is to

   (A) cut consumer spending
   (B) prevent balance of payments deficits
   (C) devalue the dollar
   (D) avoid inflationary pressures
   (E) increase the balance of trade

7. The Phase Three program contained

   (A) higher income taxes
   (B) reduced government spending
   (C) devaluation of the dollar
   (D) productivity measures
   (E) wage and price controls

8. The passage states that the unemployment rate at the time the article was written was

   (A) 6 percent   (D) a little over 4 percent
   (B) a little over 5 percent (E) 4 percent
   (C) 5 percent

PASSAGE 2

These huge waves wreak terrific damage when they crash on the shores of distant lands or continents. Under a perfectly sunny sky and from an apparently calm sea, a wall of water may break twenty or thirty feet high over beaches and waterfronts, crushing houses and drowning unsuspecting residents and bathers in its path.

How are these waves formed? When a submarine earthquake occurs, it is likely to set up a tremendous amount of shock, disturbing the quiet waters of the deep ocean. This disturbance travels to the surface and forms a huge swell in the ocean many miles across. It rolls outward in all directions, and the water lowers in the center as another swell looms up. Thus, a series of concentric swells are formed similar to those made when a coin or small pebble is dropped into a basin of water. The big difference is in the size. Each of the concentric rings of basin water traveling out toward the edge is only about an inch across and less than a quarter of an inch high. The swells in the ocean are sometimes nearly a mile wide and rise to several multiples of ten feet in height.

Many of us have heard about these waves, often referred to by their Japanese name of "tsunami." For ages they have been dreaded in the Pacific, as no shore has been free from them. An underwater earthquake in the Aleutian Islands could start a swell that would break along the shores and cause severe damage in the southern part of Chile in South America. These waves travel hundreds of miles an hour, and one can understand how they would crash as violent breakers when caused to drag in the shallow waters of a coast.

Nothing was done about tsunamis until after World War II. In 1947 a particularly bad submarine earthquake took place south of the Aleutian Islands. A few hours later, people bathing in the sun along the quiet shores of Hawaii were dashed to death and shore-line property became a mass of shambles because a series of monstrous, breaking swells crashed along the shore and drove far inland. Hundreds of lives were lost in this catastrophe, and millions upon millions of dollars' worth of damage was done.

Hawaii (at that time a territory) and other Pacific areas then asked the U.S. Coast and Geodetic Survey to attempt to forecast these killer waves. With the blessing of the government, the Coast and Geodetic Survey initiated a program in 1948 known as the Seismic Seawave Warning System, using the earthquake-monitoring facilities of the agency, together with the world seismological data center, to locate submarine earthquakes as soon as they might occur. With this information they could then tell how severe a submarine earthquake was and could set up a tracking chart, with the center over the area of the earthquake, which would show by concentric time belts the rate of travel of the resulting wave. This system would indicate when and where, along the shores of the Pacific, the swells caused by the submarine earthquakes would strike.

9. One surprising aspect of the waves discussed in the passage is the fact that they

   (A) are formed in concentric patterns
   (B) often strike during clear weather
   (C) arise under conditions of cold temperature
   (D) are produced by deep swells
   (E) may be forecast scientifically

10. The waves discussed in the passage often strike

    (A) along the coasts of the Aleutian Islands
    (B) in regions outside the area monitored by the Coast and Geodetic Survey
    (C) at great distances from their place or origin
    (D) at the same time as the occurrence of earthquakes
    (E) in areas outside the Pacific region

11. It is believed that the waves are caused by

    (A) seismic changes   (D) underwater earthquakes
    (B) concentric time belts   (E) storms
    (C) atmospheric conditions

12. The normal maximum width of the waves is approximately

    (A) five feet   (D) five miles
    (B) ten feet   (E) thirty miles
    (C) one mile

13. The U.S. Coast and Geodetic Survey set up a program to

    I. Prevent submarine earthquakes
    II. Locate submarine earthquakes
    III. Determine the severity of submarine earthquakes

    (A) I only
    (B) III only
    (C) I and II only
    (D) II and III only
    (E) I, II, and III

14. Nothing was done about the waves until

(A) deaths occurred
(B) the outbreak of World War II
(C) a solution was found
(D) millions of dollars worth of damage was incurred in Hawaii
(E) large areas in Chile were devastated

15. The movement of the waves has been measured at a speed of

(A) 30 miles an hour
(B) 40 miles an hour
(C) 50 miles an hour
(D) 100 miles an hour
(E) more than a hundred miles an hour

16. According to the passage, the waves occur most frequently in the area of

(A) the Eastern U.S. seaboard   (D) Western Europe
(B) the Pacific   (E) Asia
(C) Argentina

17. Given present wave-tracking systems, scientists can forecast all of the following *except*

(A) the severity of underwater earthquakes
(B) the wave's rate of travel
(C) when a wave will strike
(D) where a wave will strike
(E) the height of the wave

PASSAGE 3

It is indisputable that in order to fulfill its many functions, water should be clean and biologically valuable. The costs connected with the provision of biologically valuable water for food production with the maintenance of sufficiently clean water, therefore, are primarily production costs. Purely "environmental" costs seem to be in this respect only costs connected with the safeguarding of cultural, recreational and sports functions which the water courses and reservoirs fulfill both in nature and in human settlements.

The pollution problems of the atmosphere resemble those of the water only partly. So far, the supply of air has not been deficient as was the case with water, and the dimensions of the air-shed are so vast that a number of people still hold the opinion that air need not be economized. However, scientific forecasts have shown that the time may be already approaching when clear and biologically valuable air will become problem No. 1.

Air being ubiquitous, people are particularly sensitive about any reduction in the quality of the atmosphere, the increased contents of dust and gaseous exhalations, and particularly about the presence of odors. The demand for purity of atmosphere, therefore, emanates much more from the population itself than from the specific sectors of the national economy affected by a polluted or even biologically aggressive atmosphere.

The households' share in atmospheric pollution is far bigger than that of industry which, in turn, further complicates the economic problems of atmospheric purity. Some countries have already collected positive experience with the reconstruction of whole urban sectors on the basis of new heating appliances based on the combustion of solid fossil fuels; estimates of the economic consequences of such measures have also been put forward.

In contrast to water, where the maintenance of purity would seem primarily to be related to the costs of production and transport, a far higher proportion of the costs of maintaining the purity of the atmosphere derives from environmental considerations. Industrial sources of gaseous and dust emissions are well known and classified; their location can be accurately identified, which makes them controllable. With the exception, perhaps, of the elimination of sulphur dioxide, technical means and technological processes exist which can be used for the elimination of all excessive impurities of the air from the various emissions.

Atmospheric pollution caused by the private property of individuals (their dwellings, automobiles, etc.) is difficult to control. Some sources such as motor vehicles are very mobile, and they are thus capable of polluting vast territories. In this particular case, the cost of anti-pollution measures will have to be borne, to a considerable extent, by individuals, whether in the form of direct costs or indirectly in the form of taxes, dues, surcharges, etc.

The problem of noise is a typical example of an environmental problem which cannot be solved passively, i.e., merely by protective measures, but will require the adoption of active measures, i.e., direct interventions at the source. The costs of a complete protection against noise are so prohibitive as to make it unthinkable even in the economically most developed countries. At the same time it would not seem feasible, either economically or politically, to force the population to carry the costs of individual protection against noise, for example, by reinforcing the sound insulation of their homes. A solution of this problem probably cannot be found in the near future.

18. According to the passage, the population at large

    (A) is unconcerned about air pollution controls

    (B) is especially aware of problems concerning air quality and purity

    (C) regards water pollution as more serious than air pollution

    (D) has failed to recognize the economic consequences of pollution

    (E) is unwilling to make the sacrifices needed to ensure clean air

19. Scientific forecasts have shown that clear and biologically valuable air

    (A) is likely to remain abundant for some time

    (B) creates fewer economic difficulties than does water pollution

    (C) may soon be dangerously lacking

    (D) may be beyond the capacity of our technology to protect

    (E) has already become difficult to obtain

20. According to the passage, which of the following contributes *most* to atmospheric pollution?

    (A) industry   (D) mining

    (B) production   (E) waste disposal

    (C) households

21. The costs involved in the maintenance of pure water are determined primarily by

    I. production costs

    II. transport costs

    III. research costs

    (A) I only   (D) II and III only

    (B) III only   (E) I, II, and III

    (C) I and II only

22. According to the passage, atmospheric pollution caused by private property is

    (A) easy to control   (D) decreasing

    (B) impossible to control (E) negligible

    (C) difficult to control

23. According to the passage, the problem of noise can be solved through

    I. Active measures
    II. Passive measures
    III. Tax levies

  (A) I only   (D) II and III only
  (B) III only   (E) I, II, and III
  (C) I and II only

24. According to the passage, the costs of some anti-pollution measures will have to be borne by individuals because

  (A) individuals contribute to the creation of pollution
  (B) governments do not have adequate resources
  (C) industry is not willing to bear its share
  (D) individuals are more easily taxed than producers
  (E) individuals demand production, which causes pollution

25. Complete protection against noise

  (A) may be forthcoming in the near future
  (B) is impossible to achieve
  (C) may have prohibitive costs
  (D) is possible only in developed countries
  (E) has been achieved in some countries

If there is still time remaining, you may review the questions in this section only. You may not turn to any other section of the test.

Section II   Problem Solving   Time: 30 minutes

Directions: Solve each of the following problems; then indicate the correct answer on the answer sheet. [On the actual test you will be permitted to use any space available on the examination paper for scratch work.]

NOTE: A figure that appears with a problem is drawn as accurately as possible so as to provide information that may help in answering the question (unless the words "Figure not drawn to scale" appear next to the figure). Numbers in this test are real numbers.

1. A trip takes 6 hours to complete. After traveling ¼ of an hour, 1⅜ hours, and 2⅓ hours, how much time does one need to complete the trip?

   (A) 2¹⁄₁₂ hours
   (B) 2 hours, 2½ minutes
   (C) 2 hours, 5 minutes

   (D) 2⅛ hours
   (E) 2 hours, 7½ minutes

2. If a stock average was 500 points at the beginning of a week and 400 points at the end of the same week, by what percent has it decreased during the week?

   (A) 20
   (B) 22
   (C) 25

   (D) 27
   (E) 30

3. A car wash can wash 8 cars in 18 minutes. At this rate, how many cars can the car wash wash in 3 hours?

   (A) 13
   (B) 40.5
   (C) 80

   (D) 125
   (E) 405

4. If the ratio of the areas of 2 squares is 2:1, then the ratio of the perimeters of the squares is

   (A) 1:2
   (B) 1:$\sqrt{2}$
   (C) $\sqrt{2}$:1

   (D) 2:1
   (E) 4:1

5. In Leesville, 70% of the cars have whitewall tires and 25% of the cars are air-conditioned. If 20% of the cars are air-conditioned and have whitewall tires, what percentage of the cars have neither air-conditioning nor whitewall tires?

   (A) 5
   (B) 10
   (C) 15

   (D) 20
   (E) 25

6. A company issued 100,000 shares of stock. In 1970, each share of stock was worth $122.50. In 1973, each share of the stock was worth $111.10. How much less were the 100,000 shares worth in 1973 than in 1970?

(A) $114,000
(B) $1,100,040
(C) $1,140,000
(D) $114,000,000
(E) $1,140,000,000

7. A worker's daily salary varies each day. In one week he worked five days. His daily salaries were $51.90, $52.20, $49.80, $51.50, and $50.60. What was his average daily wage for the week?

(A) $50.80
(B) $51.20
(C) $51.50
(D) $51.60
(E) $255.00

8. A borrower pays 18% interest per year on the first $600 he borrows and 17% per year on the part of the loan in excess of $600. How much interest will the borrower pay on a loan of $6,000 for 1 year?

(A) $926
(B) $1,020
(C) $1,026
(D) $1,080
(E) $1,126

9. If $3x - 2y = 8$, then $4y - 6x$ is:

(A) −16
(B) −8
(C) 8
(D) 16
(E) none of these

10. It costs 10¢ a kilometer to fly and 12¢ a kilometer to drive. If you travel 200 kilometers, flying x kilometers of the distance and driving the rest, then the cost of the trip in dollars is

(A) 20
(B) 24
(C) $24 - 2x$
(D) $24 - .02x$
(E) $2,400 - 2x$

11. If two identical rectangles R_1 and R_2 form a square when placed next to each other, and the length of R_1 is x times the width of R_1, then x is

(A) 1
(B) 3/2
(C) 5/4
(D) 2
(E) 3

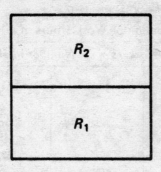

12. If the area of a square increases by 69%, then the side of the square increases by

    (A) 13%   (D) 69%
    (B) 30%   (E) 130%
    (C) 39%

13. A used car dealer sells a car for $1,380 and makes a 20% profit. How much did the car cost the dealer?

    (A) $1,100   (D) $1,180
    (B) $1,120   (E) $1,560
    (C) $1,150

14. If $x < z$ and $x < y$, which of the following statements are always true? Assume $x \geq 0$.

    I. $y < z$
    II. $x < yz$
    III. $2x < y + z$

    (A) only I
    (B) only II
    (C) only III
    (D) II and III only
    (E) I, II, and III

Use the following table for questions 15–17.

Distribution of Work Hours in a Factory

Numbers of Workers		*Number of Hours Worked*
20		45–50
15		40–44
25		35–39
16		30–34
4		0–29
80	TOTAL	3,100

15. What percentage of workers worked 40 or more hours?

(A) 18.75   (D) 40

(B) 25   (E) 43.75

(C) 33⅓

16. The number of workers who worked from 40 to 44 hours is x times the number who worked up to 29 hours, where x is

(A) $^{15}/_{16}$ (D) 5

(B) 3¾   (E) 6¼

(C) 4

17. Which of the following statements can be inferred from the table?

  I. The average number of hours worked per worker is less than 40.

 II. At least 3 worked more than 48 hours.

III. More than half of all the workers worked more than 40 hours.

(A) I only

(B) II only

(C) I and II only

(D) I and III only

(E) I, II, and III

18. A truck traveling at 70 miles per hour uses 30% more gasoline to travel a certain distance than it does when it travels at 50 miles per hour. If the truck can travel 19.5 miles on a gallon of gasoline at 50 miles per hour, how far can the truck travel on 10 gallons of gasoline at a speed of 70 miles per hour?

(A) 130   (D) 175

(B) 140   (E) 195

(C) 150

19. $\dfrac{2}{5} + \dfrac{1}{3} = \dfrac{x}{30}$, where x is

(A) 4   (D) 16

(B) 7   (E) 22

(C) 11

20. How many squares with sides ½ inch long are needed to cover a rectangle which is 4 feet long and 6 feet wide?

(A) 24   (D) 13,824

(B) 96   (E) 14,266

(C) 3,456

If there is still time remaining, you may review the questions in this section only. You may not turn to any other section of the test.

Section III   Analysis of Situations   Time: 30 minutes

Directons: Read the following passages. After you have completed each one, you will be asked to answer questions that involve determining the importance of specific factors included in the passage. When answering questions, you may consult the passage.

PASSAGE 1

The success of the Abco Corporation in the investment-conscious country of Frieland was recently the subject of a government inquiry. Frieland is a developing country about the size of New York State with a population of ten million people. It has a small but growing industrial base, and several multinational business concerns have established manufacturing plants in various parts of the country.

Government policy in **Frieland has** traditionally favored foreign investment. Leaders of all political parties **have been** virtually unanimous in their belief that foreign investment in Frieland **would contribute** to speeding that country's economic development, a major priority of both the ruling coalition and opposition parties. Of special interest to the government were those industries that exported a significant share of their total output. Since Frieland had a relatively small population, there was a limit to the amount of goods that could be produced for the local market. Also, the government did not want to encourage foreign investors to compete with local industry, even though new industries might alleviate the already high unemployment rate.

A final reason for encouraging export-intensive industries was to earn badly needed foreign exchange. Frieland had a chronic deficit in its balance of trade; that is, its imports were regularly greater than its exports. This meant that it had to use scarce foreign exchange to pay for the growing deficit. Therefore, Frieland welcomed potential investors that would promise to export a significant share of their total output. So when executives of Abco Corporation proposed to establish a shoe manufacturing plant which would be export-intensive, it received ready approval from the government.

Government support for the enterprise was given not only because of the promise to export, but also because of the high unemployment rate in the country. However, approval was given despite the fact that there was at the time surplus shoe production in Frieland, most factories having large excess capacities and underworked labor forces. It was known that Abco had promised the government, among other things, to (1) employ hundreds of workers, (2) reduce the price of shoes by some 30 percent, and (3) export more than half its output.

In return for these promises, Abco received the following concessions from the government:

(1) Land was given the company on a lease basis for a period of 99 years, rent-free.
(2) A government-owned contracting firm built the factory at low subsidized prices.
(3) The company received loans at very low interest rates for an extended period of time. These loans could be renewed at company request at lower than the prevailing market interest rate.
(4) The government trained workers at the plant at no expense to the company.

Production commenced one year after the first equipment arrived at the new plant. It took another half year to properly train the new work force to operate the sophisticated equipment which was introduced. After the "running in" period, production continued smoothly for about a year until a labor dispute occurred. It appeared that management wanted to dismiss about 10 percent of the work force owing to what a company spokesman called "a temporary slack in demand" for Abco's products. The labor union representing the company's work force refused to accept any reduction in the work force and threatened a strike if workers were terminated. After some discussion, union representatives agreed that the company might be justified in laying off some workers, but nowhere near the 10 percent figure that management desired. At any rate, the union claimed that the company must first submit its request to a joint union-management grievance committee which was authorized under the current labor agreement to deal with such disputes. Management acquiesced to the union demand. After several days of bargaining, an agreement was worked out whereby Abco would be allowed to terminate most part-time workers, amounting to only one percent of the total work force. Although the agreement brought about a temporary solution to the current problem, labor-management relations at Abco continued to be strained, as management was convinced that more workers were redundant than the union cared to admit.

After another six months, it became apparent that what management had termed "a temporary slack in demand" was in reality a failure of the company to sell the quantity of shoes that had been forecast before production began. Actual sales never reached the target quantity, and, as a result, the company lost $1 million in each of its first two years of operation. The American representatives on the board of directors—who constituted a majority—voted to terminate the company's operations in Frieland. Shortly after the vote, bankruptcy hearings began.

Because Abco was located in an underdeveloped area of the country, the government was worried about the political ramifications if production ceased. The company employed 500 workers, and quite a few shopkeepers were dependent upon their patronage. When government representatives asked Abco management what could be done to keep the company operating, they received the following answer. Management was willing to continue production if the government granted the company an additional five-million-dollar loan on favorable terms. If the government could not grant such a loan, then another alternative was to purchase the company from Abco at a "reasonable" price.

The government was in a dilemma. On the one hand, it was concerned about the political consequences if Abco should continue the bankruptcy proceedings. On the other hand, if it granted the loan, it might be setting a precedent for any other company that was in financial difficulties. Moreover, there was a certain risk involved in lending the money to a company in bad shape. The government appointed a special committee to investigate the financial condition of Abco and decide the issue.

One month later, the committee submitted its report. The major finding was that Abco had not kept any of its original promises to the government. For one thing, Abco's shoe prices were no lower than those of any of its competitors. As for exports, not only had the company failed to reach its promised goal of 50 percent, but as of the bankruptcy hearings, its exports for a five-year period only amounted to 5 percent of total output. In light of these developments, the government felt that it had to make a quick decision in the Abco affair in such a way as to avoid criticism from the opposition.

Data Evaluation Questions

Directions: The questions that follow relate to the preceding passage. Evaluate, in terms of the passage, each of the items given. Then select your answer from one of the following classifications, and blacken the corresponding space on the answer sheet.

(A) A MAJOR OBJECTIVE in making the decision: one of the goals sought by the decision maker

(B) A MAJOR FACTOR in making the decision: an aspect of the problem, specifically mentioned in the passage, that fundamentally affects and/or determines the decision

(C) A MINOR FACTOR in making the decision: a less important element bearing on or affecting a Major Factor, rather than a Major Objective directly

(D) A MAJOR ASSUMPTION in making the decision: a projection or supposition arrived at by the decision maker before considering the factors and alternatives

(E) AN UNIMPORTANT ISSUE in making the decision: an item lacking significant impact on, or relationship to, the decision

1. Ability of Abco to survive if the five-million-dollar loan was granted

2. High unemployment in Frieland

3. Dependence of shopkeepers on the existence of Abco

4. Government investment incentives granted to Abco

5. Status of Frieland as a developing country

6. Continued operation of Abco

7. Training of workers at no expense to Abco

8. Strained worker-management relations at Abco

9. Export potential of Abco

10. Political philosophy of the opposition party

11. Need for a quick decision by the government as to whether to grant the loan requested by Abco

12. Availability of government funds needed to support Abco

13. Prevention of layoffs of workers at Abco

14. Political consequence of an Abco bankruptcy

15. Frieland's small population

16. Increasing foreign exchange reserves

17. Surplus shoe production

18. Reduction of shoe prices

PASSAGE 2

In early 1957 the Conway Clock Company was considering the introduction of a new line of electric clocks in an effort to increase unit sales and thereby utilize a greater percentage of its production facilities. The new line would be sold under the brand name Concord and would be marketed in direct competition with the lower-priced models of the regular Conway line. While the total market for clocks had increased in recent years, Conway's unit sales had remained relatively constant. The company's sales manager felt that one way to increase sales was to introduce a line of non-fair-traded clocks.[1]

The Conway Company had been producing a line of quality household clocks

---

[1] The company had enforced resale price maintenance or fair trade on its regular line of clocks. Resale price maintenance is a procedure whereby a manufacturer is permitted in some states to establish, by contract, a minimum retail price below which retailers may not sell its products.

for almost a century. Throughout its existence the company had maintained an excellent reputation for the production of quality clocks. Many of its first clocks were known to be still operating in satisfactory fashion. Some were even considered family heirlooms.

In 1955 the Conway Company produced a line consisting of eight basic models. In 1956, however, four new models were added, making a total of twelve models of electric and mechanical clocks sold under the Conway name. Of these, two were alarm clocks, three were table model occasional clocks, and seven were wall clocks. Each model was produced in several different colors, with black, brown, and red the most popular ones. Styles ranged from traditional to ultramodern. The company employed a full-time designer and emphasized style in its dealer and consumer promotions.

The clock market was considered to be highly competitive. The industry was comprised of a number of firms, most of which were small or medium size. The giant in the field was General Electric with its Telechron line of electric clocks. The smaller firms sold either on a price or quality-of-workmanship basis. These firms usually produced a relatively small number of models and changed styles frequently. Conway was one of the medium-sized companies with about 5 percent of the industry's sales. The company's share of the market had been greater during the late 1920's and early 1930's, but the increase in the number of firms selling inexpensive electric clocks had cut into the company's share substantially. Because of an expanding market, however, Conway's unit sales had remained relatively constant since 1945. Dollar sales of Conway clocks approximated $7 million in 1956. The increase in dollar sales which had taken place since World War II was due almost entirely to changes in Conway's prices.

The Conway Company employed salesmen who sold to 300 distributors, most of whom were jewelry wholesalers. These wholesalers sold to over 14,000 retail outlets, of which 80 percent were jewelry stores and the rest department stores. The bulk of the company's sales to department stores was accounted for by 60 to 70 large stores. Each of the company's salesmen had about 20 large retail accounts to which he sold direct. If an outlet which had been served by one of the wholesalers was sold direct by a Conway salesman, the outlet was billed through the wholesaler so that the latter received its margin.

To back up the efforts of the salesmen, the company budgeted about $250,000 annually for advertising. About 70 percent was spent on consumer advertising and the remainder on trade advertising. Most of the consumer advertisements were placed in magazines, although some radio spots were used. The advertisements stressed the up-to-date styling and quality of the Conway clocks.

Conway clocks were priced at retail from $8.95 to $59.50, but most of the sales were in the $29 to $39 price range. The company established a policy of resale price maintenance for the Conway line to protect the small dealer. This policy was policed largely by examining dealer advertisements and collecting information from trade sources. If a dealer sold Conway merchandise at less than the fair-traded price, Conway issued a warning to the dealer. If a second violation occurred within a year, Conway sought a court injunction against the dealer to prevent future violations. Actually, Conway had little difficulty in maintaining its retail prices. The company did, however, face growing price competition from small clock manufacturers who frequently offered large credit jewelers and discount houses a special price for a volume order.

The new line of clocks under consideration in 1957 would be sold under the Concord brand and would consist solely of two electric alarm clocks and three electric wall models. The styles for these five models would be obtained from (1) previously discontinued Conway models, (2) new models developed especially for Concord, or (3) modified current Conway models, usually "stripped" versions. These clocks would have suggested list prices ranging from $6.95 to $14.95. These prices would be identical to the prices charged for the comparable Conway models. However, the Concord line would *not* be fair traded and the price to dealers would be less. (See Table 1 for a price schedule.) It was expected that many retailers would sell the Concord line at considerably less than the list price.

The only advertising planned for the Concord line was some illustrated price lists for use by company salesmen and distributors, point-of-purchase signs,

TABLE 1
EXAMPLE OF A COMPARABLE PRICE STRUCTURE ON CONWAY AND CONCORD CLOCKS

Price	Conway Model No. 102* (Fair Traded)	Concord Model No. C102 (Not Fair Traded)	
		Lots of 1–24	Lots of 25 or More
List	$10.95	$10.95	$10.95
To dealer	7.23	6.68	5.97
To distributor	5.59	5.25	4.50

* No quantity discounts offered on this model.

display racks, and consumer handouts for use by retailers. This material would be free to distributors and dealers. It was thought that many of the retailers handling the Conway line would also handle the Concord models. It was expected that the quality of the Conway models would be used as a selling point by both distributors and retailers. It was hoped that additional cut-price outlets, such as credit jewelers, large drug chain outlets, and discount houses, would be interested in the new line.

Data Evaluation Questions

Directions: The questions that follow relate to the preceding passage. Evaluate, in terms of the passage, each of the items given. Then select your answer from one of the following classifications, and blacken the corresponding space on the answer sheet.

(A) A MAJOR OBJECTIVE in making the decision: one of the goals sought by the decision maker

(B) A MAJOR FACTOR in making the decision: an aspect of the problem, specifically mentioned in the passage, that fundamentally affects and/ or determines the decision

(C) A MINOR FACTOR in making the decision: a less important element bearing on or affecting a Major Factor, rather than a Major Objective directly

(D) A MAJOR ASSUMPTION in making the decision: a projection or supposition arrived at by the decision maker before considering the factors and alternatives

(E) AN UNIMPORTANT ISSUE in making the decision: an item lacking significant impact on, or relationship to, the decision

19. The selling by wholesalers to 14,000 retail outlets

20. Utilization of excess capacity

21. Conway's declining market share

22. Conway's 100 years in business

23. The placement of most consumer ads in magazines

24. Consumer acceptance of the new line

25. Competition from small manufacturers

26. Selling new line to discount houses

27. Need to increase unit sales

28. Reputation of Conway

29. Resale price maintenance

30. Protection of the small dealer

31. Importance of styling

32. Sales to department stores

33. Existing retailers will sell Concord models

34. Checking dealer advertisements

35. Growing price competition

*If there is still time remaining, you may review the questions in this
section only. You may not turn to any other section of the test.*

Section IV Data Sufficiency   Time: 30 minutes

Directions: Each of the following problems has a question and two statements
which are labeled (1) and (2). Use the data given in (1) and (2) together with
other available information (such as the number of hours in a day, the definition
of *clockwise*, mathematical facts, etc.) to decide whether the statements are
sufficient to answer the question. Then fill in space

(A) if you can get the answer from (1) alone but not from (2) alone;

(B) if you can get the answer from (2) alone but not from (1) alone;

(C) if you can get the answer from (1) and (2) together, although neither
statement by itself suffices;

(D) if statement (1) alone suffices *and* statement (2) alone suffices;

(E) if you cannot get the answer from statements (1) and (2) together, but
need even more data.

All numbers used in this section are real numbers. A figure given for a problem is intended to provide information consistent with that in the question, but not necessarily with the additional information contained in the statements.

1. Are two triangles congruent?

   (1) Both triangles are right triangles.
   (2) Both triangles have the same perimeter.

2. Is x greater than zero?

   (1) $x^4 - 16 = 0$
   (2) $x^3 - 8 = 0$

3. If both conveyer belt A and conveyer belt B are used, they can fill a hopper with coal in one hour. How long will it take for conveyer belt A to fill the hopper without conveyer belt B?

   (1) Conveyer belt A moves twice as much coal as conveyer belt B.
   (2) Conveyer belt B would take 3 hours to fill the hopper without belt A.

4. A fly crawls around the outside of a circle once. A second fly crawls around the outside of a square once. Which fly travels further?

   (1) The diagonal of the square is equal to the diameter of the circle.
   (2) The fly crawling around the circle took more time to complete his journey than the fly crawling around the square.

5. How much did it cost the *XYZ* Corporation to insure its factory from fire in 1972?

   (1) It cost $5,000 for fire insurance in 1971.
   (2) The total amount the corporation spent for fire insurance in 1970, 1971, and 1972 was $18,000.

6. Is y larger than 1?

   (1) y is larger than 0.
   (2) $y^2 - 4 = 0$.

7. A worker is hired for 6 days. He is paid $2 more for each day of work than he was paid for the preceding day of work. How much was he paid for the first day of work?

(1) His total wages for the 6 days were $150.

(2) He was paid 150% of his first day's pay for the sixth day.

8. A car originally sold for $3,000. After a month, the car was discounted x%, and a month later the car's price was discounted y%. Is the car's price after the discounts less than $2,600?

(1) $y = 10$

(2) $x = 15$

9. What is the value of a?

(1) $a = f$
(2) $a = b$

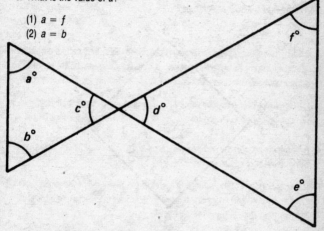

10. In triangle ABC, find z if $AB = 5$ and $y = 40$.

(1) $BC = 5$
(2) The bisector of angle B is perpendicular to AC.

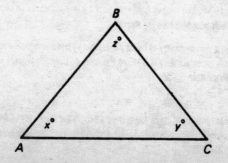

11. How much cardboard will it take to make an open cubical box with no top?

   (1) The area of the bottom of the box is 4 square feet.
   (2) The volume of the box is 8 cubic feet.

12. How many books are on a bookshelf?

   (1) The total weight of all the books on the bookshelf is 40 pounds.
   (2) The average weight of the books on the bookshelf is 2.5 pounds.

13. Is the figure *ABCD* a rectangle?

   (1) $x = 90$
   (2) $AB = CD$

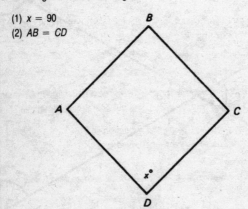

14. A sequence of numbers is given by the rule $a_n = (a_{n-1})^2$. What is a_5?

   (1) $a_1 = -1$
   (2) $a_3 = 1$

15. How much is John's weekly salary?

   (1) John's weekly salary is twice as much as Fred's weekly salary.
   (2) Fred's weekly salary is 40% of the total of Chuck's weekly salary and John's weekly salary.

16. Find $x + 2y$.

   (1) $x + y = 4$
   (2) $2x + 4y = 12$

17. Is angle *BAC* a right angle?

   (1) $x = 2y$
   (2) $y = 1.5z$

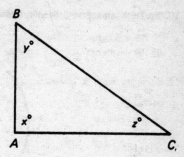

18. Is x greater than y?

   (1) $x = 2k$
   (2) $k = 2y$

19. How much profit did Toyland make selling 65 dolls if each doll cost $8?

   (1) The amount the dolls sold for was $750.
   (2) The dolls cost $7 each last year.

20. 50% of the people in Teetown have blue eyes and blond hair. What percent of the people in Teetown have blue eyes but do not have blond hair?

   (1) 70% of the people in Teetown have blond hair.
   (2) 60% of the people in Teetown have blue eyes.

21. The pentagon *ABCDE* is inscribed in the circle with center *O*. How many degrees is angle *ABC*?

   (1) The pentagon *ABCDE* is a regular pentagon.
   (2) The radius of the circle is 5 inches.

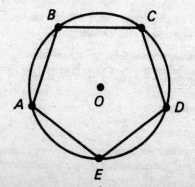

22. What is the area of the circle with center O? (AB and DE are straight lines)

(1) $DE = 5$ inches
(2) $AB = 7$ inches

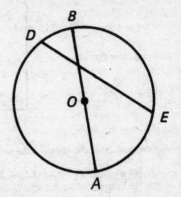

23. What is the taxable income of the Kell family in 1973? The taxable income of the Kell family in 1971 was $10,000.

(1) The Kell family had taxable income of $12,000 in 1972.
(2) The total taxable income of the Kell family for the three years 1971, 1972, and 1973 was $34,000.

24. A piece of string 6 feet long is cut into three smaller pieces. How long is the longest of the three pieces?

(1) Two pieces are the same length.
(2) One piece is 3 feet, 2 inches long.

25. If a group of 5 craftsmen take 3 hours to finish a job, how long will it take a group of 4 apprentices to do the same job?

(1) An apprentice works at ⅔ the rate of a craftsman.
(2) The 5 craftsmen and the 4 apprentices working together will take $1^{22}/_{23}$ hours to finish the job.

If there is still time remaining, you may review the questions in this section only. You may not turn to any other section of the test.

Section V Writing Ability   Time: 30 minutes

Directions: This test consists of a number of sentences, in each of which some part or the whole is underlined. Each sentence is followed by five alternative versions of the underlined portion. Select an alternative you consider both most correct and most effective according to the requirements of standard written English. Answer A is the same as the original version; if you think the original version is best, select answer A.

In considering the answer choices, be attentive to matters of grammar, diction, and syntax, as well as clarity, precision, and fluency. Do not select an answer which alters the meaning of the original sentence.

1. If he was to decide to go to college, I, for one, would recommend that he plan to go to Yale.

   (A) If he was to decide to go to college,
   (B) If he were to decide to go to college,
   (C) Had he decided to go to college,
   (D) In the event that he decides to go to college,
   (E) Supposing he was to decide to go to college,

2. Except for you and I, everyone brought a present to the party.

   (A) Except for you and I, everyone brought
   (B) With exception of you and I, everyone brought
   (C) Except for you and I, everyone had brought
   (D) Except for you and me, everyone brought
   (E) Except for you and me, everyone had brought

3. When one reads the poetry of the seventeenth century, you find a striking contrast between the philosophy of the Cavalier poets such as Suckling and the attitude of the Metaphysical poets such as Donne.

   (A) When one reads the poetry of the seventeenth century, you find
   (B) When you read the poetry of the seventeenth century, one finds
   (C) When one reads the poetry of the seventeenth century, he finds
   (D) If one reads the poetry of the 17th century, you find
   (E) As you read the poetry of the 17th century, one finds

4. Because of his broken hip, John Jones <u>has not and possibly never will be able to run</u> the mile again.

(A) has not and possibly never will be able to run
(B) has not and possibly will never be able to run
(C) has not been and possibly never would be able to run
(D) has not and possibly never would be able to run
(E) has not been able to run and possibly never will be able to run

5. <u>Had I realized how close</u> I was to failing, I would not have gone to the party.

(A) Had I realized how close
(B) If I would have realized
(C) Had I had realized how close
(D) When I realized how close
(E) If I realized how close

6. Having finished the marathon in record-breaking time, <u>the city awarded him its Citizen's Outstanding Performance Medal</u>.

(A) the city awarded him its Citizen's Outstanding Performance Medal
(B) the city awarded the Citizen's Outstanding Performance Medal to him
(C) he was awarded the Citizen's Outstanding Performance Medal by the city
(D) the Citizen's Outstanding Performance Medal was awarded to him
(E) he was awarded by the city with the Citizen's Outstanding Performance Medal

7. <u>The football team's winning it's first game of the season</u> excited the student body.

(A) The football team's winning it's first game of the season
(B) The football team having won it's first game of the season
(C) The football team's having won it's first game of the season
(D) The football team's winning its first game of the season
(E) The football team winning it's first game of the season

8. Anyone interested in the use of computers can learn much <u>if you have access to</u> a Radio Shack TRS-80 or a Pet Microcomputer.

(A) if you have access to
(B) if he has access to

    (C) if access is available to
    (D) by access to
    (E) from access to

9. No student had ought to be put into a situation where he has to choose between his loyalty to his friends and his duty to the class.

    (A) No student had ought to be put into a situation where
    (B) No student had ought to be put into a situation in which
    (C) No student should be put into a situation where
    (D) No student ought to be put into a situation in which
    (E) No student ought to be put into a situation where

10. Being a realist, I could not accept his statement that supernatural beings had caused the disturbance.

    (A) Being a realist,
    (B) Since I am a realist,
    (C) Being that I am a realist,
    (D) Being as I am a realist,
    (E) Realist that I am,

11. The reason I came late to class today is because the bus broke down.

    (A) I came late to class today is because
    (B) why I came late to class today is because
    (C) I was late to school today is because
    (D) that I was late to school today is because
    (E) I came late to class today is that

12. I have to make dinner, wash the dishes, do my homework, and then relaxing.

    (A) to make dinner, wash the dishes, do my homework, and then relaxing
    (B) to make dinner, washing the dishes, do my homework, and then relax
    (C) to make dinner, wash the dishes, doing my homework and then relaxing
    (D) to prepare dinner, wash the dishes, do my homework, and then relaxing
    (E) to make dinner, wash the dishes, do my homework, and then relax

13. The climax occurs when he asks who's in the closet.

    (A) occurs when he asks who's
    (B) is when he asks whose
    (C) occurs when he asks whose
    (D) is when he asks who'se
    (E) occurs when he asked who's

14. The grocer <u>hadn't hardly any of those kind</u> of canned goods.

    (A) hadn't hardly any of those kind
    (B) hadn't hardly any of those kinds
    (C) had hardly any of those kind
    (D) had hardly any of those kinds
    (E) had scarcely any of those kind

15. <u>Having stole the money, the police searched the thief.</u>

    (A) Having stole the money, the police searched the thief.
    (B) Having stolen the money, the thief was searched by the police.
    (C) Having stolen the money, the police searched the thief.
    (D) Having stole the money, the thief was searched by the police.
    (E) Being that he stole the money, the police searched the thief.

16. The child is <u>neither encouraged to be critical or to examine</u> all the evidence for his opinion.

    (A) neither encouraged to be critical or to examine
    (B) neither encouraged to be critical nor to examine
    (C) either encouraged to be critical or to examine
    (D) encouraged either to be critical nor to examine
    (E) not encouraged either to be critical or to examine

17. The process by which the community <u>influence the actions of its members</u> is known as social control.

    (A) influence the actions of its members
    (B) influences the actions of its members
    (C) had influenced the actions of its members
    (D) influences the actions of their members
    (E) will influence the actions of its members

18. To be sure, there would be scarcely no time left over for other things if school children <u>would have been expected to have considered</u> all sides of every matter on which they hold opinions.

    (A) would have been expected to have considered
    (B) should have been expected to have considered
    (C) were expected to consider
    (D) will be expected to have been considered
    (E) were expected to be considered

19. Depending on skillful suggestion, argument is seldom used in advertising.

   (A) Depending on skillful suggestion, argument is seldom used in advertising.
   (B) Argument is seldom used by advertisers, who depend instead on skillful suggestion.
   (C) Skillfull suggestion is depended on by advertisers instead of argument.
   (D) Suggestion, which is more skillful, is used in place of argument by advertisers.
   (E) Instead of suggestion, depending on argument is used by skillful advertisers.

20. When this war is over, no nation will either be isolated in war or peace.

   (A) either be isolated in war or peace
   (B) be either isolated in war or peace
   (C) be isolated in neither war nor peace
   (D) be isolated either in war or in peace
   (E) be isolated neither in war or peace

21. Each will be within trading distance of all the others and will be able to strike them.

   (A) within trading distance of all the others and will be able to strike them
   (B) near enough to trade with and strike all the others
   (C) trading and striking the others
   (D) within trading and striking distance of all the others
   (E) able to strike and trade with all the others

22. Examining the principal movements sweeping through the world, it can be seen that they are being accelerated by the war.

   (A) Examining the principal movements sweeping through the world, it can be seen
   (B) Having examined the principal movements sweeping through the world, it can be seen
   (C) Examining the principal movements sweeping through the world can be seen
   (D) Examining the principal movements sweeping through the world, we can see
   (E) It can be seen examining the principal movements sweeping through the world

23. However many mistakes have been made in our past, the tradition of America, not only the champion of freedom but also fair play, still lives among millions who can see light and hope scarcely anywhere else.

    (A) not only the champion of freedom but also fair play,
    (B) the champion of not only freedom but also of fair play,
    (C) the champion not only of freedom but also of fair play,
    (D) not only the champion but also freedom and fair play,
    (E) not the champion of freedom only, but also fair play,

24. In giving expression to the play instincts of the human race, new vigor and effectiveness are afforded by recreation to the body and to the mind.

    (A) new vigor and effectiveness are afforded by recreation to the body and to the mind
    (B) recreation affords new vigor and effectiveness to the body and to the mind
    (C) there are afforded new vigor and effectiveness to the body and to the mind
    (D) by recreation the body and mind are afforded new vigor and effectiveness
    (E) the body and the mind afford new vigor and effectiveness to themselves by recreation

25. Play being recognized as an important factor in improving mental and physical health and thereby reducing human misery and poverty.

    (A) Play being recognized as
    (B) By recognizing play as
    (C) Their recognizing play as
    (D) Recognition of it being
    (E) Play is recognized as

If there is still time remaining, you may review the questions in this section only. You may not turn to any other section of the test.

Section VI* Analysis of Situations   Time: 30 minutes

Directions: Read the following passages. After you have completed each one, you will be asked to answer questions that involve determining the importance of specific factors included in the passage. When answering questions, you may consult the passage.

PASSAGE 1

Mr. Ed Krim, a building contractor by profession, met with an old friend, Mr. Sam Sims, a marketing consultant. Mr. Krim was excited about a business opportunity and wanted to obtain Sims's evaluation of its prospects. Posture-mat, a small company producing foam rubber mattresses, was in financial trouble, and its owners were anxious to sell it. The company had been established some twenty years, but its market share had steadily declined over the last five years. Since Mr. Krim had no previous experience in the mattress business, he requested that his friend find out what he could about the company.

Mr. Sims first analyzed the company's resources. Its best resource was its product and brand name. Foam rubber mattresses are made of imported latex and are extremely firm, unlike synthetic rubber mattresses made of polyure-thane. However, synthetics are much cheaper than foam rubber mattresses. Latex mattresses are known for their orthopedic and anti-allergic qualities, among others. The Posturemat brand name had very nearly become a generic term for all types of rubber mattresses. Posturemat, however, was the only latex mattress produced locally.

Apart from a superior product, the company had few resources. Its equipment, while satisfactory, was old and had been fully depreciated. It operated in leased premises on a year-to-year basis, although the landlord was willing to conclude a long-term agreement on favorable terms. On the other hand, the company's labor force was experienced and dedicated and its production manager had more than ten years' experience in latex manufacturing.

Mr. Joe Caspi, president of the company, was past seventy years old and was anxious to retire. He had tried to retire previously, but had failed to train a successor. Apart from Fred Lefko, the sales manager, no one else shared responsibility for marketing or administration. Fred Lefko let Sam Sims know that if the company were sold, he had no intention of remaining. Lefko had eighteen years' experience in the mattress industry, including twelve years with Posturemat. If Lefko left the company, Krim might be hard pressed to find a suitable replacement. This was another issue that Sam Sims would have to study.

Posturemat's financial position was precarious. The company was heavily in debt and its line of credit fully extended. There was some question as to whether the company would be able to purchase enough latex to keep production going, but Mr. Caspi assured Sam Sims that the company had a bank letter of credit to purchase an additional three months' supply.

It spite of Mr. Caspi's optimism, the fact was that his company had steadily lost market share. Once the dominant mattress manufacturer, with fifty percent of the local market, its market share had declined to less than ten percent. Mr. Caspi attributed this decline to inroads made by spring mattress manufacturers, who had only begun production five years ago. Spring mattresses now accounted for seventy percent of the total market, Caspi's company ten percent, with the remaining twenty percent shared by a number of small plants producing synthetic rubber mattresses. Spring mattresses had some attributes similar to those of foam rubber, such as orthopedic qualities. They were less costly to manufacture, but sold to the consumer at about the same price as Posturemat mattresses.

Because of Posturemat's financial difficulties, it ceased advertising in newspapers and on radio. Little if any advertising had been done in other media over the past five years. As a result, retailers were reluctant to handle the product line. By contrast, two of the larger spring mattress manufacturers had advertised heavily in the mass media. One of these manufacturer's products was sold exclusively by the largest furniture chain in the country. During his study of the mattress market, a number of retailers had expressed the opinion to Mr. Sims that a whole generation of young people were largely unaware of Posturemat products because of the lack of advertising. One retailer was quoted as saying: "It is true that older people remember Posturemat, but these mattresses last for almost twenty years. The big market is not the replacement market, but sales generated by family formation. Thousands of young couples get married every year, and every marriage means another mattress sale. But these young people only see advertisements for spring mattresses. It is obviously easier for my salesman to sell a mattress which his customers have seen in countless advertisements than one which is relatively unknown."

Sims was aware of the fact that if Posturemat was ever to regain some of its lost market share, it would have to launch a major advertising program to educate young adults about the important attributes found in its products. A major question that needed an immediate answer was: "To what extent are people aware of Posturemat mattresses and their attributes?" Other questions involved the attitudes of people toward foam rubber mattresses in general and how these attitudes compared to those toward spring mattresses. Mr. Sims ordered a market research survey to obtain answers to his questions. In brief, the study revealed that a large segment of the population over twenty-five years of age was aware of Posturemat mattresses and had favorable attitudes toward their attributes. About three-quarters of these people expressed a preference for foam rubber mattresses for their children (by contrast with other mattresses for their own use). Awareness among younger segments of the population of the attributes of foam rubber mattresses in general, and of Posturemat in particular, was very low. Few young people expressed an intention to buy foam rubber mattresses.

On the basis of the preliminary research results, Krim was optimistic that he could turn the company around. In support of his belief, he cited the recognition of the company among a significant portion of the population, and the fact that they would buy a Posturemat for their children. He believed that once retailers became aware that new management had taken over the company, they would be willing to stock the product. Krim was aware that the research findings were not always in agreement with his conclusions. However, the finding that young people were relatively unaware of Posturemat did not seem to worry him. He felt that a well-designed advertising program would convince many people to buy a foam rubber mattress, rather than any competing type. Moreover, the introduction of a new management team would instill confidence among Posturemat's bankers. Credit lines would be increased, thereby improving the company's financial position. However, before making a final decision as to whether to purchase Posturemat, Mr. Krim waited for Sam Sims's final report and recommendations.

Data Evaluation Questions

Directions: The questions that follow relate to the preceding passage. Evaluate, in terms of the passage, each of the items given. Then select your answer from one of the following classifications, and blacken the corresponding space on the answer sheet.

(A) A MAJOR OBJECTIVE in making the decision: one of the goals sought by the decision maker

(B) A MAJOR FACTOR in making the decision: an aspect of the problem, specifically mentioned in the passage, that fundamentally affects and/or determines the decision

(C) A MINOR FACTOR in making the decision: a less important element bearing on or affecting a Major Factor, rather than a Major Objective directly

(D) A MAJOR ASSUMPTION in making the decision: a projection or supposition arrived at by the decision maker before considering the factors
and alternatives

(E) AN UNIMPORTANT ISSUE in making the decision: an item lacking significant impact on, or relationship to, the decision

1. Public awareness of the high quality of Posturemat mattresses

2. Joe Caspi's marketing ability

3. The anti-allergic qualities of Posturemat mattresses

4. Attitude of older consumers towards Posturemat mattresses

5. Willingness of retailers to stock Posturemat products in the future

6. Need to import latex rubber

7. Posturemat's present market share

8. Sam Sims's recommendations

9. Posturemat's present market share

10. Plausibility of changing consumer attitudes through advertising

11. Orthopedic qualities of Posturemat mattresses

12. Use of polyurethane in the production of synthetic mattresses

13. Lefko's intention to leave Posturemat

14. Age of Posturemat's manufacturing equipment

15. Likelihood that credit lines could be increased

16. Caspi's explanation for loss of market share

PASSAGE 2

In 1956 officials of the Grace Fabri-Tool Company, manufacturers of special
tools and presses for working with laminated plastic sheets[1] such as Formica,

---

[1] Laminated plastic sheets were made of specially processed papers impregnated with res-
ins and then cured under intense heat and pressure. The layers were then fused into sheets
usually about 1/16 inch thick. These sheets were bonded to plywood and hardboard and
used as a surface material on many types of domestic, commercial, and industrial furniture
and furnishings. One of the most popular applications in the home was for kitchen counter
tops.

Micarta, and Textolite, were considering possible changes in the company's distribution channels. From the company's founding in 1953, it had sold through laminated plastics distributors. Sales increased rapidly from the start, but profits were not satisfactory. This condition resulted from the difficulties encountered by distributors in providing adequate field service.

In 1942 Mr. Robert Grace had first realized the difficulties that Formica presented to the fabricator. While working in his father's shop, he was often given the job of cutting Formica and bonding it to plywood, and in time he developed considerable skill in handling the plastic material.

After serving in the armed forces and attending college, Mr. Grace decided to put his knowledge of Formica to good advantage. He persuaded the Formica Company to hire him to travel all over the country to show fabricators and cabinetmakers improved methods of cutting and forming Formica sheets. As a demonstrator, Mr. Grace arranged meetings for distributors. Typically such a meeting would attract 50 to 500 people from the cabinet shops and woodworking and plastic-fabricating plants in the distributor's area. Each meeting lasted about two hours and was generally held in a hotel in which a shop had been set up for temporary use by Mr. Grace. Distributors found that a large number of their customers and prospective customers attended these meetings because most of them had little experience in working with laminated plastic sheets and were in need of aid. Following such a meeting, it was not uncommon for a distributor to experience a 30 to 35 percent increase in Formica sales.

After two years as a Formica demonstrator, Grace felt that Formica could be fabricated more efficiently if special tools and presses were available for that purpose. The officials of the company encouraged Grace to find someone to design and produce such tools and presses, but no manufacturer was interested in his idea. Therefore, Grace decided to form his own company to design and sell the tools and presses. After completing the designs in his own workshop, he engaged a tool manufacturer to produce them.

Grace Fabri-Tool Company was formed in 1953 and was the first to introduce a line of tools for working laminated plastic sheets, but Stanley and Porter-Cable were quick to follow. Even though specially made for working plastic sheets, these tools could also be used with other materials, including wood.

The principal types of operation used in working laminated plastic sheets were sawing, drilling, routing, beveling, bonding, and forming. While all these operations except forming could be performed with ordinary shop tools, field experience indicated that carbide-tipped tools, such as those made by Grace, gave better results and lasted longer. However, such tools were about twice as expensive as ordinary carpenter's tools. Representative of the tools were the routing and trimming fixtures. The average price of the tools was about $15.

Grace Fabri-Tool Company also sold bonding and forming presses; the least expensive model initially sold for $1,650. The Grace Thermofast vacuum press used a heat process which saved a great deal of time over the conventional cold-pressure method of bonding plastic sheets (or other material such as wood veneer) to a second surface. Field tests indicated that the Grace press could complete in six minutes a bond that would require several hours using the cold-pressure method.

Forming presses were used to shape sheets of plastic in more than one plane. For example, in place of a flat plastic-covered kitchen counter top, it was not uncommon for a designer to specify an extension of the plastic sheet up the back wall and down over the front edge, or a slight ridge along the front edge of the counter top to prevent water from running off. Forming sheets in this manner required special presses which, because of their cost, could be purchased only by the large fabricators, who consequently did the bulk of this kind of work either on their own account or on a custom basis for smaller firms. Initially it was felt that the presses could be installed and operated with a minimum of instruction and would require virtually no service.

Mr. Grace was particularly fortunate in that the Formica Company continued to use his services, on an independent contractor basis, for a period of about five months after he had formed his own company. Under this arrangement he continued as a demonstrator of Formica, but was paid according to the number of demonstrations made, rather than on a straight salary basis. This arrangement subsidized his selling efforts on behalf of his own products and brought him into direct contact with prospective distributors and final users of his products. He estimated that this support was worth $10,000–$12,000 and that it was instrumental in assuring the success of the firm at a critical stage.

In view of the above arrangement, Mr. Grace decided to sell his products through laminated plastic sheet distributors. He sent letters to 50 of them with the result that 40 sent in orders. They gave the company representation in most parts of the country.

Laminated plastic sheet distributors generally sold only plastic sheets, plywood, adhesives, and seam-fillers. However, some had taken on noncompeting items to serve their customers better. Many of the customers of the distributors were relatively unacquainted with the problems of working with laminated plastic sheets and welcomed any information or tools that would help them. As a result, the Grace Fabri-Tools were added to their lines by many distributors. Not only were they better able to service their customers' needs, but it was possible for their salesmen to call on customers with something new to talk about.

Distributor interest in Grace tools continued, since for some time a new tool was added to the line almost every month. Distributors' salesmen thus had a steady stream of new items to talk about as they called on their customers. As the number of new tools increased, the need for additional ones decreased and in time the company ran out of ideas. This caused distributors' salesmen to lose their special interest in the Grace tools.

Prior to late 1955, distributors aggressively sought business. However, the demand for plastic sheets became so great after that time that distributors took most of their salesmen off the road and had them use the telephone to take orders. Even with this arrangement distributors' sales of plastic sheets increased as much as 30 percent in a year. But the sale of Grace products suffered from the lack of selling effort. Distributors spent most of their time taking orders for plastic sheets and trying to fill them. The search for funds to finance their operations became a major problem. This situation continued into 1956. However, there were some indications that it might again become necessary for distributors to get out and sell.

Sales of the Grace Company amounted to $60,000 during the last six months of 1953. The following year they rose to $350,000 and in 1955 reached $455,000. Despite the sales increases, profits suffered as a result of field service costs. The company, belatedly recognizing the need for field service on the presses and the inadequacy of distributors in this respect, leaned over backwards to remedy the situation.

By 1955 distributors found that service demands and complaints from buyers of presses were a problem. The buyer looked to the distributor to keep the press running. Yet the distributor usually had no facilities, and Grace was inadequately prepared to meet the service needs which developed. This situation resulted in long delays in completing service calls. Distributors had in the past been able to adjust customers' complaints on the spot inasmuch as they involved small tools, adhesives, plywood, and plastic sheets. Defects in these products could be detected easily, and when necessary, the product could be replaced out of stock at a small cost. This was not possible, however, with a machine costing several thousand dollars and normally shipped by the manufacturer to the customer.

Flatbed presses were originally priced at $1,650 on the assumption that service and repairs under the warranty would be a trivial expense to the company. Actual experience, however, indicated that claims made under the company's warranty could not be handled by letter or telephone and that satisfactory handling incurred expenses ranging from $200 to $300 per press. Moreover, redesign of the presses increased manufacturing costs from $400 to $500 per press. In setting a new price, the company decided to set it high enough to recover the added manufacturing costs and the estimated cost of delivering, installing the equipment, training operators, and handling service and repairs under the warranty. The new price was established at $2,975. Many distributors felt that at this price the item was too expensive to handle. Some made no effort to sell it but continued to sell the smaller tools. Others voluntarily dropped the Grace products.

With the adoption of the new installation and service policy it became necessary for the company to reconsider its distribution channels. Moreover, the desire to achieve broader distribution and more aggressive selling increased the need for reassessing existing channels.

Distributors' discounts were cut from 20 percent to 10 percent of list price, except in those cases where the distributor was able and willing to handle, install, and service presses and to train operators. A discount was allowed anyone who bought for resale. However, no discounts were allowed on direct sales by the company to users, no matter how large. It was reasoned that a user would buy only what he required whether or not quantity discounts were allowed.

In 1956 the management felt that manufacturers' representatives, together with the remaining distributors, would provide the desired coverage and selling effort. In investigating this possibility some difficulty was encountered in locating representatives who were regularly calling on prospective buyers of Grace products and who were not selling competing items. In some cases agents not calling upon potential buyers of Grace products were willing to do so and asked for the Grace line.

The representatives under consideration carried various other products. Several handled automotive items, one handled kitchen cabinets and appliances, another handled noncompeting electronic gluing equipment, and one with a very large territory was willing to handle Grace products exclusively. Some representatives for laminated plastic sheets also expressed interest in taking on Grace products. A representative was paid a 10 percent commission on all shipments of tools or presses destined for his area, even those resulting from distributor effort. However, if a representative obtained an order for shipment into the territory of another representative, the commission was to be split. The Grace Fabri-Tool Company management recognized that from 12 to 18 months would be required before a representative could be expected to develop his territory.

Data Evaluation Questions

Directions: The questions that follow relate to the preceding passage. Evaluate, in terms of the passage, each of the items given. Then select your answer from one of the following classifications, and blacken the corresponding space on the answer sheet.

    (A) A MAJOR OBJECTIVE in making the decision: one of the goals sought by the decision maker

    (B) A MAJOR FACTOR in making the decision: an aspect of the problem, specifically mentioned in the passage, that fundamentally affects and/or determines the decision

    (C) A MINOR FACTOR in making the decision: a less important element bearing on or affecting a Major Factor, rather than a Major Objective directly

    (D) A MAJOR ASSUMPTION in making the decision: a projection or supposition arrived at by the decision maker before considering the factors and alternatives

    (E) AN UNIMPORTANT ISSUE in making the decision: an item lacking significant impact on, or relationship to, the decision

17. Total cost of a Grace press

18. Adoption of a new service policy

19. Adoption of a new distribution channel

20. Working in his father's shop

21. Service expenses of $400 to $500 per press

22. Lack of selling effort

23. Desire for expanded distribution

24. Complaints from buyers

25. Possibility that manufacturers' representatives would expand coverage

26. The press being too expensive for distributors to handle

27. Cutting of distributors' discounts

28. Difficulty in finding distributors

29. The fact that some prospective representatives carried appliances

30. Easy detection of defects in Fabri-Tools

31. Delays in completing service calls

32. Lack of distributor facilities

33. Level of distributor discounts

34. Arrangement of meetings for distributors

35. Likelihood of buying regardless of quantity discounts

If there is still time remaining, you may review the questions in this section only. You may not turn to any other section of the test.

Section VII   Writing Ability   Time: 30 minutes

Directions: This test consists of a number of sentences, in each of which some part or the whole is underlined. Each sentence is followed by five alternative versions of the underlined portion. Select the alternative you consider both most correct and most effective according to the requirements of standard written English. Answer A is the same as the original version; if you think the original version is best, select answer A.

In considering the answer choices, be attentive to matters of grammar, diction, and syntax, as well as clarity, precision, and fluency. Do not select an answer which alters the meaning of the original sentence.

1. John wanted to have gone to the movies.

   (A) wanted to have gone
   (B) had wanted to have gone
   (C) wanted to go
   (D) wanted to have went
   (E) had wanted to have went

2. Knowing the cost of the Space Shuttle program, its breakdown caused the director much irritation.

   (A) Knowing the cost of the Space Shuttle program, its breakdown caused the director much irritation.
   (B) Knowing the cost of the Space Shuttle program. Its breakdown caused the director much irritation.

(C) Knowing the cost of the Space Shuttle program, the director was greatly irritated by its breakdown.
(D) By knowing the cost of the Space Shuttle program, its breakdown greatly irritated the director.
(E) Knowledge of the cost of the Space Shuttle program: its breakdown greatly irritated the director.

3. In this particular job we have discovered that to be diligent is more important than being bright.

(A) to be diligent is more important than being bright
(B) for one to be diligent is more important than being bright
(C) diligence is more important than brightness
(D) being diligent is more important than to be bright
(E) by being diligent is more important than being bright

4. On their return, they not only witnessed the sinking ship but the amazing escape of the passengers as well.

(A) not only witnessed the sinking ship but the
(B) not only witnessed the sinking ship, but the
(C) did not only witness the sinking ship, but also the
(D) witnessed not only the sinking ship but the
(E) witnessed the sinking ship and also the

5. No one but him could have told them that the thief was I.

(A) him could have told them that the thief was I
(B) he could have told them that the thief was I
(C) he could have told them that thief was me
(D) him could have told them that the thief was me
(E) he could have told them the thief was me

6. Either you transfer the data which was demanded or file a report explaining why you did not submit the overall annual figures.

(A) Either you transfer the data which was demanded
(B) You either transfer the data, which was demanded,
(C) You either transfer the data which were demanded
(D) Either you transfer the data, which was demanded,
(E) Either you transfer the data, which were demanded,

7. On entering the stadium, cheers greeted them as a sign of universal approval of their great achievement.

   (A) On entering the stadium, cheers greeted them
   (B) On entering the stadium, they were greeted by cheers
   (C) While entering the stadium, cheers greeted them
   (D) On entering the stadium cheers greeted them
   (E) On entering the stadium: cheers greeted them

8. The set of propositions which was discussed by the panel have been published in the society journal.

   (A) which was discussed by the panel have
   (B) which were discussed by the panel have
   (C) that was discussed by the panel has
   (D) which were discussed by the panel has
   (E) which was discussed, by the panel, has

9. In a great amount of the requests, there have been very few that the staff could deal with efficiently.

   (A) In a great amount of the requests, there have been very few
   (B) Out of the great amount of the requests, there have been very little
   (C) In a great amount of the requests, there has been very few
   (D) In a great number of the requests, there have been very few
   (E) Of the great number of requests, there have been very few

10. They decided to honor Mr. Wilson, who will be president of the club for ten years next Tuesday.

   (A) will be president of the club for ten years next Tuesday
   (B) shall have been president of the club for ten years next Tuesday
   (C) next Tuesday will have been president of the club for ten years
   (D) next Tuesday has been president of the club for ten years
   (E) had been president of the club for ten years next Tuesday

11. After a careful evaluation of the circumstances surrounding the incident, we decided that we neither have the authority nor the means to cope with the problem.

   (A) neither have the authority nor
   (B) neither have authority or

(C) have neither the authority nor

(D) have neither the authority or

(E) have not either the authority nor

12. Everyone of us have understood that without him helping us we would not have succeeded in our program over the past six months.

   (A) Everyone of us have understood that without him helping us

   (B) Everyone of us has understood that without his helping us

   (C) Everyone of us have understood that without his help

   (D) Everyone of us has understood that without him helping us

   (E) Every single one of us have understood that without him helping us

13. On the African continent, the incidence of vitamin deficiencies correlates positively with the level of solar radiation.

   (A) deficiencies correlates positively with

   (B) deficiencies correlate positively with

   (C) deficiencies, correlate positively with,

   (D) deficiencies correlate positively to

   (E) deficiencies correlates positively to

14. A thoroughly frightened child was seen by her cowering in the corner of the room.

   (A) A thoroughly frightened child was seen by her cowering in the corner of the room.

   (B) Cowering in the corner of the room a thoroughly frightened child was seen by her.

   (C) She saw, cowering in the corner of the room, a thoroughly frightened child.

   (D) A thoroughly frightened child, cowering in the corner of the room, was seen by her.

   (E) She saw a thoroughly frightened child who was cowering in the corner of the room.

15. If they would have taken greater care in the disposal of the nuclear waste, the disaster would not have occurred.

   (A) If they would have taken greater care

   (B) Unless they took greater care

    (C) Had they not taken **greater care**

    (D) If they had taken **greater care**

    (E) If they took greater care

16. Neither the judge nor I am ready to announce who the winner is.

    (A) Neither the judge nor I am ready to announce who the winner is.

    (B) Neither the judge nor I are ready to announce who the winner is.

    (C) Neither the judge nor I are ready to announce who is the winner.

    (D) Neither the judge nor I am ready to announce who is the winner.

    (E) Neither I or the judge are ready to announce who is the winner.

17. After adequate deliberation, the council can see scarcely any valid reason for its reviewing the request.

    (A) can see scarcely any valid reason for its

    (B) can not see scarcely any valid reason for its

    (C) can see any valid reason scarcely for its

    (D) can see scarcely any valid reason for it's

    (E) can scarcely see any valid reason for it's

18. Knowing little algebra, it was difficult to solve the problem.

    (A) it was difficult to solve the problem

    (B) the problem was difficult to solve

    (C) I found it difficult to solve the problem

    (D) the solution to the problem was difficult to solve

    (E) solving the problem was difficult

19. If she were I, she would have accepted the prize if she had won it.

    (A) were I, she would have accepted the prize if she had

    (B) was I, she would have accepted the prize if she would have

    (C) was I, she would have accepted the prize if she had

    (D) were I, she would have accepted the prize if she would have

    (E) were me, she would have accepted the prize if she had

20. We expect help in providing adequate facilities and ample funds from everybody in order to advance this vital program.

    (A) in providing adequate facilities and ample funds from everybody

    (B) in the provision of adequate facilities and ample funds from everybody

    (C) in providing adequate facilities and funds from everyone

(D) with facilities and funds from everyone

(E) from everybody in providing adequate facilities and ample funds

21. From the moment he took public office, his actions have been loaded with significance and filled with worth.

(A) been loaded with significance and filled with worth

(B) been significant and worthwhile

(C) become loaded with significance and worth

(D) to be loaded with significance and filled with worth

(E) been actions of significance and worth

22. After several days' tour, we became convinced that the climate of this deserted island was like Florida in winter.

(A) the climate of this deserted island was like Florida in winter

(B) the climate of this deserted island was like that of Florida in winter

(C) the climate of this desert Island was like Florida in winter

(D) the climate of this deserted island in winter was like Florida

(E) the climate of this desert island was as Florida in winter

23. The students have always had a most sincere interest and admiration for the important work of Professor Jakobsen.

(A) a most sincere interest and admiration for

(B) a most sincere interest in and admiration for

(C) mostly a sincere interest and admiration for

(D) a most sincere interest, and admiration for

(E) a most sincere interest and an admiration for

24. I might have provided a happier ending if I was the author of that novel.

(A) ending if I was the author of that novel

(B) ending, if I were the author of that novel

(C) ending. If I were the author of that novel

(D) ending if I had been the author of that novel

(E) ending, if I had to be the author of that novel

25. Last night, our guest lecturer spoke about the methods of controlling population growth, the dangers involved in manipulating nature, and how to calculate potential change in species' size.

(A) the dangers involved in manipulating nature, and how to calculate

(B) the dangers involved in manipulating nature and in calculating

(C) how to manipulate nature, and how to calculate

(D) the dangers involved in manipulating nature, and the method of calculating

(E) how to manipulate nature and to calculate

*If there is still time remaining, you may review the questions in this
section only. You may not turn to any other section of the test.*

Section VIII   Problem Solving   Time: 30 minutes

Directions: Solve each of the following problems; then indicate the correct
answer on the answer sheet. [On the actual test you will be permitted to use
any space available on the examination paper for scratch work.]

NOTE: A figure that appears with a problem is drawn as accurately as possible
so as to provide information that may help in answering the question (unless
the words "Figure not drawn to scale" appear next to the figure). Numbers in
this test are real numbers.

Use the following graphs for questions 1–3.

AVERAGE ANNUAL RECEIPTS AND OUTLAYS OF U.S. GOVERNMENT 1967–1970 IN PERCENTAGE

RECEIPTS

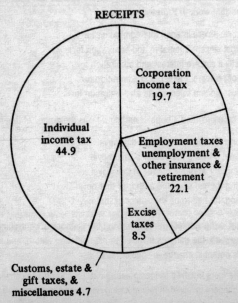

Corporation income tax 19.7

Individual income tax 44.9

Employment taxes unemployment & other insurance & retirement 22.1

Excise taxes 8.5

Customs, estate & gift taxes, & miscellaneous 4.7

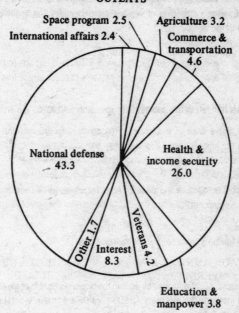

OUTLAYS

Space program 2.5   Agriculture 3.2

International affairs 2.4   Commerce & transportation 4.6

National defense 43.3

Health & income security 26.0

Other 1.7

Interest 8.3

Veterans 4.2

Education & manpower 3.8

1. If the annual average receipts from the corporation income tax during the years 1967–1970 equal x, then the average annual receipts during this period were about

  (A) $\dfrac{x}{4}$ (D) $5x$

  (B) x^2 (E) x^5

  (C) $3x$

2. The average annual combined outlay for veterans, education and manpower, and health and income security was roughly what fraction of the average annual outlays?

  (A) ¼   (D) ½

  (B) ⅓   (E) ⅔

  (C) ⅖

3. If ⅝ of the average annual outlays for agriculture was spent in the western U.S., what percentage of average annual outlays was spent on agriculture in the western U.S.?

(A) ⅝   (D) 2
(B) 1   (E) 3.2
(C) 1¼

4. The next number in the geometric progression 5,10,20 . . . is

(A) 25   (D) 40
(B) 30   (E) 50
(C) 35

5. Eggs cost 8¢ each. If the price of eggs increases by ⅛, how much will a dozen eggs cost?

(A) 90¢   (D) $1.12
(B) $1.08   (E) $1.18
(C) $1.10

6. A trapezoid *ABCD* is formed by adding the isosceles right triangle *BCE* with base 5 inches to the rectangle *ABED* where *DE* is *t* inches. What is the area of the trapezoid in square inches?

(A) $5t + 12.5$ (D) $(t + 5)^2$
(B) $5t + 25$ (E) $t^2 + 25$
(C) $2.5t + 12.5$

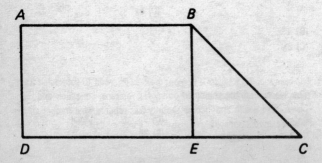

7. A manufacturer of jam wants to make a profit of $75 when he sells 300 jars of jam. It costs 65¢ each to make the first 100 jars of jam and 55¢ each to make each jar after the first 100. What price should he charge for the 300 jars of jam?

(A) $75   (D) $240

(B) $175   (E) $250

(C) $225

8. A farmer walks around the outside of a rectangular field at a constant speed. It takes him twice as long to walk the length of the field as it takes him to walk the width of the field. If he walked 300 yards when he walked around the field, what is the area of the field in square yards?

(A) 5,000   (D) 25,000

(B) 15,000   (E) 30,000

(C) 20,000

9. A company makes a profit of 7% selling goods which cost $2,000; it also makes a profit of 6% selling a machine which cost the company $5,000. How much total profit did the company make on both transactions?

(A) $300   (D) $440

(B) $400   (E) $490

(C) $420

10. If $\dfrac{x}{y} = \dfrac{3}{z}$, then $9y^2$ equals

(A) $\dfrac{x^2}{9}$ (D) $3x^2$

(B) $x^3 z$ (E) $\left(\dfrac{1}{9}\right) x^2 z^2$

(C) $x^2 z^2$

11. The operation * applied to a number gives as its result 10 subtracted from twice the number. What is *(*9)?

(A) −11   (D) 9

(B) 6   (E) 36

(C) 8

12. *ABCD* is a rectangle. The length of *BE* is 4 and the length of *EC* is 6. The area of triangle *BEA* plus the area of triangle *DCE* minus the area of triangle *AED* is

   (A) 0
   (B) .4 of the area of triangle *AEB*
   (C) .5 of the area of triangle *AED*
   (D) .5 of the area of *ABCD*
   (E) cannot be determined

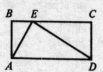

13. 36 identical chairs must be arranged in rows with the same number of chairs in each row. Each row must contain at least three chairs and there must be at least three rows. A row is parallel to the front of the room. How many different arrangements are possible?

   (A) 2   (D) 6
   (B) 4   (E) 10
   (C) 5

14. Which of the following solids has the largest volume? (*Figures are not drawn to scale.*)

   I. A cylinder of radius 5 mm and height 11 mm
      (volume of a cylinder is $\pi r^2 h$)

   II. A sphere of radius 6 mm
       (volume of a sphere is $\frac{4}{3}\pi r^3$)

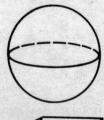

   III. A cube with edge of 9 mm
        (volume of a cube is e^3)

   (A) I
   (B) II
   (C) III
   (D) I and II
   (E) II and III

15. If .2% of x is .03, then x is

   (A) 150   (D) $6\frac{2}{3}$

   (B) $66\frac{2}{3}$ (E) 1.5

   (C) 15

16. A pension fund has a total of $1 million invested in stock of the ABC Company and bonds of the DEF Corporation. The ABC stock yields 12% in cash each year, and the DEF bonds pay 10% in cash each year. The pension fund received a total of $115,000 in cash from ABC stock and DEF bonds last year. How much money was invested in ABC stock?

   (A) $750,000.00   (D) $333,333.33

   (B) $600,000.00   (E) $250,000.00

   (C) $500,000.00

17. The ratio of chickens to pigs to horses on a farm can be expressed as the triple ratio 20:4:6. If there are 120 chickens on the farm, then the number of horses on the farm is

   (A) 4   (D) 36

   (B) 6   (E) 60

   (C) 24

18. If $x^2 - y^2 = 15$ and $x + y = 3$, then $x - y$ is

   (A) -3 (D) 5

   (B) 0   (E) cannot be determined

   (C) 3

19. Tom's salary is currently $35,000. When Tom was hired 5 years ago, his salary was $10,000. By what percentage was Tom's salary increased since he was hired?

   (A) $28\frac{4}{7}$ (D) 250

                               (E) 350

   (B) 40

   (C) 50

20. What is the area of the shaded region? The radius of the outer circle is a and the radius of each of the circles inside the large circle is $\frac{a}{3}$.

(A) 0

(D) $\left(\frac{7}{9}\right)\pi a^2$

(B) $\left(\frac{1}{3}\right)\pi a^2$

(E) $\left(\frac{8}{9}\right)\pi a^2$

(C) $\left(\frac{2}{3}\right)\pi a^2$

If there is still time remaining, you may review the questions in this section only. You may not turn to any other section of the test.

Answers

Section I   Reading Comprehension

1. **(D)**	8. **(B)**	15. **(E)**	22. **(C)**
2. **(E)**	9. **(B)**	16. **(B)**	23. **(C)**
3. **(C)**	10. **(C)**	17. **(E)**	24. **(A)**
4. **(A)**	11. **(D)**	18. **(B)**	25. **(C)**
5. **(B)**	12. **(C)**	19. **(C)**	
6. **(D)**	13. **(D)**	20. **(C)**	
7. **(E)**	14. **(D)**	21. **(C)**	

Section II   Problem Solving

1. **(B)**	6. **(C)**	11. **(D)**	16. **(B)**
2. **(A)**	7. **(B)**	12. **(B)**	17. **(A)**
3. **(C)**	8. **(C)**	13. **(C)**	18. **(C)**
4. **(C)**	9. **(A)**	14. **(C)**	19. **(E)**
5. **(E)**	10. **(D)**	15. **(E)**	20. **(D)**

Section III Analysis of Situations

1. (D)	10. (E)	19. (E)	28. (B)
2. (B)	11. (D)	20. (A)	29. (B)
3. (C)	12. (D)	21. (B)	30. (A)
4. (E)	13. (A)	22. (C)	31. (B)
5. (E)	14. (B)	23. (E)	32. (C)
6. (A)	15. (E)	24. (D)	33. (D)
7. (E)	16. (A)	25. (B)	34. (E)
8. (B)	17. (E)	26. (D)	35. (B)
9. (B)	18. (D)	27. (A)	

Section IV Data Sufficiency

1. (E)	8. (B)	15. (E)	22. (B)
2. (B)	9. (E)	16. (B)	23. (C)
3. (D)	10. (D)	17. (C)	24. (B)
4. (A)	11. (D)	18. (E)	25. (D)
5. (E)	12. (C)	19. (A)	
6. (C)	13. (E)	20. (B)	
7. (D)	14. (D)	21. (A)	

Section V Writing Ability

1. (B)	8. (B)	15. (B)	22. (D)
2. (D)	9. (D)	16. (E)	23. (C)
3. (C)	10. (A)	17. (B)	24. (B)
4. (E)	11. (E)	18. (C)	25. (E)
5. (A)	12. (E)	19. (B)	
6. (C)	13. (A)	20. (D)	
7. (D)	14. (D)	21. (D)	

Section VI Analysis of Situations

1. (B)	11. (C)	21. (C)	31. (B)
2. (E)	12. (E)	22. (B)	32. (C)
3. (C)	13. (B)	23. (A)	33. (E)
4. (C)	14. (E)	24. (B)	34. (E)
5. (D)	15. (D)	25. (D)	35. (D)
6. (E)	16. (B)	26. (B)	

7. **(B)**	17. **(B)**	27. **(E)**	
8. **(B)**	18. **(B)**	28. **(B)**	
9. **(E)**	19. **(A)**	29. **(C)**	
10. **(D)**	20. **(E)**	30. **(E)**	

Section VII   Writing Ability

1. **(C)**	8. **(D)**	15. **(D)**	22. **(B)**
2. **(C)**	9. **(E)**	16. **(A)**	23. **(B)**
3. **(C)**	10. **(C)**	17. **(A)**	24. **(D)**
4. **(D)**	11. **(C)**	18. **(C)**	25. **(D)**
5. **(A)**	12. **(B)**	19. **(A)**	
6. **(C)**	13. **(A)**	20. **(E)**	
7. **(B)**	14. **(C)**	21. **(B)**	

Section VIII   Problem Solving

1. **(D)**	6. **(A)**	11. **(B)**	16. **(A)**
2. **(B)**	7. **(E)**	12. **(A)**	17. **(D)**
3. **(D)**	8. **(A)**	13. **(C)**	18. **(D)**
4. **(D)**	9. **(D)**	14. **(B)**	19. **(D)**
5. **(B)**	10. **(C)**	15. **(C)**	20. **(D)**

ANALYSIS

Section I   Reading Comprehension

1. **(D)** This is clearly a passage dealing with the economy and economic policy. Note that (E) is too vague; an *economic policy* textbook might have been a correct answer.

2. **(E)** All of the others are given in paragraph 2.

3. **(C)** See paragraph 2: ". . . consumer and business sentiment benefited from rising public expectations that a resolution of the conflict [Vietnam] was in prospect and that East-West tensions were easing."

4. **(A)** See paragraph 3, line 1: "The underpinnings of the business expansion were to be found in part in the stimulative monetary and fiscal policies that had been pursued."

5. **(B)** See paragraph 4: ". . . there was actually a substantial deterioration in

our trade account to a sizable deficit, almost two thirds of which was with Japan.''

6. **(D)** See paragraph 5, line 1: Only (D) was mentioned.

7. **(E)** See paragraph 5, sentence 3: "The Phase Three program of wage and price restraint can contribute to dampening inflation."

8. **(B)** See paragraph 5: ". . . the unemployment rates of a bit over 5 percent . . ."

9. **(B)** See paragraph 1: "Under a perfectly sunny sky and from an apparently calm sea . . ." None of the other answer choices is particularly surprising.

10. **(C)** See the first sentence of the passage: ". . . distant lands or continents."

11. **(D)** See paragraph 2, line 1: "How are these waves formed? When a submarine earthquake occurs. . . ."

12. **(C)** See paragraph 2: "The swells in the ocean are sometimes nearly a mile wide. . . ."

13. **(D)** See paragraph 5: ". . . the Coast and Geodetic Survey initiated a program . . . to locate submarine earthquakes [and] tell how severe a submarine earthquake was. . . ."

14. **(D)** See paragraph 4.

15. **(E)** See paragraph 3: "These waves travel hundreds of miles an hour. . . ."

16. **(B)** See paragraph 3.

17. **(E)** All are mentioned in paragraph 5, except for the height of the wave.

18. **(B)** See paragraph 3, sentence 1: ". . . people are particularly sensitive about any reduction in the quality of the atmosphere. . . ."

19. **(C)** This is implied in paragraph 2.

20. **(C)** See paragraph 4: "The households' share in atmospheric pollution is far bigger than that of industry. . . ." The key word in the question is "most."

21. **(C)** Both production *and* transportation costs are important. Although paragraph 1 states that the costs of maintaining clean water are "primarily" production costs, paragraph 5 states that this problem is "related to the costs of production and transport . . ."

22. **(C)** See paragraph 6, line 1: "Atmospheric pollution caused by the private property of individuals . . . is difficult to control."

23. **(C)** See paragraph 7: both active and passive resources. No mention is made of levying taxes.

24. **(A)** See paragraph 6: "*In this particular case*, the cost of anti-pollution measures will have to be borne, to a considerable extent, by individuals. . . ." "In this particular case" refers to the situation also described in the paragraph where pollution is caused by the private property of individuals.

25. **(C)** See paragraph 7: While noise abatement is not impossible to achieve, the "costs of a complete protection against noise are so prohibitive. . . ."

Section II Problem Solving

1. **(B)** The time needed to complete the trip is $\left(6 - \frac{1}{4} - 1\frac{3}{8} - 2\frac{1}{3}\right)$ hours.
   This equals $6 - (1 + 2) - \left(\frac{1}{4} + \frac{3}{8} + \frac{1}{3}\right) = 3 - \frac{6 + 9 + 8}{24} = 3 - \frac{23}{24} = 2\frac{1}{24} = 2$ hours $2\frac{1}{2}$ minutes.

2. **(A)** The average has decreased by $500 - 400$ or 100 points during the week, so the percentage of decrease is 100/500 or 20%.

3. **(C)** Since there are 180 minutes in 3 hours, then $\frac{x}{8} = \frac{180}{18}$, where x is the number of cars washed in 3 hours. Therefore, $x = 8 \times 10 = 80$.

4. **(C)** If s and t denote the sides of the two squares, then $s^2 : t^2 = 2 : 1$, or $\frac{s^2}{t^2} = \frac{2}{1}$. Thus $\left(\frac{s}{t}\right)^2 = \frac{2}{1}$ and $\frac{s}{t} = \frac{\sqrt{2}}{1}$. Since the ratio of the perimeters is $4s : 4t = s : t$, (C) is the correct answer.

5. **(E)** The Venn diagram indicates the answer immediately. The region outside both circles denotes neither whitewall tires nor air-conditioning.

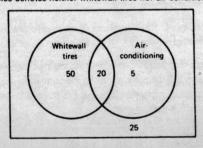

Whitewall tires

Air-conditioning

50   20   5

25

6. **(C)** Each share was worth $122.50 − $111.10 or $11.40 less in 1973 than it was in 1970. Therefore, the 100,000 shares were worth 100,000 × $11.40 or $1,140,000 less in 1973 than in 1970.

7. **(B)** Add up the daily wages to get the total wages for the week. $51.90 + 52.20 + 49.80 + 51.50 + 50.60 = $256.00. Divide $256.00 by 5 to get the average daily wage, $51.20.

8. **(C)** The interest on the first $600 is (.18) ($600) or $108 for a year. There is $5,400 of the loan in excess of $600; so he must pay (.17)(5,400) or $918 interest for the year on the $5,400. Therefore, the interest for one year will be $108 + $918 or $1,026.

9. **(A)** $4y − 6x = −2(3x − 2y) = −2(8) = −16.$

10. **(D)** Since the total distance is 200 kilometers, of which you fly x kilometers, you drive $(200 − x)$ kilometers. Therefore, the cost is $10x + (200 − x)12$, which is $10x − 12x + 2400$ or $2400 − 2x$ cents. The answer in dollars is obtained by dividing by 100, which is $(24 − .02x)$ dollars.

11. **(D)** Since the sides of the square equal the length of the rectangles, which is twice the width, the length of R_1 is 2 times its width.

12. **(B)** If A_1 denotes the increased area and A the original area, then $A_1 = 1.69A$, since A_1 is A increased by 69%. Thus, $s_1{}^2 = A_1 = 1.69A = 1.69s^2$, where s_1 is the increased side and s the original side. Since the square root of 1.69 is 1.3, we have $s_1 = 1.3s$ so s is increased by .3 or 30%.

13. **(C)** Since the dealer made a profit of 20%, he sold the car for 120% of what the car cost. Thus, if C is the cost of the car, 120% of C = $1,380 or $(\%5)C$ = $1,380. Therefore, $C = \%$ of $1,380, which is $1,150.

14. **(C)** STATEMENT I is not always true. For example, 1 is less than 5 and 1 is less than 6, but 6 is not less than 5.

    STATEMENT II is not always true, since ⅜ < ½ and ⅜ < ⅔ but ⅜ is not less than (½) (⅔) = ⅓.

    Since STATEMENT III is always true, (C) is the correct answer.

15. **(E)** The total number of workers is 80, and 35 of them work 40 or more hours. Therefore, ³⁵⁄₈₀ = .4375 = 43.75%.

16. **(B)** 15 people worked 40 to 44 hours, and 4 worked up to 29 hours. So $4x = 15$, which means $x = {}^{15}\!/_4 = 3\%$.

17. **(A)** STATEMENT I can be inferred, since the average number of hours worked is $\frac{3100}{80} = 38\frac{3}{4}$ which is less than 40.

    STATEMENT II cannot be inferred, since there is no information about the number of workers who worked over 48 hours.

    STATEMENT III is not true, since there are only 35 workers who worked 40 or more hours.

18. **(C)** The truck uses 30% more gasoline to travel the same distance at 70 mph than it does at 50 mph. Therefore, the truck requires 130% of a gallon of gasoline, which is 1.3 gallons, to travel 19.5 miles at 70 mph. So the truck will travel (10/1.3)(19.5) or 150 miles on 10 gallons of gas at 70 mph.

19. **(E)** Convert ⅖ and ⅓ into fractions with denominators of 30. Since ⅖ = ¹²/₃₀ and ⅓ = ¹⁰/₃₀, ⅖ + ⅓ = ¹²/₃₀ + ¹⁰/₃₀ = ²²/₃₀, and x is equal to 22.

20. **(D)** The area of the rectangle is $4 \times 6 = 24$ square feet. Since 1 square foot is 144 square inches, the area of the rectangle is 3,456 square inches. Each square has an area of $(\frac{1}{2})^2$ or ¼ square inches. Therefore, the number of squares needed = $3,456 \div \frac{1}{4} = 3,456 \times 4 = 13,824$.

Section III   Analysis of Situations

1. **(D)** A *Major Assumption* of the government is that Abco will stay in business if the loan is granted.

2. **(B)** High unemployment in the country is a *Major Factor*, because it is a primary consideration in the decision as to whether to approve the additional loan.

3. **(C)** The dependence of shopkeepers on the existence of Abco is a *Minor Factor* in the government's weighing of the loan decision. Although not crucial in itself, the fact that shopkeepers may be harmed by an Abco bankruptcy helps to sway the government towards a decision to grant the loan.

4. **(E)** Investment incentives (concessions) were an important factor in Abco's decision to establish a plant in Frieland, but they do not figure in the government's decision as to whether to make the loan.

5. **(E)** The fact that Frieland is a developing country is not a consideration in the selection of an alternative course of action, nor is it a major assumption made by a decision maker.

6. **(A)** Finding a way to keep Abco operating is the *Major Objective* of the government, for both economic and political reasons.

7. **(E)** The initial training of workers at government expense has no bearing on the present decision.

8. **(B)** Poor worker-management relations is a *Major Factor* in the government's decision concerning the loan. It raises the problem of whether the company can become an economically viable institution.

9. **(B)** One of the government's economic policy goals is to increase exports. It is committed to supporting those companies that can contribute to this goal. Therefore, the export potential of Abco is a *Major Factor* in the decision, supporting the alternative of granting the company further financial support.

10. **(E)** There is nothing in the passage to suggest that the political *philosophy* of the opposition party is a consideration in the government's decision as to whether to make an additional loan. Of course, the political *consequence* (question 14) is important.

11. **(D)** The existence of a deadline ("a quick decision") is mentioned in the passage. The government *believes* that a quick decision is necessary to avoid criticism from the opposition. However, there are no facts cited to support this contention.

12. **(D)** The key word is "availability." No facts are mentioned to indicate that sufficient government funds are actually available to assist Abco.

13. **(A)** One *Major Objective* of the government is to prevent increased unemployment.

14. **(B)** The political consequence of Abco's pending bankruptcy is a *Major Factor* in the government's consideration of whether to grant the additional loan.

15. **(E)** The size of the population has no weight in the consideration of any decision alternative.

16. **(A)** Frieland encouraged investment in industries that would export most of their total output, so that the country could earn badly needed foreign exchange. Increasing foreign exchange reserves was a *Major Objective* of the government.

17. **(E)** According to the passage, government approval for an Abco factory

was given "despite the fact that there was . . . surplus shoe production in Frieland." Apparently, the government chose to overlook the fact of underemployment in the shoe industry in their decision to grant approval to Abco.

18. **(D)** Abco had promised the government, among other things, to reduce shoe prices by 30 percent. This estimate was a projection supplied by management and was a *Major Assumption* of government decision makers.

19. **(E)** This fact was not related to a major decision or objective of the decision maker.

20. **(A)** The company had excess capacity and its utilization was a *Major Objective*.

21. **(B)** Although Conway's unit sales had remained constant, its share of total market had declined. Therefore, management decided to introduce a new line to increase both sales and market share.

22. **(C)** This is clearly a *Minor Factor*, having no direct influence on the company's objective.

23. **(E)** The placing of advertising is an *Unimportant Issue* not directly related to the problem.

24. **(D)** No information is given to substantiate management's *assumption* that the proposed line will be accepted by consumers.

25. **(B)** Growing price competition from small clock manufacturers led Conway management to decide on a new line which would be sold to dealers at a lower price than the existing line.

26. **(D)** Key words in the passage are "expected" and "hoped." That the line would be bought by these dealers was a *Major Assumption*.

27. **(A)** A *Major Objective* of management was to increase sales.

28. **(B)** Conway's reputation was very good. Because smaller manufacturers competed on either a price or a quality basis, reputation is an important factor to be considered.

29. **(B)** The fact that Conway's present line could not be discounted prevented the company from reaching a segment of the market that desired cheaper clocks. This was a *Major Factor* in the decision to market a line that would be discounted.

30. **(A)** Protecting the small dealer (against price competition) would have to be considered as an objective because it is the reason for the adoption of resale price maintenance.

31. **(B)** Styling was an important factor in the decision to market a new line of clocks. First, styling was important to maintain Conway's reputation for high quality. Second, styles were changed frequently by the industry. Third, advertising stressed up-to-date styling, an attribute of importance to consumers.

32. **(C)** Sales to department stores amounted to 20 percent of total wholesale sales (paragraph 5) and represented 60 to 70 out of 14,000 retail outlets. Therefore, sales to department stores is a *Minor Factor*.

33. **(D)** Conway management "thought" that existing retailers would also sell the Concord models. This supposition was considered in management's decision to market the new line of clocks.

34. **(E)** Conway policed dealer advertisements to make sure they were maintaining suggested price schedules. The mechanics of policing was not a factor related to the decision to market a new line.

35. **(B)** Growing price competition for small clock manufacturers was a major reason why management considered marketing a lower-priced line of clocks.

Section IV   Data Sufficiency

1. **(E)** A triangle with sides of lengths 3, 4, and 5 is a right triangle since $3^2 + 4^2 = 5^2$, and its perimeter is 12. A triangle with sides of lengths 2, 4⅘, and 5⅕ also has a perimeter of 12. And since $2^2 + (4⅘)^2 = (5⅕)^2$, it too is a right triangle. Therefore, two triangles can satisfy STATEMENTS (1) and (2) yet not be congruent. On the other hand, any pair of congruent right triangles satisfy STATEMENTS (1) and (2). Thus, STATEMENTS (1) and (2) together are not sufficient to answer the question.

2. **(B)** $x^3 - 8 = 0$ has only $x = 2$ as a real solution. And 2 is greater than 0, so STATEMENT (2) alone is sufficient.

   Since $x = 2$ and $x = -2$ are both solutions of $x^4 - 16 = 0$, STATEMENT (1) alone is not sufficient.

3. **(D)** STATEMENT (1) is sufficient since it implies that conveyer belt A loads ⅔ of the hopper while conveyer belt B loads only ⅓ with both work-

ing. Since conveyer belt *A* loads ⅓ of the hopper in a hour, it will take 1 ÷ ⅔ or 1½ hours to fill the hopper by itself.

STATEMENT (2) is also sufficient since it implies that conveyer belt *B* fills ⅓ of the hopper in 1 hour. Thus, conveyer belt *A* loads ⅔ in one hour, and that means conveyer belt *A* will take 1½ hours by itself.

4. **(A)** The first fly will travel a distance equal to the circumference of the circle which is π times the diameter. The second fly will travel $4s$ where s is the length of a side. Since the diagonal of a square has length $\sqrt{2}S$, the second fly will travel $4/\sqrt{2}$ times the diagonal of the square. Therefore, (1) alone is sufficient, since $4/\sqrt{2} = 4\sqrt{2}/2 = 2\sqrt{2}$ which is less than π. (2) alone is not sufficient, since one fly might have crawled faster than the other.

5. **(E)** Using (1) and (2) together, it is only possible to determine the total amount paid for fire insurance in 1970 and 1972. Since no relation is given between the amounts paid in 1970 and 1972, there is not enough information to determine the cost in 1972.

6. **(C)** (2) alone is not sufficient since both $y = 2$ and $y = -2$ satisfy $y^2 - 4 = 0$. (1) alone is not sufficient, since ½ is larger than 0 but less than 1 while 3 is larger than 0 and larger than 1. The only solution of $y^2 - 4 = 0$ which is larger than 0 is 2 which is larger than 1. Therefore, (1) and (2) are sufficient.

7. **(D)** Let $x be the amount he was paid the first day. Then he was paid $x + 2$, $x + 4$, $x + 6$, $x + 8$, and $x + 10$ dollars for the succeeding days. (1) alone is sufficient, since the total he was paid is $(6x + 30)$ dollars, and we can solve $6x + 30 = 150$ (to find that he was paid $20 for the first day). (2) alone is also sufficient. He was paid $(x + 10)$ on the sixth day, so (2) means that $(1.5)x = x + 10$ (which is the same as $x = 20$).

8. **(B)** Since 85% of $3,000 is $2,550, (2) alone is sufficient. (1) alone is not sufficient, since if x were 5% (1) would tell us the price of the car is less than $2,600. But if x were 1%, (1) would imply that the price of the car is greater than $2,600.

9. **(E)** Vertical angles are equal, so $c = d$. Since the sum of the angles in a triangle is 180°, $a + b + c = d + e + f$ which means $a + b = e + f$. If we use (1) and (2), we have $a + a = e + a$ so $e = a$. And we know the triangles are similar. However this does not give any information about

the value of a, since any two similar triangles can be made to satisfy conditions (1) and (2). Therefore, (1) and (2) together are not sufficient.

10. **(D)** (1) alone is sufficient since $BC = AB$ implies $x = y = 40$. Since the sum of the angles in a triangle is 180°, z must equal 100. (2) alone is sufficient. Let D be the point where the bisector of angle B meets AC. Then according to (2), triangle BDC is a right triangle. Since angle y is 40°, the remaining angle in triangle BDC is 50° and equals $\frac{1}{2}z$, so $z = 100$.

11. **(D)** Since there are a bottom and 4 sides, each a congruent square, the amount of cardboard needed will be $5e^2$ where e is the length of an edge of the box. So we need to find e. (1) alone is sufficient. Since the area of the bottom is e^2, (1) means $e^2 = 4$ with $e = 2$ feet. (2) alone is also sufficient. Since the volume of the box is e^3, (2) means $e^3 = 8$ and $e = 2$ feet.

12. **(C)** The average weight of the books is the total weight of all the books divided by the number of books on the shelf. Thus (1) and (2) together are sufficient. (Solve $2.5 = \frac{40}{x}$ for x, the number of books on the shelf.) (1) alone is not sufficient, nor is (2) alone sufficient.

13. **(E)** If $ABCD$ has the pairs of opposite sides equal and each angle is 90°, then it is a rectangle. But there are many quadrilaterals which have two opposite sides equal with one angle a right angle. For example, the figure has $AB = DC$ and $x = 90$, but it is not a rectangle. Therefore, (1) and (2) together are insufficient.

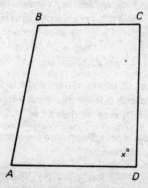

14. **(D)** (2) alone is sufficient, since if $a_3 = 1$ then $a_4 = (a_3)^2 = 1^2 = 1$; then $a_5 = (a_4)^2 = 1^2 = 1$. (1) alone is also sufficient. If $a_1 = -1$ then $a_2 =$

$(a_1)^2 = 1$, and $a_3 = (a_2)^2 = 1$, but $a_3 = 1$ is given by (2) which we know is sufficient.

15. **(E)** Let J, F and C stand for the weekly salaries of John, Fred, and Chuck. (1) says $J = 2F$ and (2) says $F = .4(C + J)$. Since there is no information given about the values of C or F, we cannot deduce the value of J. Therefore, (1) and (2) together are insufficient.

16. **(B)** STATEMENT (2) alone is sufficient. $2x + 4y = 2(x + 2y)$, so if $2x + 4y = 12$ then $2(x + 2y) = 12$ and $x + 2y = 6$.

    STATEMENT (1) alone is insufficient. If you only use STATEMENT (1) then you can get $x + 2y = x + y + y = 4 + y$ but there is no information on the value of y.

17. **(C)** Since the sum of the angles in a triangle is 180°, $x + y + z = 180$. Using STATEMENT (1) alone we have $2y + y + z = 3y + z = 180$, which is insufficient to determine y or z.

    Using STATEMENT (2) alone we have $x + 1.5z + z = x + 2.5z = 180$, which is not sufficient to determine x or z.

    However, if we use both STATEMENTS (1) and (2) we obtain $3y + z = 4.5z + z = 5.5z = 180$, so $z = \frac{2}{11}$ of 180. Now $y = \frac{3}{2}$ of z, so $y = \frac{3}{11}$ of 180, and $x = \frac{6}{11}$ of 180. Therefore, angle BAC is not a right angle and STATEMENTS (1) and (2) are sufficient.

18. **(E)** Since STATEMENT (1) only describes x and STATEMENT (2) only describes y both are needed to get an answer. Using STATEMENT (2), STATEMENT (1) becomes $x = 2k = 2 \cdot 2y = 4y$, so $x = 4y$. However, this is not sufficient, since if $y = -1$ then $x = -4$ and -4 is less than -1, but if $y = 1$ then $x = 4$ and x is greater than y.

19. **(A)** If each doll costs $8, then 65 dolls will cost $8 \times \$65 = \$520$. Using STATEMENT (1), the profit is selling price minus cost = $\$750 - \$520 = \$230$, so STATEMENT (1) alone is sufficient.

    STATEMENT (2) alone is not sufficient since you need to know what price the dolls sell for to find the profit.

20. **(B)** STATEMENT (2) alone is sufficient. 60% of the people have blue eyes and 50% of the people have blue eyes and blond hair, so 60% − 50% = 10% of the people have blue eyes but do not have blond hair.

STATEMENT (1) alone is not sufficient. Using STATEMENT (1) alone we can only find out how many people have blond hair and do not have blue eyes, in addition to what is given.

21. **(A)** The sum of the angles of the pentagon is 540°. (The sum of the angles of a polygon with n sides which is inscribed in a circle is $(n - 2)180°$.) STATEMENT (1) alone is sufficient. If the polygon is regular, all angles are equal and so angle ABC is ⅕ of 540° or 108°.

STATEMENT (2) alone is insufficient because the radius of the circle does not give any information about the angles of the pentagon.

22. **(B)** The area of a circle is πr^2, where r is the radius of the circle. Since O is a point on the line AB, AB is a diameter of the circle. Therefore, since a radius is one half of a diameter, the radius of the circle is 3.5 inches. Thus, STATEMENT (2) alone is sufficient.

STATEMENT (1) alone is insufficient since there is no relation between DE and the radius.

23. **(C)** Using STATEMENT (2) alone we have $\$10,000 + x + y = \$34,000$, where x is the taxable income for 1972 and y is the taxable income for 1973. So STATEMENT (2) alone is not sufficient.

STATEMENT (1) alone is not sufficient since no relation given between taxable income in 1972 and 1973.

STATEMENTS (1) and (2) together give the equation $\$10,000 + \$12,000 + y = \$34,000$, which means $y = \$12,000$, where y is the taxable income for 1973.

24. **(B)** STATEMENT (2) alone is sufficient. 3 feet 2 inches is more than half of 6 feet so the piece of string 3 feet 2 inches long must be longer than the other 2 pieces put together.

STATEMENT (1) alone is insufficient. There is not enough information to find the length of *any* of the three pieces of string.

25. **(D)** Let r be the fraction of the job the 4 apprentices finish in 1 hour. Then $1/r$ is the amount of time in hours that it will take the 4 apprentices to finish the job. So it is sufficient to find r. The group of 5 craftsmen finishes ⅓ of the job per hour, so each craftsman does 1/15 of the job per hour.

STATEMENT (1) alone is sufficient. An apprentice will do $\frac{2}{3}$ of $\frac{1}{15} = \frac{2}{45}$ of the job per hour, so $r = \frac{8}{45}$.

STATEMENT (2) alone is sufficient. The craftsmen and the apprentices together will finish $\frac{1}{3} + r$ of the job per hour. Since it takes them $1\frac{22}{23}$ hours to finish the job, $(\frac{1}{3} + r)(\frac{45}{23}) = 1$ which can be solved for r.

Section V   Writing Ability

1. **(B)** This corrects the misuse of the subjunctive.

2. **(D)** This corrects the error in the case of the pronoun. Choice E corrects the error in case but introduces an error in tense.

3. **(C)** The improper use of the pronouns *one* and *you* is corrected in Choice C.

4. **(E)** The omission of the past participle *been* is corrected in Choice E.

5. **(A)** No error.

6. **(C)** This corrects the dangling participle.

7. **(D)** Misuse of word. The pronoun is *its*.

8. **(B)** This corrects the unnecessary switch in the pronouns, *anyone—you*.

9. **(D)** This corrects the error in tense and in the use of adjective or adverbial clauses.

10. **(A)** No error.

11. **(E)** *The reason is that* is preferable to *The reason is because*.

12. **(E)** This corrects the error in parallel structure.

13. **(A)** No error.

14. **(D)** This corrects the double negative (*hadn't hardly*) and the misuse of *those* with *kind*.

15. **(B)** This corrects the dangling participle and the misuse of *stole* for *stolen*.

16. **(E)** This question involves two aspects of correct English. *Neither* should be followed by *nor*; *either* by *or*. Choices A and D are, therefore, incorrect. The words *neither . . . nor* and *either . . . or* should be placed before the

two items being discussed—*to be critical* and *to criticize*. Choice E meets both requirements.

17. **(B)** This question tests agreement. Agreement between subject and verb and pronoun and antecedent are both involved. *Community* (singular) needs a singular verb, *influences*. Also, the pronoun which refers to *community* should be singular (*its*). Choice B is best.

18. **(C)** *Would have been expected* is incorrect as a verb in a clause introduced by the conjunction *if. Had been expected* or *were expected* is preferable. *To have considered* does not follow correct sequence of tense and should be changed to *to consider*. Choice E changes the thought of the sentence and is illogical. Choice C is best.

19. **(B)** As presented, the sentence contains a dangling participle, *depending*. Choice B corrects this error. The other choices change the emphasis presented by the author.

20. **(D)** This question is similar to question 16. *Either . . . or* should precede the two choices offered (*in war* and *in peace.*).

21. **(D)** This phrase expresses the thought more compactly than the other four choices.

22. **(D)** Choices A and B are incorrect because of the dangling participle. Choice C is incoherent. Choice E also has a dangling phrase.

23. **(C)** Parallel structure requires that *not only . . . but also* immediately precede the words they limit.

24. **(B)** Given a choice, most authorities recommend the use of the active voice whenever possible. Thus, *affords* in Choice B is stronger than *are afforded* in Choices A, C, and D. The meaning of the sentence is changed in Choice E.

25. **(E)** This is an incomplete sentence or fragment. The sentence needs a verb to establish a principle clause. Choice E provides the verb (*is recognized*) and presents the only complete sentence in the group.

Section VI   Analysis of Situations

1. **(B)** A primary consideration in Mr. Krim's decision as to whether to buy the firm is the degree of public awareness of the company's products, since this will help determine the company's chances for future success.

2. **(E)** Caspi's marketing ability is not important to Krim's decision to buy the company, since Caspi will retire if the company is sold.

3. **(C)** While not crucial in itself, this feature of Posturemat mattresses is one of the strengths of the product and so of the company as a whole.

4. **(C)** This is a *Minor Factor*, since older consumers play only a small role in determining the present and future success of the company.

5. **(D)** Krim's assumption about retailers' attitudes is contrary to the facts given in the passage. Only if Posturemat launches an aggressive advertising campaign may retailers' attitudes change. But this is an assumption, not a fact.

6. **(E)** The importation of latex is not an issue in the decision as to whether to buy the company.

7. **(B)** Posturemat's declining market share is a *Major Factor* in the decision as to whether to buy the company. The issue is whether the decline can be halted and reversed.

8. **(B)** Although Krim had a preconceived notion of whether to buy the company, he nevertheless has asked Sims to prepare a marketing analysis upon which he will base his final decision.

9. **(E)** The ownership of the premises is not critical to the success of the firm or its viability as an enterprise.

10. **(D)** That attitudes toward foam rubber mattresses can be changed by advertising is an assumption of Mr. Krim not supported by any facts cited in the passage.

11. **(C)** The advantage or attribute of orthopedic qualities in particular is a *Minor Factor* in the decision as to whether to buy the company. The *overall* quality of Posturemat (including other attributes) would constitute a *Major Factor*.

12. **(E)** The fact that synthetic mattresses are made of polyurethane does not influence the selection of an alternative, and is related to neither a major objective nor an assumption of the decision maker.

13. **(B)** The passage states that Lefko handled the sales force of Posturemat. If he leaves, Krim will not have a single experienced manager to handle marketing and sales. Therefore, Krim must weigh the impact that Lefko's leaving would have on the management of the firm. It is, therefore, a *Major Factor*.

14. **(E)** The age of the machinery does not mean that the equipment was obsolete or useless (see paragraph 3). Therefore, the condition does not directly influence any of the decision alternatives.

15. **(D)** Krim *felt* that introduction of a new management team would instill confidence in the firm and allow for increased credit (see the last paragraph). However, no evidence is presented in the passage to support his feeling.

16. **(B)** Caspi attributed Posturemat's loss in market share to the competition of spring mattresses, which had "similar attributes" and were "less costly to manufacture, but sold at about the same price as Posturemat. . . ." Whether Posturemat would in the future successfully compete against these conditions is a *Major Factor* in the decision to buy the company.

17. **(B)** The total cost of a press was a *Major Factor* in the determination of the new price and distribution channels.

18. **(B)** Adoption of a new service policy was a *Major Factor* in the consideration of distribution channel alternatives.

19. **(A)** Adoption of a new distribution channel was a major outcome or goal sought by Mr. Grace.

20. **(E)** Working in his father's shop lacked any impact on the consideration of a new distribution channel.

21. **(C)** The price of a new press was comprised of manufacturing cost, and the costs of delivery, instruction, training, and service. Service expenses were only one consideration in the pricing and channel selection decisions.

22. **(B)** The lack of selling effort on the part of Grace's present distributors was a *Major Factor* in the decision to select a new distribution channel.

23. **(A)** Note the key word "desire." The desire for broader distribution is an outcome sought by the decision maker.

24. **(B)** Note the word "complaints." Complaints from buyers were one of several factors contributing to the outcome sought, a new distribution channel.

25. **(D)** Note the key word "possibility." Management "felt that manufacturers' representatives . . . would provide the desired coverage. . . ." The question deals with an opinion or belief. This *assumption* is important to the decision because it is related to a major advantage of a channel alternative.

26. **(B)** Although the passage states that distributors "felt" the price was high, it is not an assumption. It is explicitly stated that some distributors dropped Grace products, while others made no effort to sell them because of the high price.

27. **(E)** The fact that discounts were cut is mentioned in the passage. However, there is nothing in the passage to suggest that this action played a significant role in the decision process.

28. **(B)** The difficulty in finding representatives who were regularly calling on prospective buyers of Grace products was a major consideration in a decision alternative (to use manufacturers' representatives extensively).

29. **(C)** The fact that some prospective representatives carried appliances is a narrower consideration within the more important consideration of whether they carried competing products.

30. **(E)** Defects in Fabri-Tools was not an issue in any alternative course of action considered by Grace management.

31. **(B)** Delays in completing service calls was a major issue in the consideration to select a new distribution system.

32. **(C)** Lack of distributor facilities was one of the factors contributing to delays in completing service calls. Lack of facilities alone is not a major issue. The major issue is the resulting effect, i.e., delays in completing service calls.

33. **(E)** Although one might assume that the issue of distributor discounts is an important one, it does not appear to significantly influence the consideration of an alternative course of action on the part of a decision maker.

34. **(E)** In the past, Mr. Grace earned income for his company by arranging meetings for distributors. More recently, that effort does not play a role in Mr. Grace's decision making.

35. **(D)** It is stated in the passage that "no discounts were allowed on direct sales by the company to users, no matter how large." The decision was taken because it "was reasoned" that a quantity discount would not induce buyers to purchase more than they need.

Section VII   Writing Ability

1. **(C)** The sequence of tenses is incorrect. According to the meaning of the sentence, John's wanting comes *before*, not *after*, John's going.

2. **(C)** The participle *knowing* should be followed by *director*, the noun it modifies.

3. **(C)** Parallelism: a similar form is required on either side of the comparison.

4. **(D)** They did witness two things, *not only the sinking ship* but the *escape* as well.

5. **(A)** *But* meaning *except* is always followed by the objective pronoun, and the copula *was* takes the subjective *I*.

6. **(C)** *Either . . . or* connect *transfer* and *file*. *Data* here is plural and requires the verb *were*.

7. **(B)** A participial phrase at the beginning of a sentence must be followed by the word it modifies.

8. **(D)** The *set has been* published, while the *propositions* (individually) *were* discussed.

9. **(E)** *Requests* as a countable noun requires *number*, whereas only *a few* of them could be dealt with.

10. **(C)** The future perfect tense is required here, since the action continues from the past into the future (*next Tuesday*).

11. **(C)** *Neither . . . nor* apply to *authority* and *means* and must precede them directly.

12. **(B)** *Everyone* is singular and requires the singular *has*. The preposition *without* requires the gerund *helping* preceded by the possessive *his*.

13. **(A)** The *incidence* (singular) *correlates*. The preposition *with* is correct.

14. **(C)** This is a suspenseful sentence since what *She saw* is held off to the very last word in the sentence. Also, an active verb, *saw*, is preferable to the passive *was seen*.

15. **(D)** The correct form of the past conditional requires the past perfect in the conditional clause: *had taken*.

16. **(A)** In *neither . . . nor* constructions, the verb is matched to the noun or pronoun that immediately precedes it. The sentence is not a question, and thus does not become inverted.

17. **(A)** *Scarcely* applies to the *valid reason* and thus must precede it directly.

Scarcely, having a negative connotation, does not require a negation of the verb.

18. **(C)** This answer provides the correct subject (*I*) modified by the verbal *knowing*.

19. **(A)** No error. The sequence of tenses requires that the past perfect tense be used in the conditional clause *if she had won it*. Also, *I* is required after a form of the verb *to be*.

20. **(E)** *Everybody* is expected to help. The sense demands that *from everybody* be placed in the general position. *In the provision of* makes the sentence unnecessarily bulky.

21. **(B)** The original sentence is too wordy.

22. **(B)** The *climate* can only be compared to another climate.

23. **(B)** *Interest in* a subject and *admiration for* it: the prepositions must remain.

24. **(D)** This is a past conditional and requires the past perfect in the conditional clause. There is no punctuation before the *if*.

25. **(D)** Parallel structure demands a list of noun phrases: *the methods, the dangers,* and *the method*.

Section VIII   Problem Solving

1. **(D)** The corporation income tax accounted for 19.7% of all average annual receipts for the years 1967–1970. Since 19.7% is about 20% or ⅕, the average annual receipts were about 5 times the average annual receipts from the corporation income tax. Therefore, the answer is 5*x*.

2. **(B)** Veterans received 4.2%, education and manpower 3.8%, and health and income security 26% of the average annual outlays; so together the three categories received 4.2% + 3.8% + 26% or 34%. Since ⅓ is 33⅓%, 34% is roughly ⅓.

3. **(D)** Since ⅝ of 3.2% = 5 × .4% = 2.0%, the correct answer is (D).

4. **(D)** $\frac{10}{5} = 2 = \frac{20}{10}$, so the ratio of successive terms of the progression is 2. Therefore, the term which follows 20 is 2 times 20 or 40.

5. **(B)** Since ⅛ of 8¢ is 1¢, each egg will cost 8¢ + 1¢ or 9¢ after the price has increased. The price of a dozen eggs will be 12 × 9¢ or $1.08.

6. **(A)** The area of trapezoid *ABCD* equals the area of rectangle *ABED*, which is $t \times 5$ (since $BE = BC = 5$), plus the area of triangle *BEC*, which is $\frac{(5 \times 5)}{2}$. The answer is thus $5t + 12.5$.

7. **(E)** The selling price of the jars should equal cost + $75. The cost of making 300 jars = (100)65¢ + (200)55¢ = $65 + $110 = $175. So the selling price should be $175 + $75 or $250.

8. **(A)** Since it takes twice as long to walk the length as the width, $l = 2w$ where l is the length and w the width. The perimeter equals $2l + 2w = 3l$ = 300 yards, so the length is 100 yards and the width is 50 yards. Therefore, the area is $50 \times 100 = 5{,}000$ square yards.

9. **(D)** The company's profit = (2,000)(.07) + (5,000)(.06) = $140 + $300 = $440.

10. **(C)** Since $\frac{x}{y} = \frac{3}{z}$, $xz = 3y$ and $9y^2 = (3y)^2$; so $9y^2 = (xz)^2 = x^2z^2$.

11. **(B)** *9 is 10 subtracted from twice 9, or 2(9) − 10. So *9 is 18 − 10 = 8. Thus *(*9) will be *8. *8 is 10 subtracted from twice 8, or 16 − 10 = 6. Therefore 6 is the correct answer.

12. **(A)** The area of a triangle is 1/2 the base times the altitude. Since *ABCD* is a rectangle, the triangles *AED*, *BEA*, and *CDE* all have the same altitude (*AB*). The base of *AED* is *AD*, which is equal to the base of *ABE* (*BE*) plus the base of *CDE* (*EC*). So the area of *ABE* plus the area of *CDE* is equal to the area of *AED*. Therefore, subtracting the area of *ADE* from the sum of the areas of *ABE* and *CDE* gives a result of 0.

13. **(C)** Let *c* be the number of chairs in a row and *r* be the number of rows. Since each row must have the same number of chairs, *c* times *r* must equal 36. We need to know how many ways we can write 36 as a product of two integers each greater than or equal to three, since each way to write 36 corresponds to an acceptable arrangement of the room. (*c* must be greater than or equal to 3 since each row must contain at least 3 chairs. In the same way, *r* must be greater than or equal to 3 because there must be at least 3 rows.) Writing 36 as a product of primes, we obtain 36 = 2 × 18

$= 2 \times 2 \times 9 = 2 \times 2 \times 3 \times 3$. So 36 can be written as 1×36, 2×18, 3×12, 4×9, 6×6, 9×4, 12×3, 18×2, and 36×1. Of these possibilities, 5 (3×12, 4×9, 6×6, 9×4, and 12×3) satisfy the requirements. Therefore, there are 5 arrangements.

14. **(B)** Volume of the cube is $9 \times 9 \times 9 = 729$ cubic mm. The sphere has volume $\frac{4}{3}\pi 6 \times 6 \times 6 = 288\pi$. Since π is greater than 3, 288π is greater than 729. The volume of the cylinder is $5 \times 5 \times 11 \ \pi = 275\pi$. So the sphere has the largest volume.

You can save a lot of time in this problem if you do not change π to a decimal and then multiply the answers out.

15. **(C)** Change the percentage to a decimal to compute. Since .2% is .002, you know that $.002x = .03$. So x is $\frac{.03}{.002} = \frac{30}{2} = 15$.

16. **(A)** Let s be the amount invested in ABC stock and b be the amount invested in DEF bonds. Then $s + b = 1,000,000$ and $.12s + .10b = 115,000$. Solve $s + b = 1,000,000$ for b and you get $b = 1,000,000 - s$. Now substitute this into the second equation. The result is $.12s + .10(1,000,000 - s) = .12s - .10s + 100,000 = 115,000$. So $.02s = 15,000$, which gives $s = 15,000/.02$. Therefore, $s = \$750,000$.

17. **(D)** A triple ratio is a compact way of expressing three ratios. So the ratio of chickens to pigs to horses, $20:4:6$, means that the ratio of chickens to pigs is $20:4$ and the ratio of pigs to horses is $4:6$ and the ratio of chickens to horses is $20:6$. Thus for every 20 chickens there are 6 horses. So if there are 120 chickens, there are x horses where x satisfies the proportion $\frac{120}{20} = \frac{x}{6}$. Cross multiplying gives $20x = 720$ or $x = 36$. You can check the answer by seeing that the ratio of chickens to horses is $120:36$, which is the same ratio as $20:6$.

18. **(D)** $x^2 - y^2$ is factored into $(x + y)(x - y)$. So if $x + y$ is equal to 3, then $x^2 - y^2 = 15$ is equivalent to $3(x - y) = 15$. Dividing each side of the equation by 3, we obtain $x - y = \frac{15}{3} = 5$.

19. **(D)** His salary has increased by $\$35,000 - \$10,000 = \$25,000$. So his salary

has increased by $\dfrac{\$25,000}{\$10,000} = 2.5 = 250\%$. The question asks for the percentage of increase. His current salary is 350% of his starting salary, but his salary has not increased by $35,000. Notice that the period of 5 years has nothing to do with the correct solution.

20. **(D)** The area of a circle is π times the square of the radius of the circle. So the area of the large circle is πa^2, and the area of each of the interior circles is $\pi \left(\dfrac{a}{3}\right)^2 = \left(\dfrac{1}{9}\right)\pi a^2$. Since there are two interior circles the shaded region has area equal to $\pi a^2 - 2\left(\left(\dfrac{1}{9}\right)\pi a^2\right) = \left(1 - \dfrac{2}{9}\right)\pi a^2 = \left(\dfrac{7}{9}\right)\pi a^2$.

Evaluating Your Score

Tabulate your score for each section of Sample Test 1 according to the directions on pages 5–6 and record the results in the Self-scoring Table below. Then find your rating for each score on the Self-scoring Scale and record it in the appropriate blank.

SELF-SCORING TABLE

SECTION	SCORE	RATING
1		
2		
3		
4		
5		
6		
7		
8		

SELF-SCORING SCALE

RATING

SECTION	POOR	FAIR	GOOD	EXCELLENT
1	0–12 +	13–17 +	18–21 +	22–25
2	0–9 +	10–13 +	14–17 +	18–20
3	0–17 +	18–24 +	25–31 +	32–35
4	0–12 +	13–17 +	18–21 +	22–25
5	0–12 +	13–17 +	18–21 +	22–25
6	0–17 +	18–24 +	25–31 +	32–35
7	0–12 +	13–17 +	18–21 +	22–25
8	0–9 +	10–13 +	14–17 +	18–20

Study again the Review sections covering material in Sample Test 1 for which you had a rating of FAIR or POOR. Then go on to Sample Test 2.

To obtain an approximation of your GMAT score see page 7.

Answer Sheet—Sample Test 2

Section I
Reading
Comprehension

1. Ⓐ Ⓑ Ⓒ Ⓓ Ⓔ
2. Ⓐ Ⓑ Ⓒ Ⓓ Ⓔ
3. Ⓐ Ⓑ Ⓒ Ⓓ Ⓔ
4. Ⓐ Ⓑ Ⓒ Ⓓ Ⓔ
5. Ⓐ Ⓑ Ⓒ Ⓓ Ⓔ
6. Ⓐ Ⓑ Ⓒ Ⓓ Ⓔ
7. Ⓐ Ⓑ Ⓒ Ⓓ Ⓔ
8. Ⓐ Ⓑ Ⓒ Ⓓ Ⓔ
9. Ⓐ Ⓑ Ⓒ Ⓓ Ⓔ
10. Ⓐ Ⓑ Ⓒ Ⓓ Ⓔ
11. Ⓐ Ⓑ Ⓒ Ⓓ Ⓔ
12. Ⓐ Ⓑ Ⓒ Ⓓ Ⓔ
13. Ⓐ Ⓑ Ⓒ Ⓓ Ⓔ
14. Ⓐ Ⓑ Ⓒ Ⓓ Ⓔ
15. Ⓐ Ⓑ Ⓒ Ⓓ Ⓔ
16. Ⓐ Ⓑ Ⓒ Ⓓ Ⓔ
17. Ⓐ Ⓑ Ⓒ Ⓓ Ⓔ
18. Ⓐ Ⓑ Ⓒ Ⓓ Ⓔ
19. Ⓐ Ⓑ Ⓒ Ⓓ Ⓔ
20. Ⓐ Ⓑ Ⓒ Ⓓ Ⓔ
21. Ⓐ Ⓑ Ⓒ Ⓓ Ⓔ
22. Ⓐ Ⓑ Ⓒ Ⓓ Ⓔ
23. Ⓐ Ⓑ Ⓒ Ⓓ Ⓔ
24. Ⓐ Ⓑ Ⓒ Ⓓ Ⓔ
25. Ⓐ Ⓑ Ⓒ Ⓓ Ⓔ

Section II
Data
Sufficiency

1. Ⓐ Ⓑ Ⓒ Ⓓ Ⓔ
2. Ⓐ Ⓑ Ⓒ Ⓓ Ⓔ
3. Ⓐ Ⓑ Ⓒ Ⓓ Ⓔ
4. Ⓐ Ⓑ Ⓒ Ⓓ Ⓔ
5. Ⓐ Ⓑ Ⓒ Ⓓ Ⓔ
6. Ⓐ Ⓑ Ⓒ Ⓓ Ⓔ
7. Ⓐ Ⓑ Ⓒ Ⓓ Ⓔ
8. Ⓐ Ⓑ Ⓒ Ⓓ Ⓔ
9. Ⓐ Ⓑ Ⓒ Ⓓ Ⓔ
10. Ⓐ Ⓑ Ⓒ Ⓓ Ⓔ
11. Ⓐ Ⓑ Ⓒ Ⓓ Ⓔ
12. Ⓐ Ⓑ Ⓒ Ⓓ Ⓔ
13. Ⓐ Ⓑ Ⓒ Ⓓ Ⓔ
14. Ⓐ Ⓑ Ⓒ Ⓓ Ⓔ
15. Ⓐ Ⓑ Ⓒ Ⓓ Ⓔ
16. Ⓐ Ⓑ Ⓒ Ⓓ Ⓔ
17. Ⓐ Ⓑ Ⓒ Ⓓ Ⓔ
18. Ⓐ Ⓑ Ⓒ Ⓓ Ⓔ
19. Ⓐ Ⓑ Ⓒ Ⓓ Ⓔ
20. Ⓐ Ⓑ Ⓒ Ⓓ Ⓔ
21. Ⓐ Ⓑ Ⓒ Ⓓ Ⓔ
22. Ⓐ Ⓑ Ⓒ Ⓓ Ⓔ
23. Ⓐ Ⓑ Ⓒ Ⓓ Ⓔ
24. Ⓐ Ⓑ Ⓒ Ⓓ Ⓔ
25. Ⓐ Ⓑ Ⓒ Ⓓ Ⓔ

Section III
Problem
Solving

1. Ⓐ Ⓑ Ⓒ Ⓓ Ⓔ
2. Ⓐ Ⓑ Ⓒ Ⓓ Ⓔ
3. Ⓐ Ⓑ Ⓒ Ⓓ Ⓔ
4. Ⓐ Ⓑ Ⓒ Ⓓ Ⓔ
5. Ⓐ Ⓑ Ⓒ Ⓓ Ⓔ
6. Ⓐ Ⓑ Ⓒ Ⓓ Ⓔ
7. Ⓐ Ⓑ Ⓒ Ⓓ Ⓔ
8. Ⓐ Ⓑ Ⓒ Ⓓ Ⓔ
9. Ⓐ Ⓑ Ⓒ Ⓓ Ⓔ
10. Ⓐ Ⓑ Ⓒ Ⓓ Ⓔ
11. Ⓐ Ⓑ Ⓒ Ⓓ Ⓔ
12. Ⓐ Ⓑ Ⓒ Ⓓ Ⓔ
13. Ⓐ Ⓑ Ⓒ Ⓓ Ⓔ
14. Ⓐ Ⓑ Ⓒ Ⓓ Ⓔ
15. Ⓐ Ⓑ Ⓒ Ⓓ Ⓔ
16. Ⓐ Ⓑ Ⓒ Ⓓ Ⓔ
17. Ⓐ Ⓑ Ⓒ Ⓓ Ⓔ
18. Ⓐ Ⓑ Ⓒ Ⓓ Ⓔ
19. Ⓐ Ⓑ Ⓒ Ⓓ Ⓔ
20. Ⓐ Ⓑ Ⓒ Ⓓ Ⓔ

Section IV
Analysis
of Situations

1. Ⓐ Ⓑ Ⓒ Ⓓ Ⓔ
2. Ⓐ Ⓑ Ⓒ Ⓓ Ⓔ
3. Ⓐ Ⓑ Ⓒ Ⓓ Ⓔ
4. Ⓐ Ⓑ Ⓒ Ⓓ Ⓔ
5. Ⓐ Ⓑ Ⓒ Ⓓ Ⓔ
6. Ⓐ Ⓑ Ⓒ Ⓓ Ⓔ
7. Ⓐ Ⓑ Ⓒ Ⓓ Ⓔ
8. Ⓐ Ⓑ Ⓒ Ⓓ Ⓔ
9. Ⓐ Ⓑ Ⓒ Ⓓ Ⓔ
10. Ⓐ Ⓑ Ⓒ Ⓓ Ⓔ
11. Ⓐ Ⓑ Ⓒ Ⓓ Ⓔ
12. Ⓐ Ⓑ Ⓒ Ⓓ Ⓔ
13. Ⓐ Ⓑ Ⓒ Ⓓ Ⓔ
14. Ⓐ Ⓑ Ⓒ Ⓓ Ⓔ
15. Ⓐ Ⓑ Ⓒ Ⓓ Ⓔ
16. Ⓐ Ⓑ Ⓒ Ⓓ Ⓔ
17. Ⓐ Ⓑ Ⓒ Ⓓ Ⓔ
18. Ⓐ Ⓑ Ⓒ Ⓓ Ⓔ
19. Ⓐ Ⓑ Ⓒ Ⓓ Ⓔ
20. Ⓐ Ⓑ Ⓒ Ⓓ Ⓔ
21. Ⓐ Ⓑ Ⓒ Ⓓ Ⓔ
22. Ⓐ Ⓑ Ⓒ Ⓓ Ⓔ
23. Ⓐ Ⓑ Ⓒ Ⓓ Ⓔ
24. Ⓐ Ⓑ Ⓒ Ⓓ Ⓔ
25. Ⓐ Ⓑ Ⓒ Ⓓ Ⓔ
26. Ⓐ Ⓑ Ⓒ Ⓓ Ⓔ
27. Ⓐ Ⓑ Ⓒ Ⓓ Ⓔ
28. Ⓐ Ⓑ Ⓒ Ⓓ Ⓔ
29. Ⓐ Ⓑ Ⓒ Ⓓ Ⓔ
30. Ⓐ Ⓑ Ⓒ Ⓓ Ⓔ
31. Ⓐ Ⓑ Ⓒ Ⓓ Ⓔ
32. Ⓐ Ⓑ Ⓒ Ⓓ Ⓔ
33. Ⓐ Ⓑ Ⓒ Ⓓ Ⓔ
34. Ⓐ Ⓑ Ⓒ Ⓓ Ⓔ
35. Ⓐ Ⓑ Ⓒ Ⓓ Ⓔ

Section V
Data
Sufficiency

1. Ⓐ Ⓑ Ⓒ Ⓓ Ⓔ
2. Ⓐ Ⓑ Ⓒ Ⓓ Ⓔ
3. Ⓐ Ⓑ Ⓒ Ⓓ Ⓔ
4. Ⓐ Ⓑ Ⓒ Ⓓ Ⓔ
5. Ⓐ Ⓑ Ⓒ Ⓓ Ⓔ
6. Ⓐ Ⓑ Ⓒ Ⓓ Ⓔ
7. Ⓐ Ⓑ Ⓒ Ⓓ Ⓔ
8. Ⓐ Ⓑ Ⓒ Ⓓ Ⓔ
9. Ⓐ Ⓑ Ⓒ Ⓓ Ⓔ
10. Ⓐ Ⓑ Ⓒ Ⓓ Ⓔ
11. Ⓐ Ⓑ Ⓒ Ⓓ Ⓔ
12. Ⓐ Ⓑ Ⓒ Ⓓ Ⓔ
13. Ⓐ Ⓑ Ⓒ Ⓓ Ⓔ
14. Ⓐ Ⓑ Ⓒ Ⓓ Ⓔ
15. Ⓐ Ⓑ Ⓒ Ⓓ Ⓔ
16. Ⓐ Ⓑ Ⓒ Ⓓ Ⓔ
17. Ⓐ Ⓑ Ⓒ Ⓓ Ⓔ
18. Ⓐ Ⓑ Ⓒ Ⓓ Ⓔ
19. Ⓐ Ⓑ Ⓒ Ⓓ Ⓔ
20. Ⓐ Ⓑ Ⓒ Ⓓ Ⓔ
21. Ⓐ Ⓑ Ⓒ Ⓓ Ⓔ
22. Ⓐ Ⓑ Ⓒ Ⓓ Ⓔ
23. Ⓐ Ⓑ Ⓒ Ⓓ Ⓔ
24. Ⓐ Ⓑ Ⓒ Ⓓ Ⓔ
25. Ⓐ Ⓑ Ⓒ Ⓓ Ⓔ

Section VI
Problem
Solving

1. Ⓐ Ⓑ Ⓒ Ⓓ Ⓔ
2. Ⓐ Ⓑ Ⓒ Ⓓ Ⓔ
3. Ⓐ Ⓑ Ⓒ Ⓓ Ⓔ
4. Ⓐ Ⓑ Ⓒ Ⓓ Ⓔ
5. Ⓐ Ⓑ Ⓒ Ⓓ Ⓔ
6. Ⓐ Ⓑ Ⓒ Ⓓ Ⓔ
7. Ⓐ Ⓑ Ⓒ Ⓓ Ⓔ
8. Ⓐ Ⓑ Ⓒ Ⓓ Ⓔ
9. Ⓐ Ⓑ Ⓒ Ⓓ Ⓔ

10. Ⓐ Ⓑ Ⓒ Ⓓ Ⓔ
11. Ⓐ Ⓑ Ⓒ Ⓓ Ⓔ
12. Ⓐ Ⓑ Ⓒ Ⓓ Ⓔ
13. Ⓐ Ⓑ Ⓒ Ⓓ Ⓔ
14. Ⓐ Ⓑ Ⓒ Ⓓ Ⓔ
15. Ⓐ Ⓑ Ⓒ Ⓓ Ⓔ
16. Ⓐ Ⓑ Ⓒ Ⓓ Ⓔ
17. Ⓐ Ⓑ Ⓒ Ⓓ Ⓔ
18. Ⓐ Ⓑ Ⓒ Ⓓ Ⓔ
19. Ⓐ Ⓑ Ⓒ Ⓓ Ⓔ
20. Ⓐ Ⓑ Ⓒ Ⓓ Ⓔ

Section VII
Analysis of
Situations

1. Ⓐ Ⓑ Ⓒ Ⓓ Ⓔ
2. Ⓐ Ⓑ Ⓒ Ⓓ Ⓔ
3. Ⓐ Ⓑ Ⓒ Ⓓ Ⓔ
4. Ⓐ Ⓑ Ⓒ Ⓓ Ⓔ
5. Ⓐ Ⓑ Ⓒ Ⓓ Ⓔ
6. Ⓐ Ⓑ Ⓒ Ⓓ Ⓔ
7. Ⓐ Ⓑ Ⓒ Ⓓ Ⓔ
8. Ⓐ Ⓑ Ⓒ Ⓓ Ⓔ
9. Ⓐ Ⓑ Ⓒ Ⓓ Ⓔ
10. Ⓐ Ⓑ Ⓒ Ⓓ Ⓔ
11. Ⓐ Ⓑ Ⓒ Ⓓ Ⓔ
12. Ⓐ Ⓑ Ⓒ Ⓓ Ⓔ
13. Ⓐ Ⓑ Ⓒ Ⓓ Ⓔ
14. Ⓐ Ⓑ Ⓒ Ⓓ Ⓔ
15. Ⓐ Ⓑ Ⓒ Ⓓ Ⓔ
16. Ⓐ Ⓑ Ⓒ Ⓓ Ⓔ
17. Ⓐ Ⓑ Ⓒ Ⓓ Ⓔ
18. Ⓐ Ⓑ Ⓒ Ⓓ Ⓔ
19. Ⓐ Ⓑ Ⓒ Ⓓ Ⓔ
20. Ⓐ Ⓑ Ⓒ Ⓓ Ⓔ
21. Ⓐ Ⓑ Ⓒ Ⓓ Ⓔ
22. Ⓐ Ⓑ Ⓒ Ⓓ Ⓔ
23. Ⓐ Ⓑ Ⓒ Ⓓ Ⓔ
24. Ⓐ Ⓑ Ⓒ Ⓓ Ⓔ
25. Ⓐ Ⓑ Ⓒ Ⓓ Ⓔ
26. Ⓐ Ⓑ Ⓒ Ⓓ Ⓔ
27. Ⓐ Ⓑ Ⓒ Ⓓ Ⓔ
28. Ⓐ Ⓑ Ⓒ Ⓓ Ⓔ
29. Ⓐ Ⓑ Ⓒ Ⓓ Ⓔ
30. Ⓐ Ⓑ Ⓒ Ⓓ Ⓔ
31. Ⓐ Ⓑ Ⓒ Ⓓ Ⓔ
32. Ⓐ Ⓑ Ⓒ Ⓓ Ⓔ
33. Ⓐ Ⓑ Ⓒ Ⓓ Ⓔ
34. Ⓐ Ⓑ Ⓒ Ⓓ Ⓔ
35. Ⓐ Ⓑ Ⓒ Ⓓ Ⓔ

Section VIII
Writing
Ability

1. Ⓐ Ⓑ Ⓒ Ⓓ Ⓔ
2. Ⓐ Ⓑ Ⓒ Ⓓ Ⓔ
3. Ⓐ Ⓑ Ⓒ Ⓓ Ⓔ
4. Ⓐ Ⓑ Ⓒ Ⓓ Ⓔ
5. Ⓐ Ⓑ Ⓒ Ⓓ Ⓔ
6. Ⓐ Ⓑ Ⓒ Ⓓ Ⓔ
7. Ⓐ Ⓑ Ⓒ Ⓓ Ⓔ
8. Ⓐ Ⓑ Ⓒ Ⓓ Ⓔ
9. Ⓐ Ⓑ Ⓒ Ⓓ Ⓔ
10. Ⓐ Ⓑ Ⓒ Ⓓ Ⓔ
11. Ⓐ Ⓑ Ⓒ Ⓓ Ⓔ
12. Ⓐ Ⓑ Ⓒ Ⓓ Ⓔ
13. Ⓐ Ⓑ Ⓒ Ⓓ Ⓔ
14. Ⓐ Ⓑ Ⓒ Ⓓ Ⓔ
15. Ⓐ Ⓑ Ⓒ Ⓓ Ⓔ
16. Ⓐ Ⓑ Ⓒ Ⓓ Ⓔ
17. Ⓐ Ⓑ Ⓒ Ⓓ Ⓔ
18. Ⓐ Ⓑ Ⓒ Ⓓ Ⓔ
19. Ⓐ Ⓑ Ⓒ Ⓓ Ⓔ
20. Ⓐ Ⓑ Ⓒ Ⓓ Ⓔ
21. Ⓐ Ⓑ Ⓒ Ⓓ Ⓔ
22. Ⓐ Ⓑ Ⓒ Ⓓ Ⓔ
23. Ⓐ Ⓑ Ⓒ Ⓓ Ⓔ
24. Ⓐ Ⓑ Ⓒ Ⓓ Ⓔ
25. Ⓐ Ⓑ Ⓒ Ⓓ Ⓔ

SAMPLE TEST 2

Section I   Reading Comprehension   Time: 30 minutes

Directions: This part contains three reading passages. You are to read each one carefully. When answering the questions, you will be allowed to refer back to the passages. The questions are based on what is *stated* or *implied* in each passage.

PASSAGE 1

The following passage was written in 1964.

The main burden of assuring that the resources of the federal government are well managed falls on relatively few of the five million men and women whom it employs. Under the department and agency heads there are 8,600 political, career, military, and foreign service executives—the top managers and professionals—who exert major influence on the manner in which the rest are directed and utilized. Below their level there are other thousands with assignments of some managerial significance, but we believe that the line of demarcation selected is the best available for our purposes in this attainment.

In addition to Presidential appointees in responsible posts, the 8,600 include the three highest grades under the Classification Act; the three highest grades in the postal field service; comparable grades in the foreign service; general officers in the military service; and similar classes in other special services and in agencies or positions excepted from the Classification Act.

There is no complete inventory of positions or people in federal service at this level. The lack may be explained by separate agency statutes and personnel systems, diffusion among so many special services, and absence of any central point (short of the President himself) with jurisdiction over all upper-level personnel of the government.

This Committee considers establishment and maintenance of a central inventory of these key people and positions to be an elementary necessity, a first step in improved management throughout the Executive Branch.

Top Presidential appointees, about 500 of them, bear the brunt of translating the philosophy and aims of the current administration into practical programs. This group includes the secretaries and assistant secretaries of cabinet departments, agency heads and their deputies, heads and members of boards and commissions with fixed terms, and chiefs and directors of major bureaus, divisions, and services. Appointments to many of these politically sensitive positions are made on recommendation by department or agency heads, but all are presumably responsible to Presidential leadership.

One qualification for office at this level is that there be no basic disagreement with Presidential political philosophy, at least so far as administrative judgments and actions are concerned. Apart from the bi-partisan boards and commissions, these men are normally identified with the political party of the President, or are sympathetic to it, although there are exceptions.

There are four distinguishable kinds of top Presidential appointees, including:

—Those whom the President selects at the outset to establish immediate and effective control over the government (e.g., Cabinet secretaries, agency heads, his own White House staff and Executive Office Personnel).

—Those selected by department and agency heads in order to establish control within their respective organizations (e.g.—assistant secretaries, deputies, assistants to, and major line posts in some bureaus and divisions).

—High-level appointees who—though often requiring clearance through political or interest group channels, or both—must have known scientific or technical competence (e.g.—the Surgeon General, the Commissioner of Education).

—Those named to residual positions traditionally filled on a partisan patronage basis.

These appointees are primarily regarded as policy makers and overseers of policy execution. In practice, however, they usually have substantial responsibilities in line management, often requiring a thorough knowledge of substantive agency programs.

1. According to the passage, about how many top managerial professionals work for the federal government?

   (A) five million   (D) nine thousand
   (B) two million   (E) five hundred
   (C) twenty thousand

2. No complete inventory exists of positions in the three highest levels of government service because

   (A) no one has bothered to count them
   (B) computers cannot handle all the data
   (C) separate agency personnel systems are used
   (D) the President has never requested such information
   (E) the Classification Act prohibits such a census

3. Top Presidential appointees have as their central responsibility the

   (A) prevention of politically motivated interference with the actions of their agencies
   (B) monitoring of government actions on behalf of the President's own political party
   (C) translation of the aims of the administration into practical programs
   (D) investigation of charges of corruption within the government
   (E) maintenance of adequate controls over the rate of government spending

4. One exception to the general rule that top Presidential appointees must be in agreement with the President's political philosophy may be found in

   (A) most cabinet-level officers
   (B) members of the White House staff
   (C) bi-partisan boards and commissions
   (D) those offices filled on a patronage basis
   (E) offices requiring scientific or technical expertise

5. Applicants for Presidential appointments are usually identified with or are members of

   (A) large corporations
   (B) the foreign service
   (C) government bureaus
   (D) academic circles
   (E) the President's political party

6. Appointees that are selected directly by the President include

   (A) U.S. marshals and attorneys
   (B) military officers
   (C) agency heads
   (D) assistant secretaries
   (E) congressional committee members

7. Appointees usually have to possess expertise in

   (A) line management
   (B) military affairs
   (C) foreign affairs
   (D) strategic planning
   (E) constitutional law

8. According to the passage, Presidential appointees are regarded primarily as

   (A) political spokesmen   (D) scientific or technical experts
   (B) policy makers   (E) business executives
   (C) staff managers

9. Appointees selected by department and agency heads include

   (A) military men
   (B) cabinet secretaries
   (C) deputy secretaries
   (D) diplomats
   (E) residual position holders

PASSAGE 2

Under state fair trade acts, a producer or distributor of a good bearing his brand, trademark, or name can prescribe by contract either a minimum or stipulated resale price of that good, depending upon the particular state law. Prior to the passage of the fair trade laws, resale price maintenance agreements were considered illegal because such agreements by a producer with more than one distributor prevent price competition among those distributors. The effect is the same as if the distributors had combined and agreed to fix price.

In late 1963, forty states had fair trade laws; of these, twenty-three had "non-signer" clauses. According to the nonsigner provision, all resellers are bound by the terms of the resale price maintenance contract signed by any *one* re-seller. To be truly effective, a state fair trade law must contain a nonsigner provision; for unless the manufacturer has some control over the noncontracting price-cutter, there can be little effective control by the manufacturer over resale prices. In addition, in late 1963 special legislation in nine states made resale price maintenance with respect to alcoholic beverages either mandatory or subject to control by state liquor control agencies.

Not all branded goods are covered by the fair trade laws. Closeout sales are excepted. Exceptions are made in some of these laws on sales to colleges and libraries. Some make provisions to except damaged goods or those from which the brand or trade names have been removed or obliterated.

An obstacle to the success of fair trade is the fact that cut-price mail-order shipments of goods out of an area which has no fair trade law into a fair trade state cannot be prevented by an enforcement action under the fair trade law of the state into which the goods are shipped, for the buyer takes title to the goods in the location from which the goods are shipped. The mail-order business can thus be used to evade a state fair trade act. Likewise, an advertisement within a fair-trade state of cut prices of goods available in a non-fair-trade area has been judged not to be within the jurisdiction of the state fair trade law. Sales from within a fair-trade state to customers outside the state in a non-fair-trade area cannot, however, be made at cut prices.

Maintaining a fair-trade program is fraught with several legal problems. Responsibility for enforcement falls upon the producer or distributor, who must monitor and take legal action against the price-cutters. Legal enforcement must be continuous, vigorous, and effective; it cannot be selective. An assortment of marketing devices contrived by retailers to evade fair-trade prices, such as the granting of trading stamps in abnormally high volume or the placing of excessive value on the trade-in of durable consumer items, must be dealt with by court action. Further, utilization of fair trade prevents a manufacturer from itself selling in competition with those distributors, either wholesalers or retailers, who are governed by its fair-trade contracts, for the effect of such an arrangement is a horizontal agreement.

10. The essential purpose of fair trade legislation is to

(A) allow manufacturers to stipulate the resale price of a good
(B) allow manufacturers to bypass distributors in sales to retailers
(C) provide that manufacturers engage in fair and equal trade with distributors
(D) allow manufacturers to maintain a fair markup on their goods
(E) exempt resale items from antitrust legislation

11. A "nonsigner clause" stipulates that

(A) all resellers who sign fair trade contracts are bound by them
(B) all resellers are bound by the terms of the fair trade contract signed by one reseller
(C) resellers are not bound by law to sign fair trade contracts
(D) all branded goods are covered by the fair trade legislation
(E) "nonsigners" are exempt from the provisions of fair trade legislation

12. It can be inferred from the passage that fair trade laws would probably be most welcomed by

(A) discount stores
(B) wholesale distributors
(C) small-volume retailers
(D) import-export houses
(E) producers of raw materials

13. A direct obstacle to the success of fair trade laws is that

    (A) not all states have these laws
    (B) not all resellers are bound by the laws
    (C) cut-rate goods can be mailed from a non-fair-trade state
    (D) manufacturers may not avail themselves of all privileges given by the legislation
    (E) loss-leader selling is prohibited

14. Responsibility for enforcing fair trade laws falls on the

    (A) state   (D) manufacturer
    (B) federal government   (E) retailer
    (C) courts

15. Categories of goods exempted from fair trade laws include

    (A) pharmaceutical products   (D) items in closeout sale
    (B) alcoholic beverages   (E) private label goods
    (C) imports

16. At the time the passage was written, how many states had fair trade laws?

    (A) all states   (D) about thirty
    (B) about ten   (E) about forty
    (C) about twenty

17. Methods used by retailers to evade fair trade laws include

    (A) refusing to comply with the law
    (B) dealing with more than one supplier
    (C) giving extra trading stamps
    (D) giving extra discounts
    (E) refusing to deal with the manufacturer

PASSAGE 3

When President Carter signed the synthetic fuels bill on June 30, 1980, he said that passage of the measure, designed to speed production of synthetic oil and gas from the vast U.S. coal and shale reserves, marked "a proud day for America." If all goes according to plan, the United States will be producing two million barrels of synthetic fuels daily by 1992, enough to substantially reduce U.S. dependence on imported oil. It is "the keystone of our national energy policy," he said, which "at last is being put in place."

The bill authorizes:

—Creation of a federally owned corporation, the U.S. Synthetic Fuels Corporation, to encourage production of oil and gas from coal and oil from shale.
—The hiring of up to 300 employees. The corporation's management would be by a seven-member board nominated by the President and confirmed by the U.S. Senate.
—Expenditure of $20 billion to be used by the corporation over the next five years for loans, loan guarantees, and other incentives to private industry to meet, by 1987, a production goal equivalent to 500,000 barrels of oil a day from synthetic sources. Another $68 billion is to be made available— subject to congressional appropriation—over the following seven years to meet the two-million-barrel-a-day goal.

The government's financial backing is intended to help private utilities and pipeline and energy companies borrow funds to build synthetic fuel plants. Hundreds of these firms have indicated their intention to seek the loans. There would be no direct cost to the government unless the projects failed to operate, or the finished product was so expensive that it required a subsidy to be marketed.

The new legislation also provides $5 billion to finance solar energy projects and for conservation measures, such as improved insulation for low-income households.

Speaking at the signing ceremony, President Carter said the measure would help the United States conserve considerably more energy than at present, thus further reducing its dependence on foreign oil. In this connection, he noted that U.S. oil imports have declined by 12.9 percent in the past year, gasoline consumption fell eight percent, and total oil consumption was off by more than nine percent.

Another benefit to be derived from synthetic fuels production is the increased employment it will provide for the nation's work force. A recent study by the Department of Energy found that designing and building a 60,000 barrel-a-day plant for turning coal directly into liquid fuel will take 22 million worker-hours of engineering time. To meet the President's goal of a million barrels of coal-based liquid fuel daily by 1990 would take 17 such plants. This would mean up to 85,000 persons employed at the construction sites by the middle of the 1980s.

Although there are already a few small experimental plants making synthetic gas and oil (including gasohol) in operation in the United States, the first large-scale production is to come from the huge oil-shale deposits underlying the high plains where the states of Colorado, Wyoming, and Utah meet. The Green River formation, a 16,500-square-mile area, contains an estimated 600 billion barrels of recoverable oil, almost as much as the total of proven worldwide oil reserves. A recent congressional study found that about 400 billion barrels of oil could be recovered from this source with existing technology at prices competitive with imported oil—though not without significant technological, economic, environmental and social problems yet to be resolved.

Indeed, the environmental aspects of synthetic fuel production may hamper its development despite the plans of government and industry. The possibility that a large-scale effort would cause massive air pollution and irreparable damage to the Western landscape, as well as deplete scarce water supplies essential for crops and livestock, has raised considerable apprehension, particularly among environmentalists. They contend that increased emphasis on solar energy, along with more energy conservation, would dispel the need for synthetic fuel development. Others believe, however, that the program is too vital to the economy and security of the nation to be postponed or sidetracked. A typical supporter of an all-out effort to produce synthetic fuels is a former governor of Colorado who now heads a business group advocating energy development. In his words, "We have got to face the fact that because our country needs these resources, they must be developed."

18. According to the passage, the United States may be producing two million barrels of synthetic fuels daily by the year

(A) 1985   (D) 1994
(B) 1989   (E) 2000
(C) 1992

19. The benefits derived from synthetic fuels production include

  I. energy conservation
 II. increased employment
III. decreased pollution

(A) I only
(B) II only
(C) I and II only

(D) II and III only

(E) I, II, and III

20. Which of the following synthetic fuel sources is (are) mentioned in the passage?

   I. Fossil fuels

  II. Coal

 III. Shale

(A) I only

(B) II only

(C) I and II only

(D) II and III only

(E) I, II, and III

21. The synthetic fuels bill provides for funding a U.S. Synthetic Fuels Corporation, over a period of twelve years, in the amount of

(A) $20 billion   (D) $78 billion

(B) $30 billion   (E) $88 billion

(C) $68 billion

22. The legislation provides $5 billion to finance building of

   I. antipollution devices

  II. experimental plants

 III. solar energy projects

(A) II only

(B) III only

(C) I and II only

(D) II and III only

(E) I, II, and III

23. It is estimated that the U.S. Synthetic Fuels Corporation will hire up to

(A) 100 employees   (D) 800 employees

(B) 300 employees   (E) 1,200 employees

(C) 500 employees

24. According to the passage, those who favor solar energy over synthetic fuels development include

   I. environmentalists
  II. big business
  III. the U.S. Department of Energy

  (A) I only
  (B) III only
  (C) I and III only
  (D) II and III only
  (E) I, II, and III

25. Oil-shale deposits are concentrated in the states of

   I. Nevada
  II. Wyoming
  III. Utah

  (A) I only
  (B) III only
  (C) I and III only
  (D) II and III only
  (E) I, II, and III

If there is still time remaining, you may review the questions in this section only. You may not turn to any other section of the test.

Section II Data Sufficiency   Time: 30 minutes

Directions: Each of the following problems has a question and two statements which are labeled (1) and (2). Use the data given in (1) and (2) together with other available information (such as the number of hours in a day, the definition of *clockwise*, mathematical facts, etc.) to decide whether the statements are *sufficient* to answer the question. Then fill in space

  (A) if you can get the answer from (1) alone but not from (2) alone;

  (B) if you can get the answer from (2) alone but not from (1) alone;

  (C) if you can get the answer from (1) and (2) together, although neither statement by itself suffices;

  (D) if statement (1) alone suffices *and* statement (2) alone suffices;

(E) if you cannot get the answer from statements (1) and (2) together, but need even more data.

All numbers used in this section are real numbers. A figure given for a problem is intended to provide information consistent with that in the question, but not necessarily with the additional information contained in the statements.

1. In triangle *ABC*, find *x* if *y* = 40.

   (1) *AB* = *BC*
   (2) *z* = 100

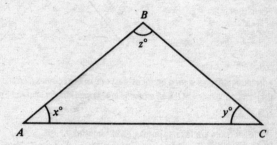

2. What is the area of the shaded part of the circle? *O* is the center of the circle.

   (1) The radius of the circle is 4.
   (2) *x* is 60.

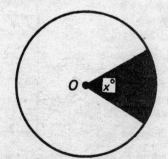

3. What was Mr. Kliman's income in 1970?

   (1) His total income for 1968, 1969, and 1970 was $41,000.
   (2) He made 20% more in 1969 than he did in 1968.

4. If l and l' are straight lines, find y.

(1) $x = 100$
(2) $z = 80$

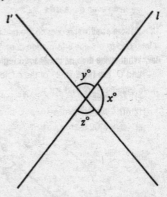

5. Fifty students have signed up for at least one of the courses German I and English I. How many of the 50 students are taking German I but not English I?

(1) 16 students are taking German I and English I.
(2) The number of students taking English I but not German I is the same as the number taking German I but not English I.

6. Is *ABCD* a square?

(1) $AD = AB$
(2) $x = 90$

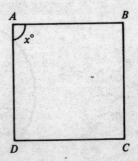

7. The *XYZ* Corporation has 7,000 employees. What is the average yearly wage of an employee of the *XYZ* Corporation?

(1) 4,000 of the employees are executives.
(2) The total amount the company pays in wages each year is $77,000,000.

8. Is $x > y$?

   (1) $(x + y)^2 > 0$
   (2) x is positive

9. What is the area of the shaded region if both circles have radius 4, and O and O' are the centers of the circles?

   (1) The area enclosed by both circles is 29π.
   (2) The line connecting O and O' is perpendicular to the line connecting B and C (B and C are the points where the two circles intersect).

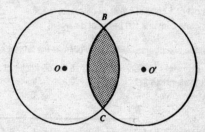

10. How long will it take to travel from A to B? It takes 4 hours to travel from A to B and back to A.

   (1) It takes 25% more time to travel from A to B than it does to travel from B to A.
   (2) C is midway between A and B, and it takes 2 hours to travel from A to C and back to A.

11. l, l', and k are straight lines. Are l and l' parallel?

   (1) $x = y$
   (2) $y = z$

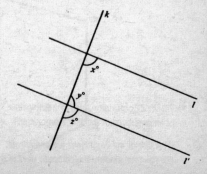

12. What is $x + y + z$?

    (1) $x + y = 3$

    (2) $x + z = 2$

13. How much cardboard will it take to make a rectangular box with a lid whose base has length 7 inches?

    (1) The width of the box will be 5 inches.

    (2) The height of the box will be 4 inches.

14. What is the profit on 15 boxes of detergent?

    (1) The cost of a crate of boxes of detergent is $50.

    (2) Each crate contains 100 boxes of detergent.

15. Which of the two figures, *ABCD* or *EFGH*, has the largest area?

    (1) The perimeter of *ABCD* is longer than the perimeter of *EFGH*.

    (2) *AC* is longer than *EG*.

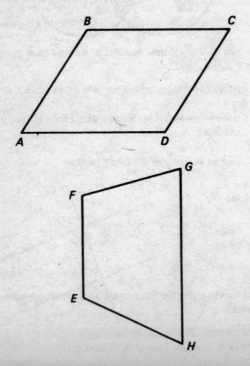

16. Is a number divisible by 9?

(1) The number is divisible by 3.
(2) The number is divisible by 27.

17. *PQRS* is a rectangle. The coordinates of the point *P* are (2,3). What is the area of *PQRS*?

(1) The coordinates of the point *S* are (2,5).
(2) The coordinates of the point *Q* are (6,3).

18. *ABCD* is a rectangle. Which region, *ABEF* or *CDFE*, has a larger area?

(1) *BE* is longer than *FD*.
(2) *BE* is longer than *CD*.

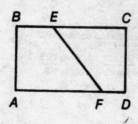

19. Is the integer *k* odd or even?

(1) k^2 is odd.
(2) $2k$ is even.

20. Does a car with 5 gallons of gas in its fuel tank have enough fuel to travel 100 miles?

(1) The car travels 25 miles on one gallon of gas.
(2) The car is driven at a speed of 50 miles per hour.

21. *ABCD* is a square. *BCO* is a semicircle. What is the area of *ABOCD*?

(1) The length of *AC* is $4\sqrt{2}$.
(2) The radius of
    the semicircle *BOC* is 2.

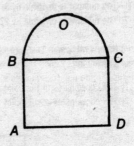

22. Do the points *P* and *Q* lie on the same circle with center (0,0)?

(1) The coordinates of point *P* are (2,3).
(2) The coordinates of point *Q* are (4,1).

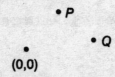

23. Did ABC Company make a profit in 1980?

(1) ABC Company made a profit in 1979.
(2) ABC Company made a profit in 1981.

24. Is 2^n divisible by 8?

(1) *n* is an odd integer.
(2) *n* is an integer greater than 5.

25. Did the price of a bushel of soybeans increase during every week of 1980?

(1) The price of a bushel of soybeans was $2 on Jan 1, 1980.
(2) The price of a bushel of soybeans was $4 on Jan 1, 1981.

*If there is still time remaining, you may review the questions in this
section only. You may not turn to any other section of the test.*

Section III   Problem Solving   Time: 30 minutes

Directions: Solve each of the following problems; then indicate the correct answer on the answer sheet. [On the actual test you will be permitted to use any space available on the examination paper for scratch work.]

NOTE: A figure that appears with a problem is drawn as accurately as possible so as to provide information that may help in answering the question (unless the words "Figure not drawn to scale" appear next to the figure). Numbers in this test are real numbers.

1. A borrower pays 6% interest on the first $500 he borrows and 5½% on the part of the loan in excess of $500. How much interest will the borrower have to pay on a loan of $5,500?

   (A) $275   (D) $305
   (B) $280   (E) $330
   (C) $302.50

2. If $2x - y = 4$, then $6x - 3y$ is

   (A) 4   (D) 10
   (B) 6   (E) 12
   (C) 8

3. The next number in the arithmetical progression 5, 11, 17, . . . is

   (A) 18   (D) 28
   (B) 22   (E) 33
   (C) 23

Use the graph on page 208 for questions 4–6.

4. In what year did the installed capacity first exceed 50 million kilowatts?

   (A) 1939   (D) 1947
   (B) 1944   (E) 1950
   (C) 1945

5. In 1952, the installed capacity of steam and internal combustion plants was about x times the installed capacity of the hydro plants where x is

   (A) ½   (D) 3
   (B) 1   (E) 4
   (C) 2

INSTALLED CAPACITY OF
ELECTRIC UTILITY GENERATING PLANTS 1920–1952

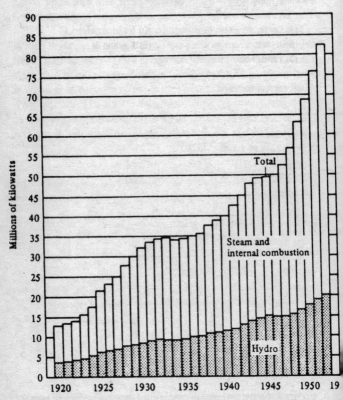

Source: Federal Power Commission

6. Which of the following statements about the installed capacity of electric utility generating plants between 1920 and 1952 can be inferred from the graph?

I. In the period 1930–39, there was less of an increase in capacity than in either of the periods 1920–1929 or 1940–1949.

II. More than $\frac{1}{5}$ of the capacity in 1925 was produced by hydro plants.

III. The increase in capacity in kilowatts between 1945 and 1952 was greater than the increase between 1925 and 1945.

(A) I only

(B) II only

(C) I and III only

(D) II and III only

(E) I, II, and III

7. A warehouse has 20 packers. Each packer can load $\frac{1}{8}$ of a box in 9 minutes. How many boxes can be loaded in $1\frac{1}{2}$ hours by all 20 packers?

(A) $1\frac{1}{4}$

(B) $10\frac{1}{4}$

(C) $12\frac{1}{2}$

(D) 20

(E) 25

8. In Motor City 90% of the population own a car, 15% own a motorcycle, and everybody owns a car or motorcycle or both. What percent of the population own a motorcycle but not a car?

(A) 5

(B) 8

(C) 9

(D) 10

(E) 15

9. Jim's weight is 140% of Marcia's weight. Bob's weight is 90% of Lee's weight. Lee weighs twice as much as Marcia. What percentage of Jim's weight is Bob's weight?

(A) $64\frac{2}{7}$

(B) $77\frac{7}{9}$

(C) 90

(D) $128\frac{4}{7}$

(E) $155\frac{5}{9}$

10. Towns A and C are connected by a straight highway which is 60 miles long. The straight-line distance between town A and town B is 50 miles, and the straight-line distance from town B to town C is 50 miles. How many miles is it from town B to the point on the highway connecting towns A and C which is closest to town B?

(A) 30

(B) 40

(C) $30\sqrt{2}$

(D) 50

(E) 60

11. A chair originally cost $50.00. The chair was offered for sale at 108% of its cost. After a week the price was discounted 10% and the chair was sold. The chair was sold for

(A) $45.00   (D) $49.50

(B) $48.60   (E) $54.00

(C) $49.00

12. A worker is paid x dollars for the first 8 hours he works each day. He is paid y dollars per hour for each hour he works in excess of 8 hours. During one week he works 8 hours on Monday, 11 hours on Tuesday, 9 hours on Wednesday, 10 hours on Thursday, and 9 hours on Friday. What is his average daily wage in dollars for the five-day week?

(A) $x + \dfrac{7}{5}y$ (D) $x + 2y$

(B) $2x + y$ (E) $5x + 7y$

(C) $\dfrac{5x + 8y}{5}$

13. A club has 8 male and 8 female members. The club is choosing a committee of 6 members. The committee must have 3 male and 3 female members. How many different committees can be chosen?

(A) 112,896   (D) 112

(B) 3,136   (E) 9

(C) 720

14. A motorcycle costs $2,500 when it is brand new. At the end of each year it is worth ⅘ of what it was at the beginning of the year. What is the motorcycle worth when it is 3 years old?

(A) $1,000   (D) $1,340

(B) $1,200   (E) $1,430

(C) $1,280

Use the table on page 211 for questions 15–17.

15. What is the cost of fuel for a 120-mile trip by automobile?

(A) $5   (D) $15

(B) $9   (E) $30

(C) $12

Type of vehicle	Cost of fuel for 200-mile trip
Automobile	$15
Motorcycle	$ 5
Bus	$20
Truck	$50
Airplane	$70

16. If the wages of a bus driver for a 200-mile trip are $70, and the only costs for a bus are the fuel and the driver's wages, how much should a bus company charge to charter a bus and driver for a 200-mile trip in order to obtain 120% of the cost?

(A) $24 (D) $104
(B) $90 (E) $108
(C) $94

17. If 3 buses, 4 automobiles, 2 motorcycles, and one truck each make a 200-mile trip, what is the average fuel cost per vehicle?

(A) $5 (D) $20
(B) $15 (E) $24
(C) $18

18. If $x + 2y = 2x + y$, then $x - y$ is equal to

(A) 0 (D) 5
(B) 2 (E) cannot be determined
(C) 4

19. 15% of the families in state x have an income of $25,000 or more. $\frac{2}{3}$ of the families with income of $25,000 or more in state x own a boat. What fraction of the families own a boat and have an income of $25,000 or more in state x?

(A) $\frac{1}{15}$ (D) $\frac{4}{21}$
(B) $\frac{1}{12}$ (E) $\frac{9}{40}$
(C) $\frac{1}{10}$

20. If the angles of a triangle are in the ratio 1:2:2, then the triangle

(A) is isosceles   (D) is equilateral

(B) is obtuse   (E) has one angle greater than 80°

(C) is a right triangle

If there is still time remaining, you may review the questions in this section only. You may not turn to any other section of the test.

Section IV   Analysis of Situations   Time: 30 minutes

Directions: Read the following passages. After you have completed each one, you will be asked to answer questions that involve determining the importance of specific factors included in the passage. When answering questions, you may consult the passage.

PASSAGE 1:

Bill Kamil was director of Tibland's national lottery. The lottery had been established twenty years before to raise funds for health, education, and welfare projects. It was owned by the state and supervised by a board of directors selected from among leading businessmen, professional people such as lawyers and educators, and government officials. Throughout its history, lottery sales had increased faster than the annual growth of population and about 20 percent faster than the annual rate of inflation. However, during the last two years, sales—while increasing—had grown at a decreasing rate. Kamil was concerned that, should this trend continue, sales would soon level off, or even decrease. He therefore called a meeting of his staff, including Fred Fishman, Marketing Manager; Arnold Fox, Operations Manager; and Ron Davis, Statistician. Fishman was responsible for the lottery program, changes in prizes, new products, pricing policy, and advertising. Fox was responsible for the distribution of lottery tickets to dealers, collection of ticket sales, and the maintenance of sales booths. Davis's main duties involved preparing monthly statistical reports on lottery sales and data analysis.

Tibland's lottery consisted of three games. The most widely played of the three was a weekly game. All the participant had to do was purchase a ticket printed with a five-digit number. Every Monday a lottery was held wherein a computer selected the winning numbers at random. In a second game, the participant checked a series of numbers in boxes printed on a standard form. He or she might choose a birthdate, his or her children's ages, or any random series of numbers. Winning numbers were also selected at random by a computer. The third game was an instant lottery. Participants scraped off the foil on part of a card which revealed a series of numbers, symbols, or pictures, depending upon the game. Winning tickets were those that contained four of a kind (first prize), three of a kind (second prize), or two of a kind (third prize).

Top on the agenda of Kamil's staff meeting was a discussion of how sales of all lottery games could be increased. Kamil especially drew the staff's attention to a sales report prepared by Ron Davis.

Lottery Sales
(100,000 units of local currency)

Year	Weekly	Lottery Lotto	Instant	Total Sales
1961	38	—	—	38
1966	111	—	—	111
1971	136	31	—	167
1976	278	174	—	452
1977	356	233	—	589
1978	467	351	78	896
1979	616	494	142	1,252
1980	822	623	140	1,585

The report showed that total lottery sales in monetary units had increased every year. However, the rate of increase had declined since 1978. Ron Davis pointed out that Lotto sales had tapered off more than those of the weekly lottery. Instant lottery sales had actually declined slightly in 1980, and early sales returns for 1981 showed a similar downward trend. In all three games, the *number* of tickets sold had declined. If the trend continued, lottery sales growth in real terms (discounted for inflation) would be negative.

Kamil requested his staff to suggest alternative courses of action that would result in (1) an *annual* increase in the sales of all three games of not less than 30 percent, (2) a ten-percent increase in the number of tickets sold, and (3) the introduction of four new instant games every year. The following discussion ensued.

Fishman: Stagnating lottery sales are owing to bad publicity surrounding the introduction of the instant game in 1978. Initially, there were many buyers who even waited on long lines to purchase tickets. Media coverage of this frantic period was extensive, but negative. Rather than emphasize the positive aspects of the lottery, the news media pointed out that most of the purchasers seemed to be members of the lower social classes. We must do all we can to stimulate sales among upper income groups.

Fox: It wasn't the media that lowered sales, but simply that the initial enthusiasm wore off. Prizes are much smaller in the instant lottery compared to the weekly, even though the ticket prices of both are nearly the same. Participants feel that they are not getting their money's worth from the instant game.

Davis: There may be a third factor. Many people who were regular purchasers of weekly lottery tickets tried the instant game. Those who were disappointed with the instant game may have stopped purchasing other lottery games as well. This would explain the decrease in the number of tickets sold.

Fishman: An increase in sales of all lottery games can be made possible by, first, attracting new buyers, and, second, increasing the rate of purchase of existing buyers. According to a recent survey, the "non buyers" of most lottery games are mainly upper-income, professional people. We can best reach these people through a direct-mail compaign. One possibility is to sell them ticket subscriptions. Instead of buying one or a few tickets at a time of a single lottery, we should offer them a half year's subscription to the weekly lottery. Subscriptions can be paid for through the mail, at great convenience to the consumer.

Fox: Subscriptions might be the answer to the weekly lottery, but they will not work for the instant and Lotto games. Moreover, a six-month subscription would cost $52. Not enough people will pay such a sum in advance. Costs for printing special tickets and circulating them through the mail would be greater than the costs of our present distribution method.

Davis: We want to reach upper-income groups; they will be willing to pay for the convenience of subscribing to a series of lotteries in advance, without having to purchase tickets at a retail outlet. Present buyers who do not choose to subscribe may continue to purchase tickets at retail locations.

Fishman: Subscriptions sales work well in Germany and a few other European countries. I do not believe there is any difference between purchases in those countries and Tibland. People buy lottery tickets for two reasons: for the fun of playing, and to fulfill some sort of dream that only a large sum of money can make real. These motives are universal.

Fox: Subscriptions may induce non-buyers to purchase lottery tickets, but sales of the instant game and Lotto will not increase. We must increase advertising expenditures by at least fifty percent to stimulate sales. I have been in this business for twenty years. Based on my experience, advertising has always been the key to sales.

Davis: We have to operate within a budget. We do not have sufficient resources to undertake a subscription campaign, while at the same time increasing advertising expenditures by fifty percent. We may also be criticized by consumer councils for spending so much of our income on advertising, rather than allocating it to public projects.

Fishman: Let's consider trying to increase sales by making the games more attractive. For instance, we could immediately institute a plan to introduce new instant games every six weeks. The Lotto game could also be improved by adding a consolation prize. These changes would do more to stimulate sales than an increase in advertising. It is the product that counts, not the advertising.

Data Evaluation Questions

Directions: The questions that follow relate to the preceding passage. Evaluate, in terms of the passage, each of the items given. Then select your answer from one of the following classifications, and blacken the corresponding space on the answer sheet.

- (A) A MAJOR OBJECTIVE in making the decision: one of the goals sought by the decision maker

- (B) A MAJOR FACTOR in making the decision: an aspect of the problem, specifically mentioned in the passage, that fundamentally affects and/ or determines the decision

- (C) A MINOR FACTOR in making the decision: a less important element bearing on or affecting a Major Factor, rather than a Major Objective directly

- (D) A MAJOR ASSUMPTION in making the decision: a projection or supposition arrived at by the decision maker before considering the factors and alternatives

- (E) AN UNIMPORTANT ISSUE in making the decision: an item lacking significant impact on, or relationship to, the decision

1. Fox's years of experience in the lottery business

2. Increasing the number of lottery games

3. Stagnating lottery sales

4. Cost of an advertising campaign

5. Increasing lottery sales by 30 percent

6. Number of tickets likely to be sold under each alternative

7. Predominance of members of the lower classes among purchasers of instant lottery tickets

8. Existence of lotteries in Tibland for the past twenty years

9. Printing costs for subscription tickets

10. Similarity of motives of purchasers of lottery tickets in Tibland and in Europe

11. Likelihood of stimulating sales through advertising

12. Attracting new buyers of lotteries

13. Amount of money available in the budget

14. Cost of proposed subscriptions to the weekly lottery game

15. Socio-economic status of members of the board of directors

16. Lotteries were held every Monday

17. Paying for subscriptions in advance

18. Selecting winning numbers at random

PASSAGE 2

Len Hibert was given the task of formulating compensation policy for overseas managers for a multinational firm operating in several Latin American countries and Europe. His company is a major manufacturer of heavy industrial equipment that has been operating in foreign markets for over 40 years. Like many early export-oriented companies, most of the international business was export with no manufacturing abroad. In recent years, the company orientation and attitudes toward the foreign operation have shifted drastically; they now have manufacturing in six different countries and the international portion of their business accounts for well over 50 percent of their annual profits. The company philosophy toward International has been shifting away from viewing the international portion as export only and trying to organize into a multinational company. This shift in philosophy and the importance of the international division has placed greater emphasis on the type and function of the international manager sent abroad. While the company has effectively utilized the typical "expatriate freewheeler" to represent them abroad (although mavericks in their management style, they have proved to be extremely effective for the company), it is now becoming more evident that there is a need for a different type of person to spend a shorter period of time abroad. Most host countries have changed their policies toward foreigners working in their countries from relatively liberal permission to operate at many levels to increasingly more restrictive policies. For example, many of the Latin American countries will not permit foreign personnel when there are qualified nationals to fulfill the tasks. The only exception is that a U.S. citizen will be given a work permit for three or four years to train a national replacement. Even in Europe, it is becoming more and more politically astute to hire nationals. For the company this has meant sending fewer people to represent their worldwide operations abroad, and further, that those who are sent abroad must be extremely capable, understand the total operation, and be effective teachers. The "right man" to go abroad is the same person with the same qualifications who would be in demand in the domestic operation as well.

The company has, historically, provided the typical inducements for moving abroad: cost of living allowances, depending on the country, from 20 percent to 30 percent of the base salary; paid vacations on an annual basis back to the United States; schooling allowances for children back in the States or in private schools; and all moving expenses including complete household furnishings. Despite such inducements there have been some real problems with prospective people the company has wanted to send abroad. Many of them center around the family. Over the years, the personnel director has kept a record of some of the typical complaints and questions raised when executives have been asked to go abroad. For example, "Will you keep us supplied with baby food in Columbia [Colombia]? You mean to pay only 20 percent premium for the sacrifice of leaving the United States? My daughter could live at home while she attends college; will you bring her back to the States and pay her living expenses? Will you pay my way back to see my own doctor if it's necessary? Will you move my new outboard cruiser? Will you move my mother-in-law, who lives with us, to Buenos Aires too?" While these questions may not seem relevant to an outsider, to the individual raising the questions they are important. It has been felt that these kinds of issues are critical in the initial decision to go abroad and are also quite important as reasons why executives return ahead of schedule. An article in *Business Week* tends to sum up the kinds of problems Len is facing.

COMPENSATION FOR OVERSEAS EXECUTIVES
TOO MUCH OR TOO LITTLE?[1]

Today, serving a hitch overseas for the company is required of almost anyone wanting company advancement. Many problems arise in sending the executive overseas, but one of the most critical is compensation. Some feel that the overseas executive or expatriate is overcompensated; others feel that, considering the sacrifice, he is undercompensated. You be the judge.

On the plus side, a man of 28 to 45 (the usual age range of overseas appointees) generally gets a boost in his career: higher pay, broader responsibilities. Major companies are sending their top-ranking younger men abroad, not employees they want to "bury."

Says a Chase Manhattan Bank executive: "A man is smart to have some overseas time if he really wants to move up the ladder." About 80 percent of those Chase sends abroad are sent for career development. The same holds for a growing number of big and medium-size international outfits. The usual hitch lasts from two to five years. And the man most apt to benefit from it is the middle manager. He will probably get control over a whole local operation. That lets him prove his general managerial ability. And, if he is successful, he returns home with higher status. A younger man is smart to go for experience—even without more pay.

A far less attractive deal involves going overseas for an indeterminate period to train a national for a job abroad. This missionary must return home to discover that a former equal has stepped above him. Usually, of course, a man over 50 goes abroad only to fill a high-ranking spot. Some big companies now provide added incentive; they allow foreign service men to retire early (often at 60) with varying retirement benefits.

The big gamble is not so much age and the assignment. It's how well a man's wife and children will adjust to the relocation. There's likely to be at least moderate strain—and there are plenty of cases where relocation has broken up marriages. Even a move to Western Europe can be difficult. "People who have strong family ties back home are poor risks," says a Jersey Standard personnel executive. Some self-examination is a must, say the pros. But too often this is ignored by the man eager to push ahead. Says one old hand in the international field: "If you're just trying to get away from it all, forget about going abroad. Your problems will magnify."

As a rule, you won't get a contract for an overseas hitch (and it's best not to

---

[1] Reprinted from the November 30, 1968, issue of *Business Week* by special permission, © 1968 by McGraw-Hill, Inc, New York, N.Y. 10020. All rights reserved.

push for one). But there are some things you will want to nail down. You should expect a foreign service premium of 15 percent to 25 percent above your base salary. This is what many of the larger outfits are paying. Note that the cost of living abroad can be higher than in the United States. For example, it may cost up to $200 a month more to rent a comparable house in Europe than in the United States. "Making a profit on a tour abroad doesn't work these days," says one pro, "except in a place like Nairobi."

Moving expenses should be paid, too. This may mean $5,000 to $6,000 (nontaxable) for moving your family to Western Europe. In addition, many companies will pay $800 to $1,000 per child per year for school expenses abroad. Some pay for one round trip a year for a college-age son or daughter studying in the United States. Quite a few companies will even help you in your search for a school and pay exceptional costs such as high tutoring fees in remote areas.

As an example,

a typical United States executive assigned in Brussels might receive in addition to his base salary: (1) a 10 percent to 25 percent premium; (2) a cost-of-living allowance of several hundred dollars a month; and (3) housing allowance which permits him to live in the best Brussels suburb at about the same cost as a more modest house at home. He drives a European sports car while his wife makes do with the American sedan the company shipped overseas for him. His children attend the best local private schools when they would have gone to public schools at home. His social circle includes some of the top business, professional, and government people in the country. His wife is able to visit some of the finest museums, concerts, and lectures in the world—if she can find time away from an active social life. And yet they both complain to their friends in the local expatriate community, to local management, and to company headquarters that they are being vastly undercompensated, are deeply unhappy, and feel that the company has done them an injustice.[2]

Len's company's compensation program is not too different from the ones discussed in the article above. His company has also had several executives return from foreign assignments within six to eight months, and in most cases after returning they have left the company. Some were not considered a loss, but there were at least one or two whom the company did not want to lose. While this has not been a major problem, certainly Len's immediate superior feels that part of the reason why some executives have returned before their assignments were up was the arm twisting done to get them to accept the assignment. They were not really enthusiastic about going abroad in the first

---

[2] Reprinted from J. Vivian, "Expatriate Executives: Overpaid but Undercompensated," *Columbia Journal of World Business*. January–February 1968, pp. 29–40. Copyright © 1968 by the Trustees of Columbia University.

place but felt obligated, and further, they were not properly prepared to face the cultural shock involved.

There is some indication that companies are cutting fringe benefits. There are several reasons for this—living conditions abroad are not as bad today as they once were, companies' philosophies have changed to the extent that advancement to higher executive positions requires involvement in the foreign operations, and there is a general feeling that there is no need to pay extra just for going overseas and doing an accepted part of a job. The *Wall Street Journal* reported that Hewlett-Packard Company has moved to eliminate cost-of-living allowances, phase out their housing subsidies, and eliminate their yearly educational allowance of up to 1,250 dollars per child. Standard Oil of California has decided to cut its premiums to U.S. executives in Venezuela from the current 28 percent to about 17 percent. IBM and DuPont are also considering reduction of their extras. While reduction of extras is occurring among some, an extensive survey by the Conference Board taken in 1974 of 267 of the largest U.S.-based international corporations showed the following: 84 percent paid their American officials abroad a premium for foreign service; 81 percent paid cost-of-living allowances for what was perceived as the higher cost of maintaining an American standard of living abroad; and 72 percent gave housing subsidies.

Another problem that many companies are having and that Len's company faces as it expands is how to deal effectively with the returning executive. In the past, the company has been able to absorb all of its returning personnel in meaningful positions at headquarters. However, as policies and changes mentioned above lead to a larger turnover in foreign executive personnel, management needs to consider the effective integration of these executives in meaningful positions when they return to the U.S. The cultural shock experienced by returning executives is a problem.

A recent study of repatriated executives from 25 international companies suggests some of the problems of integrating returning executives into regular company operations. The men interviewed were between the ages of 30 and 45, married, with an average of 3 children, and they had spent from 2 to 6 years abroad. Many had left their jobs for positions with other companies shortly after returning from abroad. The principal reason given for leaving was dissatisfaction with their new domestic assignments.

In general, most of the executives were alienated from their companies and the reasons cited were: (1) the nature of the new domestic assignment was too disagreeable; (2) the location of the domestic assignment was unacceptable to the returnee; (3) salary and fringe benefits to which the individual and his family had become accustomed while on foreign assignment were lost; and (4) the skills and experience acquired could be marketed more to the individual's advantage either domestically or internationally through another company. Finally, there were several individuals who complained of unfair discriminatory practice by the company in dealing with their objections and grievances.[3]

The findings of this study were supported by a recent incident involving a financial officer of Len's company who had been stationed in Western Europe. The Browns lived in Paris where he was responsible for overseeing the financial operations of the company in six European countries. He and his family had enjoyed their five-year stay in Paris and had become accustomed to French culture and the higher level of living there. Their children had been enrolled in private schools outside of Paris and liked the more relaxed pace of European life. The company ordered him back to the U.S. since it wanted to provide foreign experience for another executive. A new company policy of calling back executives after a four-year assignment had recently been initiated. This policy was considered necessary to provide foreign experience for as many key personnel as possible. Brown was the first to be affected.

He was ordered back to Chicago as assistant to the Vice President of Finance. In this position he had much less responsibility and authority than he had had in the European post where he reported directly to the President of European operations. As a consequence, he found his new job strange and certainly less challenging. Even though his salary had not been reduced, he was not happy in Chicago. In his European job he had operated in a number of different capacities and become very familiar with the entire European operation. He felt that the company did not appreciate him and was not effectively using his experience gained as a key European financial officer. In addition to his dissatisfaction, the lifestyle in Chicago was substantially different than that in Paris, and his whole family was upset about having to move back to the States. In fact, one daughter stayed in Europe to complete her education since she had received most of her education there and didn't want to transfer to U.S. schools. After about six months in Chicago, Brown quit and went to work with a competitor.

Part of Len's task is to determine if the new policy of rotating key personnel in foreign assignments should continue to be followed, and if so how to avoid losing men like Brown. There is no doubt that top management was upset about losing Brown, whom they considered to have been a definite asset to the organization.

Not only is there no simple solution to repatriating executives, but Len must

---

[3] For an interesting report on this problem see J. Alex Murray, "International Personnel Repatriation: Cultural Shock in Reverse," *MSU Business Topics*, Summer 1973, pp. 59–66.

COST OF LIVING INDEXES AND APARTMENT RENTS FOR SELECTED MAJOR BUSINESS CENTERS

City	Index* (New York = 100)	3-Room Apt.† Furnished (monthly)
Tokyo	130.4	$755–1,132
Frankfurt	110.1	$324–405
Zurich	106.1	$363–495
Geneva	105.3	$330–462
Brussels	100.1	$214–348
New York	100.0	$300–500
Amsterdam	92.3	$259–370
Athens	86.7	$235–370
London	82.4	$341–585
Rome	79.4	$209–296
Madrid	76.5	$270–540
São Paulo	68.0	$299–498

* The following categories of living expenses are included: shopping basket (retail food products and non-alcoholic beverages), alcoholic beverages, household supplies and operations (cleaning supplies, laundry and dry cleaning charges), personal care products, tobacco, utilities, clothing and footwear, domestic help, recreation and entertainment (TV rental fees, nightclub entertainment, theatre/concerts, cinema, dinner at a fashionable restaurant, subscription to English-language newspaper) and transportation.

† Cost of 3-bedroom apartment (living room, dining room, kitchen, bedrooms) near center of city.

Source: "Selected Cost of Living Indexes Abroad," *Sales Management*, January 7, 1974, pp. 83–85.

also deal with the negative aspects of sending men abroad because of the hardships of moving and the cost of maintaining an American style of living standard abroad at today's prices. See the table for some indication of the cost of living in different parts of the world.

Further, when Len read about the abductions in South America of U.S. executives, it was hard to believe that there wouldn't be more resistance to moving abroad, especially if the outstanding man he wants to assign abroad can see that he has as much opportunity in the States as he would have by moving. There is no doubt, however, that the trend is to keep the number of Americans overseas as low as possible and to eventually reduce the number in relation to business volume as rapidly as possible while at the same time giving as many as possible international experience. Thus the men who go to foreign operations almost always are picked for special knowledge and are expected to train nationals to replace them; this means Len must send his best. His task is to devise a policy to help solve the immediate problems as well as those he can anticipate in the future. This policy may entail recommendations for specific changes in organization and methods of control. Hopefully, the new policy will help motivate his executives to go overseas and provide him with the best possible talent abroad, talent the company will be able to effectively utilize once they return to the United States.

Data Evaluation Questions

Directions: The questions that follow relate to the preceding passage. Evaluate, in terms of the passage, each of the items given. Then select your answer from one of the following classifications, and blacken the corresponding space on the answer sheet.

(A) A MAJOR OBJECTIVE in making the decision: one of the goals sought by the decision maker

(B) A MAJOR FACTOR in making the decision: an aspect of the problem, specifically mentioned in the passage, that fundamentally affects and/ or determines the decision

(C) A MINOR FACTOR in making the decision: a less important element bearing on or affecting a Major Factor, rather than a Major Objective directly

(D) A MAJOR ASSUMPTION in making the decision: a projection or supposition arrived at by the decision maker before considering the factors and alternatives

(E) AN UNIMPORTANT ISSUE in making the decision: an item lacking significant impact on, or relationship to, the decision

19. Determining compensation policy for overseas managers

20. Production of heavy industrial equipment

21. Organizing into a multinational company

22. Location of overseas executives

23. Cost of renting a house in Europe

24. Cost of living abroad

25. Selecting personnel for overseas assignments

26. Problem of integrating returning executives

27. Disadvantages of rotating key personnel in foreign assignments

28. Number of countries in which Hibert's company operates

29. Operating abroad for over 40 years

30. Company philosophy

31. Host country policies toward foreign employees

32. Kidnappings in South America

33. Motivating executives to go overseas

34. Cultural shock experienced by expatriates

35. The Browns lived in Paris

If there is still time remaining, you may review the questions in this section only. You may not turn to any other section of the test.

Section V Data Sufficiency   Time: 30 minutes

Directions: Each of the following problems has a question and two statements which are labeled (1) and (2). Use the data given in (1) and (2) together with other available information (such as the number of hours in a day, the definition of *clockwise*, mathematical facts, etc.) to decide whether the statements are *sufficient* to answer the question. Then fill in space

(A) if you can get the answer from (1) alone but not from (2) alone;

(B) if you can get the answer from (2) alone but not from (1) alone;

(C) if you can get the answer from (1) and (2) together, although neither statement by itself suffices;

(D) if statement (1) alone suffices *and* statement (2) alone suffices;

(E) if you cannot get the answer from statements (1) and (2) together, but need even more data.

All numbers used in this section are real numbers. A figure given for a problem is intended to provide information consistent with that in the question, but not necessarily with the additional information contained in the statements.

1. Is x greater than y?

    (1) $3x = 2k$

    (2) $k = y^2$

2. Is $ABCD$ a parallelogram?

    (1) $AB = CD$

    (2) AB is parallel to CD

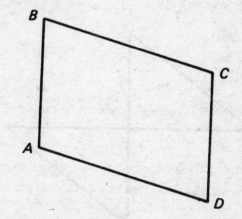

3. What was Mr. Smith's combined income for the years 1965–1970? In 1965 he made $10,000.

    (1) His average yearly income for the years 1965–1970 was $12,000.

    (2) In 1970, his income was $20,000.

4. How much profit did Walker's Emporium make selling dresses?

    (1) Each dress cost $10.

    (2) 600 dresses were sold.

5. *k* is a positive integer. Is *k* a prime number?

   (1) No integer between 2 and $\sqrt{k}$ inclusive divides *k* evenly.

   (2) No integer between 2 and $\dfrac{k}{2}$ inclusive divides *k* evenly, and *k* is greater than 5.

6. The towns A, B, and C lie on a straight line. C is between A and B. The distance from A to B is 100 miles. How far is it from A to C?

   (1) The distance from A to B is 25% more than the distance from C to B.
   (2) The distance from A to C is ¼ of the distance from C to B.

7. Is *AB* perpendicular to *CD*?

   (1) AC = BD
   (2) x = y

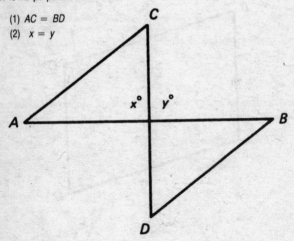

8. What is the value of x − y?

   (1) x + 2y = 6
   (2) x = y

9. The number of eligible voters is 100,000. How many eligible voters voted?

   (1) 63% of the eligible men voted.
   (2) 67% of the eligible women voted.

10. If $z = 50$, find the value of x.

(1) $RS \neq ST$
(2) $x + y = 60$

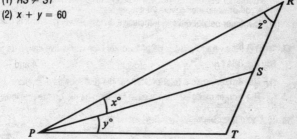

11. How much was the original cost of a car which sold for $2,300?

(1) The car was sold for a discount of 10% from its original cost.
(2) The sales tax was $150.

12. The hexagon *ABCDEF* is inscribed in the circle with center *O*. What is the length of *AB*?

(1) The radius of the circle is 4 inches.
(2) The hexagon is a regular hexagon.

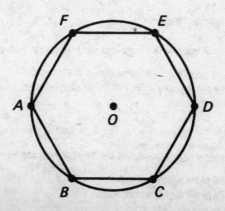

13. How many rolls of wallpaper are necessary to cover the walls of a room whose floor and ceiling are rectangles 12 feet wide and 15 feet long?

    (1) A roll of wallpaper covers 20 square feet.

    (2) There are no windows in the walls.

14. What is the average daily wage of a worker who works five days? He made $80 the first day.

    (1) The worker made a total of $400 for the first four days of work.

    (2) The worker made 20% more each day then he did on the previous day.

15. Is ABC a right triangle? $AB = 5$; $AC = 4$.

    (1) $BC = 3$

    (2) $AC = CD$

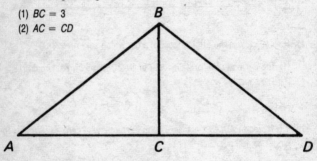

16. Did the price of energy rise last year?

    (1) If the price of energy rose last year, then the price of food would rise this year.

    (2) The price of food rose this year.

17. How much was a certain Rembrandt painting worth in January 1971?

    (1) In January 1977 the painting was worth $2,000,000.

    (2) Over the ten years 1968–1977 the painting increased in value by 10% each year.

18. A sequence of numbers $a_1, a_2, a_3, \ldots$ is given by the rule $a_n{}^2 = a_{n+1}$. Does 3 appear in the sequence?

    (1) $a_1 = 2$

    (2) $a_3 = 16$

19. Is AB greater than AC?

(1) $z > x$
(2) $AC > AD$

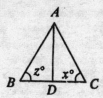

20. x and y are integers that are both less than 10. Is x greater than y?

(1) x is a multiple of 3.
(2) y is a multiple of 2.

21. Is $\dfrac{1}{x}$ greater than $\dfrac{1}{y}$?

(1) x is greater than 1.
(2) x is less than y.

22. AB intersects CD at point O. Is AB perpendicular to CD? $AC = AD$.

(1) Angle CAD is bisected by AO.
(2) $BC = AD$

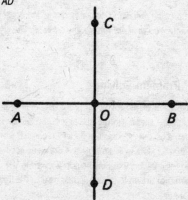

23. Plane X flies at r miles per hour from A to B. Plane Y flies at S miles per hour from B to A. Both planes take off at the same time. Which plane flies at a faster rate? Town C is between A and B.

(1) C is closer to A than it is to B.
(2) Plane X flies over C before plane Y.

24. What is the value of $x + y$?

(1) $2x + y = 4$
(2) $x + 2y = 5$

25. What is the area of the circular section AOB?
A and B are points on the circle which has
O as its center.

(1) Angle $AOB = 36°$
(2) $OB = OA$

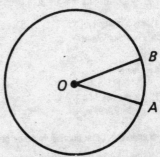

*If there is still time remaining, you may review the questions in this
section only. You may not turn to any other section of the test.*

Section VI   Problem Solving   Time: 30 minutes

Directions: Solve each of the following problems; then indicate the correct
answer on the answer sheet. [On the actual test you will be permitted to use
any space available on the examination paper for scratch work.]
NOTE: A figure that appears with a problem is drawn as accurately as possible
so as to provide information that may help in answering the question (unless
the words "Figure not drawn to scale" appear next to the figure). Numbers in
this test are real numbers.

1. If a car travels at a constant rate of 60 miles per hour, how long will it take
   to travel 255 miles?

   (A) 3¾ hours
   (B) 4 hours
   (C) 4⅛ hours

   (D) 4¼ hours
   (E) 4½ hours

2. A car currently travels 15 miles on a gallon of gas but after a tune-up the car will use only ¾ as much gas as it does now. How many miles will the car travel on a gallon of gas after the tune-up?

(A) 15   (D) 18⅔
(B) 16½   (E) 20
(C) 17½

3. Successive discounts of 20% and 15% are equal to a single discount of

(A) 30%   (D) 35%
(B) 32%   (E) 36%
(C) 34%

Use the following graphs for questions 4–7.

PER CAPITA PERSONAL HEALTH CARE EXPENDITURES

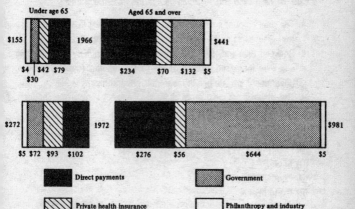

Under age 65

$155   1966

$4 $42 $79
$30

Aged 65 and over

$441

$234 $70 $132 $5

$272   1972 $981

$5 $72 $93 $102

$276 $56 $644 $5

Direct payments   Government

Private health insurance   Philanthropy and industry

Source: Social Security Bulletin

4. If there were about 20 million people 65 and over in 1966, how much did the govenment spend on personal health care for people aged 65 and over in 1966?

(A) $26 million   (D) $2.640 billion
(B) $264 million   (E) $3.6 billion
(C) $2 billion

5. Between 1966 and 1972, the per capita amount spent by the government on personal health care for those under age 65 increased by x% where x is

(A) 100   (D) 220
(B) 120   (E) 240
(C) 140

6. In 1972, the fraction contributed by philanthropy and industry towards expenditures for personal health care for those aged 65 and over was about

(A) $\frac{1}{500}$ (D) $\frac{1}{88}$
(B) $\frac{1}{196}$ (E) $\frac{2}{101}$
(C) $\frac{1}{99}$

7. Which of the following statements about expenditures for personal health care between 1966 and 1972 can be inferred from the graphs?

 I. The total amount spent for those aged 65 and over in 1972 was more than 3 times as much as the total amount spent on those under 65.
 II. Between 1966 and 1972, the amount spent per capita by those aged 65 and over increased in each of the four categories (direct payments, government, private health insurance, philanthropy).
 III. The government paid more than $\frac{1}{2}$ of the amount of expenditures for those aged 65 and over in 1972.

(A) I only
(B) II only
(C) III only
(D) I and III only
(E) II and III only

8. Oranges cost $1.00 for a crate containing 20 oranges. If oranges are sold for 6¢ each, what percent of the selling price is the profit?

(A) 5%   (D) 20%
(B) 10%   (E) 25%
(C) $16\frac{2}{3}$%

9. A hen lays $7\frac{1}{2}$ dozen eggs during the summer. There are 93 days in the summer and it costs $10 to feed the hen for the summer. How much does it cost in food for each egg produced?

(A) 10¢

(D) 13$\frac{1}{13}$¢

(B) 11$\frac{1}{9}$¢

(E) 15¢

(C) 12$\frac{3}{13}$¢

10. If the diameter of a circle has length d, the radius has length r, and the area equals a, then which of the following statements is (are) true?

I. $a = \pi d^2$

II. $d = 2r$

III. $\dfrac{a}{d} = \pi \dfrac{r}{2}$

(A) only II

(B) I and II only

(C) I and III only

(D) II and III only

(E) I, II, and III

11. If hose A can fill up a tank in 20 minutes, and hose B can fill up the same tank in 15 minutes, how long will it take for the hoses together to fill up the tank?

(A) 5 minutes

(D) 9$\frac{2}{7}$ minutes

(B) 7$\frac{1}{2}$ minutes

(E) 12 minutes

(C) 8$\frac{4}{7}$ minutes

12. If 5 men take 2 hours to dig a ditch, how long will it take 12 men to dig the ditch?

(A) 45 minutes

(D) 60 minutes

(B) 50 minutes

(E) 84 minutes

(C) 54 minutes

Use the following table for questions 13–15.

Car Production at Plant T for One Week in 1960

	Number of cars produced	Total daily wages
MONDAY	900	$30,000
TUESDAY	1200	$40,000
WEDNESDAY	1500	$52,000
THURSDAY	1400	$50,000
FRIDAY	1000	$32,000

13. What was the average number of cars produced per day for the week shown?

   (A) 1,000   (D) 1,200
   (B) 1,140   (E) 1,220
   (C) 1,180

14. What was the average cost in wages per car produced for the week?

   (A) $25   (D) $32
   (B) $26   (E) $34
   (C) $29

15. Which of the following statements about the production of cars and the wages paid for the week can be inferred from the table?

   I. ¼ of the cars were produced on Wednesday.
   II. More employees came to the plant on Friday than on Monday.
   III. ⅖ of the days accounted for ½ the wages paid for the week.

   (A) I only
   (B) II only
   (C) I and II only
   (D) I and III only
   (E) I, II, and III

16. A train travels from Cleveland to Toledo in 2 hours and 10 minutes. If the distance from Cleveland to Toledo is 150 miles, then the average speed of the train is about

   (A) 60 mph   (D) 72 mph
   (B) 66 mph   (E) 75 mph
   (C) 69 mph

17. If $x > 2$ and $y > -1$, then

   (A) $xy > -2$ (D) $-x > 2y$
   (B) $-x < 2y$ (E) $x < 2y$
   (C) $xy < -2$

18. What is the area of the rectangle $ABCD$, if the length of AC is 5 and the length of AD is 4?

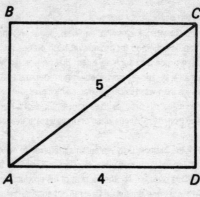

(A) 3   (D) 15
(B) 6   (E) 20
(C) 12

19. If electricity costs k¢ an hour, heat $\$d$ an hour, and water w¢ an hour, how much will all three cost for 12 hours?

(A) $12(k + d + w)$¢

(B) $\$(12k + 12d + 12w)$

(C) $\$(k + 100d + w)$

(D) $\$\left(12k + \dfrac{12d}{100} + 12w \right)$

(E) $\$(.12k + 12d + .12w)$

20. If $x = y = 2z$ and $x \cdot y \cdot z = 256$, then x equals

(A) 2   (D) $4 \sqrt[3]{2}$
(B) $2 \sqrt[3]{2}$ (E) 8
(C) 4

If there is still time remaining, you may review the questions in this section only. You may not turn to any other section of the test.

Section VII   Analysis of Situations   Time: 30 minutes

Directions: Read the following passages. After you have completed each one, you will be asked to answer questions that involve determining the importance of specific factors included in the passage. When answering questions, you may consult the passage.

PASSAGE 1

In 1967 Mr. Ed Carswell, a chemical engineer, began experimenting in his spare time with a new method for processing fresh orange juice. By 1970, he had perfected the process to such an extent that he was ready to begin production in a small way. His process enabled him to extract 18 percent more juice from oranges than was typically extracted by a pressure juicer of the type currently used in cafes. His process also removed some of the bitterness which got into the juice from the peelings when oranges were squeezed without peeling them.

Since many of the better quality restaurants preferred to serve fresh orange juice instead of canned or frozen juice, Mr. Carswell believed he could find a ready market for his product. Another appeal of his product would be that he could maintain more consistent juice flavor than haphazard restaurant juicing usually produced.

Mr. Carswell patented the process and then started production. Since his capital was limited, he began production in a small building which previously had been a woodworking shop. With the help of his brother, Mr. Carswell marketed the juice through local restaurants. The juice was distributed in glass jugs, which proved to be rather expensive because of high breakage. The new product was favorably accepted by the public, however, and the business proved to be a success.

Mr. Carswell began to receive larger and more frequent orders from his customers and their business associates. In 1972, he quit his regular job in order to devote full time to his juice business. He soon reached his capacity because of his inability to personally cover a larger area with his pickup truck. Advertising was on a small scale because of limited funds. Faced with the problems of glass jug breakage and limited advertising and distribution, Mr. Carswell approached a regional food distributor for a solution. Mr. Carswell was offered a plan whereby the distributor would advertise and distribute the product on the basis of 25 percent of gross sales. The distributor would assist Mr. Carswell in securing a loan from the local bank to expand production.

Before he had an opportunity to contact the bank to borrow money, Mr. Carswell was introduced to Mr. Bernie Lubo, a plastics engineer, who produced plastic containers. Mr. Carswell mentioned his own problems in the expansion of his business. Mr. Lubo wanted to finance expanded juice production with the understanding that plastic containers would be used for marketing the orange juice. He would lend the money interest free, but he was to receive 40 percent of the net profits for the next ten years. Distribution and advertising were to be done through a local broker for 25 percent of gross sales. The principal on Mr. Lubo's invested money was to be repaid by Mr. Carswell on a basis of 10 percent of his share of the profits. Mr. Lubo was to retain an interest in the profits of the firm until the loan was repaid, or at least for ten years.

Mr. Carswell's current sales were 10,000 gallons of juice a month. If distribution could be expanded, sales could be doubled, given the potential demand. Of the possible total sales of 20,000 a month, about 75 percent would be sold to large restaurants and the remainder to small cafeterias and luncheonettes. As soon as the juice was bottled in plastic containers, sales could also be made to household consumers. Mr. Carswell was very optimistic that sales to the final consumer through retail shops would succeed. Some initial contacts were made with a local franchiser of drive-in dairy shops. The franchiser was sure that he could sell 4,000 gallons a month through his outlets.

Mr. Carswell also calculated his potential profits. His goal was to increase sales while at the same time earning a 10 percent rate of return on his prior capital investment in equipment and other assets. The present value of Mr. Carswell's investment was $250,000. Of this sum, machinery and equipment were valued at $100,000; real estate was worth $50,000 and his patent and know-how were valued at $100,000. On the basis of this evaluation, Mr. Carswell desired a return of $25,000 above salaries and other expenses after the first year of operation.

Both the regional distributor and Mr. Bernie Lubo believed that Mr. Carswell's sales could be increased to 15,000 gallons of juice per month by the end of the first year of expanded operations. However, the extent to which production could be expanded to meet demand depended on the availability of plastic containers (which would be supplied at factory cost under Mr. Lubo's proposal), and additional machinery. Increased market coverage would be obtained under both the regional food distributor and Lubo proposals. The critical deciding factor, as Mr. Carswell understood, was which plan would maximize his return on investment beyond the minimum figure of 10 percent.

Data Evaluation Questions

Directions: The questions that follow relate to the preceding passage. Evaluate, in terms of the passage, each of the items given. Then select your answer from one of the following classifications, and blacken the corresponding space on the answer sheet.

(A) A MAJOR OBJECTIVE in making the decision: one of the goals sought by the decision maker

(B) A MAJOR FACTOR in making the decision: an aspect of the problem, specifically mentioned in the passage, that fundamentally affects and/or determines the decision

(C) A MINOR FACTOR in making the decision: a less important element bearing on or affecting a Major Factor, rather than a Major Objective directly

(D) A MAJOR ASSUMPTION in making the decision: a projection or supposition arrived at by the decision maker before considering the factors and alternatives

(E) AN UNIMPORTANT ISSUE in making the decision: an item lacking significant impact on, or relationship to, the decision

1. Cost of securing a loan

2. High breakage rate of glass jugs

3. Expansion of the business

4. Continued demand by the public for Carswell's orange juice

5. Availability of an interest-free loan

6. Possibility of doubling sales through expanded distribution

7. Current valuation of Carswell's real estate

8. Previous use of Mr. Carswell's building as a woodworking shop

9. Ten percent return on investment

10. Plausibility of monthly sales of 4,000 gallons in dairy shops

11. Small scale of current advertising

12. Availability of a loan from a local rather than a national bank

13. Sale of juice to cafeterias

14. Value of patent held by Mr. Carswell

15. Mr. Carswell's current level of sales

16. Carswell's background in chemical engineering

17. Carswell's processing method

18. Cost of plastic containers

PASSAGE 2

National Office Machines of Dayton, Ohio, manufacturers of cash registers, EDP equipment, adding machines, and other small office equipment, has recently (March, 1970) entered into a joint venture with Nippon Cash Machines of Tokyo, Japan. National Office Machines (N.O.M.) had domestic sales of over _____million dollars in 1969 and foreign sales of nearly _____ million. Besides the United States, they operate in most of Western Europe, the Mideast, and some parts of the Far East. In the past, they have had no significant sales or sales force in Japan although they were represented there by a small trading company until a few years ago. In the United States they are one of the leaders in their field and are considered to have one of the most successful and aggressive sales forces found in the this highly competitive industry.

Nippon Cash Machines (N.C.M.) is an old-line cash register manufacturing company organized in 1872. At one time, they were the major manufacturer of cash register equipment in Japan but they have been losing ground since 1950 even though they produce perhaps the best cash register in Japan. Sales in 1969 were _____yen (280 yen = 1 U.S. dollar), a 15 percent decrease over sales in 1968. The fact that they produce only cash registers is one of their major problems; the merger with N.O.M. will give them much-needed breadth in their product offerings. Another hoped-for strength to be gained from the joint venture is managerial leadership, which they sorely need.

There are 14 Japanese companies which have products that compete with Nippon, plus several foreign giants such as IBM, National Cash Register, Burroughs of the United States, and Sweda Machines of Sweden. Nippon has a small sales force of 21 men, most of whom have been with the company since shortly after World War II and a few since pre-World War II days. These salesmen have been responsible for selling to Japanese trading companies and to a few large purchasers of equipment.

Part of the joint venture agreement was doubling the sales force within a year, with N.O.M. responsible for hiring and training the new salesmen, who must all be young, college-trained Japanese nationals. The agreement also allowed for U.S. personnel in supervisory positions for an indeterminate period of time and retaining the current Nippon sales force.

One of the many sales management problems facing the Nippon/American Business Machines Corporation (N.A.B.M.C.—the name of the new joint venture) was what sales compensation plan to use, i.e., should they follow the Japanese tradition of straight salary and guaranteed employment until death with no incentive program, or the U.S. method (very successful for N.O.M. in the United States) of commissions and various incentives based on sales performance, with the ultimate threat of being fired if sales quotas continuously go unfilled.

The immediate response to the problem might well be one of using the tried and true U.S. compensation methods, since they have worked so well in the United States and are perhaps the kind of changes needed and expected from the U.S. management. N.O.M. management is convinced that salesmen selling their kinds of products in a competitive market must have strong incentives in order to produce. In fact, N.O.M. had experimented on a limited basis in the United States with straight salary about 10 years ago and it was a "bomb." Unfortunately the problem is considerably more complex than it appears on the surface.

One of the facts to be faced by N.O.M. management is the traditional labor-management relations and employment systems which exist in Japan. The roots of the system go back to Japan's feudal era, when a serf promised a lifetime of service to his lord in exchange for a lifetime of protection. By the start of the country's industrial revolution in the 1880s, an unskilled worker pledged to remain with a company all his useful life if the employer would teach him the new mechanical arts. The tradition of spending a lifetime with a single employer survives today mainly because most workers like it that way. There is little chance of being fired, pay raises are regular, and there is a strict order of job-protecting seniority.

Japanese workers at larger companies still are protected from out-right dismissal by union contracts and an industrial tradition that some personnel specialists believe has the force of law. Under this tradition, a worker can be dismissed after an initial trial period only for gross cause, such as theft or some other major infraction. As long as the company remains in business he isn't discharged, or even furloughed, simply because there isn't enough work to be done.

Besides the guarantee of employment for life, the typical Japanese worker receives many fringe benefits from the company. Just how paternalistic the typical Japanese firm can be is illustrated by a statement from the Japanese Ministry of Foreign Affairs which gives the example of "A," a male worker who is employed in a fairly representative company in Tokyo:

> To begin with, A lives in a house provided by his company, and the rent he pays is amazingly low when compared with average city rents. His daily trips between home and factory are paid by the company. A's working hours are from 9 A.M. to 5 P.M. With a break for lunch which he usually takes in the company restaurant at a very cheap price. He

often brings back to his wife food, clothing, and other miscellaneous articles that he buys at the company store at a discount ranging from 10 percent to 30 percent below city prices. The company store even supplies furniture, refrigerators, and television sets on an installment basis, for which, if necessary, A can obtain a loan from the company almost free of interest.

In case of illness, A is given free medical treatment in the company hospital, and if his indisposition extends over a number of years, the company will continue paying almost his full salary. The company maintains lodges at seaside or mountain resorts, where A can spend the holidays or an occasional weekend with the family at moderate prices. . . . It must also be remembered that when A reaches retirement age (usually 55) he will receive a lump sum retirement allowance or a pension, either of which will assure him a relatively stable living for the rest of his life.[1]

Even though "A" is only an example of a typical employee, a salesman can expect the same treatment. Job security is such an expected part of everyday life that no attempt is made to motivate the Japanese salesman in the same manner as in the United States; as a consequence, selling traditionally has been primarily an order-taking job. Except for the fact that sales work offers some travel, entry to outside executive offices, the opportunity to entertain, and similar side benefits, it provides a young man with little other incentive to surpass his basic quotas and drum up new business. The traditional Japanese bonuses (which normally amount to about two or four months' salary over the year) are no larger for salesmen than any other functional job in the company.

As a key executive in a Mitsui-affiliated engineering firm put it recently: "The typical salesman in Japan isn't required to have any particular talent." In return for meeting sales quotas, most Japanese salesmen draw a modest monthly salary, sweetened about twice a year by bonuses. Manufacturers of industrial products generally pay no commission or other incentives to boost their businesses.

Besides the problem of motivation, a foreign company faces other strange customs when trying to put together and manage a sales force. Class systems and the Japanese distribution system with its penchant for reciprocity put strain on the creative talents of the best sales managers, as Simmons, the U.S. bed-

---

[1] "Japan's Paternalistic Employment System Is Changing in Face of Tight Labor Market," *The Wall Street Journal,* March 27, 1967, p. 6. Reprinted by permission of *The Wall Street Journal,* © Dow Jones & Company, Inc. (1967). All Rights Reserved.

ding manufacturer, was quick to learn. One Simmons executive explains:

> We had no idea of the workings of the class system. Hiring a good man
> from the lower classes, for instance, could be a disaster. If he called
> on a client of a higher class, there was a good chance the client would
> be insulted. There is also a really big difference in language among the
> classes.[2]

In the field, Simmons found itself stymied by the bewildering realities of Japanese marketing, especially the traditional distribution system which operates on a philosophy of reciprocity that goes beyond mere business to the core of the Japanese character. It's involved with "on," the notion that regards a favor or any kind as a debt that must be repaid. To "wear" another's "on" in business and then turn against him is to lose face, abhorrent to most Japanese. Thus, the owner of large Western-style apartments, hotels, or developments will buy his beds from the supplier to whom he owes a favor, no matter what the competition offers.

In small department and other retail stores, where most items are handled on consignment, the bond with the supplier is even stronger. Consequently, all sales outlets are connected in a complicated web that runs from the largest supplier, with a huge national force, to the smallest local distributor, with a handful of door-to-door salesmen. The system is self-perpetuating and all but impossible to crack from the outside.

However, there is some change in attitude taking place as both workers and companies start discarding traditions for the job mobility common in the United States. Skilled workers are willing to bargain on the strength of their experience in an open labor market in an effort to get higher wages or better job opportunities; in the United States it's called "shopping around." And a few companies are showing willingness to lure workers away from other concerns. A number of companies are also plotting on how to rid themselves of some of the "deadwood" workers accumulated as a result of promotions by strict seniority.

Toyo Rayon Company, Japan's largest producer of synthetic fibers, says it will start reevaluating all its senior employees every five years with the implied threat that those who don't measure up to the company's expectations will have to accept reassignment and possibly demotion; some may even be asked

---

[2] "Simmons in Japan, No Bed of Roses," *Sales Management*, August 1, 1967, pp. 27–29. Reprinted by permission from Sales & Marketing Management magazine. Copyright 1967.

to resign. A chemical engineering and construction firm is planning to ask all its employees over 42 to negotiate a new contract with the company every two years. Pay raises and promotions will go to those the company wants to keep. For those who think they are worth more than the company is willing to pay, the company will offer "retirement" with something less than the $15,000 lump-sum payment that the average Japanese worker receives when he reaches 55.

And a few U.S. companies operating in Japan are also experimenting with incentive plans. Nitta and Company, a belting manufacturer and Japanese distributor for Chesterton Packing and Seal Company, was persuaded by Chesterton to set up a travel plan incentive for salesmen who topped their regular sales quotas. Unorthodox as the idea was for Japan, Nitta went along and, the first year, special one-week trips to Far East holiday spots like Hong Kong, Taiwan, Manila, and Macao were inaugurated. Nitta's sales of Chesterton products jumped 212 percent and this year sales are up 60 percent over 1968.

Last April, Nitta took the full step toward an American-style sales program. Under Chesterton's guidance, the company eliminated bonuses and initiated a sales commission plan.

When the first quarterly commission checks were mailed last June, the top salesmen found they had earned an average of $550 per month each, compared to original basic salaries of about $100 a month.

At first, Nitta's management had resisted any form of incentive program for its personnel, arguing that it would "disrupt" all normal business operations of the company. The virtually instantaneous success of the travel incentives in motivating previously plodding sales performances into an enthusiastic burst of initiative has prompted Nitta to consider installing some form of incentive and/or commission sales plan for its extensive non-Chesterton operations. The company is one of the largest manufacturers of industrial belting in Japan.

IBM also has made a move toward chucking the traditional Japanese sales system (i.e., salary plus bonus but no incentives). For about a year it has been working with a combination which retains the semi-annual bonus while adding commission payments on the sales over pre-set quotas.

"It's difficult to apply a straight commission system in selling computers because of the complexities of the product," an IBM-Japan official said. "Our salesmen don't get big commissions because other employees would be jealous." To head off possible ill-feeling, therefore, some non-selling IBM employees receive monetary incentives.

Most Japanese companies seem reluctant to follow IBM's and Nitta's example because they have their doubts about directing older salesmen to go beyond their usual order-taking role. High-pressure tactics are not well accepted here, and sales channels are often pretty well set by custom and long practice (e.g., a manufacturer normally deals with one trading company, which in turn sells only to customers A, B, C, and D). A salesman or trading company, for that matter, is not often encouraged to go after customer Z and get him away from a rival supplier.

Japanese companies also consider non-sales employees a tough problem to handle. With salesmen deprived of the "glamour" status often accorded by many top managements in the United States, even Nitta executives admit they have a ticklish problem in explaining how salesmen—who are considered to be just another key working group in the company with no special status—rate incentive pay and special earning opportunities.[3]

The Japanese market is becoming more competitive and there is real fear on the part of N.O.M. executives that the traditional system just won't work in a competitive market. On the other hand, the proponents of the incentive system agree that the system really has not been tested over long periods or even very adequately, since it has only been applied in a growing market. In other words, was it the incentive system which caused the successes achieved by the companies or was it market growth? Especially is there doubt since other companies following the traditional method of compensation and employee relations have also had sales increases during the same period.

The problem is further complicated for Nippon/American because they will have both new and old salesmen. The young Japanese seem eager to accept the incentive method but older men are hesitant. How do you satisfy both since you must, by agreement, retain all the sales staff? Another very critical problem lies with the nonsales employees; traditionally, all employees on the same level are treated equally whether sales, production, or staff. How do you encourage competitive, aggressive salesmanship in a market unfamiliar to such tactics, and how do you compensate salesmen in such a manner to promote more aggressive selling in the face of tradition-bound practices of paternalistic company behavior?

---

[3] "How to Put New Hustle into a Japanese Salesman," *Business Abroad*, November 27, 1967, pp. 33–34. Reprinted with permission.

Data Evaluation Questions

Directions: The questions that follow relate to the preceding passage. Evaluate, in terms of the passage, each of the items given. Then select your answer from one of the following classifications, and blacken the corresponding space on the answer sheet.

(A) A MAJOR OBJECTIVE in making the decision: one of the goals sought by the decision maker

(B) A MAJOR FACTOR in making the decision: an aspect of the problem, specifically mentioned in the passage, that fundamentally affects and/ or determines the decision

(C) A MINOR FACTOR in making the decision: a less important element bearing on or affecting a Major Factor, rather than a Major Objective directly

(D) A MAJOR ASSUMPTION in making the decision: a projection or supposition arrived at by the decision maker before considering the factors and alternatives

(E) AN UNIMPORTANT ISSUE in making the decision: an item lacking significant impact on, or relationship to, the decision

19. Motivating Japanese salesmen

20. Using U.S. compensation methods in Japan

21. Labor-management relations

22. Job security of Japanese workers

23. Retaining the current Nippon sales force

24. Doubling the sales force

25. The establishment of Nippon in 1872

26. Determining a sales compensation plan

27. Differences in American and Japanese fringe benefits

28. Understanding the Japanese class system

29. The reevaluation of senior employees by Toyo Rayon

30. Regular pay raises in Japan

31. Expanding N.C.M.'s product line

32. Selling to Japanese trading companies

33. Inproving N.C.M.'s management

34. The traditional compensation system cannot work in a competitive market

35. N.O.M.'s aggressive sales force

*If there is still time remaining, you may review the questions in this
section only. You may not turn to any other section of the test.*

Section VIII   Writing Ability   Time: 30 minutes

Directions: This test consists of a number of sentences, in each of which some
part or the whole is underlined. Each sentence is followed by five alternative
versions of the underlined portion. Select the alternative you consider both
most correct and most effective according to the requirements of standard
written English. Answer A is the same as the original version; if you think the
original version is best, select answer A.

In considering the answer choices, be attentive to matters of grammar, diction, and syntax, as well as clarity, precision, and fluency. Do not select an
answer which alters the meaning of the original sentence.

1. Although I calculate that he will be here any minute, I cannot wait much
   longer for him to arrive.

   (A) Although I calculate that he will be here
   (B) Although I reckon that he will be here
   (C) Because I calculate that he will be here
   (D) Although I think that he will be here
   (E) Because I am confident that he will be here

2. The fourteen-hour day not only has been reduced to one of ten hours but
   also, in some lines of work, to one of eight or even six.

   (A) The fourteen-hour day not only has been reduced

(B) Not only the fourteen-hour day has been reduced
(C) Not the fourteen-hour day only has been reduced
(D) The fourteen-hour day has not only been reduced
(E) The fourteen-hour day has been reduced not only

3. The trend toward a decrease is further evidenced in the longer weekend already given to employees in many business establishments.

(A) already
(B) all ready
(C) allready
(D) ready
(E) all in all

4. Using it wisely, leisure promotes health, efficiency, and happiness.

(A) Using it wisely,
(B) If used wisely,
(C) Having used it wisely,
(D) Because it is used wisely,
(E) Because of usefulness,

5. Americans are learning that their concept of a research worker, toiling alone in his laboratory and who discovers miraculous cures has been highly idealized and glamorized.

(A) toiling alone in his laboratory and who discovers miraculous cures
(B) toiling in his laboratory by himself and discovers miraculous cures
(C) toiling alone in his laboratory to discover miraculous cures,
(D) who toil alone in the laboratory and discover miraculous cures
(E) toiling in his laboratory to discover miraculous cures by himself

6. We want the teacher to be him who has the best rapport with the students.

(A) We want the teacher to be him
(B) We want the teacher to be he
(C) We want him to be the teacher
(D) We desire that the teacher be him
(E) We anticipate that the teacher will be him

7. If he were to win the medal, I for one would be disturbed.

   (A) If he were to win the medal,
   (B) If he was to win the medal,
   (C) If he wins the medal,
   (D) If he is the winner of the medal,
   (E) In the event that he wins the medal,

8. The scouts were told to take an overnight hike, pitch camp, prepare dinner, and that they should be in bed by 9 p.m.

   (A) to take an overnight hike, pitch camp, prepare dinner, and that they should be in bed by 9 p.m.
   (B) to take an overnight hike, to pitch camp, to prepare dinner, and that they should be in bed by 9 p.m.
   (C) to take an overnight hike, pitch camp, prepare dinner, and be in bed by 9 p.m.
   (D) to take an overnight hike, pitching camp, preparing dinner and going to bed by 9 p.m.
   (E) to engage in an overnight hike, pitch camp, prepare dinner, and that they should be in bed by 9 p.m.

9. The dean informed us that the applicant had not and never will be accepted by the college because of his high school record.

   (A) applicant had not and never will be accepted by the college because of his high school record
   (B) applicant had not and never would be accepted by the college because of his high school record
   (C) applicant had not been and never will be excepted by the college because of his high school record
   (D) applicant had not been and never would be excepted by the college because of his high school record
   (E) applicant had not been and never would be accepted by the college because of his high school record

10. The government's failing to keep it's pledges will earn the distrust of all the other nations in the alliance.

   (A) government's failing to keep it's pledges
   (B) government failing to keep it's pledges

(C) government's failing to keep its pledges
(D) government failing to keep its pledges
(E) governments failing to keep their pledges

11. Her brother along with her parents insist that she remain in school.

   (A) insist
   (B) insists
   (C) are insisting
   (D) were insisting
   (E) have insisted

12. Most students like to read these kind of books during their spare time.

   (A) these kind of books
   (B) these kind of book
   (C) this kind of book
   (D) this kinds of books
   (E) those kind of books

13. She not only was competent but also friendly in nature.

   (A) She not only was competent but also friendly
   (B) Not only was she competent but friendly also
   (C) She not only was competent but friendly also
   (D) She was not only competent but also friendly
   (E) She was not only competent but friendly also

14. In the normal course of events, John will graduate high school and enter college in two years.

   (A) John will graduate high school and enter
   (B) John will graduate from high school and enter
   (C) John will be graduated from high school and enter
   (D) John will be graduated from high school and enter into
   (E) John will have graduated high school and enter

15. With the exception of <u>Frank and I, everyone in the class finished</u> the assignment before the bell rang.

   (A) Frank and I, everyone in the class finished
   (B) Frank and me, everyone in the class finished
   (C) Frank and me, everyone in the class had finished
   (D) Frank and I, everyone in the class had finished
   (E) Frank and me everyone in the class finished

16. Many middle-class individuals find that they cannot obtain good medical attention, <u>despite they need it badly</u>.

   (A) despite they need it badly
   (B) despite they badly need it
   (C) in spite of they need it badly
   (D) however much they need it
   (E) therefore, they need it badly

17. During the winter of 1973, Americans <u>discovered the need to conserve energy and attempts were made to meet the crisis.</u>

   (A) discovered the need to conserve energy and attempts were made to meet the crisis
   (B) discovered the need to conserve energy and that the crisis had to be met
   (C) discovered the need to conserve energy and attempted to meet the crisis
   (D) needed to conserve energy and to meet the crisis
   (E) needed to conserve energy and attempts were made to meet the crisis

18. <u>When one eats in this restaurant, you often find</u> that the prices are high and that the food is poorly prepared.

   (A) When one eats in this restaurant, you often find
   (B) When you eat in this restaurant, one often finds
   (C) As you eat in this restaurant, you often find
   (D) If you eat in this restaurant, you often find
   (E) When one ate in this restaurant, he often found

19. Ever since the bombing of Cambodia, there has been much opposition <u>from they who maintain that it was an unauthorized war.</u>

(A) from they who maintain that it was an unauthorized war

(B) from they who maintain that it had been an unauthorized war

(C) from those who maintain that it was an unauthorized war

(D) from they maintaining that it was unauthorized

(E) from they maintaining that it had been unauthorized

20. John was <u>imminently qualified for the position because he had studied computer programming and how to operate an IBM machine.</u>

    (A) imminently qualified for the position because he had studied computer programming and how to operate an IBM machine

    (B) imminently qualified for the position because he had studied computer programming and the operation of an IBM machine

    (C) eminently qualified for the position because he had studied computer programming and how to operate an IBM machine

    (D) eminently qualified for the position because he had studied computer programming and the operation of an IBM machine

    (E) eminently qualified because he had studied computer programming and how to operate an IBM machine

21. <u>I am not to eager to go to this play because it did not get good reviews.</u>

    (A) I am not to eager to go to this play because it did not get good reviews.

    (B) Because of its poor reviews, I am not to eager to go to this play.

    (C) Because of its poor revues, I am not to eager to go to this play.

    (D) I am not to eager to go to this play because the critics did not give it good reviews.

    (E) I am not too eager to go to this play because of its poor reviews.

22. <u>It was decided by us that the emphasis would be placed on the results that might be attained.</u>

    (A) It was decided by us that the emphasis would be placed on the results that might be attained.

    (B) We decided that the emphasis would be placed on the results that might be attained.

    (C) We decided to emphasize the results that might be attained.

    (D) We decided to emphasize the results we might attain.

    (E) It was decided that we would place emphasis on the results that might be attained.

23. May I venture to say that I think this performance is the most superior I have ever heard.
    (A) May I venture to say that I think this performance is the most superior
    (B) May I venture to say that this performance is the most superior
    (C) May I say that this performance is the most superior
    (D) I think this performance is superior to any
    (E) This performance is the most superior of any

24. Completing the physical examination, the tonsils were found to be diseased.
    (A) Completing the physical examination, the tonsils were found to be diseased.
    (B) Having completed the physical examination, the tonsils were found to be diseased.
    (C) When the physical examination was completed, the tonsils were found to be diseased.
    (D) The physical examination completed, the tonsils were found to be diseased.
    (E) The physical examination found that the tonsils were diseased.

25. Today this is a totally different world than we have seen in the last decade.
    (A) than we have seen
    (B) from what we have seen
    (C) from what we seen
    (D) than what we seen
    (E) then we have seen

If there is still time remaining, you may review the questions in this section only. You may not turn to any other section of the test.

Answers

Section I   Reading Comprehension

1. (D)	8. (B)	15. (D)	22. (B)
2. (C)	9. (C)	16. (E)	23. (B)
3. (C)	10. (A)	17. (C)	24. (A)
4. (C)	11. (B)	18. (C)	25. (D)
5. (E)	12. (C)	19. (C)	
6. (C)	13. (C)	20. (D)	
7. (A)	14. (D)	21. (E)	

Section II Data Sufficiency

1. (D)	8. (E)	15. (E)	22. (C)
2. (C)	9. (A)	16. (B)	23. (E)
3. (E)	10. (A)	17. (C)	24. (B)
4. (D)	11. (C)	18. (A)	25. (E)
5. (C)	12. (E)	19. (A)	
6. (E)	13. (C)	20. (A)	
7. (B)	14. (E)	21. (D)	

Section III Problem Solving

1. (D)	6. (E)	11. (B)	16. (E)
2. (E)	7. (E)	12. (A)	17. (C)
3. (C)	8. (D)	13. (B)	18. (A)
4. (D)	9. (D)	14. (C)	19. (C)
5. (D)	10. (B)	15. (B)	20. (A)

Section IV Analysis of Situations

1. (E)	11. (D)	21. (B)	31. (B)
2. (A)	12. (A)	22. (B)	32. (D)
3. (B)	13. (B)	23. (C)	33. (A)
4. (C)	14. (C)	24. (B)	34. (B)
5. (A)	15. (E)	25. (A)	35. (E)
6. (B)	16. (E)	26. (C)	
7. (D)	17. (B)	27. (B)	
8. (E)	18. (E)	28. (E)	
9. (C)	19. (A)	29. (E)	
10. (D)	20. (E)	30. (B)	

Section V Data Sufficiency

1. (E)	8. (B)	15. (A)	22. (A)
2. (C)	9. (E)	16. (E)	23. (E)
3. (A)	10. (E)	17. (C)	24. (C)
4. (E)	11. (A)	18. (D)	25. (E)
5. (D)	12. (C)	19. (A)	
6. (D)	13. (E)	20. (E)	
7. (B)	14. (B)	21. (C)	

Section VI   Problem Solving

1. (D)	6. (B)	11. (C)	16. (C)
2. (E)	7. (C)	12. (B)	17. (B)
3. (B)	8. (C)	13. (D)	18. (C)
4. (D)	9. (B)	14. (E)	19. (E)
5. (C)	10. (D)	15. (D)	20. (E)

Section VII   Analysis of Situations

1. (B)	11. (B)	21. (B)	31. (A)
2. (B)	12. (E)	22. (C)	32. (E)
3. (A)	13. (C)	23. (B)	33. (A)
4. (D)	14. (E)	24. (A)	34. (D)
5. (B)	15. (C)	25. (E)	35. (E)
6. (D)	16. (E)	26. (A)	
7. (C)	17. (B)	27. (C)	
8. (E)	18. (C)	28. (B)	
9. (A)	19. (A)	29. (E)	
10. (D)	20. (D)	30. (C)	

Section VIII   Writing Ability

1. (D)	8. (C)	15. (C)	22. (D)
2. (E)	9. (E)	16. (D)	23. (D)
3. (A)	10. (C)	17. (C)	24. (E)
4. (B)	11. (B)	18. (C)	25. (B)
5. (C)	12. (C)	19. (C)	
6. (A)	13. (D)	20. (D)	
7. (A)	14. (D)	21. (E)	

Analysis

Section I   Reading Comprehension

1. **(D)** Note that the question asks "about how many" which requires an approximate figure. Of all the alternative answers, (D) comes closest to the 8,600 employees given in paragraph 1.

2. **(C)** See paragraph 3.

3. **(C)** See paragraph 5: "Top Presidential appointees, . . . bear the brunt of translating the philosophy and aims of the current administration into practical programs."

4. **(C)** See paragraph 6, sentence 2.

5. **(E)** See paragraph 6, last line.

6. **(C)** See paragraph 7: "Those whom the president selects. . . ." and following.

7. **(A)** See paragraph 8: ". . . they usually have substantial responsibilities in line management. . . ."

8. **(B)** Paragraph 8: "These appointees are primarily regarded as policy makers. . . ."

9. **(C)** See paragraph 7: "Those selected by department and agency heads . . ." and following.

10. **(A)** See paragraph 1.

11. **(B)** See paragraph 2: ". . . all resellers are bound by the terms of the . . . contract. . . ."

12. **(C)** This is implied throughout the passage.

13. **(C)** See paragraph 4.

14. **(D)** Paragraph 5: "Responsibility for enforcement falls upon the producer or distributor. . . ."

15. **(D)** See paragraph 3: "Closeout sales are excepted."

16. **(E)** This is found in paragraph 2.

17. **(C)** See paragraph 5: ". . . granting of trading stamps in abnormally high volume. . . ."

18. **(C)** See paragraph 1.

19. **(C)** Energy savings are mentioned in paragraph 4, employment benefits in paragraph 6. Pollution, on the contrary, would increase: see the last paragraph.

20. **(D)** Only coal and shale are mentioned.

21. **(E)** $20 billion is to be appropriated over the first five years and another

$68 billion over the following seven years, i.e. $88 billion over a period of twelve years.

22. **(B)** See paragraph 4.

23. **(B)** See paragraph 2.

24. **(A)** See the last paragraph.

25. **(D)** See paragraph 7.

Section II   Data Sufficiency

1. **(D)** (1) alone is sufficient, since if two sides of a triangle are equal, the angles opposite the equal sides are equal. Since $AB = BC$ then $x = y$, so $x = 40$. (2) alone is sufficient since the sum of the angles of a triangle is $180°$. Therefore, if $z = 100$ and $y = 40$, x must equal $180 - 100 - 40 = 40$. Therefore, each statement alone is sufficient.

2. **(C)** (1) tells us the area of the circle is $\pi 4^2 = 16\pi$. Since there are $360°$ in the whole circle, (2) tells us that the shaded area is $60/360$ or $1/6$ of the area of the circle. Thus, using both (1) and (2), we can answer the question, but since we need both the radius of the circle and the value of x, neither of them alone is sufficient. Therefore, the answer is (C).

3. **(E)** Using (1) we can find the income for 1970 if we know the income for 1968 and 1969, but (1) gives no more information about the income for 1968 and 1969. If we also use (2) we can get the income in 1969 if we know the income for 1968, but we still can't determine the income for 1968. Therefore, both together are not sufficient.

4. **(D)** Since a straight line forms an angle of $180°$ and l' is a straight line, we know $x + y = 180$. If we use (1) we get $y = 80$, so (1) alone is sufficient. When two straight lines intersect, the vertical angles are equal. So $y = z$; thus if we use (2) we get $y = 80$. Therefore, (2) alone is sufficient. Thus, each statement alone is sufficient.

5. **(C)** In the figure, x denotes the number taking German I but not English I, and y the number taking English I but not German I. From (1) we know that $x + 16 + y = 50$; from (2), $x = y$. Neither statement alone can be solved for x, but both together are sufficient (and yield $x = 17$).

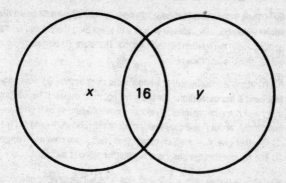

6. **(E)** (1) alone is not sufficient because it only says two sides are equal; in a square all four sides are equal. Even if we use (2) we don't know if *ABCD* is a square since *all* angles have to be right angles in a square. Therefore, both statements together are insufficient.

7. **(B)** The average yearly wage per employee is the total amount of wages divided by the number of employees. So (2) alone is sufficient since it gives the total amount of wages and we are given the number of employees. (1) alone is not sufficient, since (1) by itself does not tell us the total wages. Therefore, the answer is (B).

8. **(E)** Since the square of any nonzero number is positive, (1) says $x + y \neq$ 0 or $x \neq -y$. So (1) alone is not sufficient. If we also assume (2), we know only that x is positive and unequal to $-y$, not whether x is greater than or less than y. Thus (1) and (2) together are insufficient.

9. **(A)** Since the circles both have radius 4, the figure $OBO'C$ is a rhombus (each side is a radius) and the diagonals BC and OO' (of a rhombus) are perpendicular. So (2) does not give any new information, and is thus not sufficient alone. (1) alone is sufficient. The area of each circle is 16π since the radius of each circle is 4. If there were no shaded area, the area enclosed by both circles would be $16\pi + 16\pi = 32\pi$. Since the area enclosed by both circles is 29π, the shaded area is $32\pi - 29\pi$ or 3π. So (1) alone is sufficient but (2) alone is insufficient.

10. **(A)** Let x be the time it takes to travel from *A* to *B* and let y be the time it takes to travel from *B* to *A*. We know $x + y = 4$. (1) says x is 125% of y or $x = \frac{5}{4}y$. So using (1) we have $x + \frac{5}{4}x = 4$ which we can solve

for x. Thus, (1) alone is sufficient. (2) alone is not sufficient since we need information about the relation of x to y to solve the problem and (2) says nothing about the relation between x and y. Therefore, (1) alone is sufficient but (2) alone is insufficient.

11. **(C)** (1) alone is insufficient. If x and y were right angles, (1) would imply that l and l' are parallel, but if x and y are not right angles, (1) would imply that l and l' are not parallel. (2) alone is not sufficient since it gives information only about l' and says nothing about the relation of l and l'. (1) and (2) together give $x = z$ which means that l and l' are parallel. Therefore, (1) and (2) together are sufficient but neither alone is sufficient.

12. **(E)** If we use (1), we have $x + y + z = 3 + z$, but we have no information about z, so (1) alone is insufficient. If we use (2) alone, we have $x + y + z = y + 2$, but since we have no information about y, (2) alone is insufficient. If we use both (1) and (2), we obtain $x + y + z = y + 2 = 3 + z$. We can also add (1) and (2) to obtain $2x + y + z = 5$, but we can't find the value of $x + y + z$ without more information. So the answer is (E).

13. **(C)** We need to know the surface area of the box. Since each side is a rectangle, we know the surface area will be $2LW + 2LH + 2HW$ where H is the height of the box, L is the length, and W is the width. We are given that $L = 7$, so to answer the question we need H and W. Since (1) gives only the value of W and (2) gives only the value of H, neither alone is sufficient. But both (1) and (2) together are sufficient.

14. **(E)** The profit is the selling price minus the cost, so to answer the question we need to know both the selling price and the cost of 15 boxes of detergent. Since (1) and (2) give information only about the cost but no information about the selling price, both statements together are insufficient.

15. **(E)** (1) alone is not sufficient. A four-sided figure can have both larger perimeter and smaller area than another four-sided figure, or it could have larger perimeter and larger area. (2) alone is also insufficient since the length of one diagonal does not determine the area of a four-sided figure. (1) and (2) together are also insufficient, as shown by the figure.

(1) and (2) are both satisfied and the area of $EFGH$ is larger than $ABCD$. But (1) and (2) could still be satisfied and the area of $ABCD$ be larger than the area of $EFGH$; so the answer is (E).

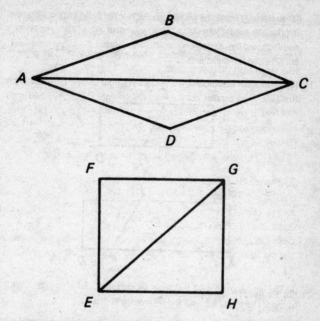

16. **(B)** Statement (1) alone is not sufficient, since 12 is divisible by 3 but 12 is not divisible by 9. Statement (2) alone is sufficient, since if a number is divisible by 27 then, because $27 = 9 \times 3$, the number must be divisible by 9.

17. **(C)** Statement (1) is not sufficient. (1) will let you figure out the length of the side *SP*; however, you need to know the length of *SR* or *PQ* to find the area. Statement (2) alone is not sufficient. (2) will allow you to find the length of *PQ*, but you also need to know the length of *SP* or *RQ*.

    Statements (1) and (2) together are sufficient.

18. **(A)** Both regions *ABEF* and *CDFE* are trapezoids, so their area is given by the formula $a\,(\frac{1}{2}[b_1 + b_2])$ where a is an altitude and b_1 and b_2 are the sides perpendicular to the altitude. Since *ABCD* is a rectangle, $AB = CD$, which means the altitudes are the same length for each region. So it is sufficient to know whether $BE + AF$ is larger than $EC + FD$.

    Statement (1) alone is sufficient, since, if *BE* is larger than *FD*, then *BC* –

BE, which is *EC*, must be smaller than *AD* − *FD* = *AF*. (*AD* = *BC* since *ABCD* is a rectangle.) So *BE* + *AF* is larger than *EC* + *FD*.

Statement (2) alone is not sufficient, since either region could be larger if *BE* is larger than *CD* (See figures).

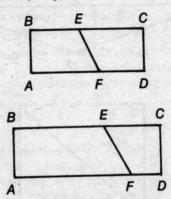

19. **(A)** The square of an even integer is always even. So if k^2 is odd, k can't be even. Therefore, k is odd and (1) alone is sufficient.

Statement (2) alone is not sufficient, since $2k$ is even for every integer k.

20. **(A)** Statement (1) alone is sufficient, since using (1) implies that the car can travel 125 miles using 5 gallons of fuel.

Statement (2) alone is not sufficient. The speed is not enough to determine how far the car can travel.

21. **(D)** The area of the region is the area of the square plus the area of the semicircle. So you must be able to determine the length of a side of the square and the length of the radius of the semicircle. Since the radius is ½ of *BC*, it is sufficient to determine either the radius or the length of a side of the square. Statement (1) alone is sufficient, since the diagonal of a square is $\sqrt{2}$ times the length of a side. Statement (2) alone is sufficient, since the length of a side of the square is twice the radius.

22. **(C)** Using statements (1) and (2), you can determine the distance from *P* to (0,0) and the distance from *Q* to (0,0). The distances are equal if and only if *P* and *Q* are on the same circle with center (0,0). Neither statement alone is sufficient, since you need to know both distances.

23. **(E)** Both statements together give no information about the year 1980.

24. **(B)** Since 2^n is n "copies" of 2 multiplied together, 2^n is divisible by 8 if and only if n is greater than or equal to 3. (This is because $8 = 2 \times 2 \times 2 = 2^3$). Therefore, (2) alone is sufficient.

    Statement (1) alone is not sufficient, because there are odd numbers less than 3 (for example, 1) and odd numbers greater than 3.

25. **(E)** The fact that the price is higher at the end of the year than it was at the beginning of the year does not imply that the price rose every week during the year. The price could have gone up and down many times during the year.

Section III   Problem Solving

1. **(D)** Since he pays 6% on the first $500, this equals (.06)(500) or $30 interest on the first $500. He is borrowing $5,500 which is $5,000 in excess of the first $500. Thus, he also pays 5½% of $5,000, which is (.055)(5,000) or $275.00. Therefore, the total interest is $305.

2. **(E)** $6x - 3y$ is $3(2x - y)$. Since $2x - y = 4$, $6x - 3y = 3 \cdot 4$ or 12.

3. **(C)** The progression is arithmetic and $11 - 5 = 6 = 17 - 11$, so every term is 6 more than the previous team. Therefore, the next term after 17 is $17 + 6$ or 23.

4. **(D)** The bar was above 50 in 1947.

5. **(D)** In 1952, hydro plants had about 21 million kilowatts, while the total capacity was about 84 million kilowatts. Therefore, the capacity of the steam and internal combustion plants in 1952 was about $(84 - 21)$ or 63 million kilowatts. Since $\frac{63}{21} = 3$, x is 3.

6. **(E)**
   STATEMENT I is true since the graph is almost horizontal between 1930 and 1939, whereas it rises between 1920 and 1929 and between 1940 and 1949.

   Since the total capacity in 1925 was less than 25 million kilowatts and the capacity of the hydro plants in 1925 was more than 5 million kilowatts, STATEMENT II can be inferred.

   STATEMENT III is also true. Between 1925 and 1945, the capacity went from about 22 million to about 50 million kilowatts, which is an increase of about 28 million kilowatts. However, the capacity in 1925 was about 83 million kilowatts, so the increase between 1945 and 1952 was about 33 million kilowatts.

Therefore, STATEMENTS I, II, and III can all be inferred from the graph.

7. **(E)** Since each packer loads ⅛ of a box in 9 minutes, the 20 packers will load ²⁰⁄₈, or 2½ boxes in 9 minutes. There are 90 minutes in 1½ hours; so the 20 packers will load 10 × 2½ or 25 boxes in 1½ hours.

8. **(D)** The entire population can be divided into three nonoverlapping parts: owns both a car and a motorcyle, owns a car but not a motorcycle, and owns a motorcycle but not a car. If we denote these categories by A, B, and C respectively, we know that $A + B + C = 100\%$. Also, since $A + B$ consists of all the people who own a car, we have $A + B = 90\%$. Therefore, C must be 10%. But C is the category of people who own a motorcycle but do not own a car.

9. **(D)** To do computations, change percentages to decimals. Let J, M, B, and L stand for Jim's, Marcia's, Bob's, and Lee's respective weights. Then we know $J = 1.4M$, $B = .9L$, and $L = 2M$. We need to know B as a percentage of J. Since $B = .9L$ and $L = 2M$, we have $B = .9 (2M) = 1.8M$. $J = 1.4M$ is equivalent to $M = 1/(1.4)J$. So $B = 1.8M = 1.8(1/(1.4))J = (1²⁄₇)J$. Converting 1²⁄₇ to a percentage, we have 1²⁄₇ = 1.28⁴⁄₇ = 128⁴⁄₇%, so (D) is the correct answer.

10. **(B)** The towns can be thought of as the vertices of a triangle.

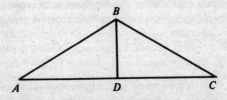

Since the distance from A to B is equal to the distance from B to C, the triangle is isosceles. The point D on AC which is closest to B is the point on AC such that BD is perpendicular to AC. (If BD were not perpendicular to AC, then there would be a point on AC closer to B than D; in the picture, E is closer to B than D is.)

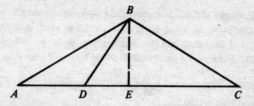

So the triangles ABD and CBD are right triangles with two corresponding sides equal. Therefore ABD is congruent to CBD. Thus $AD = DC$, and since AC is 60, AD must be 30. Since ABD is a right triangle with hypotenuse 50 and another side $= 30$, the remaining side (BD) must be 40.

11. **(B)** Since 108% of $50 $= (1.08)(50) = 54, the chair was offered for sale at $54.00. It was sold for 90% of $54 since there was a 10% discount. Therefore, the chair was sold for $(.9)($54)$ or $48.60.

12. **(A)** Here's a table of the hours worked:

	Mon.	Tues.	Wed.	Thurs.	Fri.	Wages for week
	8	8	8	8	8	$5x$
excess over 8 hrs	0	3	1	2	1	$(0 + 3 + 1 + 2 + 1)y = 7y.$

The average daily wage equals $\dfrac{(5x + 7y)}{5}$, or $x + \dfrac{7}{5}y$.

13. **(B)** There are 8 choices for the first female, then 7 choices for the second female, and 6 choices for the third female on the committee. So there are $8 \times 7 \times 6$ different ways to pick the three females in order. However, if member A is chosen first, then member B, then member C, the same three females are chosen as when C is followed by A and B is chosen last. In fact, the same three members can be chosen in $3 \times 2 \times 1$ different orders. So to find the number of different groups of 3 females, DIVIDE $8 \times 7 \times 6$ by $3 \times 2 \times 1$ to obtain 56.

In the same way, there are $8 \times 7 \times 6 = 336$ ways to choose the three males in order, but any group of three males can be put in order $3 \times 2 \times 1 = 6$ different ways. So there are $^{336}/_{6} = 56$ different groups of three males. Therefore, there are $56 \times 56 = 3,136$ different committees of 3 males and 3 females.

14. **(C)** Let x_n be what the car is worth after n years. Then we know $x_0 = \$2,500$ and $x_{n+1} = \frac{4}{5} \times x_n$. So $x_1 = \frac{4}{5} \times 2,500$, which is $\$2,000$. x_2 is $\frac{4}{5} \times 2,000$, which is 1,600, and finally x_3 is $\frac{4}{5} \times 1,600$, which is 1,280. Therefore, the car is worth $\$1,280$ at the end of three years.

OR

$$x_3 = \frac{4}{5}x_2 = \frac{4}{5}(\frac{4}{5}x_1) = (\frac{4}{5})(\frac{4}{5})(\frac{4}{5}x_0) = \frac{64}{125}x_0.$$
$(\frac{64}{125})2500 = 1280.$

15. **(B)** Since 120 miles is $\frac{3}{5}$ of 200 miles, it should cost $\frac{3}{5}$ of $\$15$ to travel 120 miles by automobile. Therefore, the cost is $\$9$.

16. **(E)** Since the only costs are $\$20$ for fuel and $\$70$ for the driver's wages, the total cost is $\$90$. Therefore, the company should charge 120% of $\$90$, which is $(1.2)(\$90)$ or $\$108$.

17. **(C)** The total fuel cost will be $3 \cdot 20 + 4 \cdot 15 + 2 \cdot 5 + 1 \cdot 50$, which is $\$180$. Since there are 10 vehicles, the average fuel cost is 180/10 or $\$18$ per vehicle.

18. **(A)** Since $x + 2y = 2x + y$, we can subtract $x + 2y$ from each side of the equation and the result is $0 = x - y$.

19. **(C)** $\frac{2}{3}$ of the 15% of the families with income over $\$25,000$ own boats. Since $\frac{2}{3}$ of 15% = 10%, $\frac{1}{10}$ of the families own boats and have an income of $\$25,000$ or more.

20. **(A)** The angles are in the ratio of 1:2:2, so 2 angles are equal to each other, and both are twice as large as the third angle of the triangle. Since a triangle with two equal angles must have the sides opposite equal, the triangle is isosceles. (Using the fact that the sum of the angles of a triangle is 180°, you can see that the angles of the triangle are 72°, 72° and 36°, so only (A) is true.)

Section IV   Analysis of Situations

1. **(E)** Fox's twenty years experience have no significant impact on the decision as to how to increase lottery sales.

2. **(A)** Increasing the number of instant lottery games was a *Major Objective* of Kamil, aimed at boosting lottery sales. *Increasing* the number of games, therefore, was an outcome sought.

3. **(B)** Note the word "stagnating." Stagnation is certainly not an outcome sought; rather, it is a condition which must be changed. The leveling off

of lottery sales is a *Major Factor* in the decision process, since it forces the lottery directors to search for means of reversing this trend.

4. **(C)** The cost of the advertising campaign, while a factor in the decision, was limited to only one of the alternatives considered in the decision as to how to increase lottery sales.

5. **(A)** Increasing sales of lottery games by at least 30 percent was a major outcome desired by Kamil.

6. **(B)** The number of tickets to be sold was a *Major Factor* associated with all decision alternatives. In paragraph 4, the situation is described. In other parts of the passage, decision alternatives such as subscriptions, increasing the number of instant games (to sell more tickets), and the introduction of consolation prizes for the Lotto, all deal with increasing the *number* of tickets sold.

7. **(D)** Fishman raised the issue that members of the lower classes were the main purchasers of instant game tickets. Although this contention appeared in the press, management had no definite evidence that non-buyers were from the upper income groups. It is possible that there were lottery ticket buyers from upper-income groups and middle-income groups as well.

8. **(E)** The long history of lottery sales in Tibland has no bearing on any of the decision alternatives.

9. **(C)** The printing costs of special tickets is a *Minor Factor*. It is only one element in the *overall cost* of the decision alternative to issue subscriptions. The other element is circulation cost. The entire cost of introducing subscriptions would be a *Major Factor*.

10. **(D)** Fishman *believed* that the purchasing behavior of lottery buyers in Europe and Tibland was similar. No facts were presented to support his contention.

11. **(D)** That advertising stimulates sales must be taken as an *assumption* in this case. The argument for more advertising is put forward by Fox, based on his "experience." He did not present any facts to show, for example, that when advertising expenditures increased, sales increased, or some similar, clearly demonstrable relationship.

12. **(A)** Attracting new buyers is one of the outcomes desired by the decision makers. See paragraph 9.

13. **(B)** According to the passage, the limited budget within which the lottery must operate would make certain expensive schemes impossible. This restriction is a *Major Factor* in selecting a decision alternative.

14. **(C)** Cost of the subscriptions is a major determinant of whether consumers will purchase them and therefore a factor in management's decision as to whether to offer the product. It is a *Minor Factor* since it relates only to one alternative.

15. **(E)** The type of people serving on the board of directors is not an element in the decision making process.

16. **(E)** The fact that lotteries were run every Monday was an *Unimportant Issue* and had no bearing on any decision alternative.

17. **(B)** A major consideration of whether to adopt the alternative of subscriptions is whether enough people would be willing to pay in advance. Fox thought not, while Davis and Fishman believed in the affirmative.

18. **(E)** While winning numbers were selected at random by computer, this fact was an *Unimportant Issue* in the decision consideration.

19. **(A)** Determining compensation policy for overseas executives is an outcome desired by Len Hibert.

20. **(E)** The fact that the company produces industrial equipment does not influence the selection of an alternative course of action.

21. **(B)** As Len's company becomes more international, more emphasis has been placed on the "type and functions" of its managers sent abroad. This importance is a *Major Factor* in determining a compensation program (a major objective).

22. **(B)** The country in which an executive will be located is a major issue in determining what his compensation will be. For example, the cost-of-living is different according to location (see the table in the passage), and executives may have to be compensated accordingly.

23. **(C)** The cost of renting a house in Europe is only one of several factors that determine the total cost of living abroad, which is a Major Factor.

24. **(B)** The cost-of-living abroad is a major determinant of an overseas executive's compensation package.

25. **(A)** In addition to determining a compensation plan, Len Hibert was re-

sponsible for selecting the "right" sort of person for overseas assignments. See the last paragraph.

26. **(C)** Returning executives "into regular company operations" is a problem. One of the causes of the problem was that the salary and benefits that the overseas executive had enjoyed were lost when he returned for domestic assignment. However, dissatisfaction with domestic salary is only one of the causes of the problem. The problem, of course, is related to the question of whether the policy of rotating key personnel in foreign assignments should continue.

27. **(B)** The disadvantages of rotating key personnel in foreign assignments are major considerations in the decision to maintain the policy. See the discussion of Mr. Brown's case in the passage.

28. **(E)** Hibert's company has manufacturing facilities in six countries. The *number* of countries is not a consideration in any alternative course of action. It is not the number of firms that is important, but rather the fact that the company has become multinational.

29. **(E)** The fact that the company has operated abroad for over 40 years is an *Unimportant Issue*. The time period is not a consideration in any decision alternative.

30. **(B)** The company philosophy of becoming more international in thought as well as in practice has created a demand for a different sort of manager. This philosophy is a *Major Factor* that affects the decision as to employee recruiting, selection, and compensation.

31. **(B)** Most host countries are becoming increasingly restrictive in their policies toward foreigners working in their countries. This is a *Major Factor* that affects the decision as to employee selection, since employees will be expected to train nationals to replace them.

32. **(D)** Increased abductions of American executives in South America led Hibert to assume that the trend would cause more resistance by personnel to work in that area.

33. **(A)** Given the mounting dissatisfaction of managers to accept overseas assignments, a *Major Objective* of Len Hibert is to formulate a new policy that will motivate key talent to fill positions abroad.

34. **(B)** A major problem in the integration of returning managers is the extent to which they experienced cultural shock abroad. The extent of this shock is a *Major Factor* to be considered in the decision to assign a returning manager to a position in the home company.

35. **(E)** The fact that the Browns lived in Paris was an *Unimportant Issue*. What was important, however, was the experience the Brown family had intergrating into French society and subsequently readjusting to the lifestyle in Chicago after Brown's transfer back to the States.

Section V   Data Sufficiency

1. **(E)**
   Since STATEMENT (1) describes only x and STATEMENT (2) describes only y, both are needed to get an answer. Using STATEMENT (2), STATEMENT (1) becomes $3x = 2k = 2y^2$, so $x = \dfrac{2y^2}{3}$. However, this is not sufficient, since if $y = -1$ then $x = \frac{2}{3}$ and x is greater than y, but if $y = 1$ then again $x = \frac{2}{3}$ but now x is less than y.

   Therefore, STATEMENTS (1) and (2) together are not sufficient.

2. **(C)**
   $ABCD$ is a parallelogram if AB is parallel to CD and BC is parallel to AD. STATEMENT (2) tells you that AB is parallel to CD, but this is not sufficient since a trapezoid has only one pair of opposite sides parallel. Thus, STATEMENT (2) alone is not sufficient.

   STATEMENT (1) alone is not sufficient since a trapezoid can have the two nonparallel sides equal.

   However, using STATEMENTS (1) and (2) together we can deduce that BC is parallel to AD, since the distance from BC to AD is equal along two different parallel lines.

3. **(A)**
   STATEMENT (1) alone is sufficient. The average is the combined income for 1965–1970 divided by 6 (the number of years). Therefore, the combined income is 6 times the average yearly income.

   STATEMENT (2) alone is not sufficient since there is no information about his income for the years 1966–1969.

4. **(E)**
   To find the profit, we must know the selling price of the dress as well as its cost. STATEMENTS (1) and (2) together are not sufficient, since there is no information about the selling price of the dresses.

5. **(D)**

   k is a prime if none of the integers 2,3,4, . . . up to $k - 1$ divide k evenly.
   STATEMENT (1) alone is sufficient since if k is not a prime then $k = (m)(n)$
   where m and n must be integers less than k. But this means either m or n
   must be less than or equal to $\sqrt{k}$, since if m and n are both larger than
   $\sqrt{k}$, $(m)(n)$ is larger than $(\sqrt{k})(\sqrt{k})$ or k. So STATEMENT (1) implies k is
   a prime.

   STATEMENT (2) alone is also sufficient, since if $k = (m)(n)$ and m and n
   are both larger than $\dfrac{k}{2}$, then $(m)(n)$ is greater than $\dfrac{k^2}{4}$; but $\dfrac{k^2}{4}$ is greater than
   k when k is larger than 5. Therefore, if no integer between 2 and $\dfrac{k}{2}$ inclusive
   divides k evenly, then k is a prime.

6. **(D)**

   Since we are given the fact that 100 miles is the distance from A to B, it is
   sufficient to find the distance from C to B. This is so, because 100 minus
   the distance from C to B is the distance from A to C. STATEMENT (1) says
   that 125% of the distance from C to B is 100 miles. Thus, we can find the
   distance from C to B, which is sufficient. Since the distance from A to C
   plus the distance from C to B is the distance from A to B, we can use
   STATEMENT (2) to set up the equation 5 times the distance from A to C
   equals 100 miles.

   Therefore, STATEMENTS (1) and (2) are each sufficient.

7. **(B)**

   STATEMENT (1) alone is not sufficient. If the segment AC is moved further
   away from the segment BD, then the angles x and y will change. So STATE-
   MENT (1) does not ensure that CD and AB are perpendicular.

   STATEMENT (2) alone is sufficient. Since AB is a straight line, $x + y$ equals
   180. Thus, if $x = y$, x and y both equal 90 and AB is perpendicular to CD.
   So the correct answer is (B).

8. **(B)**

   STATEMENT (2) alone is sufficient, since $x = y$ implies $x - y = 0$.

   STATEMENT (1) alone is not sufficient. An infinite number of pairs satisfy
   STATEMENT (1), for example, $x = 2$, $y = 2$, for which $x - y = 0$, or $x =$
   4, $y = 1$, for which $x - y = 3$.

9. **(E)**

Since there is no information on how many of the eligible voters are men or how many are women, STATEMENTS (1) and (2) together are not sufficient.

10. **(E)**

We need to find the measure of angle *PSR* or of angle *PST*. Using STATEMENT (2), we can find angle *PTR*, but STATEMENT (1) does not give any information about either of the angles needed.

11. **(A)**

STATEMENT (1) is sufficient since it means 90% of the original cost is $2,300. Thus, we can solve the equation for the original cost.

STATEMENT (2) alone is insufficient, since it gives no information about the cost.

12. **(C)**

Draw the radii from *O* to each of the vertices. These lines divide the hexagon into six triangles. STATEMENT (2) says that all the triangles are congruent since each of their pairs of corresponding sides is equal. Since there are 360° in a circle, the central angle of each triangle is 60°. And, since all radii are equal, each angle of the triangle equals 60°. Therefore, the triangles are equilateral, and *AB* is equal to the radius of the circle. Thus, if we assume STATEMENT (1), we know the length of *AB*. Without STATEMENT (1), we can't find the length of *AB*.

Also, STATEMENT (1) alone is not sufficient, since *AB* need not equal the radius unless the hexagon is regular.

13. **(E)**

We need to know the area of the walls. To find the area of the walls, we need the distance from the floor to the ceiling. Since neither STATEMENT (1) nor (2) gives any information about the height of the room, together they are not sufficient.

14. **(B)**

STATEMENT (2) alone is sufficient, since we know $80 was the amount the worker made the first day. We can use STATEMENT (2) to find his pay for each day thereafter and then find the average daily wage.

STATEMENT (1) alone is not sufficient, since there is no way to find out how much the worker made on the fifth day.

15. **(A)**

STATEMENT (1) alone is sufficient. Since $3^2 + 4^2 = 5^2$, ABC is a right triangle by the Pythagorean theorem.

STATEMENT (2) alone is not sufficient since you can choose a point D so that $AC = CD$ for *any* triangle ABC.

16. **(E)** (1) and (2) are not sufficient. The price of food could rise for other reasons besides the price of energy rising.

17. **(C)** (1) alone is obviously insufficient. To use (2) you need to know what the painting was worth at some time between 1968 and 1977. So (2) alone is insufficient, but by using (1) and (2) together you can figure out the worth of the painting in January 1971.

18. **(D)** (1) alone is sufficient since the rule enables you to compute all successive values once you know a_1. Also the rule and (1) tell you that the numbers in the sequence will always increase. Thus since $a_2 = 4$, 3 will never appear. In the same way, by using (2) and the rule for the sequence you can determine that $a_2 = 4$ and a_1 is 2 or -2, so the reasoning used above shows that 3 will never appear.

19. **(A)** (1) alone is sufficient. If $z > x$ then the side opposite angle ABC is larger than the side opposite angle ACB. (2) alone is insufficient since D can be anywhere between B and C, so you can't decide whether AD is larger or smaller than AB.

20. **(E)** If $x = 9$ and $y = 8$, then (1) and (2) would be true and $x > y$. However, if $x = 6$ and $y = 8$, (1) and (2) would still be true although $x < y$.

21. **(C)**

STATEMENT (2) alone is not sufficient. -1 is less than 2 and $1/_{-1}$ is less than $\frac{1}{2}$ but 1 is less than 2 and $1/1$ is greater than $\frac{1}{2}$.

STATEMENT (1) alone is insufficient since there is no information about y.

STATEMENTS (1) and (2) together imply that x and y are both greater than 1 and for two positive numbers x and y, if x is less than y then $1/x$ is greater than $1/y$.

22. **(A)**

STATEMENT (1) alone is sufficient. Since angle CAD is bisected by AO, the triangles AOD and AOC are congruent by side-angle-side ($AO = AO$).

Therefore, angle AOD = angle AOC. Since the sum of the angles is 180° (CD is a straight line) the two angles are right angles and AB is $\perp CD$.

STATEMENT (2) alone is insufficient. We can choose B so that $BC = AD$ whether or not $AB \perp CD$.

23. **(E)**

Since C is closer to A, if plane X is flying faster than plane Y it will certainly fly over C before plane Y. However, if plane X flies slower than plane Y, and C is very close to A, plane X would still fly over C before plane Y does. Thus, STATEMENTS (1) and (2) together are not sufficient.

24. **(C)**

STATEMENT (1) gives $x + y = 4 - x$ and since there is no further information about x, STATEMENT (1) alone is insufficient.

STATEMENT (2) alone is also insufficient because STATEMENT (2) only implies $x + y = 5 - y$. However, if you multiply STATEMENT (2) by -2 and add it to STATEMENT (1), the result is $-3y = -6$ or $y = 2$. So $x + y = 5 - 2 = 3$. Therefore, STATEMENTS (1) and (2) together are sufficient and (C) is the answer.

25. **(E)**

Since the area of a circle is πr^2, the area of the circular section AOB is the fraction $x/360$ times πr^2, where angle $AOB = x°$. (There are 360° in the entire circle.) Using STATEMENT (1), we know $x = 36$ so $(x/360)\pi r^2 = \frac{1}{10}\pi r^2$. However, STATEMENT (1) gives no information about the value of r, so STATEMENT (1) alone is insufficient.

STATEMENT (2) gives no information about the value of r, so STATEMENTS (1) and (2) together are insufficient.

Section VI   Problem Solving

1. **(D)** The car travels at 60 mph; so the time to travel 255 miles is $\dfrac{255}{60}$ hours.

Since $\dfrac{255}{60} = 4\dfrac{15}{60} = 4\dfrac{1}{4}$, it takes $4\dfrac{1}{4}$ hours.

2. **(E)** After the tune-up, the car will travel 15 miles on $\frac{3}{4}$ of a gallon of gas. So it will travel $\frac{15}{3/4}$ or $\frac{4}{3} \times 15$ or 20 miles on one gallon of gas.

3. **(B)** The price after a discount of 20% is 80% of P, the original price. After another 15% discount, the price is 85% of 80% of P or $(.85)(.80)$ P, which equals $.68P$. Therefore, after the successive discounts, the price is 68% of what it was originally, which is the same as a single discount of 32%.

4. **(D)** Since the government spent $132 per capita on personal health care for people aged 65 and over in 1966, the total expenditure by the government was $(20)(132) million, which is $2,640 million, or $2.640 billion.

5. **(C)** In 1966, the government spent $30 per capita on people under 65; by 1972 the per capita amount for those under 65 was $72. Therefore, the increase was $42. Since $\frac{42}{30} = 1.4 = 140\%$, the correct answer is (C).

6. **(B)** In 1972, philanthropy and industry contributed $5 out of the $981 per capita spent on personal health care for those aged 65 and over. Therefore, the fraction is $\frac{5}{981}$, which is about $\frac{5}{980} = \frac{1}{196}$.

7. **(C)**

STATEMENT I cannot be inferred since the graph gives only per capita amounts. The total amount will also depend on the number of people in each group.

STATEMENT II is false since private health insurance decreased from $70 to $56 per capita.

STATEMENT III is true since $644 is more than ½ of $981.

Therefore, only STATEMENT III can be inferred from the graphs.

8. **(C)** Since there are 20 oranges in a crate, a crate of oranges is sold for 20 × 6¢ or $1.20. A crate of oranges costs $1.00; so the profit on a crate is $1.20 − $1.00 or $.20. Therefore, the rate of profit $= \frac{.20}{1.20} = \frac{1}{6} = 16\frac{2}{3}\%$.

9. **(B)** $7\frac{1}{2}$ dozen is $\frac{15}{2} \times 12 = 90$, so during the summer the hen lays 90 eggs.

The food for the summer costs $10, so the cost in food per egg is

$$\frac{\$10}{90} = \frac{\$1}{9} = 11\tfrac{1}{9}\text{¢}.$$

10. **(D)**

STATEMENT I is not true since the diameter is not equal to the radius and the area of the circle is πr^2.

STATEMENT II is true since the length of a diameter is twice the length of a radius.

STATEMENT III is true since $a = \pi r^2 = \pi r(d/2) = \pi(r/2)d$. Therefore, $a/d = \pi(r/2)$.

Therefore, only STATEMENTS II and III are true.

11. **(C)** Since hose A takes 20 minutes to fill the tank, it fills up $\frac{1}{20}$ of the tank each minute. Since hose B fills up the tank in 15 minutes, it fills up $\frac{1}{15}$ of the tank each minute. Therefore, hose A and hose B together will fill up $\frac{1}{20} + \frac{1}{15}$ or $\frac{3+4}{60}$ or $\frac{7}{60}$ of the tank each minute. Thus, it will take $\frac{60}{7}$ or $8\frac{4}{7}$ minutes to fill the tank.

12. **(B)** If T is the amount of time it takes for 12 men to dig the ditch, then T = ⁵⁄₁₂ of 2 = ⁵⁄₆ of an hour. Therefore, the 12 men will take 50 minutes.

13. **(D)** The total number of cars produced was 900 + 1200 + 1500 + 1400 + 1000 or 6,000. So the average per day is $\frac{6,000}{5}$ or 1,200 cars per day.

14. **(E)** There were 6,000 cars produced and the total wages paid for the week was ($30,000 + $40,000 + $52,000 + $50,000 + $32,000) or $204,000. Therefore, the average cost in wages per car = $\frac{\$204,000}{6,000}$ = $34.

15. **(D)**

STATEMENT I is true since the total number of cars produced was 6,000 and ¼ of 6,000 is 1,500.

STATEMENT II cannot be inferred since there are no data about the number of employees. If some employees are paid more than others, there may be fewer employees present who receive higher wages.

STATEMENT III is true since $102,000 was paid on Wednesday and Thursday and $102,000 is ½ of the weekly total of $204,000.

Therefore, only STATEMENTS I and III can be inferred from the graph.

16. **(C)** The train travels 150 miles in 2 hours and 10 minutes which is $2\frac{1}{6}$ hours.

Therefore, the average speed is $\dfrac{150}{2\frac{1}{6}} = 150 \times \dfrac{6}{13} = \dfrac{900}{13} = 69\frac{3}{13}$ or about 69 miles per hour.

17. **(B)** Since $x > 2$, then $-x < -2$; but $y > -1$ implies $2y > -2$. Therefore, $-x < -2 < 2y$ so $-x < 2y$. None of the other statements is always true. (A) is false if x is 5 and $y = -\frac{1}{2}$; (C) is false if $x = 3$ and $y = -\frac{1}{2}$; (D) is false if $x = 3$ and $y = 3$, and (E) is false if $x = 3$ and $y = -\frac{1}{2}$.

18. **(C)** Since $ABCD$ is rectangle, all its angles are right angles. The area of a rectangle is length times width; and the length of AD is 4. Using the Pythagorean theorem we have $4^2 + (\text{width})^2 = 5^2$, so the $(\text{width})^2$ is $25 - 16 = 9$. Therefore, the width is 3, and the area is $4 \times 3 = 12$.

19. **(E)** The electricity costs $12k$¢ for 12 hours, the heat costs $12d$ for 12 hours, and the water costs $12w$¢ for 12 hours. So the total is $12k$¢ $+ \$12d + 12w$¢ or $\$.12k + \$12d + \$.12w$ which is $\$(.12k + 12d + .12w)$.

20. **(E)** Since $x = 2z$ and $y = 2z$, $x \cdot y \cdot z = (2z)(2z)(z) = 4z^3$; but $x \cdot y \cdot z = 256$ so $4z^3 = 256$. Therefore, $z^3 = 64$ and z is 4; so $x = 8$.

Section VII Analysis of Situations

1. **(B)** The cost of securing a loan is a *Major Factor* in making the decision.

2. **(B)** *Major Factor*. The breakage of glass jugs was a consideration in the decision to expand sales.

3. **(A)** Business expansion is clearly the *Major Objective* of Mr. Carswell.

4. **(D)** Continued public acceptance of the product is a *Major Assumption* which has led Mr. Carswell to want to expand his business.

5. **(B)** The availability of the loan was a *Major Factor* in the decision as to whether to accept Mr. Lubo's offer.

6. **(D)** The possibility of doubling his sales was a *Major Assumption* of Mr. Carswell, not an objective.

7. **(C)** Mr. Carswell's total investment was valued at $250,000, of which $50,000 was real estate. Real estate, then, was only one element in the total investment evaluation.

8. **(E)** The *previous* use of the building was of no importance to the present operation or to the decision to expand.

9. **(A)** Receiving a 10 percent rate of return is a *Major Objective* of Mr. Carswell.

10. **(D)** The franchiser was *sure* that 4,000 gallons of juice could be sold monthly through drive-in dairy shops. This figure is an estimate not substantiated by any facts cited in the passage.

11. **(B)** *Major Factor.* Mr. Carswell could advertise only on a small scale owing to lack of funds. In order to expand his business, Mr. Carswell would have to increase his advertising.

12. **(E)** The specific *source* of a business loan was an *Unimportant Issue* to Mr. Carswell.

13. **(C)** *Minor Factor.* Only 25 percent of total expected sales would be made through cafeterias.

14. **(E)** Mr. Carswell's patent—while important to protect his process—was only one part of the overall value of his business.

15. **(C)** Mr. Carswell's current sales served only as a baseline as far as expansion was concerned. Of far more importance to his decision to expand were potential sales and the expected rate of return on his investment.

16. **(E)** Carswell's background as a chemical engineer is not a consideration in any alternative course of action. It is an *Unimportant Issue*.

17. **(B)** Carswell's new method for processing orange juice had advantages over existing methods: (1) 18 percent more efficiency, (2) improved taste and flavor. Another advantage was the patent protection. The improved method was a *Major Factor* in a decision to expand operations.

18. **(C)** The *supply* of plastic containers was a major consideration because

without them production could not be expanded, nor could sales be made to household consumers. The cost of the containers is a *Minor Factor*, affecting supply.

19. **(A)** The *Major Objective* of management is to devise a plan whereby Japanese salesmen can be better motivated to sell more. This is evidenced by the fact that the Japanese company's sales had declined by 15 percent before the merger.

20. **(D)** American management was "convinced" that strong incentives would motivate Japanese salesmen. Although some companies in Japan had instituted such systems successfully, the Japanese experience was mixed, and company management believed that "the system really has not been tested . . . very adequately. . . ." (See the next to last paragraph.)

21. **(B)** The structure of labor-management relations in Japan is a major consideration in any decision to change the *status quo*.

22. **(C)** Job security is but one factor of the Japanese employment structure, so it is a *Minor Factor* in the decision process.

23. **(B)** Part of the joint-venture agreement stipulates that the Nippon sales force be maintained. This could be a major issue in management's consideration of a compensation plan.

24. **(A)** Doubling the sales force within a year was a major objective of management. See paragraph 4.

25. **(E)** The establishment date of Nippon was not an issue considered by a decision maker.

26. **(A)** Determining a sales compensation plan for Japanese salesmen was an outcome desired by management. See paragraph 5.

27. **(C)** The subject of this question is "Differences . . ." and this relates to only one issue of a compensation-fringe benefits plan, so it is a *Minor Factor*.

28. **(B)** It would be impossible for management to hire salesmen or to determine a compensation plan without understanding the class system. Since this understanding is crucial to the success or failure of a Major Objective, it is a *Minor Factor*.

29. **(E)** Toyo's reevaluation of its senior employees does not significantly influence a decision maker's consideration.

30. **(C)** Regular pay raises is one of the factors that comprise the Japanese employment structure, so it is a *Major Factor*.

31. **(A)** N.C.M. produced only cash registers. One of the reasons for the merger with N.O.M. was to expand and improve N.O.M.'s product depth. So, the product line expansion is a *Major Objective*.

32. **(E)** The fact that N.C.M. sold to trading companies was not a particular consideration in an alternative course of action. It is an *Unimportant Issue*.

33. **(A)** Another Major Objective of the merger was to improve N.C.M.'s management ability.

34. **(D)** N.O.M. executives feared that the traditional Japanese compensation system would not work in a more competitive marketplace. However, this was a *Major Assumption* on their part.

35. **(E)** That N.O.M.'s sales force was aggressive was not an issue. The consideration was how to motivate *Japanese* salesmen to become more aggressive.

Section VIII   Writing Ability

1. **(D)** Do not use *calculate* or *reckon* when you mean *think*.

2. **(E)** Since the words *but also* precede a phrase, *to one of eight or even six*, the words *not only* should precede a phrase, *to one of ten hours*. This error in parallel structure is corrected in choice E.

3. **(A)** *Already* is an adverb; *all ready* is an adjectival construction. *Allready* is a misspelling. Choices D and E do not convey the thought of the sentence.

4. **(B)** One way of correcting a dangling participle is to change the participial phrase to a clause. Choices B and D substitute clauses for the phrase. However, choice D changes the meaning of the sentence.

5. **(C)** In the underlined phrase, we find two modifiers of worker—*toiling* and *who discovers*. . . . The first is an adjective and the second a clause. This results in an error in parallel structure. Choice C corrects this by eliminating one of the modifiers of *worker*. Choice E does the same thing but creates a change in the thought of the sentence. Choice D corrects the error in parallel structure but introduces an error in agreement between subject and verb—*who* (singular) and *toil* (plural).

6. **(A)** No error.

7. **(A)** No error.

8. **(C)** This choice does not violate parallel structure.

9. **(E)** The omission of an important word (*been*) is corrected in choice E. *Excepted* (which means to *exclude*) is the wrong word to use in this sentence.

10. **(C)** Choice C corrects errors in the possessive form of *government* (needed before a verbal noun) and *it*.

11. **(B)** This corrects the error in agreement: *Her brother . . . insists.*

12. **(C)** This is also an error in agreement: *Kind* is singular and requires a singular modifier (*this*).

13. **(D)** This choice eliminates the error in parallel structure.

14. **(D)** The correct idiom is *graduate from*. The active voice is preferred to the passive used in choice C. Choice E adds an unnecessary word, *into*.

15. **(C)** This corrects the two errors in this sentence—the error in case (*me* for *I*) and the error in tense (*had finished* for *finished*).

16. **(D)** *Despite* should be used as a preposition, not as a word joining clauses.

17. **(C)** This corrects the lack of parallel structure.

18. **(C)** This was an unnecessary shift of pronoun. Do not shift from *you* to *one*. Choice D changes the meaning unnecessarily.

19. **(C)** The demonstrative pronoun *those* is needed here—*from those* (persons).

20. **(D)** Choice D corrects the error in diction and the error in parallel structure.

21. **(E)** Choice E corrects the misuse of the word *too*.

22. **(D)** Active verbs are preferred to passive verbs.

23. **(D)** The phrase *May I venture to say that* is unnecessary, as is *most* before *superior*.

24. **(E)** This answer eliminates the misplaced modifier, *completing*, and the passive verb, *were found*.

25. **(B)** The correct idiom is *different from*.

Evaluating Your Score

Tabulate your score for each section of Sample Test 2 according to the directions on pages 5–6 and record the results in the Self-scoring Table below. Then find your rating for each score on the Self-scoring Scale and record it in the appropriate blank.

SELF-SCORING TABLE

SECTION	SCORE	RATING
1		
2		
3		
4		
5		
6		
7		
8		

SELF-SCORING SCALE

RATING

SECTION	POOR	FAIR	GOOD	EXCELLENT
1	0–12 +	13–17 +	18–21 +	22–25
2	0–12 +	13–17 +	18–21 +	22–25
3	0–9 +	10–13 +	14–17 +	18–20
4	0–17 +	18–24 +	25–31 +	32–35
5	0–12 +	13–17 +	18–21 +	22–25
6	0–9 +	10–13 +	14–17 +	18–20
7	0–17 +	18–24 +	25–31 +	32–35
8	0–12 +	13–17 +	18–21 +	22–25

Study again the Review sections covering material in Sample Test 2 for which you had a rating of FAIR or POOR. Then go on to Sample Test 3.

To obtain an approximation of your actual GMAT score, see page 6.

Answer Sheet—Sample Test 3

Section I
Reading
Comprehension

1. Ⓐ Ⓑ Ⓒ Ⓓ Ⓔ
2. Ⓐ Ⓑ Ⓒ Ⓓ Ⓔ
3. Ⓐ Ⓑ Ⓒ Ⓓ Ⓔ
4. Ⓐ Ⓑ Ⓒ Ⓓ Ⓔ
5. Ⓐ Ⓑ Ⓒ Ⓓ Ⓔ
6. Ⓐ Ⓑ Ⓒ Ⓓ Ⓔ
7. Ⓐ Ⓑ Ⓒ Ⓓ Ⓔ
8. Ⓐ Ⓑ Ⓒ Ⓓ Ⓔ
9. Ⓐ Ⓑ Ⓒ Ⓓ Ⓔ
10. Ⓐ Ⓑ Ⓒ Ⓓ Ⓔ
11. Ⓐ Ⓑ Ⓒ Ⓓ Ⓔ
12. Ⓐ Ⓑ Ⓒ Ⓓ Ⓔ
13. Ⓐ Ⓑ Ⓒ Ⓓ Ⓔ
14. Ⓐ Ⓑ Ⓒ Ⓓ Ⓔ
15. Ⓐ Ⓑ Ⓒ Ⓓ Ⓔ
16. Ⓐ Ⓑ Ⓒ Ⓓ Ⓔ
17. Ⓐ Ⓑ Ⓒ Ⓓ Ⓔ
18. Ⓐ Ⓑ Ⓒ Ⓓ Ⓔ
19. Ⓐ Ⓑ Ⓒ Ⓓ Ⓔ
20. Ⓐ Ⓑ Ⓒ Ⓓ Ⓔ
21. Ⓐ Ⓑ Ⓒ Ⓓ Ⓔ
22. Ⓐ Ⓑ Ⓒ Ⓓ Ⓔ
23. Ⓐ Ⓑ Ⓒ Ⓓ Ⓔ
24. Ⓐ Ⓑ Ⓒ Ⓓ Ⓔ
25. Ⓐ Ⓑ Ⓒ Ⓓ Ⓔ

7. Ⓐ Ⓑ Ⓒ Ⓓ Ⓔ
8. Ⓐ Ⓑ Ⓒ Ⓓ Ⓔ
9. Ⓐ Ⓑ Ⓒ Ⓓ Ⓔ
10. Ⓐ Ⓑ Ⓒ Ⓓ Ⓔ
11. Ⓐ Ⓑ Ⓒ Ⓓ Ⓔ
12. Ⓐ Ⓑ Ⓒ Ⓓ Ⓔ
13. Ⓐ Ⓑ Ⓒ Ⓓ Ⓔ
14. Ⓐ Ⓑ Ⓒ Ⓓ Ⓔ
15. Ⓐ Ⓑ Ⓒ Ⓓ Ⓔ
16. Ⓐ Ⓑ Ⓒ Ⓓ Ⓔ
17. Ⓐ Ⓑ Ⓒ Ⓓ Ⓔ
18. Ⓐ Ⓑ Ⓒ Ⓓ Ⓔ
19. Ⓐ Ⓑ Ⓒ Ⓓ Ⓔ
20. Ⓐ Ⓑ Ⓒ Ⓓ Ⓔ

22. Ⓐ Ⓑ Ⓒ Ⓓ Ⓔ
23. Ⓐ Ⓑ Ⓒ Ⓓ Ⓔ
24. Ⓐ Ⓑ Ⓒ Ⓓ Ⓔ
25. Ⓐ Ⓑ Ⓒ Ⓓ Ⓔ
26. Ⓐ Ⓑ Ⓒ Ⓓ Ⓔ
27. Ⓐ Ⓑ Ⓒ Ⓓ Ⓔ
28. Ⓐ Ⓑ Ⓒ Ⓓ Ⓔ
29. Ⓐ Ⓑ Ⓒ Ⓓ Ⓔ
30. Ⓐ Ⓑ Ⓒ Ⓓ Ⓔ
31. Ⓐ Ⓑ Ⓒ Ⓓ Ⓔ
32. Ⓐ Ⓑ Ⓒ Ⓓ Ⓔ
33. Ⓐ Ⓑ Ⓒ Ⓓ Ⓔ
34. Ⓐ Ⓑ Ⓒ Ⓓ Ⓔ
35. Ⓐ Ⓑ Ⓒ Ⓓ Ⓔ

Section III
Analysis of Situations

1. Ⓐ Ⓑ Ⓒ Ⓓ Ⓔ
2. Ⓐ Ⓑ Ⓒ Ⓓ Ⓔ
3. Ⓐ Ⓑ Ⓒ Ⓓ Ⓔ
4. Ⓐ Ⓑ Ⓒ Ⓓ Ⓔ
5. Ⓐ Ⓑ Ⓒ Ⓓ Ⓔ
6. Ⓐ Ⓑ Ⓒ Ⓓ Ⓔ
7. Ⓐ Ⓑ Ⓒ Ⓓ Ⓔ
8. Ⓐ Ⓑ Ⓒ Ⓓ Ⓔ
9. Ⓐ Ⓑ Ⓒ Ⓓ Ⓔ
10. Ⓐ Ⓑ Ⓒ Ⓓ Ⓔ
11. Ⓐ Ⓑ Ⓒ Ⓓ Ⓔ
12. Ⓐ Ⓑ Ⓒ Ⓓ Ⓔ
13. Ⓐ Ⓑ Ⓒ Ⓓ Ⓔ
14. Ⓐ Ⓑ Ⓒ Ⓓ Ⓔ
15. Ⓐ Ⓑ Ⓒ Ⓓ Ⓔ
16. Ⓐ Ⓑ Ⓒ Ⓓ Ⓔ
17. Ⓐ Ⓑ Ⓒ Ⓓ Ⓔ
18. Ⓐ Ⓑ Ⓒ Ⓓ Ⓔ
19. Ⓐ Ⓑ Ⓒ Ⓓ Ⓔ
20. Ⓐ Ⓑ Ⓒ Ⓓ Ⓔ
21. Ⓐ Ⓑ Ⓒ Ⓓ Ⓔ

Section IV
Data Sufficiency

1. Ⓐ Ⓑ Ⓒ Ⓓ Ⓔ
2. Ⓐ Ⓑ Ⓒ Ⓓ Ⓔ
3. Ⓐ Ⓑ Ⓒ Ⓓ Ⓔ
4. Ⓐ Ⓑ Ⓒ Ⓓ Ⓔ
5. Ⓐ Ⓑ Ⓒ Ⓓ Ⓔ
6. Ⓐ Ⓑ Ⓒ Ⓓ Ⓔ
7. Ⓐ Ⓑ Ⓒ Ⓓ Ⓔ
8. Ⓐ Ⓑ Ⓒ Ⓓ Ⓔ
9. Ⓐ Ⓑ Ⓒ Ⓓ Ⓔ
10. Ⓐ Ⓑ Ⓒ Ⓓ Ⓔ
11. Ⓐ Ⓑ Ⓒ Ⓓ Ⓔ
12. Ⓐ Ⓑ Ⓒ Ⓓ Ⓔ
13. Ⓐ Ⓑ Ⓒ Ⓓ Ⓔ
14. Ⓐ Ⓑ Ⓒ Ⓓ Ⓔ
15. Ⓐ Ⓑ Ⓒ Ⓓ Ⓔ
16. Ⓐ Ⓑ Ⓒ Ⓓ Ⓔ
17. Ⓐ Ⓑ Ⓒ Ⓓ Ⓔ
18. Ⓐ Ⓑ Ⓒ Ⓓ Ⓔ
19. Ⓐ Ⓑ Ⓒ Ⓓ Ⓔ
20. Ⓐ Ⓑ Ⓒ Ⓓ Ⓔ
21. Ⓐ Ⓑ Ⓒ Ⓓ Ⓔ

Section II
Problem
Solving

1. Ⓐ Ⓑ Ⓒ Ⓓ Ⓔ
2. Ⓐ Ⓑ Ⓒ Ⓓ Ⓔ
3. Ⓐ Ⓑ Ⓒ Ⓓ Ⓔ
4. Ⓐ Ⓑ Ⓒ Ⓓ Ⓔ
5. Ⓐ Ⓑ Ⓒ Ⓓ Ⓔ
6. Ⓐ Ⓑ Ⓒ Ⓓ Ⓔ

22. Ⓐ Ⓑ Ⓒ Ⓓ Ⓔ
23. Ⓐ Ⓑ Ⓒ Ⓓ Ⓔ
24. Ⓐ Ⓑ Ⓒ Ⓓ Ⓔ
25. Ⓐ Ⓑ Ⓒ Ⓓ Ⓔ

Section V
Writing Ability
1. Ⓐ Ⓑ Ⓒ Ⓓ Ⓔ
2. Ⓐ Ⓑ Ⓒ Ⓓ Ⓔ
3. Ⓐ Ⓑ Ⓒ Ⓓ Ⓔ
4. Ⓐ Ⓑ Ⓒ Ⓓ Ⓔ
5. Ⓐ Ⓑ Ⓒ Ⓓ Ⓔ
6. Ⓐ Ⓑ Ⓒ Ⓓ Ⓔ
7. Ⓐ Ⓑ Ⓒ Ⓓ Ⓔ
8. Ⓐ Ⓑ Ⓒ Ⓓ Ⓔ
9. Ⓐ Ⓑ Ⓒ Ⓓ Ⓔ
10. Ⓐ Ⓑ Ⓒ Ⓓ Ⓔ
11. Ⓐ Ⓑ Ⓒ Ⓓ Ⓔ
12. Ⓐ Ⓑ Ⓒ Ⓓ Ⓔ
13. Ⓐ Ⓑ Ⓒ Ⓓ Ⓔ
14. Ⓐ Ⓑ Ⓒ Ⓓ Ⓔ
15. Ⓐ Ⓑ Ⓒ Ⓓ Ⓔ
16. Ⓐ Ⓑ Ⓒ Ⓓ Ⓔ
17. Ⓐ Ⓑ Ⓒ Ⓓ Ⓔ
18. Ⓐ Ⓑ Ⓒ Ⓓ Ⓔ
19. Ⓐ Ⓑ Ⓒ Ⓓ Ⓔ
20. Ⓐ Ⓑ Ⓒ Ⓓ Ⓔ
21. Ⓐ Ⓑ Ⓒ Ⓓ Ⓔ
22. Ⓐ Ⓑ Ⓒ Ⓓ Ⓔ
23. Ⓐ Ⓑ Ⓒ Ⓓ Ⓔ
24. Ⓐ Ⓑ Ⓒ Ⓓ Ⓔ
25. Ⓐ Ⓑ Ⓒ Ⓓ Ⓔ

Section VI
Analysis of Situations
1. Ⓐ Ⓑ Ⓒ Ⓓ Ⓔ
2. Ⓐ Ⓑ Ⓒ Ⓓ Ⓔ
3. Ⓐ Ⓑ Ⓒ Ⓓ Ⓔ
4. Ⓐ Ⓑ Ⓒ Ⓓ Ⓔ
5. Ⓐ Ⓑ Ⓒ Ⓓ Ⓔ

6. Ⓐ Ⓑ Ⓒ Ⓓ Ⓔ
7. Ⓐ Ⓑ Ⓒ Ⓓ Ⓔ
8. Ⓐ Ⓑ Ⓒ Ⓓ Ⓔ
9. Ⓐ Ⓑ Ⓒ Ⓓ Ⓔ
10. Ⓐ Ⓑ Ⓒ Ⓓ Ⓔ
11. Ⓐ Ⓑ Ⓒ Ⓓ Ⓔ
12. Ⓐ Ⓑ Ⓒ Ⓓ Ⓔ
13. Ⓐ Ⓑ Ⓒ Ⓓ Ⓔ
14. Ⓐ Ⓑ Ⓒ Ⓓ Ⓔ
15. Ⓐ Ⓑ Ⓒ Ⓓ Ⓔ
16. Ⓐ Ⓑ Ⓒ Ⓓ Ⓔ
17. Ⓐ Ⓑ Ⓒ Ⓓ Ⓔ
18. Ⓐ Ⓑ Ⓒ Ⓓ Ⓔ
19. Ⓐ Ⓑ Ⓒ Ⓓ Ⓔ
20. Ⓐ Ⓑ Ⓒ Ⓓ Ⓔ
21. Ⓐ Ⓑ Ⓒ Ⓓ Ⓔ
22. Ⓐ Ⓑ Ⓒ Ⓓ Ⓔ
23. Ⓐ Ⓑ Ⓒ Ⓓ Ⓔ
24. Ⓐ Ⓑ Ⓒ Ⓓ Ⓔ
25. Ⓐ Ⓑ Ⓒ Ⓓ Ⓔ
25. Ⓐ Ⓑ Ⓒ Ⓓ Ⓔ
26. Ⓐ Ⓑ Ⓒ Ⓓ Ⓔ
27. Ⓐ Ⓑ Ⓒ Ⓓ Ⓔ
28. Ⓐ Ⓑ Ⓒ Ⓓ Ⓔ
29. Ⓐ Ⓑ Ⓒ Ⓓ Ⓔ
30. Ⓐ Ⓑ Ⓒ Ⓓ Ⓔ
31. Ⓐ Ⓑ Ⓒ Ⓓ Ⓔ
32. Ⓐ Ⓑ Ⓒ Ⓓ Ⓔ
33. Ⓐ Ⓑ Ⓒ Ⓓ Ⓔ
34. Ⓐ Ⓑ Ⓒ Ⓓ Ⓔ
35. Ⓐ Ⓑ Ⓒ Ⓓ Ⓔ

Section VII
Reading
Comprehension
1. Ⓐ Ⓑ Ⓒ Ⓓ Ⓔ
2. Ⓐ Ⓑ Ⓒ Ⓓ Ⓔ
3. Ⓐ Ⓑ Ⓒ Ⓓ Ⓔ
4. Ⓐ Ⓑ Ⓒ Ⓓ Ⓔ
5. Ⓐ Ⓑ Ⓒ Ⓓ Ⓔ
6. Ⓐ Ⓑ Ⓒ Ⓓ Ⓔ
7. Ⓐ Ⓑ Ⓒ Ⓓ Ⓔ

8. Ⓐ Ⓑ Ⓒ Ⓓ Ⓔ
9. Ⓐ Ⓑ Ⓒ Ⓓ Ⓔ
10. Ⓐ Ⓑ Ⓒ Ⓓ Ⓔ
11. Ⓐ Ⓑ Ⓒ Ⓓ Ⓔ
12. Ⓐ Ⓑ Ⓒ Ⓓ Ⓔ
13. Ⓐ Ⓑ Ⓒ Ⓓ Ⓔ
14. Ⓐ Ⓑ Ⓒ Ⓓ Ⓔ
15. Ⓐ Ⓑ Ⓒ Ⓓ Ⓔ
16. Ⓐ Ⓑ Ⓒ Ⓓ Ⓔ
17. Ⓐ Ⓑ Ⓒ Ⓓ Ⓔ
18. Ⓐ Ⓑ Ⓒ Ⓓ Ⓔ
19. Ⓐ Ⓑ Ⓒ Ⓓ Ⓔ
20. Ⓐ Ⓑ Ⓒ Ⓓ Ⓔ
21. Ⓐ Ⓑ Ⓒ Ⓓ Ⓔ
22. Ⓐ Ⓑ Ⓒ Ⓓ Ⓔ
23. Ⓐ Ⓑ Ⓒ Ⓓ Ⓔ
24. Ⓐ Ⓑ Ⓒ Ⓓ Ⓔ
25. Ⓐ Ⓑ Ⓒ Ⓓ Ⓔ

Section VIII
Problem Solving
1. Ⓐ Ⓑ Ⓒ Ⓓ Ⓔ
2. Ⓐ Ⓑ Ⓒ Ⓓ Ⓔ
3. Ⓐ Ⓑ Ⓒ Ⓓ Ⓔ
4. Ⓐ Ⓑ Ⓒ Ⓓ Ⓔ
5. Ⓐ Ⓑ Ⓒ Ⓓ Ⓔ
6. Ⓐ Ⓑ Ⓒ Ⓓ Ⓔ
7. Ⓐ Ⓑ Ⓒ Ⓓ Ⓔ
8. Ⓐ Ⓑ Ⓒ Ⓓ Ⓔ
9. Ⓐ Ⓑ Ⓒ Ⓓ Ⓔ
10. Ⓐ Ⓑ Ⓒ Ⓓ Ⓔ
11. Ⓐ Ⓑ Ⓒ Ⓓ Ⓔ
12. Ⓐ Ⓑ Ⓒ Ⓓ Ⓔ
13. Ⓐ Ⓑ Ⓒ Ⓓ Ⓔ
14. Ⓐ Ⓑ Ⓒ Ⓓ Ⓔ
15. Ⓐ Ⓑ Ⓒ Ⓓ Ⓔ
16. Ⓐ Ⓑ Ⓒ Ⓓ Ⓔ
17. Ⓐ Ⓑ Ⓒ Ⓓ Ⓔ
18. Ⓐ Ⓑ Ⓒ Ⓓ Ⓔ
19. Ⓐ Ⓑ Ⓒ Ⓓ Ⓔ
20. Ⓐ Ⓑ Ⓒ Ⓓ Ⓔ

SAMPLE TEST 3

Section I   Reading Comprehension   Time: 30 minutes

Directions: This part contains four reading passages. You are to read each one carefully. When answering the questions, you will be able to refer to the passages. The questions are based on what is *stated* or *implied* in each passage.

PASSAGE 1

In Aachen, Germany, and environs, many children have been found to have an unusually high lead content in their blood and hair. The amount of lead in the children tested has risen above the amount found in workers in heavy-metal industries. The general public is no longer surprised that the lead has been
(5) traced to Stolberg near Aachen: Stolberg is surrounded by brass foundries and slag heaps which supply building materials to construct schoolyards and sports halls.

This is but one example. In today's Europe, cancer-stricken children outnumber adults with the disease. And in the United States, cancer kills more
(10) children between the ages of one and four than any other disease.

When Dr. John W. Gofman, professor of medical physics at the University of California and a leading nuclear critic, speaks of "ecocide" in his adversary view of nuclear technology, he means the following: A large nuclear plant like that in Kalkar, the Netherlands, would produce about 200 pounds of plutonium
(15) each year. One pound, released into the atmosphere, could cause 9 billion cases of lung cancer. This waste product must be stored for 500,000 years before it is of no further danger to man. In the anticipated reactor economy, it is estimated that there will be 10,000 tons of this material in western Europe, of which one tablespoonful of plutonium-239 represents the official maximum
(20) permissible body burden for 200,000 people. Rather than being biodegradable, plutonium destroys biological properties.

In 1972 the U.S. Occupational Safety and Health Administration ruled that the asbestos level in the work place should be lowered to 2 fibers per cubic centimeter of air, but the effective date of the ruling has been delayed until
(25) now. The International Federation of Chemical and General Workers' Unions report that the 2-fiber standard was based primarily on one study of 290 men at a British asbestos factory. But when the workers at the British factory had been reexamined by another physician, 40–70 percent had x-ray evidence of lung abnormalities. According to present medical information at the factory in

(30) question, out of a total of 29 deaths thus far, seven were caused by lung cancer and three by mesothelioma, a cancer of the lining of the chest-abdomen. An average European or American worker comes into contact with six million fibers a day. And when this man returns home at night, samples of this fireproof product are on his clothes, in his hair, in his lunchpail. "We are now, in fact, (35) finding cancer deaths within the family of the asbestos worker," states Dr. Irving Selikoff, of the Mount Sinai Medical School in New York.

It is now also clear that vinyl chloride, a gas from which the most widely used plastics are made, causes a fatal cancer of the blood-vessel cells of the liver. However, the history of the research on vinyl chloride is, in some ways, more (40) disturbing than the "Watergate cover-up." "There has been evidence of potentially serious disease among polyvinyl chloride workers for 25 years that has been incompletely appreciated and inadequately approached by medical scientists and by regulatory authorities," summed up Dr. Selikoff in the *New Scientist*. At least 17 workers have been killed by vinyl chloride because research (45) over the past 25 years was not followed up. And for over 10 years, workers have been exposed to concentrations of vinyl chloride 10 times the "safe limit" imposed by Dow Chemical Company. In the United Kingdom, a threshold limit value was set after the discovery of the causal link with osteolysis, but the limit was still higher than that set by Dow Chemical. The Germans set a new max- (50) imum level in 1970, but also higher than that set by Dow. No other section of U.S. or European industry has followed Dow's lead.

1. Which of the following titles best describes the contents of the passage?
   (A) *The Problems of Nuclear Physics*
   (B) *Advanced Technology and Cancer*
   (C) *Occupational Diseases*
   (D) *Cancer in Germany*
   (E) *The Ecology of Cancer*

2. The author provides information that would answer which of the following questions?
   (A) What sort of legislation is needed to prevent cancer?
   (B) Should nuclear plants be built?
   (C) What are some causes of lung cancer?
   (D) What are the pros and cons of nuclear energy?
   (E) Which country has the lowest incidence of occupational disease?

3. According to the author, all the following are causes of lung cancer *except*

(A) plutonium
(B) asbestos
(C) vinyl chloride

(D) osteolysis
(E) lead

4. The style of the passage is mainly
   (A) argumentative
   (B) emotional
   (C) factual
   (D) clinical
   (E) vitriolic

5. It can be inferred from the passage that the author believes that
   (A) industrialization must be halted to prevent further spread of cancer-producing agents
   (B) only voluntary, industry-wide application of antipollution devices can halt cancer
   (C) workers are partly to blame for the spread of disease because of poor work habits
   (D) more research is needed into the causes of cancer before further progress can be made
   (E) tougher legislation is needed to set lower limits of worker exposure to harmful chemicals and fibers

6. Some workers have been killed by harmful pollutants because
   (A) they failed to take the required precautions and safety measures
   (B) not enough research has been undertaken to find solutions to the pollution problem
   (C) available research was not followed up
   (D) production cannot be halted
   (E) factory owners have failed to provide safety equipment

Passage 2

The Great Glen is a 100-mile-long rift valley stretching across the Scottish Highlands from the Moray Firth in the northeast to the Firth of Lorne in the southwest, thus forming a natural link between the North Sea and the Atlantic Ocean. It is the result of a sideways slippage of the earth, a northeast-southwest trending fault of the Caledonian mountain system. During the Ice Age, Scotland was literally shoved down into the earth, and when the ice melted, the sea rose for a time, then ceased. But the land kept on rising, some 50 feet above sea level, sealing off bodies of water from the oceans and leaving bizarre, white beaches about the edges of medieval forestry.

(10)   Loch Ness, the largest freshwater lake in the British Isles and the third largest in Europe, is the principal basin of the Great Glen. It receives a quantum runoff from neighboring glens—Glen Affric, Glen Cannich, Glen Moriston, Glen Farrar, Glen Urquhart—so that the water level may rise as much as 24 inches in an hour. Any possible underground passage from the loch to the North Sea (15) has long ago been dammed by some two miles of river-brought silt, thus changing the original sea loch into a fresh-water lake. It has no curving outlines made by an indented shore or shallow bays; but, instead, its riparian walls slice straight down, giving the appearance of an enormous ditch widening to 1.5 miles and extending approximately 23 miles from Inverness in the North to Fort (20) Augustus at the southern end, where the Caledonian Canal continues on into the Atlantic. Its depth exceeds 700 feet over much of its length, with the deepest point so far discovered of 975 feet. The loch never freezes and acts like an inland Gulf Stream on its immediate environs, giving off in winter a vast amount of heat collected in the summer months. The coldest water remains at a fairly (25) constant 42 degrees, warm enough to provide a home for literally millions of migrating eels, which, according to ichthyologists, have made their home here instead of going to the sea. Along the rocky shoreline a reddish brown algae adheres to the stones, and in the shallows around the mouths of tributary rivers and burns is an abundance of freshwater weeds and organic detritus—all a (30) possible food source for eels, brown trout, salmon, and sticklebacks. Hence, the biomass of the loch is thought sufficient to support a population of large animals.

    The loch inherits its name from the Greek water goddess Nesa, whose spirit was thought to cause the many "unnatural" occurrences in the area. If "Ness" (35) is given a feminine diminutive ending, it becomes "Nessie"—the sobriquet for the Loch Ness Monster. The scientific name of *Nessiteras rhombopteryx* has been applied to Nessie by Sir Peter Scott, head of the world Wildlife Foundation and chancellor of Birmingham University. The word *Nessiteras* combines the name of the loch with the Greek word *teras*, genitive of *teratos*, which means (40) a "marvel of wonder . . . arousing awe, amazement, and often fear." The word *rhombopteryx* is a combination of the Greek *rhombos*, meaning a diamond or rhomboid shape, and the Greek *pteryx*, meaning fin or wing. The name does not link the species to any animal or group of animals known to science but applies specifically to the creature first recorded by St. Columba in 565 A.D. (45) From a zoological point of view, to base a name on photographs rather than the remains of an animal is quite unsatisfactory, however justified by the urgency to protect an endangered species and therefore permitted by the International Code of Zoological Nomenclature.

In 1933 dynamite charges shook the loch-side, tumbling boulders, tree limbs,
(50) earth, and scree into the lake. For a year the blasting intermittently continued
as steam shovels chuffed and gnawed their way through the forest, gradually
surrounding the once tranquil shoreline with the fresh macadam of a scenic
highway. Such violent activity sent reverberations down through the waters
beneath Fort Augustus, down into the deep holes off Urquhart Bay, and down
(55) into the shallows around Dores, Foyers, and Invermoriston. After the day's work
a quietude descended, but only for an uncertain time. Then something that
looked like a hump of sorts, perhaps only a wave or floating log (surely one
that had been blasted that morning) or an upturned boat, would appear, drift,
and disappear beneath a gibbous moon.

7. It can be assumed from the passage that the Loch Ness "monster" was
   thought to have been
   (A) a warm-water creature
   (B) observed in 565 A.D.
   (C) created during the ice age
   (D) fabricated during the Middle Ages
   (E) described in Greek mythology

8. The passage implies that which of the following has been offered as evi-
   dence of the existence of the Loch Ness "monster"?
   (A) Photographs of the creature
   (B) The lake's organic contents, which are suitable food for such creatures
   (C) The mild water temperature
   (D) Observations by zoologists
   (E) Discovery of the creature's remains

9. According to the passage, the surface area of Loch Ness is probably closest
   to
   (A) 1.5 square miles
   (B) 3.8 square miles
   (C) 25 square miles
   (D) 230 square miles
   (E) 345 square miles

10. The author is mainly concerned with
    (A) debunking the idea of a sea monster
    (B) describing Loch Ness and the "monster" it may contain
    (C) providing evidence for the existence of a sea monster
    (D) the scientific status of the Loch Ness "monster" myth
    (E) the geological characteristics of Scottish glens

11. When the author uses the word *ichthyologists* in line 26, he is referring to
    - (A) a Scottish clan
    - (B) zoologists who study fish
    - (C) conservationists
    - (D) wildlife experts
    - (E) geologists

12. Which of the following can be inferred from the passage?
    - (A) Loch Ness is a popular tourist resort.
    - (B) Scotland's climate is very harsh.
    - (C) Dynamite charges sealed off Loch Ness from the sea.
    - (D) The inhabitants of Loch Ness are an endangered species protected by law.
    - (E) None of the above.

PASSAGE 3

It is easy to accept Freud as an applied scientist, and, indeed he is widely regarded as the twentieth century's master clinician. However, in viewing Marx as an applied social scientist the stance needed is that of a Machiavellian operationalism. The objective is neither to bury nor to praise him. The assumption (5) is simply that he is better understood for being understood as an applied sociologist. This is in part the clear implication of Marx's *Theses on Feurbach*, which culminate in the resounding 11th thesis: "The philosophers have only interpreted the world in different ways; the point, however, is to change it." This would seem to be the tacit creed of applied scientists everywhere.

(10) Marx was no Faustian, concerned solely with understanding society, but a Promethean who sought to understand it well enough to influence and to change it. He was centrally concerned with the social problems of a lay group, the proletariat, and there can be little doubt that his work is motivated by an effort to reduce their suffering, as he saw it. His diagnosis was that their in-(15) creasing misery and alienation engendered endemic class struggle; his prognosis claimed that this would culminate in revolution; his therapeutic prescription was class consciousness and active struggle.

Here, as in assessing Durkheim or Freud, the issue is not whether this analysis is empirically correct or scientifically adequate. Furthermore, whether or not (20) this formulation seems to eviscerate Marx's revolutionary core, as critics on the left may charge, or whether the formulation provides Marx with a new veneer of academic respectability, as critics on the right may allege, is entirely irrelevant from the present standpoint. Insofar as Marx's or any other social scientist's work conforms to a generalized model of applied social science, insofar

(25) as it is professionally oriented to the values and social problems of laymen in his society, he may be treated as an applied social scientist.

Despite Durkheim's intellectualistic proclivities and rationalistic pathos, he was too much the product of European turbulence to turn his back on the travail of his culture. "Why strive for knowledge of reality, if this knowledge (30) cannot aid us in life," he asked. "Social science," he said, "can provide us with rules of action for the future." Durkheim, like Marx, conceived of science as an agency of social action, and like him was professionally oriented to the values and problems of laymen in his society. Unless one sees that Durkheim was in some part an applied social scientist, it is impossible to understand why (35) he concludes his monumental study of *Suicide* with a chapter on "Practical Consequences," and why, in the *Division of Labor*, he proposes a specific remedy for anomie.

Durkheim is today widely regarded as a model of theoretic and methodologic sophistication, and is thus usually seen only in his capacity as a pure social (40) scientist. Surely this is an incomplete view of the man who regarded the *practical* effectiveness of a science as its principal justification. To be more fully understood, Durkheim also needs to be seen as an applied sociologist. His interest in religious beliefs and organization, in crime and penology, in educational methods and organization, in suicide and anomie, are not casually (45) chosen problem areas. Nor did he select them only because they provided occasions for the development of his theoretical orientation. These areas were in his time, as they are today, problems of indigenous interest to applied sociologists in Western society, precisely because of their practical significance.

13. Which of the following best describes the author's conception of an applied social scientist?
    (A) A professional who listens to people's problems
    (B) A professional who seeks social action and change
    (C) A student of society
    (D) A proponent of class struggle
    (E) A philosopher who interprets the world in a unique way

14. According to the author, which of the following did Marx and Durkheim have in common?
    (A) A belief in the importance of class struggle
    (B) A desire to create a system of social organization
    (C) An interest in penology
    (D) Regard for the practical applications of science
    (E) A sense of the political organization of society

15. It may be inferred from the passage that the applied social scientist might be interested in all of the following subjects *except*
    (A) the theory of mechanics
    (B) how to make workers more efficient
    (C) rehabilitation of juvenile delinquents
    (D) reduction of social tensions
    (E) industrial safety

16. According to the passage, applied social science can be distinguished from pure social science by its
    (A) practical significance
    (B) universal application
    (C) cultural pluralism
    (D) objectivity
    (E) emphasis on the problems of the poor

17. Which of the following best summarizes the author's main point?
    (A) Marx and Durkheim were similar in their ideas.
    (B) Freud, Marx, and Durkheim were all social scientists.
    (C) Philosophers, among others, who are regarded as theoreticians can also be regarded as empiricists.
    (D) Marx and Durkheim were applied social scientists because they were concerned with the solution of social problems.
    (E) Pure and applied sciences have fundamentally similar objects.

18. All of the following are mentioned as topics of interest to Durkheim *except*
    (A) suicide   (D) education
    (B) psychiatry   (E) religion
    (C) crime

PASSAGE 4

Morally and culturally, American society, as reflected in our TV programs, our theatrical fare, our literature and art appears to have hit bottom.

Gen. David Sarnoff felt prompted to issue a statement in defense of the TV industry. He pointed out that there was much good in its programs that was
(5) being overlooked while its occasional derelictions were being overly stressed. It struck me that what he was saying about TV applied to other aspects of American culture as well, particularly to the theatrical productions.

Without necessarily resting on his conviction that the good outweighed the bad in American cultural activity, I saw further implications in Gen. Sarnoff's (10) declaration. Audiences needed to be sensitized more and more to the positive qualities of the entertainment and cultural media. In addition, through such increased public sensitivity, producers would be encouraged to provide even more of the fine, and less of the sordid.

Here is where questions arise. If the exemplary aspects of TV are not being (15) recognized, what is the reason for such a lack of appreciation? Similarly, and further, if the theatre, including in this term the legitimate stage, on and off Broadway as well as the moving pictures, has large measures of goodness, truth and beauty which are unappreciated, how are we to change this situation?

All in all, what should be done to encourage and condone the good, and to (20) discourage and condemn the unsavory in the American cultural pattern?

These are serious and pressing questions—serious for the survival of the American Way of Life, and pressing for immediate and adequate answers. Indeed the simple truth is that the face that America shows the world affects seriously the future of democracy all over the globe.

(25) Since the theatre in its broadest sense is a large aspect of American culture— its expression as well as its creation—I saw the urgent importance of bringing the worthwhile elements in the American Theatre to the fore. Especially was this importance impressed on me when I realized how much Hollywood was involved in exporting American life to the world, and how much Broadway with (30) all its theatres meant to the modern drama.

Then the thought of the Bible came to me in this connection. Was not the Bible the basis of Western civilization as far as morals are concerned? Why not use the Bible as guide and touchstone, as direction and goal in the matter of the cultural achievements of Western society? Thus was born "The Bible on (35) Broadway."

The birth of the idea accomplished, rearing it brought the usual difficulties of raising a child—albeit in this case a "brain" one. There was first the fact that the Bible, although the world's best seller, is not the world's best read book. Second was the current impression that "message-plays" must neces- (40) sarily be dull and unpopular. What a combination! The Bible unknown, and Broadway (in the sense of theatre with an idea) unpopular!

Still, I was drawn to the project of a series of lectures on the Bible and the contemporary theatre. What if the Bible is not well known? Teach it! Plays with a message dull? All plays by reason of their being works of art have been created (45) by their authors' selection and ordering of experience. As such, plays are proponents of ideas—and certainly they are not meant to be uninteresting.

Thus fortified, I turned to the subject of the Bible and the contemporary theatre and found it indeed appealing and full of interesting nuances.

That there are spiritual, even religious ideas, in the contemporary theatre (50) should be no cause for wonderment. It is well known that the drama had its origin in religion. The Greeks, the Romans, as well as the early Hebrews, all had forms of the drama which among the first two developed into our classical plays.

In the Middle Ages, it was the Church in the Western World that produced (55) the morality and mystery plays. With such a long history it is not surprising to find an affinity between the Bible and the Theatre.

19. The author is primarily concerned with
   (A) the declining pattern of morality in America
   (B) promoting American theatre
   (C) the role of the Bible in the contemporary theatre
   (D) comparing the theatre with other art forms
   (E) preserving the "American Way of Life"

20. With which of the following statements regarding the theatre would the author most likely agree?
   (A) The theatre does not reflect American culture.
   (B) Critics of American cultural life are biased.
   (C) While the entertainment media can be criticized, they contain much wholesome material.
   (D) The advertising media are largely to blame for criticisms leveled at the theatre.
   (E) The Bible should be used as our primary source of entertainment ideas.

21. Which of the following statements best reflects the author's own ideas?
   (A) American art forms have degenerated to a new low.
   (B) The good outweighs the bad in American cultural activity.
   (C) American culture has positive content, but it is not appreciated by the public.
   (D) Only the Biblical content of American theatre has positive meaning.
   (E) American theatre is currently dull and unpopular.

22. The author implies that he will deal with which of the following questions?
   I. What is the reason for the lack of appreciation of the theatre?
   II. To what extent have Bible themes been used in or influenced American theatrical productions?

III. What should be done to encourage the good in American culture?

(A) I only
(B) II only
(C) I and II only
(D) I and III only
(E) I, II and III

23. It can be inferred from the passage that the author's background might be in any of the following occupations *except*

(A) theatrical producer
(B) thespian
(C) humorist
(D) writer
(E) critic

24. The author implies that, if the public is made aware of the positive qualities of American entertainment, it will

   I. demand more high-quality entertainment
   II. demand less low-quality entertainment
   III. attend the theatre more often

(A) I only
(B) II only
(C) I and II only
(D) I and III only
(E) I, II, and III

25. When the author uses the expression "the Bible as guide and touchstone" in line 33, he probably means to refer to

(A) the interrelationship of the Bible and the "American Way of Life"
(B) an academic approach to researching the theatre and religion
(C) the relationship of Biblical concepts to basic ideas and values contained in theatrical productions
(D) the use of the Bible as a guide to everyday life
(E) the Bible as a source of inspiration for all

If there is still time remaining, you may review the questions in this section only. You may not turn to any other section of the test.

Section II   Problem Solving   Time: 30 minutes

Directions: Solve each of the following problems; then indicate the correct answer on the answer sheet. [On the actual test you will be permitted to use any space available on the examination paper for scratch work.]

NOTE: A figure that appears with a problem is drawn as accurately as possible so as to provide information that may help in answering the question (unless the words "Figure not drawn to scale" appear next ot the figure). Numbers in this test are real numbers.

1. If the length of a rectangle is increased by 20% and the width is decreased by 20%, then the area
   - (A) decreases by 20%
   - (B) decreases by 4%
   - (C) stays the same
   - (D) increases by 10%
   - (E) increases by 20%

2. If it is 250 miles from New York to Boston and 120 miles from New York to Hartford, what percentage of the distance from New York to Boston is the distance from New York to Hartford?
   - (A) 12%
   - (B) 24%
   - (C) 36%
   - (D) 48%
   - (E) 52%

3. The lead in a mechanical pencil is 5 inches long. After pieces $\frac{1}{8}$ of an inch long, $1\frac{3}{4}$ inches long, and $1\frac{1}{12}$ inches long are broken off, how long is the lead left in the pencil?
   - (A) 2 in.
   - (B) $2\frac{1}{24}$ in.
   - (C) $2\frac{1}{12}$ in.
   - (D) $2\frac{1}{4}$ in.
   - (E) $2\frac{1}{2}$ in.

4. It costs $1.00 each to make the first thousand copies of a record and it costs x dollars to make each subsequent copy. How many dollars will it cost to make 4800 copies of a record?
   - (A) 1,000
   - (B) 4,800
   - (C) 4,800x
   - (D) 1,000x + 3,800
   - (E) 1,000 + 3,800x

5. If a worker makes 4 boxes of labels in $1\frac{2}{3}$ hours, how many boxes of labels can he make in 50 minutes?
   - (A) 2
   - (B) $2\frac{1}{3}$
   - (C) $2\frac{2}{3}$
   - (D) $2\frac{5}{6}$
   - (E) 3

6. If $x + y = 3$ and $y/x = 2$, then y is equal to
   - (A) 0
   - (B) $\frac{1}{2}$
   - (C) 1
   - (D) $\frac{3}{2}$
   - (E) 2

7. A store buys paper towels for $9.00 a carton, each carton containing 20 rolls. The store sells a roll of paper towels for 50¢. About what percent of the cost is the selling price of a roll of paper towels?
(A) 11%
(B) 89%
(C) 100%
(D) 111%
(E) 119%

8. A history book weighs 2.4 pounds. 12 copies of the history book and 8 copies of an English book together weigh 42.8 pounds. How much will one copy of the English book weigh?
(A) 1 pound
(B) 1.4 pounds
(C) 1.75 pounds
(D) 2.88 pounds
(E) 14 pounds

9. A car goes 15 miles on a gallon of gas when it is driven at 50 miles per hour. When the car is driven at 60 miles per hour it only goes 80% as far. How far will it travel on a gallon of gas at 60 miles per hour?
(A) 12 miles
(B) 13.5 miles
(C) 16.5 miles
(D) 18.75 miles
(E) 20 miles

10. If $x + y = z$ and x and y are positive, then which of the following statements can be inferred?
  I. $x < y$
  II. $x < z$
  III. $x < 2z$

(A) I only
(B) II only
(C) I and II only
(D) II and III only
(E) I, II, and III

11. If it costs x cents to produce a single sheet of paper for the first 800 sheets and if every subsequent sheet costs $x/15$ cents, how much will it cost to produce 5,000 sheets of paper?
(A) 800x¢
(B) 1,080x¢
(C) 1,400x¢
(D) 2,430x¢
(E) 3,500x¢

12. If in 1967, 1968, and 1969 a worker received 10% more in salary each year than he did the previous year, how much more did he receive in 1969 than in 1967?

(A) 10% (D) 20%

(B) 12% (E) 21%

(C) 19%

13. If factory A turns out a cars an hour and factory B turns out b cars every 2 hours, how many cars will both factories turn out in 8 hours?

(A) $a + b$ (D) $8a + 4b$

(B) $8a$ (E) $8a + 8b$

(C) $8b$

14. If John makes a box every 5 minutes and Tim takes 7 minutes to make a box, what will be the ratio of the number of boxes produced by John to the number of boxes produced by Tim if they work 5 hours and 50 minutes?

(A) 5 to 6 (D) 7 to 5

(B) 5 to 7 (E) 2 to 1

(C) 6 to 5

15. If a store sells 3¼ crates of lettuce on Monday, 2⅙ on Tuesday, 4½ on Wednesday, and 1⅔ on Thursday, how many crates has the store sold altogether?

(A) 10 (D) 11¾

(B) 11½ (E) 12⅓

(C) 11⁷⁄₁₂

16. If $x + y > 4$ and $x < 3$, then $y > 1$ is true

(A) always (D) only if $x = 0$

(B) only if $x < 0$ (E) never

(C) only if $x > 0$

17. If 50 apprentices can finish a job in 4 hours and 30 journeymen can finish the same job in 4½ hours, how much of the job should be completed by 10 apprentices and 15 journeymen in one hour?

(A) ⅑ (D) ⅕

(B) ²⁹⁄₁₈₀ (E) ³⁹⁄₁₂₁

(C) ²⁶⁄₁₄₃

18. If 40% of all women are voters and 52% of the population are women, what percent of the population are women voters?

(A) 18.1% (D) 40

(B) 20.8% (E) 52

(C) 26.4%

19. If a bus can travel 15 miles on a gallon of gas, how many gallons of gas will it use to travel 200 miles?

(A) 10

(D) 15

(B) 12½

(E) 20⅕

(C) 13⅓

20. A tank contains 10 gallons of water. If a pump takes $15 - \dfrac{x}{10}$ minutes to pump one gallon of water out of the tank, how many minutes will it take for the pump to empty the tank?

(A) x

(D) $150 - x$

(B) $15 - 10x$

(E) $15 - 10x$

(C) $150 - 10x$

If there is still time remaining, you may review the questions in this section only. You may not turn to any other section of the test.

Section III Analysis of Situations   Time: 30 minutes

Directions: Read the following passages. After you have completed each one, you will be asked to answer questions that involve determining the importance of specific factors included in the passage. When answering questions, you may consult the passage.

PASSAGE 1

The second day of Vespucci SpA's annual sales conference in Milan threatened to end in uproar. The business equipment manufacturer's 28 salesmen had received sales manager Guido Tulli's proposal to re-assign them to new territories with angry condemnation.

Explaining the reasons behind the drastic measures, Tulli had reminded the salesmen that the company was suffering from declining sales and had a serious cash flow problem. This was mainly due to slow payments by customers. Accounts receivable were increasing at an alarming rate, he had told them.

Under Tulli's plan, the company's top salesmen were to be switched from the areas with high sales to areas that currently yielded low sales. He had explained that this would mean that the more experienced salesmen could concentrate on building up sales in the less productive regions. The less experienced salesmen could easily handle the well-developed territories.

Some of the firm's leading salesmen immediately started to object. "I have spent years building up my territory," one of them protested. "I do not see why I should have to start all over again in a new region."

Tulli pointed out that he felt that the firm's best salesmen were being wasted in these well-developed sales regions. "You are simply going to well-established customers and taking orders," he argued.

An experienced salesman contested this view, observing that he had greatly increased sales in his territory the previous year by persuading existing customers to expand the amount of their orders in business stationery.

This supported his view, retorted Tulli, that the salesmen in the well-established territories were becoming stale, and were failing to uncover new customers. "This is only natural," he added. "When I was promoted to the sales manager, I was amazed at how successful my successor was in getting new orders in my old territory. The company badly needs your experience to develop the weaker regions."

Another experienced salesman asked whether the new plan would mean that salesmen would get an extra bonus or higher commission rates for establishing new accounts. Tulli began to explain why he thought this was impractical, when he was interrupted by one of the younger salesmen who had been sitting at the back of the room quietly fuming. He told Tulli that he felt completely demotivated by the proposal to remove them from the undeveloped territories.

Tulli tried to reassure the young salesman that the company did not regard them as failures. The changes were being made simply because the company was having difficulties, and needed to boost sales quickly, he pointed out.

Tulli swallowed hard before announcing another new policy he knew was likely to upset the gathered salesmen. "The management board has also decided that in future sales commissions will be paid quarterly and only on those orders for which payments have been received from customers," he announced nervously. "As from today it will be your responsibility to raise the subject of slow payments with customers. Moreover, no new orders will be accepted from customers until all overdue payments are received."

This was too much for the salesmen to take and the meeting erupted into a noisy uproar. "Why shouldn't we be paid for orders we have succeeded in getting?" demanded one salesman furiously. "It is not our job to collect debts," protested another. "This contravenes our employment contract," shouted yet another.

The salesmen were all talking agitatedly at once when Tulli decided to close the proceedings for that day. He rushed to a nearby hotel where group managing director Leon Cavello was staying overnight. He was due to address the conference the following morning.

"Our proposals have met with even more hostility than we expected," Tulli told Cavello, relating how the meeting had broken up in disorder. "I'm afraid you will have a hard time of it tomorrow convincing them that the proposals are in everybody's interest. But I don't think we can dodge the issue now. We have to tackle it while we have them all together."

Cavello nodded gravely. His first inclination was to proceed with the proposals whether or not the salesmen approved. On the other hand, he reflected, salesmen are the key to a company's success. It might be unwise to impose a new system on them without their consent.

Cavello convinced Tulli that his plan, presented during the day at the sales meeting, could not be implemented because of the unequivocal opposition of the salesmen. A compromise plan had to be worked out. Tulli and Cavello worked long into the night putting together a plan which they believed would be acceptable to most of the salesmen and in harmony with the company's objectives.

Tulli suggested assigning quotas to salesmen in existing territories rather than shifting successful salesmen from high-sales territories. "By assigning quotas, we can measure individual performance and motivate salesmen towards a predetermined level of achievement. Annual quotas based on expected sales also help in planning production, inventory, and working capital needs. Shifting salesmen is easier under a quota system because quotas can be easily adjusted to reflect the area's potential. If a low-yielding territory has low sales potential, the quota would be relatively lower than in a high-yielding, high-potential territory."

Cavello agreed that a quota system might be the solution to their sales problem. However, quotas had some disadvantages. "Companies sometimes set lower quotas for less able salesmen, but this can be demoralizing. Better salesmen will feel that they are being discriminated against. They will not give their best effort under such a plan." Tulli insisted that a quota system would work. "We need to find a plan which will motivate our best as well as our younger, less experienced salesmen."

Cavello summarized the available options. The first option was a straight commission plan. No matter how much sales a salesman produced over his quota, he would earn the same commission rate. A second possibility was a combination of salary and commissions. "Salesmen drawing even nominal salaries tend to think as company men and they have less reason to resist sales plan changes that are justified in terms of goals." Cavello further pointed out that special incentives could be offered under such a plan, such as a new account bonus or higher commission rates for sales over 100% of quota. "By offering such incentives," Cavello added, "salesmen in less productive regions would be motivated to spend more time in building new accounts."

Tulli agreed that both options suggested by Cavello might be accepted by the salesmen. "But," he asked, "are these options better for the company than the ones I proposed today?"

Data Evaluation Questions

Directions: The questions that follow relate to the preceding passage. Evaluate, in terms of the passage, each of the items given. Then select your answer from one of the following classifications, and blacken the corresponding space on the answer sheet.

   (A) A MAJOR OBJECTIVE in making the decision: one of the goals sought by the decision maker

   (B) A MAJOR FACTOR in making the decision: an aspect of the problem, specifically mentioned in the passage, that fundamentally affects and/ or determines the decision

   (C) A MINOR FACTOR in making the decision: a less important element bearing on or affecting a Major Factor, rather than a Major Objective directly

   (D) A MAJOR ASSUMPTION in making the decision: a projection or supposition arrived at by the decision maker before considering the factors and alternatives

   (E) AN UNIMPORTANT ISSUE in making the decision: an item lacking significant impact on, or relationship to, the decision

1. Vespucci SpA's declining sales

2. Vespucci's accounts receivable problem

3. Vespucci's Italian location

4. Improved cash flow

5. Ease with which salesmen may be shifted under a quota system

6. Development of new customers

7. Late payments by customers

8. Ability of top salesmen to succeed in any territory

9. Assignment of quotas to salesmen

10. Flexibility in setting quotas at either high or low levels

11. Measurement of salesmen's individual performances

12. Likelihood that salesmen will accept Cavello's options

13. Disadvantages of sales quotas

14. Tulli's experience in dealing with salesmen

15. Number of salesmen working for Vespucci

16. Motivation of Vespucci salesmen

17. Planning production, inventory, and working capital

18. Rejection of Tulli's plan by salesmen

PASSAGE 2

Mr. Mark Davidson is the Vice-President and General Manager of the International Division of the Doltry Mining Company. His chief responsibility is choosing investment opportunities for the company, which has recently been investigating different sites for the establishment of a new mining facility. Doltry has been trying to adopt a global planning strategy whereby the enterprise makes its major business decisions of allocating limited resources by considering global opportunities and alternatives as well as future global consequences. For each project, all possible alternatives are to be sorted out and compared as to profitability potential and consequences for achieving the firm's goals. The decision should not be biased as to which country is chosen, but rather, should rest on the site's potential of profitability to the company.

In order to insure a clear, unbiased opinion, some precautions were taken. One of the major safeguards Doltry used was the replacement of the names of the countries with letters. Another safeguard implemented was to limit the amount of information given on the countries Davidson was required to choose from. Furthermore, Davidson's choices only included the three countries that Doltry felt were most viable.

Unknown to Davidson, the first alternative given, Country A, was his home country, the United States. Country B was described as a lesser developed country, and Country C was described as an advanced country.

The information given on Country A include a sizeable deficit in the current account balance. This deficit was caused, in major part, by changes in operating performance, specifically owing to the deteriorating merchandise trade. Eventually, imports had exceeded exports; thereby, a major earnings contributor was eliminated. The reason cited for this change was increased foreign competition in export markets. Other factors in the current account included services and interest income from abroad. These factors were positive—i.e., earnings exceeded payments. However, the net earnings have not been large enough to offset the deficit in the merchandise account.

Another factor even more important was the country's weak liquidity position. Foreigners questioned whether this trend would ever reverse itself. They feared Country A might not be able to meet its obligations upon demand. On a more positive note, assets still exceeded liabilities.

Mr. Davidson was further given some information on Country A's political risk. Expropriation in Country A was seldomly enacted and when it had been, adequate compensation was provided. There were few political forces hostile toward foreign enterprise. Corruption and scandal seemed abnormally high in recent years. Only a limited amount of nationalistic philosophy was observed.

In the past ten years, there were no examples of armed conflict. For the most part, law enforcement was effective. Political uncertainty was minimal, as most citizens felt fairly confident with their government. Internal violence has been minimal. There have been few armed uprisings or assassinations. While police and internal security forces are strong, they are rarely used.

Country A has experienced a small but consistent growth pattern in gross national product per capita for the last seven years. Energy consumption has been increasing quite rapidly. There is one basic language in Country A, which is used by most people, even though many nationalities coexist in this country.

Extensive political competition exists and is encouraged. Legislative effectiveness, in theory, makes good sense; in actuality, however, the laws are difficult to enforce. There have been few constitutional changes in recent years. There is a set routine with regard to changing the head of state; however, some deviations have occurred. Mr. Davidson believed that Country A was a good political and economic risk.

Mr. Davidson's second alternative was Country B, a less developed country (LDC). The balance of payments information given Davidson had been obtained from the central bank. Country B's financial situation as indicated by its balance of payments was analyzed first. Data were only available for the past three years. These data showed an extremely high deficit for the first year, slightly lower the second year, and substantially lower the third year. SEE CHART BELOW.

This deficit was caused by the development process which Country B was in the middle of. Davidson thought that, although Country B's current account was in deficit, imports were being used for industrialization. This growth process was a sign of strength.

Currect Account Balance
For Country B
In Millions of Dollars

Year 1	Year 2	Year 3
−1,028	−986	−684

For an LDC, the balance of payments data were relatively favorable. However, political risks still had to be considered. Analyzing political risks gave some insight into Country B. There were little political turmoil and no recorded takeovers of private enterprises. The possibility of expropriation was believed to be nonexistent in the near future because of the lack of mining technology and capital available in Country B. Fear of future nationalistic feelings and a conviction that natural resource endowments should be exploited for the welfare of the residents of Country B, rather than for private profit, are shared by all managers of extractive industries there. It is believed that Country B would not have sufficient skills in the techniques of mining for approximately six years. Thus, fear of expropriation would not be present for this time period. Growth in gross national product per capita was extremely high. Energy consumption per capita, however, was relatively low.

As a result of the need for capital and technology, Country B would welcome foreign investment. Latent hostility would be minimal. Political stability was strengthened by the fact that a common goal was present.

Measures of societal conflict and government processes were considered by Davidson as indicators of the political climate. Public unrest and internal violence were barely existent. There were no irregular changes in heads of state ever recorded. These were positive indications of stability. Davidson also recommended that Doltry consider investing in Country B.

Finally, Country C, considered an advanced country, was analyzed. The balance of payments statistics were quite impressive. The current account surplus was increasing rapidly and approaching one billion dollars. If Country C were a company, it would be very profitable. Exports have exceeded imports for the past nine years.

Liquidity was not a problem in Country C. There was a good amount of capital in long-term investments. The country never had trouble paying its debts on time and, therefore, never accumulated much interest costs. One of the country's top priorities was to pay debts as soon as they were due. Country C also appeared to be in an excellent position for a loan, should it need one.

The problems of Country C lie in the instability of the government. Country C's recent political independence has contributed greatly to this problem. The lack of experienced political leadership has created considerable turmoil. This lack is due to the fact that there are many small parties. There is ineffective law enforcement, and this can adversely affect production, communication, and transportation.

There have been numerous reports of public unrest. Violent rioting and many organized demonstrations have created an uneasy feeling among the citizens. Internal violence has included three assassinations in the past five years. Limited security forces have certainly been one of the main causes of Country C's problems.

Legislative ineffectiveness in both the enactment stage and the carrying-out stage has done further damage to the country. The lack of a constitution and the irregular changes in heads of state have made Country C unstable. Although Country C has a strong economy, its political instability led Davidson to submit a negative recommendation as an investment opportunity.

Data Evaluation Questions

Directions: The questions that follow relate to the preceding passage. Evaluate, in terms of the passage, each of the items given. Then select your answer from one of the following classifications, and blacken the corresponding space on the answer sheet.

(A) A MAJOR OBJECTIVE in making the decision: one of the goals sought by the decision maker

(B) A MAJOR FACTOR in making the decision: an aspect of the problem, specifically mentioned in the passage, that fundamentally affects and/or determines the decision

(C) A MINOR FACTOR in making the decision: a less important element bearing on or affecting a Major Factor, rather than a Major Objective directly

(D) A MAJOR ASSUMPTION in making the decision: a projection or supposition arrived at by the decision maker before considering the factors and alternatives

(E) AN UNIMPORTANT ISSUE in making the decision: an item lacking significant impact on, or relationship to, the decision

19. Global planning strategy

20. Country A's deteriorating merchandise trade balance

21. Expropriation in Country A

22. Country A's liquidity position

23. Country A's political risk

24. Only one language in Country A

25. Country A, a good political risk

26. Likelihood of expropriation in Country B

27. Country B, a Less Developed Country

28. Country B's balance of payments position

29. Measures of societal conflict

30. Changes in heads of state

31. Selecting investment opportunities

32. Instability of Country C's government

33. Number of political parties in Country C

34. Country A was Davidson's home country

35. The number of political parties

If there is still time remaining, you may review the questions in this section only. You may not turn to any other section of the test.

Section IV   Data Sufficiency   Time: 30 minutes

Directions: Each of the following problems has a question and two statements which are labeled (1) and (2). Use the data given in (1) and (2) together with other available information (such as the number of hours in a day, the definition of *clockwise*, mathematical facts, etc.) to decide whether the statements are *sufficient* to answer the question. Then fill in space

(A) if you can get the answer from (1) alone but not from (2) alone;

(B) if you can get the answer from (2) alone but not from (1) alone;

(C) if you can get the answer from (1) and (2) together, although neither statement by itself suffices;

(D) if statement (1) alone suffices *and* statement (2) alone suffices;

(E) if you cannot get the answer from statements (1) and (2) together, but need even more data.

All numbers used in this section are real numbers. A figure given for a problem is intended to provide information consistent with that in the question, but not necessarily with the additional information contained in the statements.

1. A piece of wood 5 feet long is cut into three smaller pieces. How long is the longest of the three pieces?
   (1) One piece is 2 feet 7 inches long.
   (2) One piece is 7 inches longer than another piece and the remaining piece is 5 inches long.

2. *AC* is a diameter of the circle. *ACD* is a straight line. What is the value of *x*?
   (1) $AB = BC$　　　　　　　　　　(2)　$x = 2y$

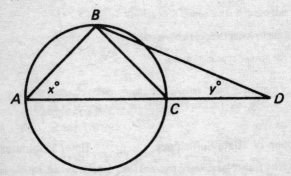

3. What is the value of *y*?
   (1) $x + 2y = 6$　　　　　　　　　　(2) $y^2 - 2y + 1 = 0$

4. Two pipes, *A* and *B*, empty into a reservoir. Pipe *A* can fill the reservoir in 30 minutes by itself. How long will it take for pipe *A* and pipe *B* together to fill up the reservoir?

(1) By itself, pipe *B* can fill the reservoir in 20 minutes.

(2) Pipe *B* has a larger cross-sectional area than pipe *A*.

5. *AB* is perpendicular to *CO*. Is *A* or *B* closer to *C*?

   (1) *OA* is less than *OB*.

   (2) *ACBD* is not a parallelogram.

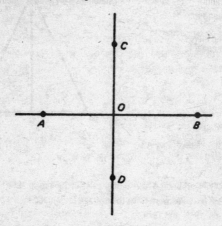

6. Is *xy* greater than 1? *x* and *y* are both positive.

   (1) *x* is less than 1.   (2) *y* is greater than 1.

7. Does *x* = *y*?

   (1) *z* = *u*   (2) *ABCD* is a parallelogram.

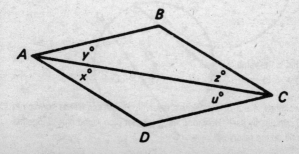

8. Train T leaves town A for town B and travels at a constant rate of speed. At the same time, train S leaves town B for town A and also travels at a constant rate of speed. Town C is between A and B. Which train is traveling faster? Towns A, C, B lie on a straight line.
   (1) Train S arrives at town C before train T.
   (2) C is closer to A than to B.

9. Does $x = y$?
   (1) BD is perpendicular to AC.
   (2) AB is equal to BC.

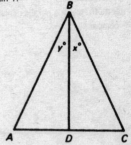

10. What is the value of $x + y$?
    (1) $x - y = 4$ (2) $3x + 3y = 4$

11. Did the XYZ Corporation have higher sales in 1968 or in 1969?
    (1) In 1968 the sales were twice the average (arithmetic mean) of the sales in 1968, 1969, and 1970.
    (2) In 1970, the sales were three times those in 1969.

12. AB and CD are both chords of the circle with center O. Which is longer, AB or CD?
    (1) Arc AEB is smaller than arc CFD.
    (2) The area of the circular segment $CAEBD$ is larger than the area of circular segment $ACFDB$.

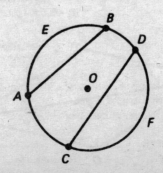

13. Is *ABDC* a square?

   (1) *BC* is perpendicular to *AD*.   (2) *BE = EC*.

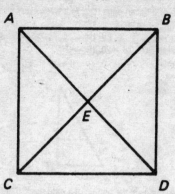

14. *k* is an integer. Is *k* divisible by 12?

   (1) *k* is divisible by 4.   (2) *k* is divisible by 3.

15. How far is it from *A* to *B*?

   (1) It is 15 miles from *A* to *C*.   (2) It is 25 miles from *C* to *B*.

16. Was Melissa Brown's novel published?

   (1) If Melissa Brown's novel was published she would receive at least $1,000 in royalties during 1978.

   (2) Melissa Brown's income for 1978 was over $1,000.

17. Is *x* an even integer? Assume *n* and *p* are integers.

   (1) $x = (n + p)^2$ (2) $x = 2n + 10p$

18. Did the price of lumber rise by more than 10% last year?

   (1) Lumber exports increased by 20%.

   (2) The amount of timber cut decreased by 10%.

19. Find the value of *z* if *x* = 3.

   (1) $z = (x + 3)^4$ (2) $z = 2x + y$

20. What was the price of a dozen eggs during the 15th week of the year 1977?
   (1) During the first week of 1977 the price of a dozen eggs was 75¢.
   (2) The price of a dozen eggs rose 1¢ a week every week during the first four months of 1977.

21. Is *DE* parallel to *BC*? *DB* = *AD*.
   (1) *AE* = *EC*   (2) *DB* = *EC*

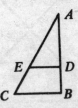

22. There are two drains in the bottom of a water tank. If drain 1 is opened and drain 2 is closed a full tank will be empty in 15 minutes. How long will it take to empty a full tank if drain 1 and drain 2 are both opened?
   (1) If drain 1 is closed and drain 2 is opened it takes 20 minutes to empty a full tank.
   (2) In 3 minutes as much water flows through drain 1 as flows through drain 2 in 4 minutes.

23. Is $x > y$?
   (1) $\dfrac{x}{y} = \dfrac{5}{4}$ (2) $x^2 > y^2$

24. Does every bird fly?
   (1) Tigers do not fly.   (2) Ostriches do not fly.

25. Find $x + 2y$.
   (1) $x - y = 12$ (2) $3x - 3y = 36$

If there is still time remaining, you may review the questions in this section only. You may not turn to any other section of the test.

Section V   Writing Ability   Time: 30 minutes

Directions: This test consists of a number of sentences, in each of which some part or the whole is underlined. Each sentence is followed by five alternative versions of the underlined portion. Select the alternative you consider both most correct and most effective according to the requirements of standard written English. Answer A is the same as the original version; if you think the original version is best, select answer A.

In considering the answer choices, be attentive to matters of grammar, diction, and syntax, as well as clarity, precision, and fluency. Do not select an answer which alters the meaning of the original sentence.

1. Since neither of the agencies had submitted the necessary documentation, each were required to reapply for the grant the following year.
   (A) each were required to reapply for the grant the following year
   (B) each were required, the following year, to reapply for the grant
   (C) each was required to reapply for the grant the following year
   (D) both were required to reapply, the following year, for the grant
   (E) it was required to reapply for the grant the following year

2. Stationary missile launching sites are frequently criticized by military experts on the ground that, in comparison to mobile units, they are the most vulnerable to preemptive attack.
   (A) they are the most   (D) stationary sites are most
   (B) such sites are the most   (E) they are more
   (C) they are rather

3. The qualities needed in a president are scarcely tested in today's political campaigns, which call instead for showmanship, good looks, and being able to seem eloquent while saying nothing.
   (A) being able to seem eloquent   (D) a certain eloquence
   (B) the ability to seem eloquent   (E) that he seem eloquent
   (C) having eloquence

4. Anyone who would speak with authority on the poets of the Renaissance must have a broad acquaintance with the writers of classical antiquity.
   (A) Anyone who would speak   (D) Anyone desirous for speaking
   (B) If one would speak   (E) Those who have a wish to speak
   (C) He which would speak

5. <u>Having chosen to demand an immediate vote on the issue</u>, because of his belief that a sizable majority was within easy reach.
   - (A) Having chosen to demand an immediate vote on the issue
   - (B) An immediate vote on the issue having been demanded
   - (C) He had chosen to demand an immediate vote on the issue
   - (D) His demand had been for an immediate vote to be held on the issue
   - (E) He had chosen that a vote on the issue should be held immediately

6. In its final report, the commission proposed, among other measures, <u>that the legal drinking age be raised</u> from eighteen to twenty-one.
   - (A) that the legal drinking age be raised
   - (B) a rise of the legal drinking age
   - (C) that the legal drinking age should be raised
   - (D) raising the age of drinking legally
   - (E) to raise legally the drinking age

7. Since neither <u>her nor the Dean were willing</u> to veto the curriculum changes, they went into effect as of September 1.
   - (A) her nor the Dean were willing
   - (B) she nor the Dean was willing
   - (C) her nor the Dean wished
   - (D) she or the Dean was willing
   - (E) she nor the Dean were willing

8. <u>A broad range of opinions was represented between</u> the various members of the steering committee.
   - (A) A broad range of opinions was represented between
   - (B) A broad range of opinions were represented between
   - (C) A broad range of opinions had been held by
   - (D) A broad range of opinions was represented among
   - (E) Varying opinions were represented by

9. Undaunted by the political repercussions of his decision, <u>the new gasoline rationing plan was announced by the Governor</u> at the state office building last Friday.
   - (A) the new gasoline rationing plan was announced by the Governor
   - (B) the Governor's new gasoline rationing plan was announced
   - (C) the Governor made the announcement concerning the new gasoline rationing plan
   - (D) the new gasoline rationing plan of the Governor was announced
   - (E) the Governor announced the new gasoline rationing plan

10. Mario had already swum five laps when I jumped into the pool.
    (A) had already swum five laps when I
    (B) already swam five laps when I
    (C) already swam five laps when I had
    (D) had already swum five laps when I had
    (E) had already swam five laps when I

11. Despite their avowed opposition to the strike, no one from among the dozens of nonunion workers were willing to cross the picket line.
    (A) from among the dozens of nonunion workers were willing
    (B) of the dozens of nonunion workers were willing
    (C) was willing from among the dozens of nonunion workers
    (D) from among the dozens of nonunion workers was willing
    (E) from the dozens of nonunion workers were willing

12. According to one recent survey, gasoline economy, low price, and safety have replaced style and comfort as leading factors in the choice of a new car.
    (A) and safety have replaced
    (B) and safe driving have replaced
    (C) and safety has replaced
    (D) as well as safety has replaced
    (E) along with safety have replaced

13. The poetry of George Herbert is regarded by many critics as equal in quality, though less influential, than the work of his more famous contemporary John Donne.
    (A) equal in quality, though less influential, than the work
    (B) equal in quality to, though less influential than, the work
    (C) qualitatively equal, though less influential than, that
    (D) equal in quality, though less influential, then the work
    (E) of equal quality, though of less influence, than that

14. If it is the present administration whom we should blame for the economic crisis, the first step toward a solution is to reject the incumbent at the polls this November.
    (A) whom we should blame   (D) who should be blamed
    (B) whom is to blame   (E) who one should blame
    (C) who we should blame

15. The assembly speaker has called for a shorter fall session of the legislature in hopes that less amendments of a purely symbolic nature will be proposed by the state's lawmakers.
    (A) in hopes that less amendments of a
    (B) hoping that fewer amendments that have a
    (C) in hopes that fewer amendments of a
    (D) in order that less amendments of a
    (E) in hope that fewer amendments of

16. One of the costliest engineering projects ever undertaken, both public and private funds have been needed to support the space shuttle program.
    (A) One of the costliest engineering projects ever undertaken, both public and private funds have been needed to support the space shuttle program.
    (B) One of the costliest engineering projects ever undertaken, support for the space shuttle program has come from both public and private funds.
    (C) The space shuttle program has been supported by both public and private funds, one of the costliest engineering projects ever undertaken.
    (D) From both public and private funds support has come for one of the costliest engineering projects ever undertaken; namely, the space shuttle program.
    (E) Both public and private funds have been needed to support the space shuttle program, one of the costliest engineering projects ever undertaken.

17. Parker's testimony made it clear that he appointed Ryan before he had become aware of Ryan's alleged underworld connections.
    (A) he appointed Ryan before he had become aware
    (B) he appointed Ryan before his awareness
    (C) he had appointed Ryan prior to his having become aware
    (D) his appointment of Ryan preceded awareness
    (E) he had appointed Ryan before becoming aware

18. Despite its being smaller in size than are conventional automobile engines, the new Alcock Engine can still deliver the horsepower needed for most short-distance city driving.
    (A) Despite its being smaller in size than are

(B) In spite of its being smaller than

(C) Although smaller than

(D) Despite its size relative to

(E) Though not comparable in size to

19. Seventy-four applications were received, of whom the better were selected for detailed review.

    (A) of whom the better were selected

    (B) from which were selected the better

    (C) the best of which were selected

    (D) from whom were selected the best

    (E) from which they selected the best

20. If the British government had had no fear of the increasing hostility of the Indian populace, Gandhi's nonviolent tactics would have availed little.

    (A) If the British government had had no fear of

    (B) If the British government did not fear

    (C) Had the British government no fear

    (D) If the British government did not have fear of

    (E) Would the British government not have feared

21. The official imposition of "Lysenkoism" on Soviet biologists, with its chilling effects on scientists in countless related fields, illustrate vividly the dangers of government interference with science.

    (A) illustrate vividly the dangers of government interference with science

    (B) illustrate the dangers of government interference with science vividly

    (C) illustrates vividly the dangers of government interference with science

    (D) vividly illustrate the dangers of government interference with science

    (E) vividly illustrates how dangerous can be government interference with science

22. Health care costs have been forced upward less by increases in the salaries of nurses, technicians, and other personnel than by increases in the amounts spent on diagnostic machinery and electronic equipment.

    (A) than by increases in the amounts

    (B) than the amounts

    (C) but by increases in the amounts

    (D) and more by increases in the amounts

    (E) than by funds

23. The press secretary announced that neither himself nor the President would be available for questions until they had had more time to examine the report.
    - (A) neither himself nor the President would be
    - (B) neither he or the President was
    - (C) neither he nor the President would be
    - (D) he and the President will not be
    - (E) he nor the President would be

24. In routine cases, the Civilian Review Board receives all complaints about police misconduct, weighs the evidence and the seriousness of the charges, and then it decides whether a formal inquiry is needed.
    - (A) then it decides whether a formal inquiry is needed
    - (B) then decides if a formal inquiry would be needed
    - (C) then it decides whether to hold a formal inquiry
    - (D) then decides whether a formal inquiry is needed
    - (E) decides at that point if a formal inquiry is needed or not

25. Current scientific theory suggests that the dinosaurs were, in fact, one of the most spectacularly successful groups of organisms ever developed in the course of evolution.
    - (A) groups of organisms ever developed
    - (B) group of organisms that have been developed
    - (C) groups of organisms to ever be developed
    - (D) group of organisms to be developed
    - (E) groups of organism developed

If there is still time remaining, you may review the questions in this section only. You may not turn to any other section of the test.

Section VI   Analysis of Situations   Time: 30 minutes

Directions: Read the following passages. After you have completed each one, you will be asked to answer questions that involve determining the importance of specific factors included in the passage. When answering questions, you may consult the passage.

PASSAGE 1

Luigi Cappa was beginning to wonder what had made him give up a smoothly running job in New York to tackle what had turned out to be a baffling problem in southern Italy.

He was a U.S. citizen, and if he had stayed with his company he might have had a seat on the board within two years.

Then an uncle in Turin, in northern Italy, had written to Cappa, imploring him to come and run his printing plant near Palermo in Sicily, which produced transfer designs and other specialized printing, some of it for export.

Cappa was 28 years old, unmarried and ambitious. The offer had appealed to him in several ways.

First, there was the chance to be his own boss immediately. Second, there was the challenge, as Cappa saw it, of bringing U.S. know-how to the Italian family firm. Third, there was the satisfaction of returning as a man of some authority to the country where his own father had been born.

He was a believer in scientific management. He also believed that people everywhere are basically alike and will respond in about the same way to the carrot of cash rewards and the stick of firm leadership.

After only a few months in Palermo, he knew differently. Cappa's uncle had set up the plant five years previously with the active encouragement of the Italian government. But the 300-strong labor force still had no loyalty to the company from the distant north. The workers dreamed of orange groves rather than production targets.

Indeed, on one occasion Cappa had found a worker blissfully cleaning equipment from one of the printing machines in an orange grove near the plant. When he had ordered him back into the plant the man had looked astonished and replied: "Why should I work inside when I can do my job here?"

Productivity was very low. When Cappa had visited a local barber, who knew that he worked in the printing plant but did not know he was the boss, the man had said: "Sir, can you get me a job with the printing company so that I no longer have to work?"

As Cappa walked round the plant he saw plenty of modern machines. He also saw a workforce that yearned to be out in the sun, and wondered how he could get his employees to change their attitudes.

First, he tried using his personal appeal as an American-Italian. That did not work. He would have been more successful, he ruefully admitted to himself, had he been born in Palermo.

He instituted production committees, which were supposed to generate their own ideas on improving productivity. He worked at them very hard but they too were a dismal failure.

When managers sat on the committees the workers seemed struck dumb, failing to produce constructive ideas. Then, when Cappa gave the committee more autonomy to run its own affairs, the members used the time allocated for meetings to leave the factory and take a siesta outside.

Cappa decided that a bonus system relating pay directly to output was the only solution. At first the union opposed this, saying it was the kind of piecework they had been fighting against. Then, to Cappa's surprise, they gave in. He thought he had won a victory.

If so, it was a hollow one. The workers began demanding the bonus as a right, whether or not they had worked extra hours or produced more. When Cappa refused to pay, the workers went on strike.

Cappa felt that he was dealing with forces beyond his control, with people whom he could not fully understand.

"They just don't seem to want to participate," he wrote to a friend in New York. "If you give them the chance to run their own affairs, they take advantage of it. If you offer them a carrot, they eat half your arm as well. And if you wave a stick, they strike."

Cappa's friend replied that he should investigate the possibility of instituting a system of co-determination management. Co-determination management gives workers a part in making decisions within the firm in areas that are traditionally the prerogative of management. What the system amounts to—in practical terms—is that it allows workers to have some managerial authority in deciding corporate policy, and in some cases, objectives. Once a decision is made in principle to institute such a system, the next step is to work out just how much authority management is willing to share with the workers and in what policy areas.

Cappa decided to give co-determination a try as a last resort. Rather than dictate specific areas in which to implement co-determination, Cappa felt that it would be best to consult with workers' committees and then make a joint decision. At first, the workers expressed some interest in the plan, but when they asked Cappa to explain how the system would add to their pay, he was taken aback. Cappa tried to explain to the workers that they would gain decision-making authority, not only on the plant floor but in policy-making. He further explained that they would have some power to influence, for example, whether profits should be re-invested in the company, or distributed to shareholders. In reply, the workers' representatives said that they had no interest in having responsibility for managerial decisions because they had enough problems of their own. With that response, Cappa realized that his co-determination scheme had no chance of being accepted by the workers.

Cappa seemed to have reached a dead end. He could advise his uncle to concentrate production in Turin and get rid of the Palermo plant. But then he would have to return to the U.S. without a job and with a feeling of defeat.

Alternatively, Cappa could find a way of motivating his workers. But *how*, he asked himself for the thousandth time.

Data Evaluation Questions

Directions: The questions that follow relate to the preceding passage. Evaluate, in terms of the passage, each of the items given. Then select your answer from one of the following classifications, and blacken the corresponding space on the answer sheet.

(A) A MAJOR OBJECTIVE in making the decision: one of the goals sought by the decision maker

(B) A MAJOR FACTOR in making the decision: an aspect of the problem, specifically mentioned in the passage, that fundamentally affects and/or determines the decision

(C) A MINOR FACTOR in making the decision: a less important element bearing on or affecting a Major Factor, rather than a Major Objective directly

(D) A MAJOR ASSUMPTION in making the decision: a projection or supposition arrived at by the decision maker before considering the factors and alternatives

(E) AN UNIMPORTANT ISSUE in making the decision: an item lacking significant impact on, or relationship to, the decision

1. Location of company headquarters in northern Italy

2. Basic similarity of the motivations of people everywhere

3. Increasing the motivation of the Sicilian workers

4. Low worker productivity

5. Likelihood that higher pay would improve output

6. Cappa's U.S. citizenship

7. Degree of worker loyalty to the company

8. Usefulness of cash rewards in motivating employees

9. Desire of workers to run their own affairs

10. Relating pay to output

11. Quality of the machines used in the factory

12. Proximity of orange groves to the plant

13. Cappa's desire to meet with workers' committees before settling on a plan

14. Cappa's high degree of personal ambition

15. Power of the union to influence worker attitudes and behavior

PASSAGE 2

Mr. Frank Kennedy, Chief Operating Executive of the Best Detergent Company, is upset over the sales records for 1981. To his dismay, although profits have increased, sales have decreased. Mr. Kennedy is concerned because, in his opinion, if sales continue to drop, a fall in profits cannot be far behind. Mr. Kennedy attributes this drop in sales to the failure of his company to introduce new or improved products and to the fact that most of his company's lines are in the maturation stage of the product's life cycle.

Mr. Kennedy's basic strategy for running the Best Detergent Company is one that leans towards simple company survival as compared to profit maximization. Because of his age (63) and the fact that he will retire in two years, Kennedy does not want to take any unnecessary risks. He wants to leave the company in good standing.

In order to solve this problem, Mr. Kennedy met with Chris Simmons, Vice-President of Marketing, who wants to introduce a new product, and with Roger Decker, Vice-President of the International Division of the Best Detergent Company, who wants to improve an already established product. Mr. Kennedy feels he can trust these two men to come up with an idea that will pull sales back up. Of course, the final decision as to which strategy will be used will be left up to Mr. Kennedy. Kennedy emphasized to these two men that the goal of this project was to increase sales in order that the desired profit level be maintained for at least the next two years or more, as Mr. Simmons and Mr. Decker will be at the company for at least ten more years. A poor recommendation not only may hurt the company, but may hurt the professional reputation of these two men as well.

Chris Simmons, Vice-President of Marketing, is pondering the possibility of introducing a new and what he feels to be superior fabric softener. His research consultants have been working on this product for the past 18 months. Tests were done to see how well the fabric softener did its job. The fabric softener was concentrated and, therefore, only a small amount was needed; this made it economical. Its fragrance was pleasing, and it rinsed well out of the clothes as it softened them. The product had another desirable trait—although its color was blue, the softener did not stain if directly spilled on an article of clothing. Most blue softeners on the market today do stain. The product would be sold in 16-ounce containers.

Since the Best Detergent Company is a multinational corporation, management desires products that will sell well in other countries. Mr. Simmons feels that this fabric softener will do well not only in the United States, but also in France, England, and Italy, the three countries Best operates in. Simmons feels the quality of this product is so superb that it will be a welcome change from all the average softeners available at the present time.

In Mr. Simmons' opinion, the introduction of a new product will help change the company's image from one of the established products to one of contemporary, up-to-the-minute innovations. According to Mr. Simmons, stagnation of product lines is a major problem of the company. The introduction of a new fabric softener will solve this problem of stagnation, and it is the feeling of Mr. Simmons that this product will not only meet Mr. Kennedy's requirement for profit level, but will exceed it. Mr. Simmons is anxious to get his product on the market as soon as possible. Being number one with a new product line can very well influence the success of the product. If this product were first on the market, it would, as a result of lack of competition, obtain higher-than-average profits. It is the opinion of Mr. Simmons that success of this product is inevitable because when consumers see the Best name, they will associate it with the quality detergent products that the Best Company is known for.

Mr. Simmons' last point to persuade Mr. Kennedy to use this option is the amount of time, energy, and money spent on research and development for this product. If this product is not marketed, all effort to produce a superior product may be lost because of the fact that another company may develop a similar product or may steal the idea.

With a little advertising, this fabric softener could increase profits greatly as little money would be spent on other marketing functions. For instance, no money would be spent to develop new distribution channels, as marketing channels and promotional arrangements—which have been the result of years of work—have been established both in the United States and in France, England, and Italy.

On the other hand, Roger Decker does not think establishing a new product line is the answer to the dilemma. Mr. Decker feels that improving an established product is more what Mr. Kennedy is looking for. Decker also thinks more profits and greater success will be gained this way.

Mr. Decker would like to improve one of the company's best-selling detergents by adding a fabric softener to the actual detergent. Many other companies have done this in the past and have met with great success. As yet, Best Detergents has failed to enter this market.

Mr. Decker feels that this method of dealing with the problem is better than creating a new product. Less risks are involved, and the product already has a steady following of consumers. In addition to this, Mr. Decker has discovered through a study that was done that people prefer one laundry product to do the jobs of both cleaning and softening. More importantly, the foreign market is not as interested in softening agents as they are in cleansers. If a cleaning product were to have a softener in it, there is a good chance that European consumers will buy and be satisfied with the product. They will not, according to Mr. Decker, buy a separate fabric softener.

Mr. Decker is against the fabric softener idea basically because of his idea of what the Best Detergent Company is. Mr. Decker feels that what Best does best is make detergents. To establish a fabric softener product line would be out of the jurisdiction of the Best Company. Best has always dealt with powdered laundry detergents. They do not have the knowledge, experience, nor the facilities to deal with a liquid product.

Mr. Decker is aware of the high rate of new product failures in the consumer goods industry. Losses due to new product failure in the detergent industry are also substantial, not to mention the fact that a product failure will mar the hard-earned reputation of the Best Detergent lines already established. This, as a result, could stop consumers from purchasing other Best products and may push them into trying other brands of detergents.

Going with past records, Mr. Decker knows that whenever Best has introduced an established product as "New and Improved," sales have increased. There is consumer attraction to those products which can offer something new. Furthermore, to discredit Mr. Simmons' argument further, Mr. Decker feels that additional research and development would be useful in the objective of incorporating a softener into an established detergent. In this way some of the money, time, and energy already spent on R&D will be salvaged.

Mr. Decker estimated that it would take about 18 months of intensive development to commercialize a detergent containing a softener. Projected total costs of the commercialization were $2 million. This figure included $750,000 for development and testing, and the rest for marketing expenses, including $1 million for advertising. On the other hand, launching a new product, as Mr. Simmons proposed, would take two years, and its cost would be double that of the improved product. Much of the added expense would be allocated to marketing functions, especially advertising. Mr. Decker believed that at least $2 million would have to be allocated to advertising, of which $1 million would be spent on a television campaign, to successfully commercialize a new product.

Mr. Simmons did not refute Mr. Decker's estimates. He countered that a new product could contribute five times the sales of an existing, even if improved, product. The increased sales and profit contribution would more than pay for the additional marketing expenses incurred.

Data Evaluation Questions

Directions: The questions that follow relate to the preceding passage. Evaluate, in terms of the passage, each of the items given. Then select your answer from one of the following classifications, and blacken the corresponding space on the answer sheet.

(A) A MAJOR OBJECTIVE in making the decision: one of the goals sought by the decision maker

(B) A MAJOR FACTOR in making the decision: an aspect of the problem, specifically mentioned in the passage, that fundamentally affects and/ or determines the decision

(C) A MINOR FACTOR in making the decision: a less important element bearing on or affecting a Major Factor, rather than a Major Objective directly

(D) A MAJOR ASSUMPTION in making the decision: a projection or supposition arrived at by the decision maker before considering the factors and alternatives

(E) AN UNIMPORTANT ISSUE in making the decision: an item lacking significant impact on, or relationship to, the decision

16. Introduction of a fabric softener

17. Attributes of a fabric softener

18. Best Detergent, a multinational company

19. Modernizing the company's image

20. Developing products as fast as possible

21. Survival of the Best Detergent Company

22. Mr. Kennedy's plans to retire in two years

23. Increasing sales of the Best Detergent Company

24. Stagnation of product lines

25. Development time of the fabric softener

26. Costs of advertising

27. Marketing ability of Simmons and Decker

28. Color of the fabric softener

29. Competition in the detergent industry

30. Rate of new product failure of consumer goods

31. Television advertising expenses

32. Size of the product package

33. Professional reputation of Decker and Simmons

34. Best Detergent's operation in four countries

35. Probability of the fabric softener's succeeding

If there is still time remaining, you may review the questions in this section only. You may not turn to any other section of the test.

Section VII   Reading Comprehension   Time: 30 minutes

Directions: This part contains four reading passages. You are to read each one carefully. When answering the questions, you will be allowed to refer back to the passages. The questions are based on what is *stated* or *implied* in each passage.

PASSAGE 1

A newly issued report reveals in facts and figures what should have been known in principle, that quite a lot of business companies are going to go under during the coming decade, as tariff walls are progressively dismantled. Labor and capital valued at $12 billion are to be made idle through the impact
(5) of duty-free imports. As a result, 35,000 workers will be displaced. Some will move to other jobs and other departments within the same firm. Around 15,000 will have to leave the firm now employing them and work elsewhere.

The report is measuring exclusively the influence of free trade with Europe. The authors do not take into account the expected expansion of production
(10) over the coming years. On the other hand, they are not sure that even the export predictions they make will be achieved. For this presupposes that a suitable business climate lets the pressure to increase productivity materialize.

There are two reasons why this scenario may not happen. The first one is that industry on the whole is not taking the initiatives necessary to adapt fully
(15) to the new price situation it will be facing as time goes by.

This is another way of saying that the manufacturers do not realize what lies ahead. The government is to blame for not making the position absolutely clear. It should be saying that in ten years time tariffs on all industrial goods imported from Europe will be eliminated. There will be no adjustment assistance for
(20) manufacturers who cannot adapt to this situation.

The second obstacle to adjustment is not stressed in the same way in the report; it is the attitude of the service sector. Not only are service industries unaware that the Common Market treaty concerns them too, they are artificially insulated from the physical pressures of international competition. The man-
(25) ufacturing sector has been forced to apply its nose to the grindstone for some time now, by the increasingly stringent import-liberalization program.

The ancillary services on which the factories depend show a growing indifference to their work obligations. They seem unaware that overmanned ships, underutilized container equipment in the ports, and repeated work stoppages
(30) slow the country's attempts to narrow the trade gap. The remedy is to cut the fees charged by these services so as to reduce their earnings—in exactly the same way that earnings in industrial undertakings are reduced by the tariff reduction program embodied in the treaty with the European Community.

There is no point in dismissing 15,000 industrial workers from their present
(35) jobs during the coming ten years if all the gain in productivity is wasted by costly harbor, transport, financial, administrative and other services. The free trade treaty is their concern as well. Surplus staff should be removed, if need

be, from all workplaces, not just from the factories. Efficiency is everybody's business.

1. The attitude of the report, as described in the passage, may best be expressed as
   (A) harshly condemnatory, because industry is not more responsive to the business climate
   (B) optimistic that government will induce industry to make needed changes
   (C) critical of labor unions
   (D) pessimistic that anything can be done to reduce the trade gap
   (E) objective in assessing the influence of free trade on employment

2. What is the meaning of *free trade* in line 8?
   (A) unlimited sale of goods in Europe
   (B) trade on a barter basis
   (C) the elimination of tariffs
   (D) sale of price-discounted goods to European countries
   (E) trade with only the so-called "free countries," i.e., Western Europe

3. It can be inferred that the term *adjustment assistance* in line 19 refers mainly to
   (A) unemployment compensation
   (B) some sort of financial assistance to manufacturers hurt by free trade
   (C) help in relocating plants to Europe
   (D) aid in reducing work stoppages
   (E) subsidy payments to increase exports

4. The author's central recommendation seems to be that
   (A) unemployment should be avoided at all costs
   (B) redundant labor should be removed in all sectors
   (C) government should control the service sector
   (D) tariffs should not be lowered
   (E) workers should be retrained

5. Which of the following titles best describes the content of the passage?
   (A) *The Prospects of Free Trade*
   (B) *Government Intervention in World Trade*
   (C) *Trade with the Common Market*

(D) *What Lies Ahead?*
(E) *Unemployment and Adjustment Assistance*

PASSAGE 2

The fundamental objectives of sociology are the same as those of science generally—discovery and explanation. To *discover* the essential data of social behavior and the connections among the data is the first objective of sociology. To *explain* the data and the connections is the second and larger objective.
(5) Science makes its advances in terms of both of these objectives. Sometimes it is the discovery of a new element or set of elements that marks a major breakthrough in the history of a scientific discipline. Closely related to such discovery is the discovery of relationships of data that had never been noted before. All of this is, as we know, of immense importance in science. But the
(10) drama of discovery, in this sense, can sometimes lead us to overlook the greater importance of explanation of what is revealed by the data. Sometimes decades, even centuries, pass before known connections and relationships are actually explained. Discovery and explanation are the two great interpenetrating, interacting realms of science.
(15) The order of reality that interests the scientists is the *empirical* order, that is, the order of data and phenomena revealed to us through observation or experience. To be precise or explicit about what is, and is not, revealed by observation is not always easy, to be sure. And often it is necessary for our natural powers of observation to be supplemented by the most intricate of
(20) mechanical aids for a given object to become "empirical" in the sense just used. That the electron is not as immediately visible as is the mountain range does not mean, obviously, that it is any less empirical. That social behavior does not lend itself to as quick and accurate description as, say, chemical behavior of gases and compounds does not mean that social roles, statuses,
(25) and attitudes are any less empirical than molecules and tissues. What is empirical and observable today may have been nonexistent in scientific consciousness a decade ago. Moreover, the empirical is often data *inferred* from direct observation. All of this is clear enough, and we should make no pretense that there are not often shadow areas between the empirical and the nonem-
(30) pirical. Nevertheless, the first point to make about any science, physical or social, is that its world of data is the empirical world. A very large amount of scientific energy goes merely into the work of expanding the frontiers, through discovery, of the known, observable, empirical world.

From observation or discovery we move to *explanation*. The explanation

(35) sought by the scientist is, of course, not at all like the explanation sought by the theologian or metaphysician. The scientist is not interested—not, that is, in his role of scientist—in ultimate, transcendental, or divine causes of what he sets himself to explain. He is interested in explanations that are as empirical as the data themselves. If it is the high incidence of crime in a certain part of (40) a large city that requires explanation, the scientist is obliged to offer his explanation in terms of factors which are empirically real as the phenomenon of crime itself. He does not explain the problem, for example, in terms of references to the will of God, demons, or original sin. A satisfactory explanation is not only one that is empirical, however, but one that can be stated in the terms (45) of a *causal proposition*. Description is an indispensable point of beginning, but description is not explanation. It is well to stress this point, for there are all too many scientists, or would-be scientists, who are primarily concerned with data gathering, data counting, and data describing, and who seem to forget that such operations, however useful, are but the first step. Until we have accounted (50) for the problem at hand, explained it causally by referring the data to some principle or generalization already established, or to some new principle or generalization, we have not explained anything.

6. According to the passage, scientists are not interested in theological explanations because
   (A) scientists tend to be atheists
   (B) theology cannot explain change
   (C) theological explanations are not empirical
   (D) theology cannot explain social behavior
   (E) scientists are concerned primarily with data gathering

7. The major objective of the passage is to
   (A) show that explanation is more important than discovery
   (B) prove that sociology is a science
   (C) explain the major objectives of sociology
   (D) discuss scientific method
   (E) describe social behavior

8. Which of the following statements best agrees with the author's position?
   (A) Science is the formulation of unverified hypotheses.
   (B) Explanation is inferred from data.
   (C) Causation is a basis for explanation.
   (D) Generalization is a prerequisite for explanation.
   (E) Empiricism is the science of discovery.

9. Judging from the contents of the passage, the final step in a study of social behavior would be to
   (A) discover the problem
   (B) establish principles
   (C) offer an explanation of the data by determining causation
   (D) collect data
   (E) establish generalizations

10. According to the passage, which of the following activities contribute to the advance of science?
    I. Finding data relationships
    II. Expanding the limits of the empirical
    III. Establishing ultimate causes of phenomena

    (A) I only   (D) I and III only
    (B) II only   (E) I, II, and III
    (C) I and II only

11. The author's main point in the first paragraph may best be described by which of the following statements?
    (A) Science and sociology are interdisciplinary.
    (B) The first objective of sociology is discovery.
    (C) Discovery without explanation is meaningless.
    (D) Both discovery and explanation are fundamental to building a science.
    (E) It takes a long time before relationships of data are discovered.

PASSAGE 3

A polytheist always has favorites among the gods, determined by his own temperament, age, and condition, as well as his own interest, temporary or permanent. If it is true that everybody loves a lover, then Venus will be a popular deity with all. But from lovers she will elicit special devotion. In ancient Rome,
(5) when a young couple went out together to see a procession or other show, they would of course pay great respect to Venus, when her image appeared on the screen. Instead of saying, "Isn't love wonderful?" they would say, "Great art thou, O Venus." In a polytheistic society you could tell a good deal about a person's frame of mind by the gods he favored, so that to tell a girl you were
(10) trying to woo that you thought Venus overrated was hardly the way to win her heart. But in any case, a lovesick youth or maiden would be spontaneously supplicating Venus.

The Greeks liked to present their deities in human form; it was natural to

them to symbolize the gods as human beings glorified, idealized. But this fact
(15) is also capable of misleading us. We might suppose that the ancients were
really worshipping only themselves; that they were, like Narcissus, beholding
their own image in a pool, so that their worship was *anthropocentric* (man-
centered) rather than *theocentric* (god-centered). We are in danger of assuming
that they were simply constructing the god in their own image. This is not
(20) necessarily so. The gods must always be symbolized in one form or another.
To give them a human form is one way of doing this, technically called *anthropomorphism* (from the Greek *anthropos*, a man, and *morphé*, form). People
of certain temperaments and within certain types of culture seem to be more
inclined to it than are others. It is, however, more noticeable in others than in
(25) oneself, and those who affect to despise it are sometimes conspicuous for their
addiction to it. A German once said an Englishman's idea of God is an Englishman twelve feet tall. Such disparagement of anthropomorphism occurred
in the ancient world, too. The Celts, for instance, despised Greek practice in
this matter, preferring to use animals and other such symbols. The Egyptians
(30) favored more abstract and stylized symbols, among which a well-known example is the solar disk, a symbol of Rà, the sun-god.

Professor C. S. Lewis tells of an Oxford undergraduate he knew who, prig-
gishly despising the conventional images of God, thought he was overcoming
anthropomorphism by thinking of the Deity as infinite vapor or smoke. Of course
(35) even the bearded-old-man image can be a better symbol of Deity than ever
could be the image, even if this were psychologically possible, of an unlimited
smog.

What is really characteristic of all polytheism, however, is not the worship of
idols or humanity or forests or stars; it is, rather, the worship of innumerable
(40) *powers* that confront and affect us. The powers are held to be valuable in
themselves; that is why they are to be worshipped. But the values conflict. The
gods do not cooperate, so you have to play them off against each other. Suppose you want rain. You know of two gods, the dry-god who sends drought
and the wet-god who sends rain. You do not suppose that you can just pray
(45) to the wet-god to get busy, and simply ignore the dry-god. If you do so, the
latter may be offended, so that no matter how hard the wet-god tries to oblige
you, the dry-god will do his best to wither everything. Because both gods are
powerful you must take both into consideration, begging the wet-god to be
generous and beseeching the dry-god to stay his hand.

12. It can be inferred from the passage that polytheism means a belief in
    (A) Greek gods

(B) more than one god
(C) a god-centered world
(D) powerful deities
(E) infinite numbers of gods

13. The author's statement in lines 8–9 that "you could tell a good deal about a person's frame of mind by the gods he favored" means that
(A) those who believed in gods were superstitious
(B) worship was either anthropocentric or theocentric
(C) gods were chosen to represent a given way of life
(D) the way a person thinks depends on the power of deities
(E) in certain cultures, the gods served as representations of what people thought of themselves

14. It may be inferred from the passage that the author would most likely agree that ancient cultures
    I. symbolized their deities only in human form
   II. symbolized the gods in many forms
  III. were mainly self-worshippers
(A) I only   (D) I and III only
(B) II only   (E) I, II, and III
(C) I and II only

15. The main point the author makes about anthropomorphism in lines 21–24 is that
(A) certain cultures are inclined to anthropomorphism
(B) those who demean anthropomorphism may themselves practice it
(C) the disparagement of anthropomorphism is common to both ancient and modern cultures
(D) the Germans tend to be more theocentric than the English
(E) anthropomorphism is a practice common to all cultures

16. It may be inferred from the last paragraph that polytheism entails
(A) a commonality of interests among the deities
(B) predictable consequences
(C) incoherence and conflict among the "powers"
(D) an orderly universe
(E) worshipping one god at a time

PASSAGE 4

The following passage was written in 1970.

It appears that the easiest kind of occupation is that of the forecaster. If a dismal future is forecasted, and remedial actions are taken, and the future turns out better than predicted—the forecaster can claim that disaster was avoided because he was listened to. If, however, his pessimism was well founded, the
(5) forecaster can take credit for being an able predictor of future events. In this last case, if corrective action was taken—but failed—the forecaster can claim that the amount of action was insufficient, too late, or of the wrong kind.

One reason that the forecasting business has, in itself, become a growth industry is that every institution must plan ahead to stay ahead. Everyone today
(10) seems to be interested in gaining whatever insights are possible as to the trends of the near future. Unfortunately, many of the people that are telling us about the nature of expected changes are basing their predictions on an irrational interpretation of recent past events, and not on factual data. Most of these popular forecasts are inspirational but not very actionable.

(15) If we flash back to the early 1960s we can quickly retrace the course of events which are the basis for many popular predictions. John Gardner, in his then recently published book, *Self Renewal*, commented that many Americans were operating on the principal of "whatever is—is right." However, within a few years this mood drastically changed. Radical student movements, Vietnam
(20) peace marches, Civil Rights demonstrations, Women's Liberation, Consumerism, Ecology, and other events tended to make Gardner's doctrine no longer descriptive of Americans. Within a period of less than five years the rapidity of change in attitudes and values was overwhelming. We suddenly began to question everything and anything—from the institution of marriage to the govern-
(25) ment's right to engage in war.

The key question is not what happened but why it happened. To answer this question we must take account of the important factors which induced change, and attach to each its due weight. Also, we must attempt to specify how these factors interrelated and interacted with each other. Of course, this is very dif-
(30) ficult because of the number of factors involved, and their far-reaching impact. If we analyze just one factor at a time, we may reach fuzzy or erroneous conclusions. For example, let us illustrate the advantage of structuring the interconnections between interrelated factors. Suppose that you are in charge of a program to build low-income housing. You are working diligently to provide
(35) decent homes for poverty-stricken people. You are praised for your far-sighted genuine concern, having been quoted as saying that your housing projects will

help eliminate poverty. You finally succeed, but your success has the unintended result of increasing poverty. Why? Low-income housing merely draws more poor people into an area where very few jobs exist; this creates an even (40) worse supply-and-demand situation for jobs; and the city's poverty problems are worsened.

In essence, we are saying that to arrive at any meaningful conclusion when studying a problem, we must first list all the factors which influence the final result or outcome, and the interrelation between these factors. The housing (45) case demonstrates that a series of short-run answers to a problem may create worse problems in the long run.

17. With which of the following statements would the author be most likely to agree?
   (A) Forecasting is a dismal business.
   (B) Forecasters are generally pessimistic.
   (C) There is a growing demand for forecasters.
   (D) Forecasting is inspirational.
   (E) Forecasters are always right.

18. Which of the following statements may be inferred from the first paragraph of the passage?
   I. Forecasting may help to avert calamities.
   II. Forecasters are adept at hedging.
   III. Forecasting should be improved.
   (A) I only   (D) I and III only
   (B) II only   (E) I, II, and III
   (C) I and II only

19. Which of the following statements best describes the point the author is trying to make in his description of the housing case?
   (A) Housing projects cannot eliminate poverty.
   (B) Poor people resent low-income housing.
   (C) The project was not a long-run solution to the poverty problem.
   (D) The project director was guilty of "fuzzy" thinking.
   (E) The project evidently suffered from cost overruns.

20. The author's main purpose in the passage is to
   (A) introduce new hypotheses
   (B) describe his experiences

    (C) discuss the early 1960s

    (D) explain the housing case

    (E) improve the art of forecasting

21. According to the passage, Gardner's thesis

    (A) is not operative today

    (B) is operative today

    (C) was operative in the early 1960s

    (D) was never operative

    (E) is completely false

22. It can be inferred from the passage that the attitude of "whatever is—is right" was succeeded by an attitude of

    (A) "whatever is—is always wrong"

    (B) "whatever is—should be questioned"

    (C) "whatever is—should be opposed"

    (D) "whatever is—is meaningless"

    (E) "whatever is—should remain"

23. It is the author's opinion that to improve forecasting there must be better

    (A) interpretation of causal factors

    (B) description of events

    (C) insights into trends

    (D) interpretation of facts

    (E) statistical analysis of data

24. The author exhorts forecasters to

    (A) analyze one fact at a time

    (B) plan ahead to stay ahead

    (C) base predictions on past events

    (D) quickly retrace the course of events

    (E) analyze all interrelated causal factors

25. According to the passage, the author's attitude towards the environmental changes mentioned in lines 18–25 is one of

    (A) ambivalence

    (B) disapproval

    (C) approval

(D) consternation

(E) surprise

If there is still time remaining, you may review the questions in this section only. You may not turn to any other section of the test.

Section VIII Problem Solving   Time: 30 minutes

Directions: Solve each of the following problems; then indicate the correct answer on your answer sheet. [On the actual exam you will be permitted to use any space available on the examination paper for scratch work.]

NOTE: A figure that appears with a problem is drawn as accurately as possible so as to provide information that may help in answering the question (unless the words "Figure not drawn to scale" appear next to the figure). Numbers in this test are real numbers.

1. .03 times .05 is

   (A) 15%

   (B) 1.5%

   (C) .15%

   (D) .015%

   (E) .0015%

2. Which of the following are possible values for the angles of a parallelogram?

   I. 90°, 90°, 90°, 90°

   II. 40°, 70°, 50°, 140°

   III. 50°, 130°, 50°, 130°

   (A) I only

   (B) II only

   (C) I and III only

   (D) II and III only

   (E) I, II, and III

3. For every novel in the school library there are two science books; for each science book there are seven economics books. Express the ratio of economics books to science books to novels in the school library as a triple ratio.

   (A) 7:2:1

   (B) 7:1:2

   (C) 14:7:2

   (D) 14:2:1

   (E) 14:2:7

4. A store has a parking lot which contains 70 parking spaces. Each row in the parking lot contains the same number of parking spaces. The store has bought additional property in order to build an addition to the store. When the addition is built, 2 parking spaces will be lost from each row; however, 4 more rows will be added to the parking lot. After the addition is built, the parking lot will still have 70 parking spaces, and each row will contain the same number of parking spaces as every other row. How many rows were in the parking lot before the addition was built?

(A) 5   (D) 10
(B) 6   (E) 14
(C) 7

5. Which of the following numbers is the closest to 0 (zero)?

(A) $(1 - .9)^2$ (D) $(.09)$
(B) $1 - (.9)^2$ (E) $(.09)^2$
(C) $\dfrac{1}{1 - .9}$

6. If the shaded area is one half the area of triangle ABC and angle ABC is a right angle, then the length of line segment AD is

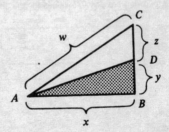

(A) $\frac{1}{2}w$ (D) $\sqrt{w^2 - 3y^2}$
(B) $\frac{1}{2}(w + x)$ (E) $\sqrt{y^2 + z^2}$
(C) $\sqrt{2x^2 + z^2}$

7. There are 50 employees in the office of ABC company. Of these, 22 have taken an accounting course, 15 have taken a course in finance, and 14 have taken a marketing course. Nine of the employees have taken exactly two

of the courses, and one employee has taken all three of the courses. How many of the 50 employees have taken none of the courses?

(A) 0 (D) 11
(B) 9 (E) 26
(C) 10

8. If $x + y = 4$ and $x - y = 3$, then $x + 2y$ is

(A) ½ (D) 4½
(B) 3.5 (E) 7½
(C) 4

9. How much interest will $2,000 earn at an annual rate of 8% in one year if the interest is compounded every 6 months?

(A) $160.00 (D) $332.80
(B) $163.20 (E) $2,163.20
(C) $249.73

10. If BC is parallel to AD and CE is perpendicular to AD, then the area of $ABCD$ is

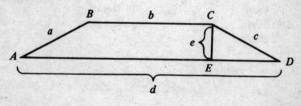

(A) bd (D) $e(b + d)$
(B) $bd + ac$ (E) $.5eb + .5ed$
(C) ed

11. A company makes a profit of 6% on its first $1,000 of sales each day, and 5% on all sales in excess of $1,000 for that day. How many dollars in profit will the company make in a day when sales are $6,000?

(A) $250 (D) $320
(B) $300 (E) $360
(C) $310

12. If 15 men working independently and at the same rate can manufacture 27 baskets in an hour, how many baskets would 45 men working independently and at the same rate manufacture in 40 minutes?
    (A) 27
    (B) 35
    (C) 40
    (D) 54
    (E) 81

13. A conveyer belt moves grain at the rate of 2 tons in 5 minutes and a second conveyer belt moves grain at the rate of 3 tons in 7 minutes. How many minutes will it take to move 20 tons of grain using both conveyer belts?
    (A) 12
    (B) 16⁴⁄₇
    (C) 18³⁄₂₆
    (D) 21
    (E) 24⁴⁄₂₉

14. A field is rectangular and its width is ⅓ as long as its length. What is the area of the field if the length of the field is 120 yards?
    (A) 480 square yards
    (B) 2,400 square yards
    (C) 4,800 square yards
    (D) 5,000 square yards
    (E) 7,200 square yards

15. If the price of steak is currently $1.00 a pound, and the price triples every 6 months, how long will it be until the price of steak is $81.00 a pound?
    (A) 1 year
    (B) 2 years
    (C) 2½ years
    (D) 13 years
    (E) 13½ years

16. If $\dfrac{x}{y} = \dfrac{2}{3}$, then $\dfrac{y^2}{x^2}$ is

    (A) $\dfrac{4}{9}$
    (B) $\dfrac{2}{3}$
    (C) $\dfrac{3}{2}$
    (D) $\dfrac{9}{4}$
    (E) $\dfrac{5}{2}$

17. The entry following a_n in a sequence is determined by the rule $(a_n - 1)^2$. If 1 is an entry in the sequence, the next three entries are
    (A) 0, −1, 2
    (B) 0, −1, 1
    (C) 0, 1, 2
    (D) 2, 3, 4
    (E) 0, 1, 0

18. An employer pays 3 workers X, Y, and Z a total of $610 a week. X is paid 125% of the amount Y is paid and 80% of the amount Z is paid. How much does X make a week?

   (A) $150
   (B) $175
   (C) $180
   (D) $195
   (E) $200

19. What is the maximum number of points of intersection of two circles which have unequal radii?

   (A) none
   (B) 1
   (C) 2
   (D) 3
   (E) infinite

20. If the area of a rectangle is equal to the area of a square, then the perimeter of the rectangle must be

   (A) ½ the perimeter of the square
   (B) equal to the perimeter of the square
   (C) equal to twice the perimeter of the square
   (D) equal to the square root of the perimeter of the square
   (E) none of the above

If there is still time remaining, you may review the questions in this section only. You may not turn to any other section of the test.

ANSWERS

Section I Reading Comprehension

1. **(B)**	8. **(A)**	15. **(A)**	22. **(B)**
2. **(C)**	9. **(C)**	16. **(A)**	23. **(C)**
3. **(D)**	10. **(B)**	17. **(D)**	24. **(C)**
4. **(C)**	11. **(B)**	18. **(B)**	25. **(C)**
5. **(E)**	12. **(E)**	19. **(C)**	
6. **(C)**	13. **(B)**	20. **(C)**	
7. **(B)**	14. **(D)**	21. **(C)**	

Section II   Problem Solving

1. (B)	6. (E)	11. (B)	16. (A)
2. (D)	7. (D)	12. (E)	17. (B)
3. (B)	8. (C)	13. (D)	18. (B)
4. (E)	9. (A)	14. (D)	19. (C)
5. (A)	10. (D)	15. (C)	20. (D)

Section III   Analysis of Situations

1. (B)	11. (A)	21. (C)	31. (A)
2. (B)	12. (D)	22. (B)	32. (B)
3. (E)	13. (B)	23. (B)	33. (C)
4. (A)	14. (E)	24. (E)	34. (E)
5. (C)	15. (E)	25. (D)	35. (C)
6. (A)	16. (A)	26. (B)	
7. (C)	17. (B)	27. (E)	
8. (D)	18. (B)	28. (B)	
9. (A)	19. (A)	29. (B)	
10. (E)	20. (C)	30. (C)	

Section IV   Data Sufficiency

1. (D)	8. (C)	15. (E)	22. (D)
2. (A)	9. (C)	16. (E)	23. (E)
3. (B)	10. (B)	17. (B)	24. (B)
4. (A)	11. (A)	18. (E)	25. (E)
5. (A)	12. (D)	19. (A)	
6. (E)	13. (E)	20. (C)	
7. (C)	14. (C)	21. (A)	

Section V   Writing Ability

1. (C)	8. (D)	15. (C)	22. (A)
2. (E)	9. (E)	16. (E)	23. (C)
3. (B)	10. (A)	17. (E)	24. (D)
4. (A)	11. (D)	18. (C)	25. (A)
5. (C)	12. (A)	19. (C)	
6. (A)	13. (B)	20. (A)	
7. (B)	14. (A)	21. (C)	

Section VI Analysis of Situations

1. (B)	11. (E)	21. (A)	31. (C)
2. (D)	12. (E)	22. (B)	32. (E)
3. (A)	13. (C)	23. (A)	33. (B)
4. (B)	14. (C)	24. (B)	34. (E)
5. (D)	15. (B)	25. (B)	35. (D)
6. (E)	16. (A)	26. (C)	
7. (B)	17. (B)	27. (D)	
8. (D)	18. (B)	28. (C)	
9. (D)	19. (D)	29. (B)	
10. (A)	20. (A)	30. (E)	

Section VII Reading Comprehension

1. (E)	8. (C)	15. (B)	22. (B)
2. (C)	9. (C)	16. (C)	23. (A)
3. (B)	10. (C)	17. (C)	24. (E)
4. (B)	11. (D)	18. (B)	25. (A)
5. (A)	12. (B)	19. (C)	
6. (C)	13. (E)	20. (E)	
7. (C)	14. (B)	21. (C)	

Section VIII Problem Solving

1. (C)	6. (D)	11. (C)	16. (D)
2. (C)	7. (C)	12. (D)	17. (E)
3. (D)	8. (D)	13. (E)	18. (E)
4. (D)	9. (B)	14. (C)	19. (C)
5. (E)	10. (E)	15. (B)	20. (E)

ANALYSIS

Section I Reading Comprehension

1. **(B)** The passage deals with the harmful effects of certain production processes on workers and others.

2. **(C)** This answer is clear from paragraph 4 of the passage.

3. **(D)** Osteolysis is not mentioned as a cause. (A) can be found in lines 13–15; (B) in lines 22ff.; (C) in lines 37–38; and (E) in lines 2ff.

4. **(C)** The author does not argue for remedial action in the passage, but merely presents the facts concerning cancer-producing occupational hazards.

5. **(E)** This is implied in lines 40ff. Existing legislated-maximum levels of vinyl chloride exposure are higher than that set by Dow Chemical and apparently higher than a medically permissible safe limit.

6. **(C)** The passage relates that at least 17 workers were killed because of the failure by authorities to follow up on available research. See lines 44–45.

7. **(B)** The passage states that "a creature" was first observed by St. Columba in 565 A.D. See line 44.

8. **(A)** The statement beginning on line 45 indicates that the name of the monster is based on a specific shape and form (as discussed in lines 33ff.) taken from a photograph of the animal.

9. **(C)** In lines 18–19, the dimensions of the lake are given as approximately 23 miles long, with a maximum width of 1.5 miles. Therefore, answers (A) and (B) are almost certainly too small, while answers (D) and (E) are much too large.

10. **(B)** Most of the passage deals with the origins of Loch Ness and with the so-called "monster" within.

11. **(B)** Ichthyologists are zoologists who study fish.

12. **(E)** None can be inferred from the passage.

13. **(B)** Lines 7–8 quote Marx as saying that philosophers only want to interpret the world, when what should be done is to change it. Change, the author states in line 9, is the "creed of applied scientists everywhere."

14. **(D)** Durkheim also valued the application of science rather than theoretical constructs alone. See lines 40–42.

15. **(A)** Items (B) through (E) deal with *applied* problems, which are the main concern of the social scientist, according to the passage.

16. **(A)** See lines 40–42.

17. **(D)** This point is stressed in lines 5–6, 12, 18ff., 31–33, 40, and 46ff.

18. **(B)** All but choice (B) are mentioned in the last paragraph.

19. **(C)** While the author is concerned with the moral and cultural aspects of American society (lines 1, 21–25), his major concern is to show how the Bible has been used as a guide for some theatrical productions. See especially lines 31–35, and 49ff.

20. **(C)** This central theme of the author's concern is contained in lines 3–13.

21. **(C)** Statements (A) and (B) were not originally voiced by the author, but rather by Gen. Sarnoff. See lines 1–2, 8–10. Statements (D) and (E) are taken out of context. See lines 31–41. Statement (C) reflects the author's own ideas. See lines 14–18.

22. **(B)** Question I is found in lines 14–18, question III in lines 19–20. However, the author does not present evidence that he intends to answer them. Only answers to question II are implied throughout. See lines 42–48.

23. **(C)** The author does not state his background or profession, but it might be any of the choices except (C), since there are no traces of humor in this passage.

24. **(C)** Both these ideas are implied in lines 10–13.

25. **(C)** Examined in context, (C) is the most probable answer. See lines 32–35.

Section II Problem Solving

1. **(B)** Let L be the original length and W the original width. The new length is 120% of L which is $(1.2)L$; the new width is 80% of W which is $(.8)W$. The area of a rectangle is length times width, so the original area is LW and the new area is $(1.2)(L)(.8)W$ or $(.96)LW$. Since the new area is 96% of the original area, the area has decreased by 4%.

2. **(D)** The distance from New York to Hartford divided by the distance from New York to Boston is $\dfrac{120}{250}$ or .48, and .48 = 48%.

3. **(B)** The amount broken off is $\dfrac{1}{8} + 1\dfrac{3}{4} + 1\dfrac{1}{12}$ inches. Since $\dfrac{1}{8} + 1\dfrac{3}{4} + 1\dfrac{1}{12} = \dfrac{3}{24} + \dfrac{42}{24} + \dfrac{26}{24} = \dfrac{71}{24}$ and the lead was 5 inches long to begin with, the amount left $= 5 - \dfrac{71}{24} = \dfrac{120}{24} - \dfrac{71}{24} = \dfrac{49}{24} = 2\dfrac{1}{24}$ inches.

4. **(E)** The first 1,000 copies cost $1 each; so altogether they will cost $1,000. The remaining 3,800 copies (4,800 − 1,000) cost x dollars each; so their cost is $3,800x. Therefore, the total cost of all 4,800 copies is $1,000 + $3,800x.

5. **(A)** Since $1\frac{2}{3}$ hours is 100 minutes, 50 minutes is ½ of $1\frac{2}{3}$ hours. Therefore, he should make half as much in 50 minutes as he does in $1\frac{2}{3}$ hours. Since he made 4 boxes in $1\frac{2}{3}$ hours, he makes 2 boxes in 50 minutes.

6. **(E)** Since $\frac{y}{x} = 2$, $y = 2x$. Therefore, $x + y = x + 2x = 3x$ which equals 3. So $3x = 3$, which means $x = 1$. Thus, $y = 2$ because $y = 2x$.

7. **(D)** Since there are 20 rolls in a carton and a carton costs $9, each roll costs $\frac{1}{20}$ of $9 which is 45¢. The roll sells for 50¢, so the selling price divided by the cost is $\frac{50}{45} = \frac{10}{9}$, which is about 111%. (Or divide the total income by the total cost: $\frac{20 \times .50}{9} = \frac{10}{9} = 111\%$.)

8. **(C)** 12 copies of the history book weigh (12)(2.4) or 28.8 pounds. Since the total weight of the books is 42.8 pounds, the weight of the English books is 42.8 − 28.8 or 14 pounds. Therefore, each English book weighs $\frac{14}{8}$ or 1.75 pounds.

9. **(A)** Let x be the number of miles the car travels on a gallon of gas when driven at 60 miles an hour. Then 80% of 15 is x; so $\frac{4}{5} \cdot 15 = x$ and $x = 12$.

10. **(D)**
    STATEMENT I cannot be inferred since if $x = 2$ and $y = 1$, then x and y are positive but x is not less than y.

    STATEMENT II is true since $x + y = z$ and y is positive so $x < z$.

    STATEMENT III is true. z is positive since it is the sum of two positive numbers and so $z < 2z$. Since we know $x < z$ and $z < 2z$, then $x < 2z$.

    Therefore, only STATEMENTS II and III can be inferred.

11. **(B)** The first 800 sheets cost $800x$ ¢. The remaining 4,200 sheets cost $\frac{x}{15}$ ¢ apiece which comes to $(4,200)\left(\frac{x}{15}\right)$ ¢ or $280x$ ¢. Therefore, the total cost of the 5,000 sheets of paper is $800x$ ¢ + $280x$ ¢, which is $1,080x$ ¢.

12. **(E)** Let S denote the worker's salary in 1967. In 1968 he received 110% of S which is $(1.1)S$, and in 1969 he received 110% of $(1.1)S$ which is $(1.1)(1.1)S$ or 1.21 S. Therefore, he received 21% more in 1969 than he did in 1967.

13. **(D)** Factory A turns out $8a$ cars in 8 hours. Since factory B turns out b cars in 2 hours, it turns out $4b$ cars in 8 hours. Therefore, the total is $8a + 4b$.

14. **(D)** In 35 minutes John makes 7 boxes and Tim makes 5. The required ratio, 7 to 5, is constant no matter how long they work.

15. **(C)** The total number of crates sold is $3\frac{1}{4} + 2\frac{1}{6} + 4\frac{1}{2} + 1\frac{2}{3}$ which is equal to $\frac{39}{12} + \frac{26}{12} + \frac{54}{12} + \frac{20}{12} = \frac{139}{12} = 11\frac{7}{12}$. A shorter method would be to add the integral parts of each of the numbers $3 + 2 + 4 + 1 = 10$. Next add the fractional parts $\frac{1}{4} + \frac{1}{6} + \frac{1}{2} + \frac{2}{3}$. Using 12 as a common denominator you get $\frac{(3 + 2 + 6 + 8)}{12}$ which is $\frac{19}{12} = 1\frac{7}{12}$. Therefore, the answer is $10 + 1\frac{7}{12} = 11\frac{7}{12}$.

16. **(A)** If $x + y$ exceeds 4 and x is less than 3, it is clear that y must exceed 1.

17. **(B)** Since 10 is $\frac{1}{5}$ of 50, the 10 apprentices should do $\frac{1}{5}$ as much work as 50 apprentices. 50 apprentices did the job in 4 hours, so in 1 hour 50 apprentices will do $\frac{1}{4}$ of the job. Therefore, 10 apprentices should do $\frac{1}{5}$ of $\frac{1}{4} = \frac{1}{20}$ of the job in an hour.

Since 15 is $\frac{1}{2}$ of 30, 15 journeymen will do half as much work as 30 journeymen. The 30 journeymen finished the job in $4\frac{1}{2}$ hours, so in 1 hour they will do $\frac{2}{9}$ of the job. Therefore, 15 journeymen will do $\frac{1}{2}$ of $\frac{2}{9} = \frac{1}{9}$ of

the job in an hour. So both groups will do $\frac{1}{20} + \frac{1}{9} = \frac{9}{180} + \frac{20}{180} = \frac{29}{180}$

of the job in an hour.

18. **(B)** 40% of the 52% of the population who are women are voters. So (.40) (.52) = .2080 = 20.8% of the population are women voters.

19. **(C)** The amount of gas needed for a bus to travel 200 miles if the bus travels 15 miles on a gallon is $\frac{200}{15}$ or $13\frac{1}{3}$ gallons.

20. **(D)** The time required to pump 10 gallons of water out of the tank is $(10)\left(15 - \frac{x}{10}\right)$ which equals $150 - x$ minutes.

Section III   Analysis of Situations

1. **(B)** The company had two major problems. The first mentioned in the passage was declining sales. The only explanation found in the passage was that salesmen had not developed enough new customers. Declining sales was a *Major Factor* in Tulli's decision to reassign salesmen, although one can argue whether his decision was correct. The second problem was the factor of increasing accounts receivable, because of slow customer payments. The problem, in turn, was a symptom of declining sales.

2. **(B)** As pointed out above, increasing accounts receivables was a major company problem and was a *Major Factor* in Tulli's decision to reassign salesmen and to change the company's compensation policy.

3. **(E)** The nationality of the company is an *Unimportant Issue*.

4. **(A)** The cash shortage is the problem uppermost in management's considerations. This condition was the primary issue which led to the change in compensation policy and the reassignment of salesmen.

5. **(C)** As one of the advantages attached by Tulli to a quota system, this is a *Minor Factor* in the decision process.

6. **(A)** *Major Objective.* The development of new customers by both experienced and less experienced salesmen was an outcome desired by Tulli.

7. **(C)** *Minor Factor.* The cash flow problem was caused by slow payments by customers. See paragraph 2 and the answers to questions 1 and 5.

8. **(D)** *Major Assumption.* Under Tulli's plan, top salesmen were to be reassigned from high to low-sales areas. The underlying assumption of Tulli was that these salesmen would succeed in low-sales territories as well. However, low sales in a territory may be more owing to a lack of potential in the territory, rather than to a lack of experience or skill on the part of the salesman.

9. **(A)** *Major Objective.* Tulli suggested assigning quotas to salesmen as a solution to the incentive problem. Cavello agreed in principle to Tulli's proposal and added some variations of his own as stated in paragraph 17ff.

10. **(E)** *Unimportant Issue.* The quota rate does not influence the decision as to whether to adopt a quota system. The issue is whether a quota system will motivate salesmen to produce more sales.

11. **(A)** Through a quota system the individual performance of salesmen can be measured. This is one of the outcomes desired by Tulli.

12. **(D)** *Major Assumption.* That salesmen will accept Cavello's options is a *belief* held by Tulli. See the last paragraph.

13. **(B)** *Major Factor.* The disadvantages of sales quotas were considered by Cavello as factors that could determine the success or failure of a possible course of action (the quota option).

14. **(E)** *Unimportant Issue.* Nothing is stated in the passage which relates Tulli's experience in dealing with salesmen to the decision process.

15. **(E)** *Unimportant Issue.* The number of salesmen—although mentioned in the passage—is unrelated to the decision process.

16. **(A)** A major prerequisite of the sales plan alternatives was that they must motivate both experienced and less experienced salesmen.

17. **(B)** Tulli's suggested plan of assigning quotas to salesmen's existing territories, rather than changing a salesman's territory, also had a side-benefit. The additional benefit was that a quota system could help in planning production, inventory, and working capital needs. However, this benefit was a *Minor Factor* in the decision to adopt the plan; certainly subsidiary to the major consideration of the plan's effect on the performance and morale of the salesmen. See paragraph 16.

18. **(B)** Carvello concluded—and succeeded in convincing Tulli—that Tulli's reorganization plan would not be accepted by the salesmen. This was based not on mere conjecture or supposition, but on the hostility of the salesmen demonstrated during the sales meeting. The hostility was a *Major Factor* in the decision to consider Carvello's options.

19. **(A)** Adoption of a global planning strategy is a *Major Objective* of Doltry Mining.

20. **(C)** A Major Factor in the consideration of whether to invest in Country A is the condition of its current account balance. Since merchandise is but one part or component of the current account deficit, it is a *Minor Factor*.

21. **(C)** Expropriation is one consideration of political risk and, therefore, a *Minor Factor*.

22. **(B)** Country A's liquidity position was a major consideration in Mr. Davidson's decision.

23. **(B)** Political risk is a major consideration in the investment decision.

24. **(E)** The reader is not told how language is considered or weighed in an alternative course of action. Therefore, it is an *Unimportant Issue*.

25. **(D)** Davidson's *belief* that Country A is a good political risk was based on little public unrest, political competition, and few constitutional changes of government.

26. **(B)** It was *believed* that the likelihood of expropriation in Country B was nonexistent. The key word in the question is "likelihood."

27. **(E)** It is not clear whether the fact that Country B is a less developed country (LDC) was a major or minor consideration by Davidson.

28. **(B)** Balance of payments data are a *Major Factor* in the investment decision by management.

29. **(B)** Measures of societal conflict were considered as indicators of the political climate.

30. **(C)** Changes in heads of state is one component of the governmental processes (a Major Factor).

31. **(A)** Davidson's goal or task was selecting investment opportunities.

32. **(B)** Country C's instability was a major consideration in Davidson's decision not to recommend investment there.

33. **(C)** The number of political parties in Country C is one component of political processes, a major factor.

34. **(E)** As the identity of Country A was disguised, the fact that it was Davidson's home country did not play any part in the investment decision.

35. **(C)** The number of political parties is a function of political leadership. For example, it is mentioned in the passage (paragraph 16) that Country C has many small parties because of a lack of political leadership. this lack of leadership is a contributor to political instability—a Major Factor in an investment decision. Therefore, the *number* of political parties is a part of a Major Factor and thus a *Minor Factor*.

Section IV   Data Sufficiency

1. **(D)**

   STATEMENT (1) alone is sufficient. 2 feet 7 inches is more than half of 5 feet, so the piece which is 2 feet 7 inches long must be longer than the other two pieces put together.

   STATEMENT (2) alone is sufficient. Since one piece is 5 inches long, the sum of the lengths of the remaining two pieces is 4 feet, 7 inches. Since one piece is 7 inches longer than the other, $L + (L + 7$ in.$) = 4$ ft. 7 in., where L is the length of the smaller of the two remaining pieces. Solving the equation yields $L + 7$ in. as the length of the longest piece.

2. **(A)** Since AC is a diameter, angle ABC is inscribed in a semicircle and is therefore a right angle.

   STATEMENT (1) alone is sufficient since it implies the two other angles in the triangle must be equal. Since the sum of the angles of a triangle is 180°, we can deduce that $x = 45$.

   STATEMENT (2) alone is not sufficient. There is no information about the angle ABD; so STATEMENT (2) cannot be used to find the angles of triangle ABD.

3. **(B)**

   STATEMENT (2) alone is sufficient, $y^2 - 2y + 1$ equals $(y - 1)^2$, so the only solution is $(y - 1)^2 = 0$ is $y = 1$.

STATEMENT (1) alone is not sufficient. $x + 2y = 6$ implies $y = 3 - \dfrac{x}{2}$, but there are no data given about the value of x.

4. **(A)**

STATEMENT (1) alone is sufficient. Pipe A fills up $\dfrac{1}{30}$ of the reservoir per minute. STATEMENT (1) says pipe B fills up $\dfrac{1}{20}$ of the reservoir per minute, so A and B together fill up $\dfrac{1}{20} + \dfrac{1}{30}$ or $\dfrac{5}{60}$ or $\dfrac{1}{12}$ of the reservoir. Therefore, together pipe A and pipe B will take 12 minutes to fill the reservoir.

STATEMENT (2) alone is not sufficient. There is no information about how long it takes pipe B to fill the reservoir.

5. **(A)**

STATEMENT (1) alone is sufficient. Draw the lines AC and BC; then AOC and BOC are right triangles, since AB is perpendicular to CO. By the Pythagorean theorem, $(AC)^2 = (AO)^2 + (CO)^2$ and $(BC)^2 = (OB)^2 + (CO)^2$; so if AO is less than OB, then AC is less than BC.

STATEMENT (2) alone is not sufficient. There is no restriction on where the point D is.

6. **(E)**

STATEMENTS (1) and (2) together are not sufficient. If $x = \frac{1}{2}$ and $y = 3$, then xy is greater than 1, but if $x = \frac{1}{2}$ and $y = \frac{3}{2}$, then xy is less than 1.

7. **(C)**

STATEMENT (1) alone is not sufficient. By choosing B and D differently we can have either $x = y$ or $x \neq y$ and still have $z = u$.

STATEMENT (2) alone is not sufficient. It implies that $x = z$ and $y = u$, but gives no information to compare x and y. STATEMENTS (1) and (2) together, however, yield $x = y$.

8. **(C)**

STATEMENT (1) alone is not sufficient. If town C were closer to B, even if S were going slower than T, S could arrive at C first. But if you also use STATEMENT (2), then train S must be traveling faster than train T, since it is further than B to C than it is from A to C.

So STATEMENTS (1) and (2) together are sufficient.

STATEMENT (2) alone is insufficient since it gives no information about the trains.

9. **(C)**

STATEMENT (2) alone is not sufficient, since D can be any point if we assume only STATEMENT (2).

STATEMENT (1) alone is not sufficient. Depending on the position of point C, x and y can be equal or unequal. For example, in both of the following triangles BD is perpendicular to AC.

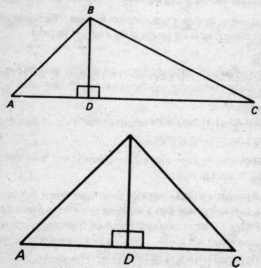

If STATEMENTS (1) and (2) are both true, then $x = y$. The triangles ABD and BDC are both right triangles with two pairs of corresponding sides equal; the triangles are therefore congruent and $x = y$.

10. **(B)**

STATEMENT (2) alone is sufficient, since $3x + 3y$ is $3(x + y)$. (Therefore, if $3x + 3y = 4$, then $x + y = \frac{4}{3}$.)

STATEMENT (1) alone is not sufficient, since you need another equation besides $x - y = 4$ to find the values of x and y.

11. **(A)**
   STATEMENT (1) alone is sufficient. We know that the total of sales for 1968, 1969, and 1970 is three times the average and that sales in 1968 were twice the average. Then the total of sales in 1969 and 1970 was equal to the average. Therefore, sales were less in 1969 than in 1968.

   STATEMENT (2) alone is insufficient, since it does not relate sales in 1969 to sales in 1968.

12. **(D)**
   Since the length of the arc of the circle is proportional to the length of the chord connecting the endpoints, STATEMENT (1) alone is sufficient.

   STATEMENT (2) alone is sufficient, since the areas of the circular segments are proportional to the squares of the lengths of the chord.

13. **(E)**
   STATEMENTS (1) and (2) together are not sufficient, since the points A and D can be moved and STATEMENTS (1) and (2) still be satisfied.

14. **(C)**
   STATEMENT (1) alone is not sufficient, since 24 and 16 are both divisible by 4 but only 24 is divisible by 12.

   STATEMENT (2) alone is not sufficient, since 24 and 15 are divisible by 3 but 15 is not divisible by 12.

   STATEMENT (1) implies that $k = 4m$ for some integer m. If you assume STATEMENT (2), then since k is divisible by 3, either 4 or m is divisible by 3. Since 4 is not divisible by 3, m must be. Therefore, $m = 3j$, where j is some integer and $k = 4 \times 3j$ or $12j$. So k is divisible by 12. Therefore, STATEMENTS (1) and (2) together are sufficient.

15. **(E)**
   STATEMENTS (1) and (2) together are not sufficient, because there is no information about the location of C relative to the locations of A and B.

16. **(E)** Obviously a single statement is not sufficient. However, since Ms. Brown could have other sources of income, even both statements together are not sufficient. If you answered (C) you are making the additional assumption that Ms. Brown's only source of income was royalties from the novel.

17. **(B)** An even integer is an integer divisible by 2. Since $2n + 10p$ is 2 times

$(n + 5p)$ using (2) lets you deduce that x is even. (1) by itself is not sufficient. If n were 2 and p were 3, $(n + p)^2$ would be 25 which is not even, but by choosing n to be 2 and p to be 4, $(n + p)^2$ is 36 which is even.

18. **(E)** Both statements give facts that *might* explain why the price of lumber rose. However, even using both statements you can't deduce what happened to the price of lumber.

19. **(A)** Since you know $x = 3$, statement (1) alone is sufficient. However, since no information is given about the value of y, statement (2) is insufficient.

20. **(C)** You need (1) to know what the price was at the beginning of 1977. Using (2) you could then compute the price during the fifteenth week. Either statement alone is insufficient. You should not actually compute the price since it would only waste time.

21. **(A)** (1) alone is sufficient since the line connecting the midpoints of 2 sides of a triangle is parallel to the third side. (2) alone is insufficient. In an isosceles triangle statement (2) would imply that ED is parallel to BC, but in a non-isosceles triangle, (2) would imply that ED and BC are not parallel.

22. **(D)** (1) alone is sufficient. For example, with both drains open, $\frac{1}{15} + \frac{1}{20}$ of the tank would be emptied each minute. You should not waste any time solving the problem. Remember, you only have to decide whether there is enough information to let you answer the question.

   (2) alone is also sufficient. You can deduce (1) from (2) and from the fact that drain 1 alone takes 15 minutes to empty the tank, and we just saw that (1) alone is sufficient.

23. **(E)** If you answered incorrectly you probably assumed that x and y were positive. If $x = 5$ and $y = 4$, then (1) and (2) are both true and $x > y$. However, if $x = -5$ and $y = -4$, (1) and (2) are both true but $x < y$.

24. **(B)** (2) alone is sufficient since ostriches are birds. (1) alone is not sufficient since tigers are not birds.

25. **(E)** Since the equation in (2) has exactly the same solutions as the equation in (1), $3(x - y) = 3x - 3y$ and $3(12) = 36$, you can't determine x and y even by using both (1) and (2). If $x = 12$ and $y = 0$, then (1) and (2) are true and $x + 2y = 12$, but if $x = 6$ and $y = -6$, (1) and (2) are again true but $x + 2y = -6$.

Section V   Writing Ability

1. **(C)** The pronoun *each* is singular, and requires the singular verb *was required*.

2. **(E)** When only two things are being compared (in this case, stationary sites and mobile units), the word *more* rather than *most* should be used.

3. **(B)** To maintain parallel structure, a phrase beginning with a noun (*ability*) is needed.

4. **(A)** The original wording is the clearest and simplest.

5. **(C)** As originally written, the sentence is a fragment, since it lacks an independent subject and verb. Choice (C) supplies them (*He had chosen*).

6. **(A)** No error.

7. **(B)** The pronoun *she* is needed, since it is part of the compound subject of the verb *was willing*; the verb must be singular to agree with the nearest subject (*Dean*).

8. **(D)** Use *among* when three or more people or things are involved.

9. **(E)** The underlined phrase must begin with *the Governor*; otherwise, the phrase which precedes it has no clear reference. Choice (C) is verbose and rather vague.

10. **(A)** No error.

11. **(D)** The pronoun *no one* is singular, and requires the singular verb *was*. Choice (C) is awkward in comparison to choice (D).

12. **(A)** The sentence is correct as originally written. Note that the compound subject ("X, Y, and Z") requires a plural verb—in this case, *have replaced*.

13. **(B)** The comparative phrases *equal . . . to* and *less . . . than* must be complete in order for the sentence to make sense.

14. **(A)** Correct as originally written. The pronoun *whom* is correct, since it is the object of the verb *should blame*.

15. **(C)** Use *fewer* for countable items (such as amendments); use *less* for noncountable substances (for example, sand, water, or time).

16. **(E)** The phrase beginning *One of the costliest* must be adjacent to the phrase *the space shuttle program*, in order to make the reference clear.

17. **(E)** The past perfect tense *had appointed* is needed to clarify the order in which the events occurred.

18. **(C)** The other choices are verbose, vague, or both.

19. **(C)** Use the pronoun *whom* only for people, never for things. Choice (E) introduces *they*, a pronoun without a reference. *Best* is needed here.

20. **(A)** No error. In most *if* clauses, the past subjunctive form of the verb—with *had*—must be used.

21. **(C)** The singular verb *illustrates* is needed, since the subject is the singular *imposition*.

22. **(A)** Correct as originally written. Parallelism calls for repetition of the pronoun *by* (*less by . . . than by . . .*).

23. **(C)** The pronoun should be *he,* since it is part of the compound subject of the verb *would be.*

24. **(D)** The pronoun *it* is unnecessary, since the subject of the verb—*the Civilian Review Board*—has already appeared.

25. **(A)** No error.

Section VI Analysis of Situations

1. **(B)** The workers had no loyalty to the company from the "distant north." This was a *Major Factor* as far as their will to work was concerned.

2. **(D)** This was an assumption initially made by Cappa upon which he developed his managerial style. It was erroneous, of course.

3. **(A)** Motivating the workers is Cappa's *Major Objective.*

4. **(B)** Low productivity, caused mainly by lack of motivation, is a *Major Factor.*

5. **(D)** Cappa's desire to institute a bonus system (that failed) was not supported by any evidence that it could succeed.

6. **(E)** The fact that Cappa was a U.S. citizen had no apparent impact on the major problem of motivating workers or on his deciding whether to return to the U.S.

7. **(B)** Worker loyalty—or lack of it—was a *Major Factor* in determining what sort of plan would motivate workers to increase productivity.

8. **(D)** Cappa *believed* that people everywhere are alike and will respond to cash incentives. This was an unsupported assumption on his part.

9. **(D)** Cappa *believed* that productivity would increase if workers received more authority. This assumption was not based on any facts given in the passage.

10. **(A)** Relating pay to output was a *Major Objective* desired by Cappa. Its purpose was to increase productivity, another major objective.

11. **(E)** The quality of the machinery was not a factor in any alternative course of action.

12. **(E)** Nothing in the passage mentions the location of the orange groves as an element in the decision process.

13. **(C)** Cappa tried to establish co-determination in order to increase worker motivation—an objective. Meeting with the committees was a less important consideration than implementing co-determination itself.

14. **(C)** Cappa's ambitions were a *Minor Factor* in Cappa's decision to leave for Italy. Note the three reasons for his accepting his uncle's proposition, as given in the passage: (1) the chance to be his own boss, (2) his wish to bring U.S. know-how to the firm, and (3) his desire to return to his father's homeland with some personal authority. Ambition is probably connected with these three factors, but it is of lesser importance.

15. **(B)** Cappa's plans had been stymied on more than one occasion by the recalcitrance of the union. Therefore, the power of the union was a *Major Factor* which Cappa had to take into consideration in making his final decision.

16. **(A)** The introduction of a fabric softener was a *Major Objective* of Mr. Simmons.

17. **(B)** The product attributes of the fabric softener were important considerations in the decision to develop the product (or not).

18. **(B)** Because Best Detergent operates abroad, its management desired the development of products that could be sold in all markets served by the firm.

19. **(D)** Mr. Simmons believed that introduction of a new product would change the company's image from "one of established products to one of contemporary, up-to-the-minute innovations."

20. **(A)** Mr. Simmons was "anxious to get his product on the market as soon as possible." Developing products quickly was a goal of a decision maker.

21. **(A)** The *Major Objective* of Best Detergent was "simple company survival."

22. **(B)** The fact that Mr. Kennedy planned to retire in two years influenced the direction of the company in that he did not "want to take any unnecessary risks." Therefore, decision making would tend to be risk averting, or conservative.

23. **(A)** One of Mr. Kennedy's goals was to "increase sales in order that the desired profit level be maintained. . . ."

24. **(B)** The introduction of new products was motivated by the stagnation of product lines, "a major problem of the company."

25. **(B)** The actual amount of time necessary to develop a fabric softener is a major consideration which influences the attainment of a Major Objective— the quick development of products.

26. **(C)** Advertising is only one component of total commercialization costs, which is a Major Factor.

27. **(D)** Mr. Kennedy "feels" that Simmons and Decker will determine ways to improve Best Detergent's slumping sales.

28. **(C)** The blue color of the fabric softener was secondary to the fact that the product did not stain.

29. **(B)** The intensity of competition is a major consideration in the decision to speed the development of a fabric softener.

30. **(E)** The rate of new product failure in the *consumer goods* industry is not a consideration, but rather the new product failure in the *detergent* industry.

31. **(C)** The expense of advertising on television is one component of development and marketing costs. Total development costs is a Major Factor.

32. **(E)** The size of the product package was not a consideration in the choice of an alternative course of action.

33. **(B)** If the reputation of the decision makers may be affected by the outcome of their decisions—as stated in the passage—then certainly this fact will influence the decision-making process.

34. **(E)** It is not the *number* of countries in which Best Detergent operates that

is important, but rather the fact that company management desires to develop products that can be sold abroad as well.

35. **(D)** Mr. Simmons "believed" that the success of his proposed product was "inevitable" because of the strength of the Best name.

Section VII Reading Comprehension

1. **(E)** The report (on which the passage is based) is certainly not optimistic (B), but rather pessimistic in its assessment, although not specifically about the trade gap (D). Nor can the report be characterized as harshly condemnatory (A) or critical of labor unions (C). After all, as pointed out in the passage, it is labor that will suffer. The answer is (E). This is specifically supported by the first and second paragraphs.

2. **(C)** Free trade is the reduction or elimination of tariffs and duties on exports. See lines 3 and 16–19.

3. **(B)** Manufacturers that cannot increase productivity in order to lower prices will not be able to compete with duty-free imports, and will not receive adjustment assistance, i.e., subsidies or some other financial payments to buttress them in the face of foreign competition.

4. **(B)** The author's recommendation is that redundant labor should be removed. See lines 36–38.

5. **(A)** Even though the subject of trade with the Common Market (C) is discussed, the major thrust of the passage is on the consequences of free trade—in this case, with the Common Market.

6. **(C)** This is stated in paragraph 3 of the passage.

7. **(C)** The major objective is to explain the objectives of sociology, which are the same as those of science. See line 1.

8. **(C)** A discussion of this point is given in paragraph 3. The other answers are either factually incorrect or incomplete.

9. **(C)** The final step or objective of science—according to the passage—is explanation (line 4), best stated as a causal proposition. See lines 43–45.

10. **(C)** I and II are mentioned in the first and second paragraphs. III is mentioned in lines 36–38 as one of the activities in which the scientist is *not* interested.

11. **(D)** Answers (B) and (E) are mentioned in the passage, but are secondary in importance to (D). Answer (C) is not correct, and answer (A) is not mentioned in the passage.

12. **(B)** This is mentioned in the first and the final paragraphs. In any case, the prefix *poly* means many and the suffix *theist* means one who believes in a god or gods.

13. **(E)** Answers (A), (B) and (D) cannot be inferred from the passage. Answer (C) is roughly consonant with what the author has to say, but (E) is a stronger example of the question statement.

14. **(B)** I is incorrect since they worshipped gods in both human and other forms. See lines 26ff.

15. **(B)** Although the author states that certain cultures are more inclined to anthropocentric worship (A), he mentions it while making the point that there are those who attribute it to others, even though practicing it themselves.

16. **(C)** The paragraph indicates that if the universe is partly controlled by the "wet-god" (it rains), then the "dry-god" lacks control. This is an example of incoherence. If you pray for rain, you must also pray to prevent the "dry-god" from exercising his powers, an example of potential conflict. Hence there is hardly a commonality of interests or order in a polytheistic system.

17. **(C)** This statement is made in lines 8–9. While it would seem that (E) is implied in the first paragraph, this thought is negated in lines 13–14.

18. **(B)** The first paragraph illustrates the author's belief that if a forecaster predicts a dismal future, no matter what the outcome, he can claim credit for action taken (if it worked), or disassociate himself from a wrong decision.

19. **(C)** While the project director might be guilty of "fuzzy" thinking (D), the main point the author is trying to make is that the housing project was a short-term solution to what was essentially a long-run problem. This point is also stated in lines 44–46.

20. **(E)** Clearly, the author's primary purpose is to point out some of the problems in forecasting and how they might be eliminated.

21. **(C)** Gardner's thesis is discussed in lines 16–18. His thesis was that in the early 1960s (when his book was written), Americans were operating on the

basis of a no-questioning value system. According to the passage, this value system changed after several years, but we cannot infer that it is not operative today (A), for it may have changed again since the passage was written. For the same reason, we cannot infer that the thesis applies today.

22. **(B)** Answer (B) can be inferred from the examples given in lines 19–22 and also the statement contained in lines 22–25. Answer (A) is unacceptable because of the word "always"—this does not appear in the passage.

23. **(A)** This opinion is explicitly stated in lines 26 and 27.

24. **(E)** This exhortation is stated in lines 42–44.

25. **(A)** The author makes no comment about these environmental changes, except that they represent a change in attitudes and values of the population. The author makes no value judgment of his own, so we can say that his attitude is one of ambivalence.

Section VIII Problem Solving

1. **(C)** Remember that the decimal point of the product of two decimals is placed so that the number of decimal places in the product is equal to the total of the number of decimal places in all of the numbers multiplied. Since .03 and .05 each have 2 decimal places, their product must have 4 (2 + 2) decimal places. Because 3 times 5 is 15, you need to add 2 zeros to get the correct number of decimal places, so the product of .03 and .05 is .0015. To change a decimal to a percentage you multiply by 100 (just move the decimal point 2 places to the right), so .0015 is .15%.

2. **(C)** Since a parallelogram is a 4-sided polygon, the sum of the angles of a parallelogram must be $(4 - 2)180° = 360°$. (A diagonal divides a parallelogram into 2 triangles and the sum of each triangle's angles is 180°.) Since the sum of the angles in II is not 360°, II is not possible. But I and III both consist of angles whose sum is 360°.

3. **(D)** If you know two ratios A : B and B : C, you can combine them into a triple ratio if B is the same number and represents the same quantity in both ratios. We know that the ratio of economics books to science books is 7 : 1 and that the ratio of novels to science books is 1 : 2. However, we can't combine this into the triple ratio 7 : 1 : 2 since 1 in the first ratio represents science books and 1 in the second ratio represents novels. We need science

books as the middle term in the triple ratio, so express the second ratio as: the ratio of science books to novels is 2:1. Now, the ratio of economics books to science books is 7:1 and the ratio of science books to novels is 2:1. Since a ratio is unchanged if both sides are multiplied by the same positive number, we can also express the ratio of economics books to science books as 14:2. Finally, we can combine these into the triple ratio 14:2:1 of economics books to science books to novels.

4. **(D)** Call s the number of spaces in each row and r the number of rows in the parking lot before the addition is built. The parking lot had 70 parking spaces, so $sr = 70$. Since after the addition is built there are 4 more rows, 2 less spaces in each row, and a total of 70 spaces, we know that $(s - 2)(r + 4) = 70$. You could solve these two equations by algebra, but there is a faster method. Since the number of rows and the number of spaces must be positive integers, you are looking for a way to write 70 as the product of two factors s and r with the additional property that $s - 2$ and $r + 4$ also have 70 as their product. Writing 70 as a product of primes, we get $70 = 2 \times 35 = 2 \times 5 \times 7$. Therefore, the only possibilities for s and r are listed here:

s	r	s	r
1	70	10	7
2	35	14	5
5	14	35	2
7	10	70	1

Now just check whether any pair of solutions (s, r) has the property that $s - 2$ and $r + 4$ is a solution. For example, if $s = 5$ and $r = 14$, then $s - 2 = 3$ and $r + 4 = 18$, which are not solutions. But if $s = 7$ and $r = 10$, then $s - 2 = 5$ and $r + 4 = 14$, which is also a solution. It is easy to see this is the only solution that works. So before the addition was built, there were 10 rows each with 7 spaces.

5. **(E)** Since all the expressions give positive results, we need to find the smallest number. (C) can be easily eliminated because the numerator is larger than the denominator, so the result is larger than 1. Since (A) and (E) are squares, simply compare the quantities being squared. (A) $= (.1)^2$ and (E) $= (.09)^2$, so (E) is smaller than (A).

Numbers between 0 and 1 become smaller when squared, so (E), which is

$(.09)^2$, is smaller than (D), which is .09. Since (B) is .19, it is larger than (E) also. Therefore (E) is the smallest number and is the closest to 0.

6. **(D)** Since angle ABC is a right angle, we know the length of AD squared is equal to the sum of y^2 and x^2. However, none of the answers given is $\sqrt{x^2 + y^2}$. The area of triangle ABC is $\frac{1}{2}x(y + z)$, and the area of triangle ABD, which is $\frac{1}{2}xy$, must be one half of $\frac{1}{2}x(y + z)$. So $\frac{1}{2}xy + \frac{1}{2}xz = \frac{1}{2}xy$, which can be solved to give $y = z$. Since angle ABC is a right angle, $w^2 = (y + z)^2 + x^2 = (2y)^2 + x^2$. So $w^2 = 4y^2 + x^2$. Since we want $x^2 + y^2$, we subtract $3y^2$ from each side to get $w^2 - 3y^2 = y^2 + x^2$. Therefore, the length of AD squared is $w^2 - 3y^2$.

7. **(C)** A picture helps.

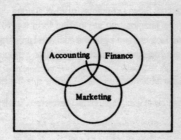

We want to know how many people are not in any of the sets.

The easy way to do this is find the number in at least one of the sets and subtract this number from 50. To find the number of employees in at least one set, *do not count the same employee more than once*. If you add 22, 15, and 14, any employee who took exactly two of the courses will be counted twice and employees who took all three courses will be counted three times. So the number who took at least one course = the number in Accounting + the number in Finance + the number in Marketing − number who took exactly two courses − 2 times the number who took all three courses = $22 + 15 + 14 − 9 − (2 \text{ times } 1) = 51 − 9 − 2 = 40$. Since 40 of the employees took at least one course, $50 − 40 = 10$ took none of the courses.

8. **(D)** Add $x + y = 4$ to $x − y = 3$ to obtain $2x = 7$. Therefore, $x = 3\frac{1}{2}$. Since $x + y = 4$, y must be $4 − 3\frac{1}{2} = \frac{1}{2}$. So $x + 2y = 3\frac{1}{2} + 2(\frac{1}{2}) = 4\frac{1}{2}$.

9. **(B)** The interest is compounded every 6 months. At the end of the first 6 months the interest earned is $2,000(.08)(1/2) = $80. (Don't forget to change 6 months into 1/2 year since 8% is the annual—yearly—rate.) Since the interest is compounded, $2,080 is the amount earning interest for the final 6 months of the year. So the interest earned during the final 6 months of the year is $2,080(.08)(1/2) = $83.20. Therefore, the total interest earned is $80 + $83.20 = $163.20.

10. **(E)** Since BC is parallel to AD, the figure $ABCD$ is a trapezoid. The area of a trapezoid is the average of the parallel sides times an altitude. Since CE is perpendicular to AD, e is an altitude. So the area is $e(1/2)(b + d) = (1/2)\,eb + (1/2)ed$. Since $1/2 = .5$, (E) is the correct answer.

11. **(C)** The profit is 6% of $1,000 plus 5% of $6,000 − $1,000 which is $(.06)(\$1,000) + (.05)(\$5,000)$. Therefore, the profit equals $60 + $250, which is $310.

12. **(D)** Since the number of baskets manufactured in an hour is proportional to the number of workers, $\dfrac{15}{45} = \dfrac{27}{x}$, where x is the number of baskets manufactured by 45 men in an hour. Therefore, x is 81. Since 40 minutes is $\dfrac{2}{3}$ of an hour, 45 men will make $\dfrac{2}{3}$ of 81 or 54 baskets in 40 minutes.

13. **(E)** The first belt lifts $\dfrac{2}{5}$ of a ton per minute and the second belt lifts $\dfrac{3}{7}$ of a ton per minute, so both belts together will lift $\dfrac{2}{5} + \dfrac{3}{7} = \dfrac{29}{35}$ of a ton per minute. Therefore, using both belts it will take $\dfrac{20}{29/35} = \dfrac{35}{29} \times 20 = \dfrac{700}{29}$ or $24\dfrac{4}{29}$ minutes to lift 20 tons.

14. **(C)** Since the width is ⅓ of the length and the length is 120 yards, the width of the field is 40 yards. The area of a rectangle is length times width, so the area of the field is 120 yards time 40 yards, which is 4,800 square yards.

15. **(B)** The price will be $3.00 a pound 6 months from now and $9.00 a pound a year from now. The price is a geometric progression of the form 3^j where j is the number of 6-month periods which have passed. Since $3^4 = 81$,

after 4 six-month periods, the price will be $81.00 a pound. Therefore, the answer is two years, since 24 months is 2 years.

16. **(D)** Since $\frac{x}{y} = \frac{2}{3}$, $\frac{y}{x}$, which is the reciprocal of $\frac{x}{y}$, must be equal to $\frac{3}{2}$. Also, $\frac{y^2}{x^2}$ is equal to $\left(\frac{y}{x}\right)^2$, so $\frac{y^2}{x^2}$ is equal to $\frac{9}{4}$.

17. **(E)** Starting with $a_n = 1$ the rule $(a_n - 1)^2 = (1 - 1)^2 = 0^2 = 0$ so the next entry is 0. Using 0 as a_n gives $(0 - 1)^2 = (-1)^2 = 1$ so the second entry is 1. Since using 1 as a_n gives 0 as the next entry, the entries after 1 should be 0, 1, 0.

18. **(E)** X is paid 125%, or $\frac{5}{4}$ of Y's salary, so Y makes $\frac{4}{5}$ of what X makes. X makes 80% or $\frac{4}{5}$ of Z's salary, so Z makes $\frac{5}{4}$ of what X makes. Thus, the total salary of X, Y, and Z is the total of X's salary, $\frac{4}{5}$ of X's salary and $\frac{5}{4}$ X's salary. Therefore, the total is $\frac{61}{20}$ of X's salary. Since the total of the salaries is $610, X makes $\frac{20}{61}$ of $610, or $200.

19. **(C)** Since the radii are unequal, the circles cannot be identical, thus (E) is incorrect. If two circles intersect in 3 points they must be identical, so (D) is also incorrect. Two different circles can intersect in 2 points without being identical, so (C) is the correct answer.

20. **(E)** Let L be the length and W be the width of the rectangle, and let S be the length of a side of the square. It is given that $LW = S^2$. A relation must be found between $2L + 2W$ and $4S$. It is possible to construct squares and rectangles so that (A), (B), (C), or (D) is false, so (E) is correct. For example, if the rectangle is a square, then the two figures are identical and (A), (C) and (D) are false. If the rectangle is not equal to a square, then the perimeter of the rectangle is larger than the perimeter of the square, so (B) is also false.

Evaluating Your Score

Tabulate your score for each section of Sample Test 3 according to the directions on pages 5–6 and record the results in the Self-scoring Table below. Then find your rating for each score on the Self-scoring Scale and record it in the appropriate blank.

SELF-SCORING TABLE

SECTION	SCORE	RATING
1		
2		
3		
4		
5		
6		
7		
8		

SELF-SCORING SCALE

RATING

SECTION	POOR	FAIR	GOOD	EXCELLENT
1	0–12 +	13–17 +	18–21 +	22–25
2	0–9 +	10–13 +	14–17 +	18–20
3	0–20 +	21–27 +	28–35 +	36–40
4	0–12 +	13–17 +	18–21 +	22–25
5	0–12 +	13–17 +	18–21 +	22–25
6	0–20 +	21–27 +	28–35 +	36–40
7	0–12 +	13–17 +	18–21 +	22–25
8	0–9 +	10–13 +	14–17 +	18–20

Study again the Review sections covering material in Sample Test 3 for which you had a rating of FAIR or POOR.

To obtain an approximation of your actual GMAT score, see page 6.